Routledge Revivals

Social Security

First Published in 1943, *Social Security* critically examines the arrangements for providing pensions, insurance benefits, allowances and compensation to the vast mass of wage earners and their dependants. Divided into two parts, it discusses crucial themes like the fundamentals of social security; unemployment and health insurance; pension schemes for widows, orphans, the blind, and the aged; the system of workmen's compensation; superannuation schemes; pensions for the members of armed forces and civilians suffering war injuries and public assistance and the work of the assistance board. This comprehensive book is a must read for scholars and researchers of political economy, British economy, and labour economics.

Social Security

Edited by William A. Robson

Routledge
Taylor & Francis Group

First published in 1943
by George Allen & Unwin Ltd.

This edition first published in 2022 by Routledge
2 Park Square, Milton Park, Abingdon, Oxon, OX14 4RN

and by Routledge
605 Third Avenue, New York, NY 10017

Routledge is an imprint of the Taylor & Francis Group, an informa business

Publisher's Note
The publisher has gone to great lengths to ensure the quality of this reprint but points out that some imperfections in the original copies may be apparent.

Disclaimer
The publisher has made every effort to trace copyright holders and welcomes correspondence from those they have been unable to contact.

A Library of Congress record exists under LCCN: 43013692

ISBN: 978-1-032-20518-2 (hbk)
ISBN: 978-1-003-26398-2 (ebk)
ISBN: 978-1-032-20519-9 (pbk)

Book DOI 10.4324/9781003263982

SOCIAL SECURITY

Edited by

WILLIAM A. ROBSON

Professor of Public Administration in the University of London

Published for the

FABIAN SOCIETY

by

GEORGE ALLEN & UNWIN LTD

London

First Published 1943
Revised Second Edition 1945
Revised Third Edition 1948

BOOK
PRODUCTION
WAR ECONOMY
STANDARD

THE PAPER AND BINDING OF THIS BOOK
CONFORM TO THE AUTHORISED ECONOMY
STANDARD

Printed in Great Britain
by T. and A. CONSTABLE LTD., Hopetoun Street,
Printers to the University of Edinburgh

CONTENTS

PART TWO: THE FUTURE

PREFACE TO THE THIRD EDITION

THE preparation of this book began early in 1941, some months before the appointment of what became known as the Beveridge Committee. The book was first published in 1943, and the second edition appeared in 1945. The purpose of those who contributed to it, the methods by which they tackled the problem, and the course of events through these formative years of British social insurance policy were fully described in the preface to the first and second editions, which is now omitted.

Since the appearance of the second edition the discussion of national policy has culminated in a series of Acts of Parliament which have created an entirely new structure of social insurance and much else besides. Parliament has passed the Disabled Persons Act, 1944; the Ministry of National Insurance Act, 1945; the Family Allowances Act, 1945; the National Insurance (Industrial Injuries) Act, 1946; the National Insurance Act, 1946, and the National Health Service Act, 1946. The Ministry of National Insurance has been established with a Minister of Cabinet rank in charge. A further measure is expected to deal with Public Assistance. These momentous changes have given a new impetus to the study of social insurance. In view of the fact that policy has now been largely decided and embodied in legislation, it is desirable that attention and study should be directed increasingly towards a consideration of the practical problems involved in working out the new system.

The previous editions contained an Epilogue by Mr. R. W. B. Clarke discussing the proposals embodied in the Coalition White Papers on Social Insurance and Workmen's Compensation.[1] This chapter had become obsolete and it was not possible for the author to write a new one. I therefore invited Lord Beveridge to contribute a fresh Epilogue. Lord Beveridge is not a member of the Fabian Society, but this did not deter him from accepting our invitation any more than it precluded us from seeking his co-operation on this and other occasions. We are therefore able to include in the present edition his concluding

[1] Cmd. 6550 and 6551.

chapter, in which the legislation is compared with his Report on Social Insurance and Allied Services and also with some of the ideas put forward in this book and in the evidence submitted to the Beveridge Committee by the Social Security Sub-Committee of the Fabian Society.[1]

The reader will find that the Fabian contributors to the present volume do not agree either with the new scheme or with Lord Beveridge on the subject of rent. We remain unrepentant advocates of a special rent allowance as an element of benefit. Lord Beveridge recognises the fundamental impossibility of making adequate provision by means of flat rate benefits which do not take into account the large variations in rent paid by insured persons. He attempts, however, to avoid the problem so far as insurance benefits are concerned by shifting the burden of dealing with this difficulty to the housing authorities. This view does not commend itself to us. So far as my knowledge goes no country has at any time produced such a "free market in housing" as to iron out the differences in rents between town and country or between large towns and small towns. If it were politically practical and economically desirable to subsidise rents as part of housing policy, that might be a satisfactory alternative to taking the rent element into consideration in providing national insurance benefits and similar payments. There are, however, substantial arguments against a subsidy of this kind, since earnings on the whole vary in a manner which follows the general trends respecting rent differentials in different parts of the country.[2] Moreover, no such scheme would appear to have any serious chance of acceptance. For these reasons we feel that the rejection of the Fabian proposal to include a rent allowance in social insurance benefit is in no way justified.

There are other differences of emphasis between the outlook of the Epilogue and that of the earlier chapters, but in general I would reiterate the statement which I made in the original preface that on most of the fundamental questions the author of the Beveridge Report and the authors of these chapters see eye to eye in principle, despite minor variations in detail.

With events moving so swiftly in the realm of practical affairs

[1] This evidence is reproduced in the Appendix.

[2] Wage rates, for example, are higher in provincial towns than in the country, and higher in London than in the provincial towns.

it is inevitable in a book of this kind that some of the chapters should not approach the subject in quite the same way as the authors would have done if they had written them today rather than in 1942 or 1943. A substantial amount of revision has been made and it is hoped the detailed information has been brought up to date. In any event we are concerned with general principles rather than with minor details and our main arguments therefore remain unaffected by small changes in current practice.

The general case for specific contributions to the National Insurance Funds by insured persons and their employers has been strengthened by recent experience of the disadvantages of direct taxation of working-class incomes. The wage-earning classes clearly dislike income tax; it appears to diminish their incentives to work; and for this reason we regard indirect taxation, of which insurance contributions are a special type, more sympathetically.

Nevertheless, the doubts expressed by Mr. Clarke concerning the level of contributions proposed under the Beveridge scheme apply *a fortiori* to the much higher contributions to be imposed under the new legislation. These seem indeed to us far too high. Again, the disparity in the Beveridge Report between the expenditure on children by way of family allowances and the expenditure on the old and unproductive members of the community has been greatly exacerbated by the Government's remarkable generosity in reducing (or eliminating altogether for some pensioners) the transitional period for the payment of retirement pensions at the new and enhanced rates of benefit.

The most striking fact about the estimated annual expenditure on income-maintenance services, such as national insurance and family allowances, is indeed the relative proportions allocated to the old and the young respectively. In the first year of the National Insurance Act, the aged will receive £268 millions in retirement pensions, non-contributory and supplementary pensions; this will rise to nearly £450 millions in the next twenty years. Family allowances, on the other hand, cost £60 millions a year (plus say £50 millions for children's allowances in kind) and there will be no automatic tendency for this to rise. In the Beveridge Plan (which was by no means niggardly to pensioners) the amount of cash paid out each year in children's allowances by the middle 'sixties would have been one-third of the amount paid in retirement pensions; under the present legislation the proportion will be less than one-seventh. This distribution is indeed difficult to defend.

In this connection I would refer to the evidence given to the Royal Commission on Population by the Population Committee of the Fabian Society, of which I was Chairman. The Committee severely criticised the scheme of family allowances recently introduced by the Government on the ground of its inadequacy to afford effective assistance to the financial burden of parenthood. The scheme provides for a family of three children a sum of 10/- a week, subject to income tax in appropriate cases which would, at present rates, leave a net weekly sum of 5/6 to the parents. "What this almost derisive contribution to family finances is intended to achieve we do not know. It can scarcely be expected to have any perceptible influence on the birthrate." [1] The Population Committee recommended to the Royal Commission payment of an average sum of 10/- a week (at 1942 prices) for each child, including the first, provided that suitable arrangements are made to cover the extra cost of rent (subject to an upper limit) occasioned by the addition of children to the household. The Fabian Population Committee also pointed out the fundamental difference in the nature of the burden imposed on the community by the aged and the young respectively. "The young dependants will eventually repay to the community during the years of their economic productivity all that they have consumed and more. The burden of the dependent aged is of an entirely different character. It consists in the allocation of resources to the support of persons who will not at any future time make a return in terms of productivity. The health, happiness and welfare of the aged is an end in itself and cannot be justified from the standpoint of present or future economic productivity."

It is greatly to be hoped that steps will be taken in the near future to remedy this disparity between the treatment of the old and the young.

Our criticism of this and other features of the new schemes in no way overshadows the tremendous satisfaction we feel at seeing these great projects securely anchored in the statute book. The continuous effort which the Fabian Society has made during the

[1] *Population and the People* (edited by W. A. Robson). Published by the Fabian Society and Allen & Unwin, p. 13.

past fifty years for the removal of poverty has certainly played a large part in changing the intellectual climate of our time. The Society has devoted a great part of its energy and ability to developing radical solutions for the problem of poverty. It has taken the initiative in propounding constructive policies and working out detailed plans far ahead of contemporary opinion. The authors of this volume may reasonably feel that in the sphere of social security they have carried on the traditions laid down by the Webbs and other leading Fabians of the last generation; and that their efforts have borne fruit.

WILLIAM A. ROBSON.

LONDON, *March* 1947.

INTRODUCTION: PRESENT PRINCIPLES

By WILLIAM A. ROBSON

THE object of this book is twofold. First, to examine critically the existing arrangements for providing pensions, insurance benefits, allowances and compensation to the vast mass of wage-earners and their dependants; and second, to discuss the fundamentals of a social security scheme at once comprehensive, unified, consistent and based on intelligible principles.

The first of these tasks is essayed in Part I; the second in Part II. In the several chapters comprising Part I of the book, the reader will find a critical exposition of Unemployment and Health Insurance, the Pension Schemes for Widows Orphans, the Blind and the Aged, the system of Workmen's Compensation, Superannuation Schemes, Pensions for members of the Forces and for Civilians suffering War Injuries, Public Assistance and the work of the Assistance Board. There is also an account of Industrial Assurance.

Before approaching these concise but detailed outlines, the reader may find it useful to consider certain general aspects of the subject which I will attempt to set out here. Broadly speaking, the schemes with which we are concerned represent the legislative effort of the past fifty years to meet the needs of the mass of the people in time of distress. Like nearly all social reforms in Britain, the arrangements have grown up piecemeal, with no attempt to introduce completeness, consistency or symmetry. Most of the schemes reveal the sudden spurts of intense interest in one particular category of persons, following and followed by long periods of indifference, which are typical of English Parliamentary methods. Most of them show a persistent reluctance to consider the relation between different aspects of the same problem—let alone co-ordinate them—which can only be attributed to sheer laziness of mind.

Yet although the arrangements were brought into operation piecemeal, and at no time related to any coherent body of general principle, we might well expect half a century's legislation in this clearly defined field to disclose the existence of well-marked tendencies which, consciously or unconsciously, were the outcome of strongly held ideas and powerful social forces. This indeed we find to be the case.

The earliest of the schemes, in point of time (if we leave aside Public Assistance, which derives from the Elizabethan Poor Law), is Workmen's Compensation, which first found its way to the statute book in 1897, to be supplemented and expanded in 1906 and 1923. The Workmen's Compensation Act, 1897, contained two very important principles which involved a drastic departure from nineteenth-century thinking on the subject of industrial accidents. The first of these was the abandonment of the atomic conception of society, which regarded each individual as a separate atom, unrelated to any other atom. Its place was taken by a recognition of the family as the rudimentary unit of social need. The Fatal Accidents Act, 1846, had already made a slight inroad on the nineteenth-century doctrine that the wage-earner's rights, his earning power, and continued existence, were matters which concerned only him and no one else, by enabling his dependants to sue in cases where he would have been able to do so had he survived; but the first occasion on which an explicit acknowledgment of family needs was made in modern legislation was in the Workmen's Compensation Act. Parliament declared that where a workman is killed when at work, or dies in consequence of an industrial accident or disease, all the members of his family who were wholly or in part dependent upon his earnings can claim compensation. And where young children are left, the amount of compensation will vary in accordance with the period during which they are presumed to remain dependent.

Family responsibilities have been recognised in practically all the subsequent schemes, with the notorious and indefensible exception of National Health Insurance. Benefit can be claimed for a wide range of dependants in Unemployment Insurance; additional allowances for children are attached to Widows' Pensions; women receive Widows' Pensions by virtue of their husband's insurance; Orphans' Pensions derive from the insurance of their parents; persons drawing Unemployment Assistance and Supplementary Old Age Pensions receive allowances for wives and children.

It is quite certain that the acceptance by the State of family responsibilities has come to stay, so far as this sphere of public administration is concerned; and that social security will move towards a fuller and more adequate recognition by the State of family reponsibilities than is at present accorded to them. Family allowances and the extension of Health Insurance benefits to cover dependants are the two most conspicuous needs in this direction.

At the same time, a parallel movement has been in progress in the opposite direction. The household means test and similar devices for calculating the ability of members of a household to assist one of its members who happens to be in distress has come to be the most hated expression in the entire vocabulary of social administration. It has been abandoned, modified or undermined in one service after another, until it manages to maintain a precarious and uncertain foothold only in Public Assistance and, to a lesser extent, Unemployment Assistance. Thus, there is at once a weakening in the obligation of the members of a family towards one another, and a stronger emphasis placed on the duty of the State to cater for family needs. There is no inconsistency in these two parallel movements.

The second important principle embodied in Workmen's Compensation is the notion of "absolute risk" in place of the confused medley of doctrines by the light—or darkness—of which the common law Judges refused to impose any liability on employers for the death of, or injuries to, their workmen, except in a small minority of cases where, broadly speaking, a clear moral guilt could be shown to fall on the management: as, for example, where the employer personally interfered with the man's work, or provided unsafe premises or defective plant which caused the accident, or chose his workmen carelessly.

The limited area within which the employer's liability was recognised at common law was still further reduced after 1840 by the doctrine of common employment, which the Judges admitted for the first time as a good defence in the case of *Priestley* v. *Fowler*. "The principle is that a servant, when he engages to serve a master, undertakes as between himself and his master to run all the ordinary risks of the service, and this includes the risk of negligence on the part of a fellow-servant, whenever he is acting in the discharge of his duty as a servant of him who is the common master of both." [1] This cruel doctrine ruled out an enormous number of accidents due to the carelessness of a fellow-workman, especially on the railways, where a locomotive driver or guard on a train was held to be a fellow-servant of a signalman who set the points wrongly, or even of a traffic superintendent in charge at a distant station.

The Workmen's Compensation Act instituted the idea of absolute risk by abolishing the necessity for the workman or his dependants to prove negligence or moral culpability on the part of the employer. All that the claimant had to show was that the workman had suffered "personal injury by accident arising out of and in the course of the employment." In short, the employer's liability on the one hand, and the employee's right to compensation on the other, arise from the risks inherent in the occupation itself.

This was a substantial advance both in common sense and social justice; but the practical advantages of the legislation were greatly curtailed by the failure of Parliament to provide any machinery of public administration to ensure the effective and economical satisfaction of claims for compensation. All that the Workmen's Compensation Acts do is to confer certain legal rights to compensation on workmen or their dependants, and to leave them to enforce those rights as best they can, either by agreement with the employer or in arbitration proceedings, which in most cases go before the County Court Judges, and thence, on appeal, to the Higher Courts. Even forty or fifty years ago it would not have required much intelligence to infer that in a sustained series of conflicts in the Courts between workmen and their employers the latter would inevitably possess great advantages, partly on account of their superior resources in money, knowledge of their rights, professional skill, and ability to wait, but also to no small extent by reason of the traditional hostility towards working men displayed by the Judges during the nineteenth century.

Few people could have foreseen, however, the fantastic manner in which the legal decisions on Workmen's Compensation claims would proliferate year by year so as to form a veritable jungle of case-law, through which neither light nor warmth can penetrate. There are literally thousands of judicial decisions on the meaning of the words "personal injury by accident arising out of and in

[1] *Hutchinson* v. *York and Newcastle Railway* (1850), 5 Ex. p. 343 at p. 352.

the course of the employment"; and yet the torrent shows no signs of abating, despite frequent protests from the House of Lords sitting in its judicial capacity. The vast mass of decisions has, indeed, served to strengthen the stream of litigation rather than to diminish it, by adding to the number of "competing analogies" which can be invoked in aid of one side or the other.

Money, time and professional skill are squandered in a scandalous manner in settling these claims. The fundamental reason is that, instead of a claim for compensation being determined on the grounds of public interest, it is opposed and obstructed at every stage by the adverse interest of the employer or his insurance company. The resources of the legal and medical professions are devoted to the ignoble and socially misguided purpose of resisting the payment of compensation to an injured workman or his dependants.

The whole system is utterly wrong in principle and highly detrimental to the welfare of the very people whom it is supposed to serve. Even where the workman gets his compensation, there is no attempt to provide him with the medical and industrial rehabilitation services which should form the keystone of a reasonable scheme of Workmen's Compensation. If the case does not come into Court, the workman and his dependants are often worse served than if it does.

The lump sum for which the weekly payment may be commuted at the employer's option, or which is payable in all cases where dependants are left by a deceased workman, has nothing whatever to commend it from the standpoint of social security. It has, indeed, the very opposite effect; for the possession of a comparatively large sum of money by persons who are accustomed to handle only weekly wages or housekeeping allowances lulls them into a false sense of security; and when the brief moment of opulence has passed, they are thrust back into a far worse condition, both mentally and economically, than before the accident.

The system of Workmen's Compensation as it now exists is indefensible; and such it will remain until the adverse interest of the employer or his insurance company or mutual trade association is removed, and the determination of the claim carried out by an administrative tribunal or commission having regard only to the public interest in the injured man or his dependants. It is, moreover, essential that the settlement of the monetary aspect of the claim should be accompanied by properly organised efforts to perform the far more important task of rehabilitating an injured workman physically, mentally and industrially.

It can be seen that Workmen's Compensation represents an intermediate stage between the old common law rights on the one hand, which were entirely inadequate to deal with the new dangers arising out of the machine age, and, on the other hand, the social insurance schemes of the twentieth century, which, despite their imperfections, are at least based on the principles of public administration, public interest and public finance, as distinct from private negotiation, private disputes, private interests and private finance.

The next step of any consequence after the establishment of Workmen's Compensation was the introduction of Old Age Pensions in 1908.

Hitherto the only public provision for the relief of destitution in old age was the Poor Law. Now for the first time a system was introduced whereby a fixed sum of money was to be paid each week to persons of either sex who had attained 70 years of age, if they fulfilled certain statutory conditions relating to nationality, residence and means. The recipient was entitled to the payment as of right; it was not dependent upon the determination of a relieving officer; the receipt of it imposed no disqualification or loss of status, and it was in no way connected with the hated stigma of the Poor Law.

The earlier Old Age Pensions scheme must be regarded, indeed, as a revolt against the Poor Law rather than as a forerunner of the insurance schemes of later years. The Poor Law was in process of being subjected to a devastating public enquiry by the Royal Commission on the Poor Laws set up in 1905, and although the Commission did not report until 1909 it was clear to the Liberal Government of the day that neither the Boards of Guardians nor the Poor Law which they administered were likely to emerge with credit from the enquiry.

The Old Age Pensions Act, 1908, was a step in the direction of removing from the Guardians a substantial bloc of their regular clientele. It was thus an anticipation of the movement for the break-up of the Poor Law recommended by the celebrated Minority Report of the Royal Commission. It bore no signs of the "insurance" principle found in the later schemes.

The Act of 1908, as Mrs. Clarke points out, was "strongly moralistic."[1] It barred from pension rights anyone who had failed to work according to his ability, opportunity and need, for the maintenance of himself and those legally dependent on him, although this disqualification would not apply if he had during the preceding ten years made provision against old age, sickness, infirmity or unemployment. The weaker brethren who had been sentenced to imprisonment without the option of a fine, those who had been detained under the Inebriates Act, the inmates of Poor Law institutions and criminal lunatic asylums, were rigorously excluded from passing through the silver gates and entering into that state of pensionable beatitude into which it had pleased Parliament to summon the worthy.

Nevertheless, Mrs. Clarke is right in stating that in the first Old Age Pensions Act are to be found the seeds of the idea, which has proved so powerful in the twentieth century, of State responsibility for the well-being of individual members of the community. "A man might receive a State pension without loss of respectability. Henceforth society's punitive attitude towards the poor diminished, while its sense of liability increased."[2]

The subsequent legislation bifurcates into two main streams. One stream flows from the original Old Age Pensions Act and is based on the principle of non-contributory pensions payable from the age of 70 onwards, subject to certain tests as to means, nationality, and residence. The other stream flows from the so-called "insurance" principle, first introduced in regard to other contingencies in 1911, but not applied to old age until 1925, when contributory pensions were created for widows, orphans, and old persons between the ages of 65 and 70 who satisfied certain "insurance" conditions. This Contributory Old Age Pensions scheme was grafted on to the National Health Insurance scheme for the purposes both of contributions and central administration. At the age of 70 the two streams are joined, for the contributory pensions are then merged in the non-contributory pensions. In addition to the two main streams there is a tributary in the shape of the Supplementary Pensions, which are based on a means test.

It is all incredibly and senselessly complicated. The Old

[1] *post*, p. 167. [2] *post*, p. 168.

Age Pensions Act, 1936, is administered by the Customs and Excise, in conjunction with local pension committees. The Contributory Old Age Pensions are administered by the Ministry of Health working through its own local officers. Persons claiming under the earlier legislation must not have private means in excess of a certain maximum income. If they have an income below that figure, the pension will be reduced in accordance with a statutory table. Those who can claim a Contributory Old Age Pension between the ages of 65 and 70 or a Widow's Pension become entitled thereafter to a pension under the Old Age Pensions Act, 1936, at the full rate of 10/- a week without regard to any test of means. Over and above these arrangements are the Supplementary Pensions administered in cases of need by the Assistance Board.

The complexity of the provisions and the disintegration of the administrative machinery are not due merely to the fact that the various schemes have been introduced piecemeal at different times. They are due also to the fact that they have not been informed by consistent principles, and that no attempt has been made to reconcile them. It is a case of chaotic administration reflecting chaotic ideas.

In 1911 the first National Insurance Act was passed. This introduced at one stroke a widespread scheme of health insurance and a tentative measure of unemployment insurance for a few industries known to be especially liable to seasonal unemployment.

The system of National Health Insurance has undergone only very slight changes in the thirty years which have passed since Mr. Lloyd George forced it through Parliament in the teeth of strenuous opposition. It remains today substantially what it was then. It has not, however, stood the test of time, for it is regarded by almost everyone who is in any way concerned with it as highly inadequate from every point of view.

The Health Insurance system was the first of the so-called "insurance" schemes; and the tenacity with which it has clung to this notion is at the root of most of its defects. The term "insurance" is, of course, borrowed from commercial transactions by means of which private individuals enter into voluntary contracts to guard themselves against financial loss arising from certain contingencies. It was applied all too lightly to State-organised schemes which bear a very different character.

In the first place, participation in the State insurance schemes is compulsory and not voluntary. In the second place, they are not wholly or even mainly supported by the contributions of the beneficiaries, since there has always been an equal levy on employers and a grant from the State of varying proportions. In the third place, the contribution is not adjusted to the risk.

Mrs. Williams observes in the course of her careful survey that although most of the schemes have an actuarial basis, none is true insurance, not because they are all subsidised by the State, " but because there is not the same degree of relationship between risk and premium as would satisfy actuarial criteria, and because the liability of premiums and benefits to constant legislative change renders them only superficially the subject of a contractual obligation." [1]

National Health Insurance is the scheme which most fully satisfies actuarial criteria. It is also—and largely for that reason—the most defective scheme now in operation. The Contributory Old Age Pension scheme could also be designated more definitely as an actuarial system than most of the other schemes because there are fewer incalculable factors to be taken into account in estimating the risk than in the other cases, but even this scheme "contains several features which have social rather than actuarial justification or which have been admitted because they corresponded with the general idea of what is fair." [2]

The contribution from the insured person is clearly a specifically allocated tax. The contribution from the employer is equally clearly a tax on employment which certainly does not ultimately fall on the employer.

Despite the fact that the insurance analogy does not hold good on a close analysis over most of the ground, there were certain political advantages thirty years ago in presenting the health and unemployment schemes under this guise. The "insurance contributions" enabled a form of direct taxation to be levied on the vast mass of the wage-earners, who would certainly have fiercely resented and resisted any attempt to bring down the income tax to the level of their wages. It was also made possible to entitle the "insured contributors" to receive benefits as of right, provided they satisfied the qualifying conditions, and not at the discretion of an official or administrative organ. The insurance schemes

[1] *post*, p. 237. [2] *post*, p. 245.

were in consequence clearly distinguished from the Poor Law and eleemosynary arrangements which had hitherto held the field and which were regarded with mistrust and dislike by the people.

The National Health Insurance scheme, as already stated, is more nearly based on "insurance" principles than any of the other so-called insurance schemes, with the possible exception of Contributory Old Age Pensions. The contribution of the State, derived from general taxation, amounts to a smaller proportion of the expenditure than is the case with the other schemes. The Approved Societies which administer a large part of the scheme are permitted to exercise a selective choice over the composition of their membership, and since the funds available for additional benefits depends on the income of a society in relation to the demands of its members for the standard benefits, there is a partial relation between contributions, benefits and risks which is not found in the other schemes.

But this very adherence to "insurance" principles constitutes the basic weakness of the National Health Insurance system. The cash benefits are hopelessly inadequate and deter sick wage-earners from going "on the panel," and therefore to some extent even from consulting their doctors for fear they will be forced on the panel. Sickness is almost certain to absorb any savings which may have been accumulated, and an insured person is often compelled to seek public assistance in order to supplement the cash benefits payable under the Health Insurance scheme. The reason the benefits are so low is that they are calculated on "actuarial" principles rather than on reasons of social security or of public health.

The distinction between sickness benefit and disablement benefit, again, is based merely on the difference between short-term and long-term illness or disability. There is no rational ground for paying benefit at a lower rate to a man or woman after he or she has been sick for more than 26 weeks, but the reduction is imposed for "actuarial" reasons in order to balance the fund.

There is no justification whatever, from the standpoint of social security or the national health, in excluding the wife, children and other dependants of an insured contributor from benefits either in cash or kind, and immense disadvantages of the most glaring sort result from leaving them outside the scheme and without any other provision in case of sickness or disability. The reason they are excluded is doubtless to be found in the practice of commercial insurance, in the field of life, accident, health and endowment assurance, which usually requires a premium to be paid in respect of each person entitled to benefit.

The Health scheme, like all the others, is based primarily on employment: in order, one may assume, that contributions can be levied on employers and employees and the fiction of insurance be maintained. This very fact has militated against the inclusion of dependants, because, as Mrs. Clarke points out, while it is logical to ask an employer to contribute towards sickness provisions for his employees, it is not logical to ask him to increase his contributions so as to enable their wives and children to be included.[1] Thus it comes about that "National Health Insurance is not national in the sense that our education is national; it is not available to the whole nation. It is not even available to all persons in the lower income groups." [2]

Maternity benefit reveals the strangest and most senseless anomalies of National Health Insurance, particularly in a community such as our own, in which the declining birth-rate ought to be one of our principal preoccupations in the sphere of social legislation. If the mother is a married woman and herself insured, she receives a double benefit of £4, regardless of whether her husband is or is not insured. If she is unmarried and insured, she receives only a single benefit of £2, although her need is probably greater than that of a married woman. If she is married and not insured, but her husband is an insured contributor, a single benefit only is again payable.

No special provision is made for pregnancy, which is left to be treated as sickness. The Ministry of Health has decided, however, that simple pregnancy may not be regarded as sickness within the meaning of the National Health Insurance Acts. Some doctors put expectant mothers "on the panel" a few weeks before confinement, but unless complications exist it is more or less a matter of chance.

The service in kind provided under National Health Insurance bears distinct signs of the rudimentary notions concerning public health prevalent in the first decade of the twentieth century. Medical benefit offers an insured person the type of treatment which a general practitioner with a working-class practice would

[1] *post*, p. 93. [2] *post*, p. 92.

normally give to patients paying a fee of, say, between 1s. 6d. and half a crown a visit. According to the Hippocratic tradition, doctors do not measure the service they give by the fee which the patient can pay; but in the long run the economic factor operates in the medical profession under present conditions no less potently than in other spheres.

The insured contributors to the Health Insurance scheme are not entitled to specialist treatment, or to any form of hospitalisation; nor is a woman entitled to the services of a doctor or midwife upon her confinement, except by paying for them out of her maternity benefit. Medical benefit does not include dental or optical treatment, though these are provided to a limited degree by some Approved Societies as additional benefits.

The inadequacy of the National Health Insurance scheme in these respects is reflected in the vast recent growth of the Hospital Saving Association, a voluntary organisation comprising several million members, and consisting largely of working men and women who by this means seek to ensure for themselves and their families the provision of hospital facilities in case of need.

It is these considerations which lead to the conclusion that "National Health Insurance is inadequate not only because it is limited to one section of the community but because it is integrated in a medical system based on obsolescent methods and values." [1]

Even within the limited conceptions embodied in the scheme, much greater equity, efficiency, and economy could have been obtained if the administration of the entire cash benefit side had been taken over by the Government instead of being confided to the Approved Societies.

These bodies, consisting of friendly societies, trade unions, commercial insurance companies, collecting societies and so forth, comprise a great variety of institutions of every kind and size. The only conditions which they must fulfil in order to become approved is that they may not be conducted for profit and must be under the exclusive control of their members.

The handing over of a large part of the administration of National Health Insurance to the Approved Societies has deprived the scheme of much of its potential usefulness. It has prevented the collection of any statistical information relating to the health of the insured part of the population, because the societies are

[1] *post*, p. 103.

not based on geographical divisions. It has led to the separation of cash benefits from medical benefit in water-tight compartments without regard to the single object which should be the common aim of both. It has immensely strengthened the Industrial Assurance business of the great commercial companies who, by conducting National Health Insurance work through Approved Society branches, thereby secure an entry into millions of working-class homes which they are able to turn to good account for themselves. It has led to the continuance of Health Insurance on the primitive lines on which it originated, and retarded its development into something better.

This last-mentioned point requires special emphasis, because whereas all the other pension and insurance schemes have developed considerably during the past thirty years,[1] National Health Insurance has virtually stood still. It has rested, not on its laurels, but on the bleak outlines of its original plan. Those responsible for its administration have indulged in a fantastic elaboration of detail: in the following pages the reader will learn of the compensation to doctors in the West Riding being adjusted according to the number of patients living along "gated roads"; of the mass of *paperasserie* which results from the intricate control over prescriptions, the removal of patients and the keeping of accounts. Yet during all these years there has been a failure to consider the essential purposes which a national health insurance system should serve, or the extent to which those purposes are served by the present scheme.

Unemployment Insurance may be regarded as the most important of all the schemes dealt with in the following pages, for the simple reason that unemployment has been the outstanding economic and social problem which Britain has had to face during the twentieth century. With the significant exception of the years during the war of 1914-18 and re the Second World War, it has been a chronic disease of industry, a running sore in the body politic. At no other time has capitalism been able to offer anything approaching full employment of the labour resources of the nation despite all manner of schemes of public works, government subsidisation of industry, a vast housing

[1] Compare Unemployment Insurance, of which Mrs. Rackham writes that in the 30 years which have passed since those early beginnings, frequent changes and extensions have taken place, so that the scheme of today is hardly recognisable as that of 1911. See Chapter IV, p. 125 *et seq.*

programme financed by the State, the introduction of a tariff, and various other devices advocated as remedies for the sovereign ill of the British people.

The assumption underlying Unemployment Insurance was that unemployment is a phenomenon of short duration. On this basis it can be ameliorated, though not prevented, by means of regular cash benefits which, though not adequate to maintain the worker's standard of life, will at least avoid the demoralisation of compelling able-bodied men and women to accept poor relief.

The introduction of Unemployment Insurance also implied a recognition of the fact that unemployment is not caused, as had hitherto been commonly alleged by the better-off classes who were not subject to its miseries, either by a reluctance to work or by some moral defect or vocational incapacity on the part of its victims. In declaring it to be an insurable risk, Parliament once and for all disposed of the myth that unemployment is a form of industrial malingering, and placed it in the category of involuntary contingencies.

Thirty years of bitter experience have demonstrated the futility of attempting to regard unemployment as an insurable risk. No risk can be insurable if its probable incidence cannot be foreseen within fairly narrow limits. And under capitalism it is quite impossible to foresee the incidence of unemployment, and, therefore, to provide for it in advance by means of a nicely calculated system of contributions and benefits. "Every year," Mrs. Williams points out, "the Unemployment Insurance Statutory Committee has carefully scanned the economic horizon in the attempt to foretell the economic weather. In every case its prognostications have proved incorrect, not because its arguments were unsound, but because it was impossible for it to foretell that certain events would happen and consequently it could not estimate their probable effects on the incidence of unemployment. The Committee has itself realised the impossibility of its task and has made its estimates only because of the need of having some working hypothesis on which to base its recommendations." [1]

It would require an entire book to describe all the changes and vicissitudes through which the Unemployment Insurance system has passed since its inception in 1911. The scope of the

[1] *post*, p. 229.

scheme, the rates of contribution and of benefit, the conditions under which benefit is payable, the disqualifications to which claimants are subject, the share of expenditure borne by the State: these and many other features have been subject to frequent alteration.

The principal element in the history of the past thirty years has, however, been the struggle to maintain the "insurance" basis of the scheme in the face of liabilities far greater than any which could be met by "actuarial" means. This struggle reached its climax with the appointment of the Royal Commission on Unemployment Insurance in 1930, whose terms of reference were to make recommendations with regard to (1) the future scope of the Unemployment Insurance scheme, "the provisions which it should contain and the means by which it may be made solvent and self-supporting," and (2) the arrangements which should be made outside the scheme for the unemployed who are capable of and available for work.

In 1934 a new step of great importance was taken by the setting up of the Unemployment Assistance Board. It was originally designed to assist the long-term unemployed who could no longer be supported by means of unemployment benefit without abandoning the "insurance" principle; and who could not be dealt with by the Public Assistance authorities without jeopardising the stability of local government finance. The Assistance Board, as it was later renamed, has subsequently had entrusted to it many other functions not related to the unemployed.

The original intention was to set up a central organ which would be independent of day-to-day Parliamentary control, the object being to remove unemployment from the exigencies of political party pressure. The hope of "taking politics out of politics" was obviously doomed to disappointment, and the Parliamentary uproar which followed the initial stages of the Board's work is not likely to be forgotten. The additional functions which have been conferred on the Assistance Board since the outbreak of war have resulted in its becoming the principal organ of the central government for making allowances and payments to the civilian population. No less than 8 Ministers of the Crown have answered questions about the Board! Yet the Board itself is not answerable to Parliament. Its constitutional position is highly unsatisfactory, and the Board might not survive any considerable strain which it may have to endure.

The Poor Law itself underwent a substantial transformation in 1929, when the Local Government Act abolished the Boards of Guardians and transferred their functions to County and County Borough Councils. The break-up of the Poor Law, the necessity for which was so powerfully advocated by Mr. and Mrs. Webb in the celebrated Minority Report of the Royal Commission on the Poor Laws, 1905-9, was not achieved by the legislation of 1929; but an important step in that direction was taken by the merging of Public Assistance administration in the general system of local government, and a still greater stride forward made by the power conferred on local authorities to declare (in the schemes they were required to submit to the Minister of Health) that, in the case of services which could be provided either under the Poor Law or under the Public Health Acts or similar legislation, they should be deemed to be provided under the relevant social service Act and not by way of public assistance.

While, therefore, the Poor Law has not been finally broken up, and the principles which were laid down in 1601 are still in operation, its administration has been transformed and humanised almost beyond recognition compared with the state of affairs which existed during the nineteenth century. Of still greater importance is the fact that large classes of the community who were formerly dependent on poor relief are now provided for by other means. These include the aged, the blind, the able-bodied unemployed, the mentally defective, the widows and orphans, the sick and disabled. As Mr. Marshall shows, the provision made for these categories by other agencies is in many cases so inadequate that it is still necessary for the Public Assistance authorities to supplement their allowances by the grant of poor relief; but despite this, the effective scope of their jurisdiction has greatly diminished. It is to this diminished sphere of operations that we should look in estimating the extent to which the Poor Law has been broken up.

In 1925 there was passed the first of the Acts to provide pensions for widows and their dependent children, orphans, and old persons between 65 and 70 years of age. Here again the contributory principle was adopted, and the new pensions were grafted on to the arrangements already in existence under the National Health Insurance Act.

The main significance of the new development was the much fuller recognition which it accorded to the family responsibilities of the wage-earner. For the first time provision was made, by means of compulsory State organisation and subsidisation by the National Exchequer, for the wives and children of men whose death has deprived the household of its main source of income.

The new scheme did not take a strictly functional view of widows' pensions. For example, a woman could not become entitled to such a pension by virtue of her own insurance, though she might suffer severe financial loss by the death of her husband, who might be employed in a non-insurable occupation. On the other hand, the wives of insured men can draw pensions even if they are able to earn their own livelihood and are without dependent children or other encumbrances.

With this legislation there is a final abandonment of the idea that the wage-earner can properly be expected to make provision, by his own unaided efforts and habits of thrift, to meet the major contingencies of life caused by death, old age, sickness and unemployment. The inadequate wages earned by large numbers of workpeople makes it difficult or impossible for them to meet even the current needs of the household for rent, food, clothing, fuel and other necessaries, not to mention drink, tobacco and amusements. To expect them in addition to make provision for the future is merely quixotic. The irregularity of employment of a vast section of both well-paid and ill-paid workers would alone suffice to make voluntary and unaided action impracticable.

The abandonment of this idea was due partly to a decline in the belief that destitution is caused by the special forms of moral culpability, or the absence of certain Victorian virtues, generally associated with poverty during the nineteenth century. It gradually dawned on the better-off classes that to expect the mass of the wage-earners to safeguard themselves against extreme misery and want in time of distress was about as sensible as to expect them to cure themselves of sickness without the aid of a doctor.

The acceptance by the State of the obligation to make provision, through compulsory organisation and a limited degree of subsidisation, against the contingencies of sickness, widowhood, orphanhood, old age and unemployment, was thus based both on a change in the moral attitude towards poverty and on a new understanding of the economic causes underlying its most common manifestations. To the rise of the social sciences, to the pioneering work of the great social investigators such as Booth, Sidney and Beatrice Webb, and Rowntree, to the Fabian Society and the Labour Movement generally, must be ascribed a large part of the difference in the moral and intellectual climate of the past twenty or thirty years, as compared with that of the Victorian era.

This change in outlook has affected not only the better-off and privileged sections of society, but also to an even greater extent the working classes themselves. They have ceased to feel guilty of the deadly sins of poverty and insolvency. The stigma which formerly attached to the acceptance of poor relief from the Guardians is no longer felt strongly, or perhaps even at all, by those who take Public Assistance from the County or County Borough Council, or allowances of one kind or another from the Assistance Board. There is a widespread feeling among applicants that they are entitled to the benefits provided by the insurance schemes, and that they have paid for them.

It is undeniable that the various benefits and pensions are paid as of right: for claims are firmly based on the new rights conferred by social legislation. The other belief is true to a lesser extent, for although the insured workers contribute towards the cost of the schemes, their share does not amount to even as much as one-half of the total expenditure.

So far as entitlement is concerned, it would seem, indeed, that the pendulum has swung too far in the opposite direction. The "insurance" principle which has been so mistakenly emphasised in the schemes has tended to produce a political psychology which regards the State as a kind of penny-in-the-slot machine, in which you put a coin and draw out your packet of chocolate. That attitude produces many political disadvantages. It overlooks the fact that although your penny released the drawer, the chocolate which was in it cost far more than a penny; and the extra cost was borne by others. It overlooks the fact that in a system of social security many people must put pennies into slots without drawing anything out. It puts all the stress on the rights of the citizen against the State, and little or none on his obligations towards the community.

Despite the emergence of the new economic, political and moral ideas to which reference has been made above, and the creation of new types of social administration which were both the cause and the consequence of changes in the world of thought, it is strange to find how incomplete and compartmental the treatment of social security has been.

The most striking omission is the lack of any provision prior to 1946 for family allowances for dependent children during the time when the wage-earner is at work. An allowance towards the burden of child-rearing is made in Workmen's Compensation, Unemployment Insurance, Widows' Pensions, Public Assistance, pensions for members of the Armed Forces and civilians suffering war injuries or war service injuries, Unemployment Assistance, and Supplementary Pensions. But when the breadwinner of the household was at work no cash provision was made for his dependent children, although their presence may make all the difference between a household falling below the poverty line or enjoying a degree of comparative comfort. Yet the State has been far from ignoring children during the present century. The development of municipal education; the creation of maternity and child welfare clinics; the successive improvements in the hours of work and conditions of employment for juveniles secured by the Factories Act, 1937, and other industrial legislation; the protection afforded to children against cruelty or neglect by their parents or guardians by the Children Act; the attempt to deal with juvenile delinquency by specially appropriate methods: all these measures show a considerable degree of solicitude on the part of Parliament and the public for the welfare of the young. Nevertheless, there was before 1946 no response to the unanswerable plea which has been made with eloquence and force by the advocates of family allowances.

The provision of allowances for children in the Income Tax law only serves to sharpen the contrast between the treatment of the working classes in this matter and that accorded to the better-off sections of the community. It is probable that the main obstacle to the introduction of a system of allowances for children has been the opposition of the trade unions, whose attitude is based on the fear that family allowances would undermine the strength of collective bargaining and drive a wedge between the men with children and those without.

Such an apprehension would justify opposition to any scheme of family allowances based on wage differentiation. But it is difficult to see in what way it can explain the long-continued hostility of the trade unions towards family allowances paid entirely by the State out of taxation, or even financed on a tripartite basis in a similar manner to the social insurance schemes.

Another striking omission in the present arrangements is the lack of any public provision to meet the cost of burial. But here there is a simple explanation. The field has been captured by commercial interests and voluntary organisations, and the State has unwisely acquiesced in that conquest.

The chapter by Mr. Ginsburg shows the extraordinary dimensions of the business conducted by the collecting societies and the assurance companies engaged in the class of business which is known as Industrial Assurance. At the end of 1938 there were no less than 100 million policies in existence in Great Britain, representing a premium income of £72 millions: an average of 2/9 a week from each of the ten million families contributing to this enormous total. The aggregate sum assured is approximately £1,600 millions.

This vast mountain of small insurance policies has been built up through the incessant ant-like activities of an army of full-time insurance agents numbering 50,000 or 60,000, employed by about 150 collecting societies (of which all but half a dozen are of negligible size) and a slightly larger number of commercial insurance companies trading for profit.

The motive which has prompted the people of Britain to indulge in this orgy of small-scale voluntary life insurance is an ever-present sense of the need to make provision against the crippling expense caused by a death in the household, if the humiliation of a pauper's funeral is to be avoided. It is difficult to overestimate the depth of the horror, fear and aversion with which the thought of a pauper's grave is regarded after three centuries of Poor Law administration; and in most places the only alternative to this is a funeral provided at high charges by an undertaker trading for profit, and attended with elaborate paraphernalia. The emotions aroused by a bereavement and a desire to earn the esteem of neighbours conspire to induce most working-class households to incur an exorbitant outlay on such an occasion; and it is to meet this that the mass of the wage-earners and persons of similar income spend each year on provision against death as much as the whole public expenditure on elementary and secondary education. The 2/9 per week which is the average weekly payment for each family compares with 1/10 per week for the contribution by an adult man for health and unemployment insurance, widows', orphans' and old age contributory pensions.

Mr. Ginsburg describes the manner in which the companies goad their agents to obtain new business, regardless of the needs of the assured or their ability to pay additional premiums; and he explains the reason why a continuous expansion is the necessary economic basis of the present system. He shows that the policies in force far exceed any reasonable coverage required to ensure decent burial; that poor people are persuaded to enter into far heavier commitments than they can afford; and that the rate of lapse is in consequence excessively high.[1]

It is impossible to survey this field of activity without concluding that the State has been gravely at fault in not making the public provision of funeral benefit a part of the national system of social security. It is painfully clear that the mass of working-class homes are mulcted of huge sums each year to provide against a universal contingency which could be better provided by public administration at a fraction of the cost; and that the present system should not be permitted to continue unchallenged for a day longer.

When the insurance schemes were first introduced, they were all based on the fact of employment. That is to say, the obligation to be insured fell on persons employed under a contract of employment or apprenticeship at a rate of remuneration not exceeding £160 a year. From 1918 even the class of voluntary contributors admitted to health insurance consisted of persons who had previously been engaged in insurable employment for a specified time.

With the gradual recognition of the fact that the need for social security depends primarily on financial status rather than on a particular economic relationship, the scope of the schemes

[1] In 1937, for example, no less than six million policies were voluntarily dropped by their owners, and in five million of these cases the policy lapsed shortly after it was started and no surrender value was paid by the Company.

has been widened so as to include not only persons of similar incomes who are not employed in the technical sense, but also persons in somewhat higher income groups who comprise the lower middle class. Legislation passed in 1937 enables men whose income does not exceed £400, and women with not more than £250 a year, to become voluntary contributors in respect of the widows', orphans' and contributory old age pensions; while in 1941 the income limit for compulsory insurance was raised to £420 a year. These Acts brought into the schemes a very large proportion of the black-coated workers.

A more extensive provision in a different direction has been made not only for wage-earners, but for both the lower and higher grades of salaried employees, by means of Superannuation schemes.

The growth of Superannuation is one of the features of the period under review. Prior to the commencement of the present century, few occupations outside the Civil Service, public education, and Poor Law administration offered any facilities to their members to provide against the vicissitudes of old age, retirement and death. Now, as Miss Cohen's investigations show, there are some 2,500,000 persons participating in superannuation schemes of one kind or another. These include (in addition to civil servants, local government officers and teachers employed by local education authorities) more than 800,000 administrative and salaried workers, clerical and sales assistants, and a slightly larger number of wage-earners.

The superannuation schemes which cover this substantial section of the administrative, professional and clerical employees, and to a less significant extent the manual workers in selected occupations, number several thousand and vary considerably in character. There are statutory and non-statutory schemes; there are those which require the employee to pay contributions and those in which the employer alone is responsible for bearing the entire cost. There are variations in the rates of benefit and the conditions under which it is payable. The most satisfactory schemes make provision not only for retirement in old age, but also for the man or woman who is compelled to give up work on account of sickness, and for the dependants of deceased employees.

The essential feature of superannuation is that the pension is related to the recipient's length of service and his rate of salary. In this it affords a sharp contrast to the statutory Old Age Pensions schemes and other social insurance arrangements, in which the rate of benefit bears no relation to the previous earnings of the applicant. In so far as the main object of social security is the maintenance of people at or near their accustomed standard of life during periods of economic strain or financial decline, this is far more nearly achieved by means of superannuation than by any of the social insurance schemes. In the United States, the social security scheme introduced by President Roosevelt provides contributory pensions based on individual earnings and with benefits corresponding thereto; but nothing similar has so far been attempted on a national scale in this country.

The growth of superannuation in Britain indicates, however, the extent to which employment of a more or less permanent nature has been established in a variety of occupations. Broadly speaking, the scope of superannuation is almost co-terminous with those organisations, both public or private, which are able to offer their employees—or at least a substantial proportion of them—full-time service during the whole working life until a recognised retiring age is reached. In this, as in other respects, certain commercial and industrial firms, in addition to an extensive range of public and private institutions, are beginning to assimilate their terms of employment to the conditions offered by the Civil Service.

The arrangements whereby pensions are available to blind persons from the age of 40 constitutes only one aspect of the special provision which has been made for a severely handicapped group whose needs have been urged with unusual ability and whose claims to sympathy and practical aid have met with a ready response from the British Government and people. There is, indeed, no other handicapped group which has received anything like the same degree of consideration or interest, though there are several which stand in great need of it. Doubt is expressed by persons specially cognisant of the blind whether their welfare is best served by segregating them for special treatment in so marked a fashion, instead of dealing with them as a particular category of partially disabled persons. In this, as in so many other instances, Parliament has been unable to rise to the height of a general proposition; and even now the pensions which are paid to the blind at 40 years old are "old age" pensions!

The most conspicuous fact about the public provision for the blind is, however, the relatively extensive effort which has been made to supplement payments in cash by services in kind; and to make such services as constructive as possible. Mr. Eagar makes it clear that much remains to be done for the blind in the fields of education, training, employment and general welfare; but, taking them all in all, the combined efforts of the local authorities and the central departments in this sphere represent a far higher level of achievement in the provision of services than anything which has been attempted in the case of the sick or the disabled, the unemployed, the aged, the orphans, the widows, or even the expectant and nursing mothers.

The compartmental thinking which has characterised the several schemes of social insurance is reflected in the fantastic array of administrative bodies which were charged with administering them. Unemployment Insurance was the responsibility of the Ministry of Labour and National Service; Health Insurance that of the Ministry of Health in conjunction with local insurance committees and the Approved Societies. Non-Contributory Old Age Pensions were administered by the Customs and Excise and the local pension committees; Contributory Old Age Pensions, Widows' and Orphans' Pensions by the Ministry of Health; Supplementary Old Age Pensions by the Assistance Board. The Ministry of Pensions deals with the pensions of all ex-Service men or their dependants; but the War Office, Admiralty and Air Ministry look after the pensions of men serving in the Forces. The Ministry of Pensions is also responsible for pensions to civilians suffering from war injuries or war service injuries. The Home Office is nominally in charge of Workmen's Compensation. The Assistance Board looks after Unemployment Assistance and a number of other functions which have recently been assigned to them. Public Assistance is in the hands of the County and County Borough Councils, supervised by the Ministry of Health.

This medley of authorities is as chaotic, illogical and inefficient as anything which existed in the eighteenth or nineteenth centuries, and at which we now smile pityingly when we read an account by a novelist or historian. It is truly amazing that such a hotch-potch of authorities should have been allowed to continue year after year without so much as a protest in Parliament. It apparently required a second World War to produce the mental activity in Westminster and Whitehall necessary to set on foot even an enquiry into the subject.

The disintegration of administrative power among so many unco-ordinated authorities is not a matter of interest merely to social reformers or students of government. It has spelt disappointment, fatigue and exasperation to thousands of old, sick, infirm, out-of-work and destitute persons who have been sent from one local office to another, badgered from pillar to post by officials whose main object is sometimes to try to pass on the marginal cases to someone else.

At the Parliamentary level no political party appears to have grasped the need for planning in this field of State action, nor to have envisaged the various insurance, relief and pension schemes as related aspects of the single problem of Social Security.

Yet none of the parties has been fundamentally hostile or unsympathetic to the idea of social security; and none of them can claim exclusive credit for what has been achieved. The Conservative Party introduced Workmen's Compensation and the Widows', Orphans' and Contributory Old Age Pensions Act, although the latter scheme is said to have been prepared by the second Labour Government when in office. The Liberal Government of 1906 initiated Old Age Pensions, National Health and Unemployment Insurance. The Labour Party did not establish any of the schemes in its two short periods of office, but it has pressed continuously for better treatment of the ex-Serviceman, the unemployed, the aged, and workers suffering industrial injuries, with a not unappreciable effect on both legislation and administration.

The final verdict on the half-century of growth, whose results are surveyed in the following chapters, is that the social security schemes described therein were introduced experimentally and have somehow never developed into maturity. Their faults were not corrected nor their virtues encouraged. They have remained in a state of arrested development attended by the usual evils associated with that condition.

The time has clearly come when we should recast the whole range of services, bring them up to date, infuse them with modern doctrines, organise them on consistent principles, place them in a definite relationship with one another, integrate the machinery of central and local administration, and inform the entire system by constructive ideas.

The manner in which that task can best be accomplished is discussed in Part II of the book.

Chapter I

PUBLIC ASSISTANCE

By HERBERT W. MARSHALL

Historical: Family Responsibility and Principle of Destitution

The present Public Assistance system originated in the Elizabethan Poor Law, which dates back to 1601. The erroneous impression still persists to some extent that the "poor law" was abolished in 1929 when the Guardians of the Poor—the local bodies elected to administer it—were abolished, but all that actually happened was that the machinery, brought up to date here and there, was placed under the direction of the County and County Borough Councils, and the law governing the grant of relief was merely consolidated into the Poor Law Act, 1930. The fact is, therefore, that the main principles of the Poor Law of 1601 are still in being,[1] but that other social legislation has lessened the scope of the law.

The first principle of the system is contained in Section 14 of the Poor Law Act, 1930, which re-enacted Section VII of the Poor Relief Act of 1601, viz.:

> "It shall be the duty of the father, grandfather, mother, grandmother, husband or child, of a poor, old, blind, lame, or impotent person, or other poor person, not able to work, if possessed of sufficient means, to relieve and maintain that person."

The duty of the local authority to relieve then follows in Section 15. From Section 14 there arises the principle that relief may be given by a local authority only to the destitute—that is, only to those persons whose personal or family resources are insufficient to meet their immediate need.[1] Whilst no statutory definition of destitution exists, the former Local Government Board expressed the view that "in determining whether a person

[1] But see now Pensions and Determination of Needs Act, 1943, pp. 49, 51 and 56.

is destitute or not, it must be remembered that a person may be destitute in respect of the want of some particular necessity of life without being destitute in all respects."[1] Since then, legislation has provided that certain kinds of income (National Health Insurance benefit, Friendly Society sick pay, Disability pensions) shall be ignored to some extent in considering the grant of relief, and the position therefore now arises that a man may be technically "destitute" but yet have means which formerly would have disqualified him from receiving relief. It is likewise permissible for capital assets to be ignored to some extent —a principle entirely abhorrent to the original Poor Law system.

From the principles of the original Poor Law there followed—quite logically—the requirement that, before relief could be granted, the circumstances of the applicant and the household in which he resided must be taken into consideration, i.e. the "family" or "household" means test. But this requirement has been materially changed in "household" cases by the operation of the Pensions and Determination of Needs Act, 1943.

Despite this latest modification of the law, however, the fundamental principles of the Poor Law are still applicable to some types of cases, although several classes which formerly had to turn to the Poor Law for assistance when in need have been, by other social legislation, removed from its scope.

Administrative Machinery

Since 1930 the local administration of the Poor Law has been the duty of County Borough and County Councils in England and Wales, and the actual machinery consists of a committee (which may be charged solely with Poor Law functions or may be another committee of the Council) to whom the Poor Law work is delegated, together with a number of sub-committees. The majority of authorities have appointed a separate Public Assistance Committee consisting usually of elected members of the Council plus a number, not exceeding one-third of the total, of persons co-opted from outside the Council. The principle of co-option is optional, and in some instances has not been exercised. All Poor Law functions are delegated to the Public

[1] Circular of Local Government Board, 18th March 1910.

Assistance Committee (as it is usually called) except the power of raising a rate, but the degree of executive power varies according to the terms of the scheme drawn up by each Council and approved by the Ministry of Health.

The Minister of Health is charged with the central direction and control of all matters relating to the administration of poor relief, but has no power to interfere in any individual case for the purpose of ordering or varying the amount of relief. In Scotland, where the practice has always differed somewhat, the applicant has a right of appeal to the Scottish Office against the decision of the local authority. The Minister of Health's powers are exercised by the issue of regulations which have the force of law, and consist principally of two Orders—the Public Assistance Order, 1930, and the Relief Regulation Order, 1930 (as amended from time to time)—and he also has a number of General Inspectors whose duty it is to visit authorities and inspect any aspect of their Poor Law administration and report his findings to the Minister. The Inspectors have no power to give directions to an authority, and any representations which may be necessary are made by the Secretary of the Ministry to the Clerk of the authority. A considerable measure of control is exercised by the central authority in the grant or refusal of sanction to loans for capital expenditure in connection with institutional relief; and so far as out-relief is concerned, the accounts of the authority are subject to the scrutiny of the Minister's Auditor, who has powers of surcharge or disallowance where he considers payments of relief to be illegal or excessive. The Minister also has the power to direct an authority to appoint officers, and certain senior officers may not be dismissed, or their remuneration reduced, without his sanction, and he may also define the duties of any such officers.

The local administrative machinery differs between County Boroughs and County Councils, and also varies considerably between individual authorities. In county boroughs the administration is carried out by a committee and a series of sub-committees, and the area is divided into a number of small relief districts with a "Relieving" Officer in charge of each district. The usual practice is that a sub-committee has charge of one or more relief districts and adjudicates and makes orders in the cases from that district submitted to it through the Relieving

Officer, and there is usually a central sub-committee which acts as a supervising and appeals committee from the local relief sub-committees.

In counties the Councils are required to appoint, in addition to a Public Assistance Committee, Guardians' Committees for appropriate areas of the county, and to delegate to such committees the duties of dealing with applications for relief in that area, and the management of any Poor Law institution therein, but the Guardians' Committees have no power to appoint or dismiss an officer without the approval of the Public Assistance Committee.

The local relief sub-committees (in county boroughs) and the Guardians' Committees (in counties) have executive powers to deal with applications for relief within the terms of rules laid down by the Public Assistance Committee, and it is usual also for the Committee to prescribe scales of relief for the guidance of the sub-committees, but there is no strict legal authority for these scales of relief. Each case, technically, is required to be dealt with on its merits according to the individual circumstances, but authorities find it necessary for the sake of uniformity and administrative convenience to lay down a guiding scale. The local relief sub-committees have considerable discretion in dealing with individual cases, and it should be noted that the decision on any particular case *rests with the Committee* and not with the officer, although the latter is under no obligation to carry out any order which may, in his opinion, be illegal. This system contrasts with the methods of the Assistance Board, where the decision on the amount to be paid to an applicant *lies with the officer*, within the Regulations approved by the Board. The Public Assistance sub-committees are frequently drawn from persons actually residing amongst the people they are required to relieve; and whilst this has the advantage that the members often have an intimate knowledge of the cases brought before them, and also that the applicant can always air a grievance by approaching his local member, it has the somewhat serious disadvantage of leaving the way open to pressure upon a local member from reasons other than pure necessity—e.g. political feeling—particularly if the member is an elected one. This sub-committee system, which originated under the former Boards of Guardians, has, since the transfer of the Poor Law to the Councils, tended to break down for two reasons: firstly, the members of the Council, being also concerned with other aspects of Council work, have less time than had the *ad hoc* Guardians to devote to attendance at relief committees; and secondly, the large increase in out-relief cases in times of acute depression makes it impossible for a committee to examine every case in detail. Largely as a result of these defects, the local administration in some areas, notably in London and some other large counties and county boroughs, has been considerably altered, with the approval of the Ministry of Health, by the abolition of the local relief sub-committees and the appointment of paid officers, known as Adjudicating Officers, whose function it is to consider the applications for relief submitted by the Relieving Officer and to assess the amount to be paid according to a fixed scale of relief prescribed by the Council, any variation from the scale, or appeals against his decision, being submitted to a committee of the Council. This system, whilst departing from the long-established democratic control of the grant of relief, has advantages in that it ensures that all applications are speedily dealt with and that relief may be paid immediately in cash. Under the sub-committee system delays occur, and a Relieving Officer has power only to relieve "in kind" pending submission of the case to the sub-committee.

The Adjudicating Officer system is similar to the system adopted by the Assistance Board, with one improvement: the applicant has a right of appeal to a democratically elected committee instead of a nominated tribunal. In practice, the latter tend to legalistic interpretations of the Board's regulations rather than to that easing of the administration where necessary which ought to be the aim of a service devoted solely to the assistance of those in need. It is extremely difficult, if not impossible, so to frame regulations that every type of case and every variation of circumstances is adequately covered, and it is essential that some officer or body must have discretion to deal with cases which do not fit in the framework so as to prevent injustice. In this respect the Public Assistance system is superior to the Assistance Board. The Advisory Committees appointed by the Assistance Board have no real analogy to the local sub-committees of the Public Assistance Committee. The latter have real power to make decisions and to order relief to persons in need. Under suitable conditions and with good personnel they are probably superior, in fact, to the Adjudicating Officer system or the system of the Assistance Board—but the Advisory Committees, besides being undemocratic in that they are nominated, are purely advisory in capacity. They have no power, and the Board may disregard their advice if they choose. In any case, they are concerned only with general questions, not with allowances to individual cases.

The chief official for the local administration of the Poor Law is the Public Assistance Officer, who in some instances is also the Clerk of the Council. The Public Assistance Officer is responsible to the Council for the administration of the service in the area; he is required to advise them on the law and practice, and to supervise the officials and see that the regulations of the Council and the Minister are properly observed. For the purposes of the actual grant of relief, however, the key official is the District Relieving Officer. This much-maligned officer, a direct descendant of the Elizabethan parish officer and of the Dickensian beadle, is, in fact, in a position to make or mar the local administration. He is required to receive any application for relief in his district; to record the required information; personally to visit the house of the applicant and investigate the accuracy of the information given; to report upon the application to his Relief Committee, and to carry out the decision of that committee. He is also required by law to grant orders for the admission of destitute persons to institutions and hospitals. The duties of the District Relieving Officer sharply contrast with the duties of an Area Officer of the Assistance Board; the former must personally investigate an application made to him and carry out the orders of the Committee and (usually) pay the money. The Area Officer, however, has the case investigated by a subordinate official and merely makes—or approves—a decision upon the information collated, and this decision is then communicated to the Ministry of Labour or the Pension Authority, and payment is actually made, not by the Board, but by the Employment Exchange or the Post Office. Equipped as he is with statutory powers to relieve distress arising in sudden or urgent necessity, irrespective of the Council, the Relieving Officer is by his personality and his attitude to his duties in a position to colour local administration with humanity and sympathy, or, on the other hand, a narrow interpretation of his work may lead to harsh results and give rise to that atmosphere of deterrence which it was the aim of Chadwick's Commissioners to enforce in the grant of outdoor relief.

In any final reform or break-up of the Poor Law system, the statutory duties at present exercised by the Relieving Officers in the grant of emergency relief must be preserved. The question of the machinery through which they should be performed is a matter of some difficulty, as with the transfer of cases to other agencies the residual cases remaining to be dealt with may not justify the existence of a separate administration merely to fill the gaps left by other authorities. The most important point is that the Relieving Officer's function of relieving urgent need is exercised locally and must in the nature of things remain so; the present larger areas and more widely separated offices of the Assistance Board are, for example, scarcely sufficient to deal with this aspect of relief efficiently. It is essential to make sure that the needs and convenience of the public should have preference over any purely administrative considerations.

Prior to 1930 the Poor Law system was the only "assistance" authority affording relief on the basis of need. Whilst, due to its local organisation, wide variations in scales of relief and standards of administration existed, it could be said with truth that one and the same principle applied throughout the country. Significant changes have, however, been introduced since that date, affecting both standards of relief and administration. The process actually commenced in 1931 when, in the transitional payments scheme adopted as an emergency economy measure, unemployed persons who had exhausted their right to standard Unemployment benefit were required to submit their claims for further assistance to the Public Assistance authorities, who had to investigate and assess their needs on the same basis as was used for persons of similar classes receiving Public Assistance from the rates. The expenditure, however, still remained the responsibility of the National Exchequer, and payment of the amounts determined by the local committees was made by the Employment Exchanges. It is unnecessary to dwell upon the disastrous result of this policy upon local administration in many areas where unemployment was rife; suffice it to say that the regulations were largely ignored and payments were authorised with little regard to Public Assistance standards of need. Directly as a result of the bitter controversy which arose from the transitional payments administration, the Unemployment Assistance Board was established, and so there came into being a centrally controlled organisation, with local offices, applying a test of need on lines prescribed by Parliament, differing in principle from the Public Assistance system, and applicable to one class of persons only, viz. the unemployed falling within the scope of the Widows', Orphans' and Old Age Contributory Pensions Acts. The Board was required to administer a fixed scale of assistance, with allowances from income on a scale practically unknown in ordinary Public Assistance administration, and so uniformity in the treatment of cases—impossible to achieve under the local authority system because no common standards existed or had been laid down by the central authority—was established.

An agitation afterwards began for the augmentation of Old Age Pensions, resulting in 1940 in handing over to the Board (now the Assistance Board) the work of supplementing Old Age Pensions on similar lines to the system adopted for Unemployment Assistance. Thus a further large section of the community formerly having recourse to the local rates for relief when necessary was taken away from the Public Assistance authorities and placed under a national organisation giving uniform treatment throughout the country. More recently still, the Determination of Needs Act, 1941, has made a drastic change in the principles of the test of need to be applied by the Board, which has had the effect of replacing very largely the "household" test of need by one limited to the resources of the applicant only.

There are now, therefore, two Assistance authorities covering the country, working side by side, each with its own administrative organisation and staffs: in the case of the Board, being based on traditional Civil Service lines, conditions of service and remuneration; and in the case of the Public Assistance authorities, following local conditions, varying considerably between area and area in standards of efficiency, conditions of service and remuneration of officials. One of the immediate effects of this dual system is to throw into high relief two objections which have always been taken to the local Public Assistance system, viz.: (i.) that the incidence of its charge varies between area and area, the wealthier residential towns being at an advantage over the highly rated industrial areas with a high percentage of Public Assistance cases; and (ii.) that similar cases under different authorities may be dealt with in quite different ways and on varying standards of relief. The changes made by the Determination of Needs Act, 1941, in the principles of the Board's test of need, placed the Public Assistance authorities in a very anomalous, and rather invidious, position. For example, whilst the Board in dealing with an unemployed man practically ignored the income of relatives residing with him and made no claim against those of his relatives who resided elsewhere, the Public Assistance authorities had, when the same person fell sick and sought relief, to take into account the resources of his family, and, in addition, had to endeavour to obtain contributions from the relatives residing elsewhere.

This position has now [1] been materially affected by the passing of the Pensions and Determination of Needs Act, 1943, which, amongst other things, applies to applicants for public assistance, the same Rules for determining need in "household" cases as are used by the Assistance Board.[2] Briefly, the Rules provide that, in the case of an applicant who is a member of a household, the resources of persons residing with him or her (except the husband or wife or dependant of the applicant) are no longer to be regarded as the resources of the applicant, contrary to the original poor law requirement that the income of the applicant's household must be taken into consideration. Thereafter, the Rules lay down fixed amounts which are to be regarded as contributions by members of households to the household expenses, and in some circumstances provide that no such contributions are to be regarded as payable.

The aim of this curious example of piecemeal legislation is apparently to obtain uniformity of treatment as between similar classes of persons applying for assistance to the Board or to the local authorities, and to bring about uniform action between the various local authorities themselves. But in applying the Rules, the Act expressly preserves the discretion of Authorities under the Poor Law. Moreover, it does not prescribe any uniform scale of relief payments to be used by Authorities, so that, even though the Rules are strictly applied, there is no certainty—little

[1] 1st November 1943.

[2] Determination of Needs Act, 1941 (First Schedule). See *post* pp. 150-1.

likelihood in fact—that identical cases under different Authorities will receive the same amount of relief. There is much to be said for a discretionary power in the grant of assistance, but it cannot lead to uniformity. Apart from this, however, the new Rules ought to improve considerably the position of applicants for public assistance who reside with adult relatives.

The operation of the Family Allowances Act, 1945, raises the somewhat controversial question of whether the allowances payable under the Act ought to be taken into account or disregarded in considering applications for assistance on the ground of need. Under the existing Poor Law system there is no legal authority to disregard them, nor do the Regulations of the Assistance Board provide otherwise. But the allowances are payable without regard to the income of the parent, or its source, and to take them into account when assessing relief or assistance means that the parent who is most in need will be deprived of the advantage of the additional income, whilst the parent whose income may be adequate or more than adequate has the allowances in addition. Legislation has already accepted the principle that some payments from public funds may be disregarded wholly or in part in considering applications for further assistance, but with the extended benefits shortly to be provided under the new National Insurance scheme, the point will soon be reached at which the community will be faced with the problem of deciding where the ultimate line must be drawn between those for whom it deems adequate provision has already been made, and those for whom further help is necessary. There is not much logic in ignoring 5/- Friendly Society pay or 10/6 National Health sick pay and yet taking into account 5/- granted to a parent as a family allowance. For many practical purposes it would be better if all other payments from public funds were suspended during any period the recipient needed "public" or "national assistance"—provided always that the scale of such assistance was upon a wholly adequate basis—but whether such a proposal would be politic is another matter. The "disregards" already provided by legislation are a compromise, and as the scale of insurance benefits becomes more comprehensive the community will ultimately have to resolve the dilemma in which it will be placed in administering a national scale of assistance based on need. The problem is one which will confront the framers of any new national scheme, which is designed to replace the present residual provisions of the Poor Law system.

The contacts between the local authorities and other agencies—e.g. Assistance Board, Ministry of Labour, Ministry of Health Insurance Department, Customs and Excise, etc.—have with each piece of legislation become more complicated, and, for the sake of the people who have recourse to these agencies, ought to be simplified.

At present, during consideration of questions of scope, insurability, availability for work, qualification for pension, etc., persons who have an unquestionable right to the particular grant they apply for may have to be relieved by the local authority until the appropriate agency has decided the case, and then the local authority must proceed to claim back the money so granted. If the non-Poor Law services do not deal immediately with a case, either from lack of time or delay in procedure or for some other cause, the person affected can always, as a last resort, fall back for the time being on the Poor Law system. Thus the Poor Law system is in the rather invidious position that it *must* deal with the immediate necessities of the situation, even though the position may have arisen from the neglect or indifference of another agency which rightly should deal with the case. This seems to have a twofold effect: it makes for elasticity in the Poor Law system (a good thing in any social service), but, on the other hand, creates a sense of lack of urgency on the part of other services which ought to be dealing with the cases.

Cases now dealt with by the Public Assistance Service

The legacy left to the new Public Assistance service in 1930 from the 300-years-old Poor Law system grows gradually smaller with the passing of each piece of new social legislation. The original duty of the Poor Law to relieve "the old, blind, lame, impotent and other poor person not able to work" has now been lessened by the transfer of most of the old to the Assistance Board under the scheme for Supplementary Pensions; the blind are already dealt with by Blind Welfare Committees under the Blind

Persons Acts; and the able-bodied unemployed persons, who, according to the letter of the Poor Law, should have been "set to work," have mostly been transferred from the ambit of the Poor Law to the Assistance Board. The present Public Assistance service is, therefore, a kind of residuary legatee of the social services, and the cases falling to it form a miscellany rather than a number of clearly defined classes.

1. *Persons applying for Public Assistance pending Assistance from Other Sources.*—It frequently happens that there is a hiatus of some weeks between an application being presented for Old Age or Widow's Pension, Unemployment Assistance, National Health Insurance Benefit or Workmen's Compensation, and the admission of the claim. In many such cases the person concerned has no means to carry on and has no alternative but to seek temporary help from the Public Assistance Committee. This is often distasteful to the applicant, who has no desire to go to the Relieving Officer, and it is a source of trouble to the local authority, who have to investigate the case and grant relief, and then obtain repayment.

2. *Persons applying for Supplementation of Amounts received from Other Sources.*—The supplementation of grants from other public sources forms a considerable item in local Public Assistance expenditure.

Supplementation of Widows' Pensions.—Until recently the supplementation of widows' pensions was a considerable item in poor law expenditure, but the Pensions and Determination of Needs Act, 1943, provides [1] that pensionable widows with children in respect of whom children's allowances are payable are entitled to apply for supplementation from the Assistance Board. But pensionable widows under 60 without children or widows without pension are still left to the Poor Law when in need of assistance.

Supplementation of Workmen's Compensation.—Workmen's Compensation is very difficult; the weekly payments are not related to the need of the family affected, and frequently fall below the actual necessities of life, although in cases of death the lump sum payments make provision for the support of dependants. But

[1] From 1st September 1943.

presumably if a system of family allowances were adopted for those in wage-earning employment, compensation would also be adjusted accordingly. It is still probable that in some cases supplementary grants would be needed, and these would have to be dealt with by a "residual" authority [1] similar to the assistance now provided by the Public Assistance authorities.

Supplementation of National Health Insurance Benefit.—Unless National Health Insurance benefit is related to actual need, some supplementation will always be necessary, and in the absence of any other provision these cases have to be dealt with by the Public Assistance service. The raising of benefit to a level more consistent with general standards of life would, of course, eliminate many of the present demands for supplementation.

3. *Public Assistance to Unemployed Able-bodied Persons.*—Formerly the relief of unemployed persons and their dependants was a major Public Assistance problem, but with the passing of the Unemployment Assistance Act in 1934 the bulk of the problem was transferred to the Assistance Board. There is, however, still a residue of cases which fall to the Public Assistance authority, although a diminishing one because of the widening of the scope of insurance. Most of these are persons whose record of industrial employment has been so poor that they have not gained an insurable status within the wide terms of the Contributory Pensions Acts, whilst others are individuals who have not gained an insurable status by reason of their employment being outside the scope of the Acts, e.g. small traders who fail in business, hawkers, etc. These cases are forced, therefore, to turn to the local authorities for assistance in time of need, and they are in the unfortunate position of being "unemployed" workers in the wide sense of the term but unable to participate in the benefits provided by the State for the unemployed, merely because of a technicality. Many of them would, when in employment, contribute through taxation to the funds of the Assistance Board, which are provided by the State and are not, like the Unemployment Insurance Fund, on an actuarial basis. The numbers are comparatively small and the differentiation so meaningless that a remedy should be found. The present system means that an unemployed non-insured person receives assistance from a local

[1] The phrase " residual authority " is used to describe an authority maintaining persons left over from all other statutory provisions.

authority on a different (and frequently lower) scale [1] than the persons dealt with by the Board.

4. *Public Assistance Emergency Relief.*—So long as the possibility of strikes or lockouts on a large scale exists, there must be some emergency machinery available for preventing destitution amongst the people affected. The present legal position is that there is no authority for relief of an able-bodied man who has a job at reasonable wages and who absents himself therefrom, but Public Assistance Committees must prevent destitution amongst the wives and families of the workmen concerned. They may, however, only grant relief in kind to such an extent as will prevent absolute need. If the man himself is so reduced by want as to be in danger of starving, he too may be granted relief in kind, but he is liable to be proceeded against under the Vagrancy Acts. In times of widespread industrial disputes, this duty to relieve is one of great importance and involves local authorities in a vast amount of work, and not infrequently attracts to them a deal of odium both from the workpeople and the ratepayers.

Any ultimate reform of Public Assistance must have regard to this class of relief. Whether the present machinery of the Assistance Board would be adequate to meet a national emergency of this character is open to doubt, but there is strong argument in favour of making the charge a national one. At present, in a national dispute in the coal trade, for instance, the cost of the relief falls entirely upon the coal-mining areas—areas which normally have a higher rate of Public Assistance expenditure than the non-industrial regions.

5. *Public Assistance to the Sick.*—Probably the largest single class of persons now left to the local authorities is the sick poor, and they may be divided into the following groups:

(*a*) Persons normally working and falling temporarily sick, whose income is so reduced thereby that they need assistance until able to resume work.

[1] In comparing scales it should be borne in mind that there is often a difference in method : the Assistance Board apply their scale as an automatic calculation subject to a limited discretion above the maximum, but many local authorities regard their scale as a maximum *within* which cases should be dealt with. The result is that some cases are deemed to be adequately dealt with at a point lower than the maximum. Only in exceptional cases is the maximum exceeded.

(*b*) Persons unemployed and normally receiving Insurance benefit or Unemployment Assistance, falling temporarily sick and thereby declared for the time being "out of scope" of the Board's regulations, and who must, therefore, turn to the Public Assistance authority until sufficiently recovered to be again regarded as "available for employment."

(*c*) Persons permanently incapacitated who have insufficient income to maintain themselves.

(*d*) Old age pensioners requiring medical care or special nourishment and nursing facilities.

The majority of persons in the first two groups, and a smaller proportion of those in the third, are persons receiving National Health Insurance benefit which is inadequate for their needs. The new standard rate of National Health Insurance benefit is 18/- per week for a man, so it is obvious that a married man, unless he has other income, cannot manage without help. The benefit is, of course, quite unrelated to need. The chronic sick are in an even worse position, because the National Health Insurance Disablement benefit is even less.

As a matter of public policy it is desirable to facilitate the return to work and health of persons normally in employment who are temporarily sick, but the present system means that such supplementation as is possible under the Public Assistance system is frequently no more than sufficient to maintain a subsistence level for a person in *good* health, and does not really suffice in those cases where extra food and nourishment are needed to speed recovery. The possibility of paying adequate sick maintenance allowances under the present National Health Insurance system is a matter for urgent consideration.

Persons transferred during sickness from the Assistance Board to Public Assistance suffer under an anomaly which now arises (and will become more acute with the abolition of the family means test by the Assistance Board) in districts where the Public Assistance scale of relief is low.[1] It sometimes occurs that a person receiving Unemployment Assistance who falls sick receives less from the local authority than he was receiving from the Board when in good health.

6. *Residual Classes.*—After all the main classes of the needy have been absorbed into their various appropriate agencies, there

[1] See footnote to para. 2.

remains, and always will to some extent remain, a miscellany of cases which cannot be drawn into any general classification. For example, there are:

(*a*) Widows not entitled to pension.

(*b*) Feeble-minded persons not requiring institutional treatment.

(*c*) Dependants of imprisoned persons.

(*d*) Dependants of persons admitted to hospital or mental institution.

These last three groups must clearly be dealt with by some local accessible authority invested with a considerable amount of discretion in the way it may deal with them.

(*e*) Deserted wives and children. Deserted wives have, of course, a right of action under the Summary Jurisdiction Acts for maintenance orders against their husbands, but cases frequently arise where these orders are not obtainable for such reasons as that the husband's whereabouts are unknown, or the wife has committed adultery, or she is the deserting party. Even if an order is obtained it may not be paid, or if paid may need supplementing. Deserted children may, of course, be dealt with by admission to Children's Homes.

District Medical Service

In addition to providing assistance in cash, or by admission to an institution, public assistance authorities also are required to afford medical relief where necessary in the form of the services of a medical practitioner and the supply of the requisite drugs and appliances. The system varies: in many areas, medical men are engaged upon a salary or contract basis to attend to the needs of the poor in a particular district; in other areas arrangements giving free choice of doctor on National Health Insurance panel lines have been made. Persons in receipt of outdoor relief, and others who are without the means of providing themselves with medical attention, are entitled to the services of the District Medical Officer, as also are blind pensioners assisted under the Blind Persons Acts, and supplementary pensioners and their dependants receiving cash assistance from the Assistance Board, if not qualified for medical benefit under the National Health Insurance Acts.

Originally the only public medical service available to the

poor—apart from voluntary and charitable dispensaries—the scope and importance of the Poor Law medical service has been greatly lessened by the development of the National Health Insurance medical service and the growth of the public health movement.

Recovery of Relief

Under the Poor Law it is the duty of a public assistance authority to recover from the "father, grandfather, mother, grandmother, husband or child" of a person relieved, if possessed of sufficient means, amounts towards the cost of out-relief or institutional treatment given. The position became very anomalous upon the setting up of the Assistance Board, which, whilst affording assistance to persons upon a basis of need, was not required to obtain any contributions towards the cost of such assistance either from the person assisted or his relatives. The Determination of Needs Act, 1941, made the position of Public Assistance Authorities more invidious still. The Pensions and Determination of Needs Act, 1943, however, in addition to enabling local authorities to deal with household income on the same lines as the Assistance Board, also provides that an order for the maintenance of a person who has attained 16 years may not be obtained against a member of the same household (except the husband or wife of the poor person). But it does not affect the power of an Authority to obtain contributions from relatives not living with the applicant. In practice, this means that whilst a relative may escape liability if he resides in the same household as the person receiving outdoor relief, he immediately becomes liable on leaving it, and vice versa. In some instances the relative living with the applicant may be financially better placed than the one who lives elsewhere. Yet the former has been practically relieved of his liability, while the latter's liability continues. Further, an Authority may grant assistance either by way of outdoor relief or by admission to an institution. If, in any particular case, the Authority deems institutional treatment to be suitable, then all the appropriate relatives, whether they have been living in the applicant's household or not, immediately become liable to contribute towards the cost of maintenance according to their ability to do so.

The Minister of Health has expressed the view [1] that, in the

[1] Circular 2833.

exercise of their discretion, local authorities could avoid obvious inequity as between one relative and another, but it is still left to local authorities to apply the law. One large Public Assistance Authority—anticipating future legislation perhaps—has already passed a resolution to the effect that claims for maintenance (apart from any claim against the person assisted) be made only against husbands and wives and against parents in respect of children under 16.

Clearly, the law covering the liability of persons to contribute towards the maintenance of their indigent relatives badly needs tidying up.

Indoor or Institutional Relief

It is the duty of the Public Assistance authority to provide accommodation in institutions for cases considered to require relief in that form, but to comprehend the existing system it is necessary to understand its origin. Following the report of the Royal Commission of 1834, a systematic building of "workhouses" was undertaken, designed primarily—and this should be borne in mind in considering the present position—for the "setting to work" of unemployed able-bodied persons, but having attached to these institutions primitive sick wards or infirmaries. The atmosphere of the original workhouse was designedly repressive or deterrent, and the system was unsuccessful in dealing with the problem of the able-bodied poor at that time. During the latter period of the administration of the Poor Law by Boards of Guardians, some of the larger and more progressive Boards greatly improved both the buildings and administration of their institutions and developed the sick wards to such an extent that they became, or formed the nucleus of, most of the present-day municipal or county hospitals. Tradition, however, dies hard, particularly when associated with a deterrent system, and the so-called "stigma" clung to these hospitals. Partly for this reason, upon the transfer of the Poor Law functions to the Councils, provision was made for the transfer of the former Poor Law hospitals to the Public Health and Hospitals Departments and for their separation both from the administrative provisions of the Poor Law Act and from the actual administration of the parts of the institution which continued to deal with persons accommodated for reasons other than sickness.

The hospital aspect of the administration should be regarded more as a matter of public health than as "assistance," and the problem with which Public Assistance authorities have to deal is really one of providing accommodation for aged and infirm persons who become unable to maintain themselves in homes of their own, and able-bodied persons who from various causes—improvidence, misfortune, crime, etc.—lose temporarily or permanently the means to maintain a household, and the children of these persons and others who may have been deserted or are orphans.

Present tendencies are for the ratio of aged and infirm persons to increase compared with the so-called "able-bodied" group, but the line between the two classes is often difficult to define, as also is the line between the aged and infirm class and the chronic sick in hospital wards. Between the two latter classes there is, in fact, much coming and going between the institutions and the hospitals.

The principal officers of an institution are the Master and Matron, whose duties are prescribed by Order and include the government and control, subject to the Management Committee, of the institution and the staff, the admission and discharge of inmates, and generally the domestic or housekeeping part of the administration. There must also be a Medical Officer, who, according to the needs of the institution, may be part time or whole time and either resident or non-resident, and (where there are more than 100 sick-beds) also a Superintendent Nurse, who is sometimes confused with the Matron where the latter is a lay administrative officer. The customary method for persons to be admitted is by application to a Relieving Officer, who, upon being satisfied of the destitution of the applicant, issues an order addressed to the Master to admit the case. The Master has, however, powers to admit in case of emergency without a Relieving Officer's order. An inmate may take his discharge from the institution upon giving due notice, and a patient in the hospital wards may, of course, be discharged therefrom by the Medical Officer, but if he is destitute this may mean merely that he is transferred to the "house" or non-sick portion of the institution.

The principal criticisms of Poor Law institutions arise from two main factors. First, buildings designed in accordance with the constructional ideas and to meet the requirements of another age are still in constant use—modernised to a limited extent, but incapable of conversion into really suitable buildings from present-day standards. Second, the unhomelike conditions which inevitably prevail in institutions dealing with large numbers of persons. A glimpse of the dining hall or a dormitory of one of the larger Poor Law institutions—spick and span, efficiently organised and ordered though they be—reveals the atmosphere which results from massing together large numbers of unfortunate people of all types.

The history of the Poor Law system has left its mark upon the institutional relief side of the administration as it has done on outdoor relief. The Commissioners set up in 1834, and their successors, the Local Government Board, found it necessary for the development of the institutional service to issue a host of orders and regulations to be observed by Guardians in their administration, dealing with the most minute details of institution management, and the pith of these regulations still exists in parts of the Public Assistance Order, 1930. The result is, therefore, that even today County and County Borough Councils, which are deemed fit to manage and control, practically without restriction, institutions and hospitals provided under other Acts, are still, according to the letter of the law, bound in managing Poor Law institutions by the rigid regulations yet remaining in force.

Some considerable developments have taken place since 1930 in the care of children in institutions. According to the Poor Law regulations, children, except tiny infants and sick children, were not to be retained in workhouses, and separate Homes, either grouped together or scattered in various parts of the district, were provided by the Guardians, and it must be acknowledged that in many instances these Children's Homes reached a very high standard and performed a very valuable social service. However, upon the transfer to the Councils, some authorities, following perhaps the suggestions of the Minority Report of the Royal Commission of 1908, placed the administration of their Homes under the Education Committee, although, as the law had not been altered, the administration was technically subject to the general control of the Public Assistance Committee and the expenditure formed part of the expenditure of the latter committee. In practice this has tended to remove whatever prejudice still remains against the Poor Law Homes, and has resulted—in at least one instance—in the development of the Homes not only as a purely residential institution, but as a nursery school and training centre.

Education Committees have more recently become the local authorities for the purposes of the Children Act, and children are committed to their care by the Magistrates for various reasons, e.g. neglect by the parents, etc. Whilst—quite rightly—objection has been taken to the use of the Poor Law Homes as Remand Homes for children with criminal tendencies, they can be, and are being, utilised for other children committed permanently to the care of the Education Committees—an example of co-ordination in administration which is all too rare.

In addition to the institutions and Children's Homes already dealt with, Public Assistance authorities may also send poor persons to Convalescent Homes and special institutions of various types (Epileptic Colonies and the like). The institutions are mostly non-Poor Law institutions, and the patients are simply maintained there at the expense of the particular Public Assistance authority.

The field of outdoor, or home, assistance, impinges upon the field of institutional or indoor relief at many points; the admission of a father of a family to an institution for treatment creates questions as to the maintenance of his family; the admission of a wife raises difficulties in the care of her husband and children. There is a small class of cases in which the whole family is accustomed to go periodically into an institution for maintenance. Under existing law, in the latter case, the husband or wife may not be discharged from the institution without the rest of the family, and this frequently raises the problem of granting outdoor relief immediately on discharge without the persons concerned having obtained proper accommodation outside the institution. There must necessarily be considerable liaison between the institutional authority and the authority charged with granting relief outside.

This aspect of assistance also raises the very difficult question of vagrancy—one of the most intractable social problems. Deterrence has been tried and found wanting; tendencies at present are towards more humane and sympathetic treatment, but it remains to be seen whether this will solve the problem. No doubt a general raising of educational standards, coupled with an improved system of social security, will ultimately help in stamping out the problem of the itinerant vagrant. But in many cases at present the mere grant of monetary allowances is no cure.

Miscellaneous Functions

In considering any final break-up of the Poor Law system, there are two minor functions which must be dealt with.

(*a*) *Persons of Unsound Mind.*—It is one of the tragedies of social policy of the past that the removal of persons of unsound mind to institutions has been associated with the old Poor Law, with the result that the idea of shame in connection with mental breakdown has been fostered, hampering the remedial side of mental treatment. It is still the duty of the Relieving Officer (and the Police!) to obtain the certification and removal of any person requiring mental treatment in an institution, except that in certain circumstances under the Mental Treatment Act, 1930, the patient may be admitted under other arrangements. There are practical difficulties to overcome, as there must always be available a local officer for this purpose and the number of cases does not in most areas justify the appointment of an official solely for this work. Perhaps an officer attached to a local hospital would be the most appropriate person to whom these duties might be transferred.

(*b*) *Burials.*—It is also the duty of the local authority under the Poor Law Acts to bury the body of any person requiring burial in the area, where there is no other means of so doing. This duty might reasonably be attached to the local Registrar of Cemeteries, or the Medical Officer of Health's Department.

Although the oldest of our public social services—perhaps, indeed, because of it—the Poor Law system is the least popular. The so-called "stigma" arising from historical origins and harsh administration of past decades still lingers in the minds of some sections of the public, but the feeling is more prevalent amongst people who have never come into actual contact with present Public Assistance administration than amongst its clientele. In fact, it would be readily admitted by many people who have had recourse to the service in recent years that they have discovered in many instances enlightened, human and constructive administration, and a high sense of social responsibility, among Public Assistance and Relieving Officers. This change in the attitude of the Public Assistance administration is reflected in the widespread change of name to "Social Welfare" made by local authorities in recent months. At the same time, the local Councils would be the first to admit that the constant shrinkage of Poor Law functions, and particularly their replacement by services founded on a more popular basis, makes it increasingly difficult to justify some of the more archaic parts of the Public Assistance system, or to resist the constant political pressure to abolish the Poor Law altogether. The best of administrators lose heart if they are constantly faced with difficulties arising from anachronisms in their service. Any consideration, therefore, of the reconstruction of the social services must, in dealing with the Poor Law, take into account not only the anomalies and overlapping which at present form such a feature of the administrative landscape, but also the attitude of the public generally both to the scope of the Poor Law and to the principles upon which it is based.

Chapter II

WORKMEN'S COMPENSATION

By ROSALIND CHAMBERS

Introduction

A workman[1] who meets with an accident arising out of his employment may be able to obtain some kind of compensation by one of three methods. He may, in certain circumstances to be more fully considered later, bring an action for damages caused by the negligence of his employers; or he may bring an action under the Employers' Liability Act of 1880; or (and this is by far the most generally used method) he may make a claim under the Workmen's Compensation Acts, 1906-25. This chapter is really concerned with the last of these three methods, but as they are to some extent bound up with each other, it will be necessary as an introduction to deal briefly with the other two.

Action at Common Law

Until 1880 the injured workman could only obtain compensation by bringing—and winning—a common law action against his employers. To be successful in this he had to prove personal negligence[2] on the part of the employer; if the accident were due to the negligence of a fellow-servant, he would generally find his claim barred by the doctrine of "common employment."[3] This doctrine, the result of various legal decisions in the first half of the nineteenth century, is still good law, though its effect has been modified in recent years by certain decisions which have narrowed the scope of common employment.[4] As industry increased in scope and complexity it was clearly more and more

[1] In this chapter " workman " refers to workers of either sex.

[2] " Negligence," i.e. the failure to observe proper precautions in the conduct of his business either personally or by not taking care to engage reasonably competent workmen or to provide efficient machinery and keep it in proper repair.

[3] " Common employment " : where several servants are working for the same employer in the same undertaking they are said to be in common employment and to have undertaken as part of their bargain with the employer to run the risks which may arise from the carelessness of their fellow-servants.

[4] *Metcalfe* v. *London Passenger Transport Board*, 55 T.L.R. 700. *Radcliffe* v. *Ribble Motor Services Ltd.*, [1939] A.C. 215.

likely that where an accident in, for example, a large factory involved negligence at all, it would be due to the carelessness or wrongdoing of a workman rather than the personal negligence of the employer. This defence cannot be pleaded where the accident is due to a breach of a statutory duty. When an Act of Parliament requires that certain precautions shall be taken or certain conditions observed, for example in workplaces governed by the Factories Act or the Mines Acts, the employer is absolutely responsible for seeing that such requirements are fulfilled; and if they are not, and an accident results, an action can be brought by the injured workman for negligence against the employer, even though the latter may have delegated the duty of carrying out statutory requirements to a fellow-servant of the injured workman.

Another defence that may be set up when a common law action is brought in cases of accident is that known as "volenti non fit injuria," which in effect means that the injured workman is said to have known of the risks of his employment and to have accepted them. This defence again cannot be pleaded when a breach of a statutory duty is involved, but a third defence is available. This is "contributory negligence," and renders an injured workman's action ineffective if the evidence shows that he was partially responsible for the accident that caused his injury, in so far that without his negligence the accident would not have happened.

It will be seen, therefore, that it is not very easy for an injured workman to succeed in an action at common law, and when such an action was his only remedy the vast majority of industrial accidents were entirely uncompensated. If the workman was killed outright or died as the result of an accident caused by the negligence of his employer, all right of action died with him, and though his family might be ruined by his death, they had no claim to any compensation. This was to some extent remedied by the Fatal Accidents Act of 1846 (Lord Campbell's Act), a statute "extremely characteristic of English legislation . . . instead of abolishing the barbarous rule which was the root of the mischief complained of, it created a new and anomalous kind of right and remedy, by way of exception." [1]

Entitled an "Act for compensating the families of Persons

[1] Pollock on *Torts*, 14th ed., p. 56.

killed by Accidents," it confers a right of action on the personal representatives of a person whose death has been caused by the wrongful act of another, in all cases where such a right would have existed if death had not occurred. Any action under the Act must be brought within twelve months of the accident and must be for the benefit of the wife, husband, parent or child of the deceased person,[1] and the claimants must have suffered some appreciable pecuniary loss by his death. It should be noted that if a common law action is successful, the injured workman may, and probably will, get much more generous compensation than if he makes a claim under the Workmen's Compensation or Employers' Liability Acts; there is no statutory limit on damages and they are assessed by the Court. For this reason, where there is an element of doubt in an accident case, insurance companies and other organisations will sometimes hurry through the payment of compensation under the Workmen's Compensation Act with unusual promptitude, for, once an injured person has accepted and received one form of compensation, he is debarred from applying for another. Should he be unsuccessful in an action for damages he may, however, ask the Judge to assess his claim for the purpose of claiming Workmen's Compensation. He must decide there and then whether he will take this course or whether he will risk an appeal to a Higher Court on his original action. To require workmen to make so momentous a decision without time for consultation and advice is a most unsatisfactory feature of the Compensation scheme.

Employers' Liability

The Employers' Liability Act, which must be briefly considered next, was passed in 1880. It rendered the defence of common employment no longer available in certain kinds of action—namely, where an accident was caused:

(1) By some defect in the ways, works, machinery or plant connected with or used in the employer's business.

(2) By negligence of a fellow-servant exercising the duties of a superintendent.

[1] "parent" includes father and mother and grandparents, stepfather and stepmother; "child" includes son and daughter, grandchildren and stepchildren. Illegitimate children are included by the Law Reform Misc. Provisions Act, 1934.

The defences of common employment, contributory negligence, and acceptance of the risk are open to the employer, as in other common law actions.

(3) By a workman's obedience to orders or directions issued negligently by a fellow-servant whom he was bound to obey.

(4) By the act or omission of a fellow-servant in obedience to rules or instructions.

(5) By the negligence of a fellow-servant who had control or charge of any signal, points, locomotive engine or train upon a railway.

This Act "appears in the light of later developments to be a tentative and imperfect piece of legislation,"[1] and it is very little used today, especially since the legal decisions in the higher Courts which have modified the doctrine of common employment, thus rendering an action at common law less difficult. The Employers' Liability Act applies to all manual workers, including agricultural workers, but not to domestic servants. An action for damages under the Act must be begun within six months of the accident, and damages recoverable are limited to a lump sum equal to three years' earnings. As a result of a legal decision in 1882[2] it was declared legal for a workman "to contract out of the Act," a decision very much resented by the workmen. These limitations, together with the fact that the defences of contributory negligence and "volenti non fit injuria" were still open to the employer, made the Act from the beginning doubtfully useful, and, after the Workmen's Compensation Acts were passed, fewer and fewer claims were made under it, and it is unnecessary to discuss it in further detail.

A New Principle Introduced

In 1897 an entirely new principle was introduced into the scheme of compensation for industrial accidents. No longer is the employer's negligence a necessary condition for the award of damages; the workman was given an absolute right to compensation for "personal injury by accident arising out of and in the course of his employment." Even the workman's own negligence does not necessarily render him ineligible for compensation. Where the workman has been guilty of serious and wilful misconduct and meets with an accident, he is disqualified from recovering compensation, unless death or serious and permanent disablement results.

[1] *Workmen's Compensation*, Wilson and Levy, vol. i. p. 37.
[2] *Griffiths* v. *Earl of Dudley*, (1882) 9 Q.B. 357.

The first Act applied only to workmen employed in or about railways, in factories, mines, engineering works, quarries or on buildings over thirty feet high. In 1906 it was extended to cover the vast majority of workmen employed under a contract of service. In 1923, following a Report of the Holman Gregory Committee, another Act was passed, and the legislation was consolidated in 1925. This last Act is the basis of the present system. Certain minor Acts have followed it, but the only ones which call for remark are the Nicholson Act of 1934, which introduced the principle of compulsory insurance in a very limited degree, and the war-time Act of 1940, which raised the weekly payments and extended the award of children's allowances.

Workmen's Compensation differs from the other social security schemes in that there is no State-administering authority and very little State control. In this Great Britain differs from most other countries which have schemes of Workmen's Compensation. In this country there is an obligation on employers to pay compensation to workmen injured at work, but the way in which they meet their obligations is their own concern. There is no compulsory insurance except in the mining industry, although the majority of the employers are probably covered by insurance, either through ordinary commercial insurance companies or by mutual indemnity associations of employers. When a claim for compensation is disputed by the employer or his insurance company, it is heard first by the County Court Judge, and if an appeal is lodged by either side the case is taken to the higher Courts. An enormous amount of litigation on this subject takes place every year, and a great deal of money is spent on legal, medical and administrative expenses. The Holman Gregory Committee reported in 1920 that "during the last five or six years the employers had to pay £100 in premium for every £48 paid out in benefits to the injured workmen." In 1936, 63·66% of the income from premiums was expended in payments of compensation or damages, while 33·31% went into payment for commission and expenses of management. It should be noted that the 63·66% included legal and medical expenses, which were a large amount, so that the injured workmen's compensation did not represent anything like this proportion of the income from premiums. In countries where there is a greater measure of State control and administration the ratio of expenses is very much lower, and the volume of litigation much smaller, and it is suggested that the independence of the system is one of the chief defects in the British scheme of Workmen's Compensation.

Scope of Workmen's Compensation

To turn now to the scope and operation of the scheme. The principal Act applies to all persons working under a contract of service or apprenticeship, including clerical workers and persons engaged in plying for hire with any vehicle or vessel, who are remunerated by a fixed sum or by a share in the earnings. There are no age limits as in the case of Unemployment and National Health Insurance; a centenarian or a child of five, if working under a contract of service, would not be disqualified from receiving compensation merely by reason of age or youth. The exceptions under the Act are casual workers, employed otherwise than for the purpose of the employer's trade or business; members of the Police Force; outworkers; or members of the employer's family dwelling in his house.

The 1925 Act did not apply to non-manual workers earning more than £350 per annum, but by an Act which came into force on 1st January 1942 this limit was raised to £420, thus bringing Workmen's Compensation into line with Unemployment and National Health Insurance in this respect.

As already stated, the Employers' Liability Act allowed employers and workmen to contract out of the scheme, and this practice was also allowed, subject to certain safeguards, by the Workmen's Compensation Act of 1897. Under the present Act, however, the employer can only avoid liability if he satisfies the Registrar of Friendly Societies that he has a scheme of compensation in operation which provides scales of benefit to the workman not less favourable than those to which they would be entitled under the Act, and also that a majority (to be ascertained by ballot) of the workers are in favour of such a scheme.

Personal Injury by Accident

Compensation is awarded to workers covered by the Act for "personal injury by accident arising out of and in the course of employment." The intention of Parliament as here expressed seems to the layman fairly clear; yet the interpretation of these apparently simple words has produced volumes of Court cases and, as Sir Henry Slesser points out, has proved one of the most fruitful sources of revenue to young barristers. It has also resulted in a considerable amount of hardship and injustice to the injured worker, whose economic and educational disabilities may put him at a grave disadvantage when he is confronted with all the legal resources available to a large insurance company or employers' association, unless he is protected by a trade union or has other legal aid.

The term "accident" has been defined as "any unexpected injury resulting to the workman in the course of his employment from any unlooked-for mishap or occurrence,"[1] and certain cases of blood-poisoning and other bacteriological infection have been held to come within the definition, where it could be shown that the workman's employment brought him into contact with such bacteria. Again, where a workman is already suffering from a disease—e.g. heart disease—and subsequently dies or is disabled thereby, if it can be shown that the work he was doing was sufficient, having regard to his condition, to cause death or disablement he may claim compensation as the victim of an accident. It is not necessary to prove that any abnormal exertion or strain was present, but merely that the work upon which the worker was engaged caused the accident.[2] Further, an assault by a fellow-worker or a stranger, or death or injury from lightning or other natural agencies, may be termed "accidents" entitling their victims to compensation if they arose out of employment.

"Arising out of and in the course of Employment"

The words "arising out of and in the course of employment" have given rise to a vast volume of litigation. To arise out of the employment, the accident must be sustained while the injured person is engaged in doing something which it was his duty as part of his employment to do; and to be in the course of his employment it must take place during the time he is engaged in his employment. A domestic servant who lives on the master's premises will be said to be continuously engaged in his employer's service. Any accident occurring to him would arise in the course of employment (unless it took place during his free time, when he was engaged on his own business or pleasure), but it

1 *Fenton* v. *Thorley*, [1903] A.C. 765.
2 *McFarlane* v. *Hutton*, [1926] 20 B. 222.

would not necessarily arise out of it. If during the spare moments of the working day he occupies himself with his own concerns and not with something incidental to his employment, and an accident takes place, it will not arise "out of" the employment, and the workman will not be entitled to compensation.[1]

It is also possible that an accident will entitle its victim to compensation even though it takes place after he has finished his day's work and is on his way home, or before he has reached his place of employment and is on his way thither. Compensation will only be payable in such cases if the workman was required by the terms of his employment to be in the place where the accident happened—e.g. if he was coming to his work or leaving it by a train or bus provided by his employer which was the normal method of travelling. The worker who mounts his bicycle to ride home and is knocked down and injured by a motor-lorry just outside the factory gates will not be entitled to compensation, because his employer did not require him to travel home in this manner, nor to incur this particular risk, although it is perfectly true that but for his work he would not have been injured. It is not surprising that workmen become confused when they are confronted with these distinctions, and it is fairly certain that a good many perfectly legitimate claims are not pressed, because the claimants are without proper legal advice and are discouraged by a refusal of the employer's insurance company in the first place. Another reason for disqualification from compensation is where the workman is injured while doing something which, though it was for his employer's purposes, was entirely outside the scope of his (the workman's) proper work. He may also fail to recover compensation if it is held that the accident took place as a result of his running an unnecessary risk, or "adding a peril" to his employment.

Industrial Diseases

Compensation may be claimed by a workman in the same way as for accident if he is suffering from certain industrial diseases, provided it can be shown that the disease was attributable to his work. In Schedule III to the 1925 Act a list of these diseases is given, together with a list of the occupations which might cause them. The list of occupational diseases included in

[1] *Gilbert* v. *Coles*, [1931] 24 B. 481.

this schedule is not exhaustive. The Secretary of State has power to make orders extending the provision for compensation to other diseases and other processes, and has in fact made a large number of orders of this kind. A sufferer from any of the scheduled diseases, if he is employed in the particular occupation scheduled against it, will be assumed, in the absence of evidence to the contrary, to have contracted the disease as a result of his employment and will be entitled to compensation as for an accident. These diseases include various kinds of poisoning which may result from working with certain noxious substances, and also such widely different afflictions as anthrax and writer's cramp. In most cases the workman who claims compensation for an industrial disease must obtain a certificate from the certifying surgeon for the district (whose name and address should appear posted up in the factory or workplace) and then make a claim. An appeal from the certifying surgeon's decision lies to a Medical Referee. Provision is made for the compensation to be shared among more than one employer where it can be shown that the disease was of gradual onset and partly contracted when the workman was in the service of a previous employer or employers. It should also, perhaps, be pointed out that "non-scheduled" diseases may also be compensatable, if the workman suffering from such a disease can show satisfactorily that the incapacity resulting from it is due to an accident arising out of and in the course of his employment. The occupation need not be the actual cause of the disease; it is only necessary to show that the incapacitating effects were brought about by some incident connected with the employment. For example, where a workman had suffered from heart disease for some time and while at work died as a result of a heart attack, it was held that there was a sufficient connection between the employment and the fatal illness to constitute an accident and entitle the dependants to compensation.

Method of Claiming Compensation

In the great majority of cases, the accident is a straightforward one, and clearly arose out of and in the course of employment. Before compensation can be obtained, notice of the accident must be given as soon as practicable after its occurrence, and before the workman has voluntarily left the employment, and may be given either verbally or in writing to the employer himself or to a supervisor or foreman under whom the workman is employed. Failure to give notice in this way may debar the workman from taking proceedings to enforce his claim for compensation. It is submitted that thus to put the entire responsibility of giving notice of the accident upon the workman may result in injustice, particularly in small establishments, where the workman may easily be quite ignorant of the requirements of the Act. Such cases have come to the notice of the writer on several occasions; the injured persons have been young girls employed, usually not in factories, but in shops or hotels. They had no one to advise them and had never heard of the Workmen's Compensation Act; all they knew was that they were injured, their wages had ceased and no National Health benefit was forthcoming. But for the lucky chance that someone with knowledge of the Act came across them, they would have given no notice of the accident and made no claim for compensation, and presumably none would have been forthcoming. In premises coming under the Factories Act, the law requires that an accident book be kept, in which particulars of industrial accidents must be entered. If this entry is made as soon as practicable after the accident takes place, it will be sufficient notice of the accident for the purpose of obtaining Workmen's Compensation.

After giving notice, a claim must be made by the injured workman or his dependants. This claim must be made within six months of the accident, or, in the case of death, dependants must claim within six months of the date of death. Failure to make such a claim, unless it is found by the arbitrator to be due to a reasonable cause, may debar the claimant from recovering compensation. Here again the law is hard upon the workman who has no one to advise him or her. Where the workman is a member of a good trade union his interests will be safeguarded by the union and no difficulty is likely to arise. But, according to Wilson and Levy, the proportion of trade union members is only about one-third of all insured workers, and as far as women are concerned, the number is much lower. Welfare workers and industrial nurses have several times asked the writer how they are to advise injured persons—generally women or girls — who know nothing of Workmen's Compensation and do not belong to a trade union. The customary reply is, of course, "Urge them to join a trade union," but this is not always immediately practicable. The fact remains that the lack of an administering authority and the placing of all responsibility for giving notice of an accident and making a claim on the worker and not at all upon the employer sometimes results in great hardship.

Basis and Amount of Compensation

If the prescribed procedure is satisfactorily followed, however, and the case is a straightforward one, compensation will be duly paid, and the basis and amount of this must now be considered. First, it should be made clear that the compensation takes the form of cash payments only. No provision whatever is made for medical treatment, surgical appliances or the rehabilitation of the injured workman. The scheme merely gives monetary compensation for loss of earning capacity, it is not concerned with the earner's pain and suffering, with his restoration to health, nor with his reinstatement in the community as a physically fit and useful citizen. In this, the British system lags far behind the practice of many other countries, including some of the Dominions.

In France, Germany, Estonia, Russia, and certain provinces of Canada and some States of the U.S.A., provision, varying in extent, is made for the vocational rehabilitation of the injured workman; in these countries, and also in Belgium, Holland (before the German occupation at all events), Switzerland and Japan, medical and hospital treatment, including in most cases the provision of surgical appliances, is given. The ratio between compensation and wages is also higher in nearly all these countries than in Great Britain, as it is usually at least 66⅔% of the weekly earnings instead of 50%. It is clear, therefore, that there is small ground for complacency on the part of this country. "Workmen's Compensation in England, even if viewed solely from the angle of weekly benefits, does not bear comparison with the corresponding legislation abroad . . . the lack of adequate statutory medical benefits and the absence of systematic provision for modern methods of medical and social rehabilitation reduce the actual compensation to a scale far below the international standard." [1]

[1] Wilson and Levy, *Workmen's Compensation*, vol. ii. pp. 107-8.

Compensation when Death Results from the Accident

Compensation is payable in case of death by a lump sum and children's allowances; in case of permanent or temporary incapacity by weekly cash payments, which may, in certain circumstances to be considered later, be redeemed by a lump sum. The weekly cash payments vary according to whether the incapacity is total or partial.

Where a workman is killed by an industrial accident, and leaves no dependants, the compensation is limited to the payment of £15 to cover funeral expenses.

Where adult dependants are left they are entitled to a lump sum representing three years' earnings by the workman or £200, whichever is the larger, with a maximum of £300; if, besides adult dependants, the workman has children under 15 dependent upon him, an allowance will be payable in respect of each child, calculated as follows: 15% of the workman's average weekly earnings, multiplied by the number of weeks between the date of death and the child's 15th birthday. Where the workman's wages were less than £1 a week, £1 will be taken as the figure; and where they were more than £2 a week, the latter figure will be substituted. The total compensation payable to dependants must not exceed £600.

Cases of Total or Partial Incapacity

When the workman is disabled as the result of an accident but not killed, the compensation to which he is entitled depends upon whether he is totally or partially disabled and also upon the amount of his wages before the accident took place. Unless the accident disables the workman for four weeks or more he will not be entitled to any compensation for the first three days of incapacity.

In case of total incapacity, if the workman's weekly wages were 50/- a week or over, he is entitled during incapacity (unless he agrees to a lump sum in commutation) to a weekly payment equal to half his average weekly earnings up to a maximum of not more than 30/-. This is increased by two temporary Acts: the Supplementary Allowances Act, 1940, and the Temporary Increases Act, 1943,[1] so that the maximum is now 35/- for the first thirteen weeks of incapacity and 40/- for succeeding weeks.

[1] These Acts apply to all accidents which took place after 1st January 1924.

Where the average earnings were less than 50/- the workmen's compensation amounts to a weekly payment equal to half his pre-accident earnings, plus an additional sum equal to one-half of the difference between the weekly payments and either the sum of 25/- or the average weekly payments, whichever is the less. This complicated formula may be illustrated by an example. Suppose an injured workman were earning on an average 38/- a week. He would be entitled to compensation amounting to half his earnings, i.e. 19/- plus 3/- (half the difference between 19/- and 25/-) or 22/- in all; and this amount is augmented under the 1940 and 1943 Acts by a further 5/- or 10/- a week, according to the duration of incapacity.

In the case of partial incapacity, i.e. where the workman is still able to earn something, though less than before the accident, he is entitled, if his pre-accident earnings were 50/- a week or more, to compensation amounting to one-half of the difference between his earnings before and after the accident. Under the principal Act the amount is limited to 30/-, but under the 1940 and 1943 Acts an additional allowance is given based on the proportion which the weekly payment he is receiving bears to the maximum weekly payment in his case. If the workman's pre-accident earnings were less than 50/- a week, his compensation will bear the same proportion to the difference between his pre-accident and actual or possible post-accident earnings as the weekly payment for total disablement bore or would have borne to the pre-accident earnings. A supplementary allowance is given under the two later Acts, based on the same principles as in the case of workers earning more than 50/-.

The 1940 and 1943 Acts make further provision for a male workman who is incapacitated by accident and who has a wife and children dependent on him; he is awarded an allowance for his wife of 5/- a week for the first thirteen weeks and 10/- for succeeding weeks and an allowance of 5/- for each child under the age of 15, or 16 if receiving full-time instruction in a school. But the additional allowances, both as regards children and as regards the workman himself, are limited by the fact that the total compensation payable, including the 1940 and 1943 additions, must not be more than seven-eighths of the average weekly earnings of the workman at the time of the accident.

The 1943 Act also raises the lump sum compensation for the

dependants of a deceased workman from a maximum of £300 to £400, and from £200 to £300, and substitutes £700 for £600 as the maximum amount payable in lump sum and children's allowances together.

It should also be noted that a workman who is incapacitated by an accident when he is under 21 years of age and before he has reached his full earning capacity may, after six months have passed since the accident, apply for an increase in the weekly payments proportional to what he would probably have been earning if it had not been for the accident. If he makes his claim before or within six months of becoming 21, and if it is considered reasonable, the weekly payment will be increased.

Partial Incapacity Sometimes Treated as Total Incapacity

In certain circumstances it is possible that, although a workman is only partially incapacitated, he may be awarded compensation as though he were totally incapacitated; this is the case if an injured workman can satisfy the County Court Judge (*a*) that, having regard to all the circumstances, it is probable that he would, but for the continuing effects of the injury, be able to obtain work in the same grade in the same class of employment as before the accident; or (*b*) that his failure to obtain employment is a consequence wholly or mainly of the injury. Section 9 (1) 4 of the Act of 1931 states that the workman must satisfy the Judge that he has taken all reasonable steps to obtain employment, and he must not be in receipt of Unemployment benefit. This provision was intended to help the workman who had partially recovered, but has never been at all satisfactory. It is very difficult to satisfy the Courts that the workman's failure to obtain work is due "mainly to the effects of the injury" and not to the state of the labour market, or that he has taken all reasonable steps to obtain employment.

The position has been to some extent improved by the House of Lords decision in *Ingham* v. *Barstow* (1938), where it was ruled that the responsibility rested with the employer to show that the workman had not taken "all reasonable steps" to obtain employment. But the workman may still have to register at the Employment Exchange and explore all sorts of avenues which might lead to work, keeping a record of his efforts, though he knows, and the Exchange officials probably know and the friends whom he has approached know, that there is no work available which he could undertake.

Inadequacy of Present Amount of Compensation

It is clear that even with the increased allowances made by the Acts the amount of compensation is quite inadequate—especially for the skilled workman who has been earning perhaps £8 or more a week. A maximum of 35/- a week personal allowance, even with the addition of children's allowances, is an absurd sum for such a man, especially when it is remembered that the compensation includes no provision at all for medical or surgical treatment, nor for rehabilitation in working life. It should also be noted that the allowance is based on the "average weekly earnings" of the injured workman, not on his wage level; therefore weeks of unemployment or short time or holiday periods will count against him and bring down the amount of his compensation, so that he may receive considerably less than he justifiably thinks he is entitled to—having been told that he will get 50% of his weekly earnings.

Recording of Agreements

The majority of claims for compensation are settled by agreement between the workman or his representatives and the employer—either the employer personally or his insurance company or mutual indemnity association. The Act provides that when a claim is settled by agreement the terms of this shall be sent to the Registrar of the County Court for record; where the agreement is for a lump sum, whether this is instead of weekly payments or in commutation of them, it will not be legally enforceable unless it is recorded. The protection to the workman's interests thus given is more apparent than real. A very large number of agreements are unrecorded because the workmen do not know about the provisions for recording, and the employers—or more usually the insurance companies—will take the risk of an unrecorded agreement. It is apparently possible for an employer to pay compensation for some time under an unrecorded agreement, and then dispute any liability, denying both the accident and the employment; [1] it is therefore prudent for the

[1] Batt, *Law of Master and Servant*, 3rd ed., p. 444.

workman to insist on the agreement being recorded. If he has a good trade union behind him, they will probably look after his interests in this respect, but, as already stated, far too few workmen are protected in this way.

"Lump Sum" Agreements

Any agreement for a lump sum by way of compensation must, according to the Act, be registered, and it is necessary now to examine the circumstances under which redemption or commutation of weekly payments may be made. While the injured workman is receiving weekly payments he may be required to undergo medical examination by the employer's doctor from time to time, subject to certain State regulations as to the times and frequency of such examinations. If the employer considers that the workman has completely or partly recovered, he may apply to the County Court Judge to have the compensation stopped or reduced; and if he has made weekly payments for not less than six months, and the workman is still incapacitated, the employer may in the same way apply to have the weekly payments commuted for a lump sum. The workman must agree to such commutation after six months, and in the case of permanent incapacity the lump sum for a person over 21 must be enough to purchase a Post Office annuity equal to three-quarters of the annual value of the weekly payments. For persons under 21, the sum will be settled by the Court. It is also open to the employer to apply for commutation of the weekly payments at any time—before they have begun at all, if desired. An agreement of this sort must be registered in the County Court if it is to be enforceable, and the Registrar has power to refuse to register it if he considers it inadequate or thinks it may have been obtained by improper means. Unfortunately, the extent to which, and the manner in which, Registrars use their power varies greatly from district to district. It is in connection with these lump sum agreements that some of the worst abuses occur in connection with our present scheme of Workmen's Compensation. It is by no means uncommon for insurance companies through their enterprising and persuasive agents to suggest to an injured workman after he has been receiving weekly payments for a few weeks that a great deal of trouble would be saved to all parties if he were to agree to commutation of the compensation for a lump sum. Injured workmen are often unduly optimistic as to their chances of recovery in the near future, and also those who have been living on a relatively small income are sometimes dazzled by the offer of a quite small lump sum, which "sounds a lot," and agree to commute their weekly payments for ridiculously inadequate amounts. Such agreements are not registered in the County Courts, for in the absence of a trade union or other protection the workmen are frequently ignorant of the requirements of the Act, and the employers or their insurance companies do not invariably enlighten them. The present writer has come into contact with several instances where injured workers—generally women—had been exploited in this way because they had no one to advise them. In some cases it was possible to obtain a more equitable settlement, which was duly registered, but in others the victims had been terrified by the idea of "going to Court" and nothing more could be done. Some form of protection of legal interests is nowhere more needed than in the matter of lump sum agreements.

Declaration of Liability

Compensation will cease to be paid when the workman has "fully recovered" from his injury, and a resumption of work at his former wages and in his former job will normally be taken to show full recovery. But with certain injuries, although the sufferer may have apparently recovered and may remain fit for his former employment for a longer or shorter time, the effects of the injury may show themselves at a later date, and he may again become incapacitated. Where there is a probability of this happening, the workman may ask the County Court for a suspensory award or a declaration of liability, which, if granted, will have the effect of keeping his claim open so that his compensation may be renewed if he should again be incapacitated from the effects of his original accident. Here again the ignorance of the workman as to these provisions may prevent him from benefiting from them.

How the Employer Meets his Liabilities

As already mentioned, Workmen's Compensation does not, in Great Britain, form part of the national system of Social Insurance as it does in many countries. There is no national fund to which the employer, the worker and the State all contribute. The Act lays the obligation on the employer, but, except in the mining industry, makes no provision as to how he shall meet his obligations. Many employers insure against compensation risks either in ordinary insurance companies or with mutual indemnity associations, probably covering the majority of the workers covered by the Act, but they are not compelled to insure in most industries. By the Workmen's Compensation (Coal Mines) Act of 1934, however, all employers in this industry must insure against their liability for accidents to their workers. Compulsory insurance is also included in some of the special schemes dealing with industrial diseases, e.g. the scheme for the sandstone industry.

The cases where the insolvency of uninsured employers makes it impossible for the worker to obtain, at any rate, the full amount of his compensation may be but a relatively small proportion of the total claims, but it is probable that there are a considerable number, particularly among small employers, in times of trade depression. It is impossible really to say how many of these hard cases there may be, for where it is clear that the employer is unable to meet his obligations it is not worth fighting him, and thus no claim is ever made. It is clear, however, that even if there are only a few—or relatively few—such cases, the workmen thus deprived of their rights are in a particularly cruel position, with no hope of redress. It is no consolation to the perhaps hopelessly crippled workman to know that his insolvent, uninsured employer has incurred an obligation which he is quite unable to meet. Compulsory insurance is in operation in nearly all other countries which have schemes of Workmen's Compensation, and it was advocated for this country by the Holman Gregory Committee on Workmen's Compensation, which estimated that in 1919 there were about 250,000 uninsured employers in Great Britain. Their recommendation as to compulsory insurance was not, however, adopted by the Government.

Disputed Claims

Where the employer is duly insured, the great majority of claims are settled by agreement. But in cases where the accident for which compensation is claimed is a serious one, causing a long period of disability, a very considerable proportion are the subject of litigation. Where this happens, the workman is obviously in a weaker position than the employer. Unless he has proper legal advice, he is sometimes forced by the fear of not getting anything to accept inadequate compensation rather than face Court proceedings, where he may be confronted with able Counsel before whose cross-examination he is likely to become bewildered and appear at a disadvantage. He is already suffering from an injury which incapacitates him from earning his living, and he is claiming the compensation to which he thinks he is entitled. Yet he is faced by a powerful organisation whose chief object appears to be to prevent him from succeeding in his claim. And it cannot be denied that the commercial insurance companies are primarily interested, not in justice to the workman, but in their own profits. On several occasions in the experience of the present writer, insurance companies have made offers of ridiculous amounts to injured workmen. When it became clear that the claimants had adequate legal advisers who were prepared to take up their claims, these offers were substantially increased. It is clear that until legal protection, through trade unions or other organisations, is very much more complete than it is at present, the danger of exploitation will remain—unless the system of settling claims is altered. Even where the workman is supported by his trade union, where excellent legal advice and assistance are generally available, a wealthy insurance company or mutual indemnity association is frequently in a considerably stronger financial position to bear the costs of carrying disputed cases perhaps to the House of Lords than is a trade union of working men and women.

From the evidence given before the various Committees and Commissions on Workmen's Compensation it appears that the majority of employers are in favour of the present system of insurance. Not all, however; in some cases employers would be perfectly ready to meet claims for compensation if it rested with them, but as they have insured against their liability with a commercial insurance company who deal with compensation claims, the matter is out of their hands, whatever their feelings may be.

Again, where a claim by a seriously injured workman is contested, delayed and perhaps finally defeated, the victim's fellow-workmen will know all about it, and it will certainly not make for good relations in the factory, nor for the popularity of the employer. Many employers must surely know this and dislike the system which necessitates it.

In foreign countries and in the Dominions the extent to which the system of Workmen's Compensation is State-controlled varies, but in very few is it so entirely independent as in Great Britain. A recommendation was made by the Holman Gregory Committee that, while a State-administered system was undesirable, a Commissioner for Workmen's Compensation should be appointed to supervise the whole field and to advise and pronounce on doubtful and difficult questions. But this recommendation, in common with most of the others made by this Committee, has never been put into effect.

Accident Prevention

One further point requires mention—the relation of compensation for accidents to the prevention of accidents. Workmen's Compensation as organised in this country offers very little incentive to the employers to make any great efforts to reduce the industrial accident rate, after risks have been covered by insurance. Little in the way of merit or schedule rating (i.e. the lowering or raising of premiums in accordance with the adoption and efficiency of safety measures) is in force here, though the experience of the United States seems to show that it is a valuable incentive to accident prevention. It must be stated, however, that a Home Office Memorandum presented to the latest Commission on Workmen's Compensation—the Hetherington Commission—was not in favour of merit rating, on the grounds that in a country with a highly developed system of safety legislation a very high percentage of industrial accidents was due to the personal factor or "accident proneness" of the workmen and would not be appreciably affected by merit rating. Even if this is true—and there are varying opinions about it—merit rating based on the steps taken by an employer to prevent the occurrence of accidents would encourage the careful employer, who feels a responsibility for his workers' safety, to adopt safety measures.

Great Britain was for long regarded as one of the leading countries in the field of social legislation—as she was certainly one of the pioneers. But so far as compensation for industrial accidents is concerned, even a cursory survey shows that, while much has been accomplished since 1880 when the Employers' Liability Act was passed, the present legislation is very imperfect and by no means ensures justice to the victims. Not only is our system inadequate in itself, but it lags far behind that of most other countries, some of which instituted social services much later than did Great Britain. It is clear that if we have made some advance on the road to social justice we still have a long way to go.

National Insurance (Industrial Injuries) Act, 1946

The workmen's compensation scheme described above will cease to be effective when the Industrial Injuries Act comes into force in 1948. Compensation for industrial injury will then change from being an obligation on the employer and will become an insurance to which worker, employer and the State all contribute, which will be administered by the Ministry of National Insurance. Many other changes will take place in the scheme, the most important of which are briefly outlined below.

A Contributory Scheme

Voluntary Insurance by the employer with a private insurance company or mutual indemnity association will cease and worker and employer alike will contribute compulsorily to the State Insurance Fund, in the following proportions:—

	Worker.	Employer.
Man (over 18)	4d. weekly	4d. weekly
Women ,,	3d. ,,	3d. ,,
Boys (under 18)	2½d. ,,	2½d. ,,
Girls ,,	2d. ,,	2d. ,,

The classes of workers covered by the Act are wider than those in the old scheme, e.g.—public employees are included; but children under the compulsory school leaving age are outside it, except where regulations may be made to include them.

"Accidents Arising Out, and in the Course, of Employment"

This formula is still used as the basis for deciding claims to benefit. As the Minister of National Insurance said in his speech on the Second Reading: "We have looked at many alternative phrases which have been suggested to us as substitutes for these familiar words, but I am bound to say that after full consideration we have decided that it is better to retain the words we have already in the Act. Not the least of our reasons for doing so was the fact that the phrase has been fully examined and interpreted by the Courts and its meaning is now, I think, reasonably clear and certain."

In the new Act it is specifically stated that an accident occurring in the course of the injured person's employment shall, in the absence of evidence to the contrary, be deemed to arise out of it; also that where an accident occurs while the injured person is travelling in transport provided by the employer, the benefit may be payable even though there was no obligation to use such transport.

Forms of Benefit

The benefit payable to the injured worker takes two forms:—

(*a*) Injury benefit which lasts 156 days, at the rate of 45/- weekly for workers over 18, 33/7 for those between 17 and 18 and 22/6 for those under 17.

(*b*) Disablement benefit, which is paid after the end of the 156 days, where the injured person is still suffering from "loss of faculty" which is likely to be permanent, or is substantial, i.e. not less than 20%; or where loss of faculty recurs at some time after the end of the injury benefit period.

In the assessment of disablement benefit a radical change takes place. Benefits are no longer to be related, as under the Workmen's Compensation Acts, to loss of earning capacity, but to the degree of disability suffered, and this benefit will therefore not vary with changes in earnings, nor cease entirely if the injured person, though still disabled, reaches his former wage level.

In the new scheme disability is assessed on broadly the same principles as are used in calculating disability for the purpose of War pensions; the injured person's condition will be compared with a physically and mentally normal person of the same age and sex. "A prescribed loss of faculty" will be taken as representing 100% disablement and lesser disability will be assessed accordingly. It should be noted that 100% disablement will not necessarily mean complete loss of earning power, though, of course, sometimes this will be the case; but whether it is or not, the injured person will still draw the rate for full disablement. Where the disability is assessed at less than 20% the benefit takes the form of a gratuity of not less than £150. This is the only example of anything like the old "lump-sum agreement" which is to be found in the scheme. Where a higher degree of disablement exists an industrial pension is awarded ranging from 45/- weekly (where disablement is 100%) to 9/-. This may be increased where the pensioner is totally and permanently incapacitated (i.e. is prevented by his injury from earning more than £52 a year), by an additional allowance of not more than £1 weekly. In special cases, and where the last-mentioned allowance is *not* awarded, a hardship allowance of 11/3 may be paid in addition to the industrial pension, provided the total payment does not exceed 45/-. Beyond this a constant attendance allowance of up to £1 a week, or in very exceptional cases £2 a week, can be awarded where the nature and degree of disability makes such provision necessary, i.e. where the disabled person requires an attendant to be constantly with him.

Dependants' Allowances

These are payable to one adult dependant at the rate of 16/- a week and to the eldest or only child of the injured persons at 7/6 a week; younger children of course come under the Family Allowances scheme.

Death Benefit

When the injured person dies as the result of the accident, death benefit may be awarded to the widow or widower (where the latter has been mainly dependent upon the deceased person), children and possibly other relatives. A widow's pension amounts to 20/- or 30/- according to age and circumstances, with a gratuity on re-marriage, when, naturally, the pension ceases; the allowance to the only or eldest child is 7/6 a week.

It should be noted that benefit may be forfeited in certain circumstances, one of which is where the injured person fails to comply with the regulation requiring medical examination or treatment, or where he obstructs or misconducts himself in connection with such treatment.

Determination of Claims

Fundamental changes are made in the new scheme in regard to administration. The procedure whereby disputed claims were heard by the County Court Judges with a possible appeal to Higher Courts, is abolished and new machinery established to deal with different kinds of disputes.

An Industrial Injuries Commissioner, with Deputy Commissioners, as necessary, are to be appointed, with general responsibility for the scheme under the Minister of National Insurance; these officers are to be Barristers or Advocates of not less than ten years' standing. Insurance officers will also be appointed for such areas as the Minister may direct, who will decide in the first instance on claims to benefit. An appeal will lie from their decision, or they may themselves refer questions to a Local Appeal Tribunal, consisting of representatives of employers and employed with a Chairman appointed by the Minister. The claimant, or an Association of employed persons acting on his behalf, or the Insurance Officer, may appeal to the Commissioner against the Local Tribunal's decision. The Commissioner's decision is final. For deciding questions relating to loss of faculty and payment of disablement benefit, Medical Boards consisting of two or more doctors will be established, from whose decisions an appeal may be made to a Medical Appeal Tribunal consisting of a Chairman and two doctors. Where questions of temporary disablement arise, reference may be made to a single doctor appointed by the Minister, with an appeal to the Medical Appeal Tribunal.

Industrial Diseases

Provision is made in the new scheme as in the old for the treatment of occupational diseases as accidents, provided that the Minister is satisfied that a particular disease should be so treated, having regard to its causes and incidence and other relevant considerations, and that "the disease is such that the attribution of particular cases to the nature of the employment can be established or presumed with reasonable certainty." Regulations may be made for special provisions relating to industrial diseases, particularly in regard to certain respiratory diseases.

Conclusion

This bare outline is perhaps enough to show that the new scheme is in many respects a great advance on the former provisions. A few points may be commented on a little more fully.

For the first time, the workman will contribute to the benefits which he will receive. Some criticism has been aroused by this provision on the ground that the risks of occupation are the responsibility of the employer and that he alone should bear the financial responsibility for compensating the injured workman. It was, however, pointed out in the Debate on the Bill that the right of bringing an action for damages for negligence against the employer still remains, where an accident appears to be the employer's fault, but that most accidents are either no one's fault or due to the negligence or possibly misconduct of a worker; and that a contributory scheme was therefore fair and reasonable. A more convincing defence of the contribution by the worker is perhaps the contention that workers and employers alike will participate in the administration of the scheme, by sitting on the Appeal Tribunals, and that they should therefore both contribute to its cost.

It will be remembered that the Beveridge Scheme proposed a special levy of extra contributions from employers in specially dangerous trades. This suggestion has not been adopted. It would in fact be difficult to implement satisfactorily.

The change in the basis of assessment has already been referred to and is particularly welcome. The earlier scheme, whereby a workman who had suffered a severe injury might draw no compensation at all if he were able—or if he were judged to be able—to earn at his former rate, was manifestly unfair and likely to have extremely bad moral and psychological effects.

By substituting a system of Medical Boards and other Appeal Tribunals for the County Courts in disputed cases the volume of litigation heard year by year in regard to Workmen's Compensation will disappear, to the advantage of all, except perhaps the legal profession. The abolition of insurance on a commercial basis and its inclusion in the national scheme will also be welcomed by most people, especially by social workers who have had experience of the difficulties encountered by injured persons in settling their claims.

Another advance on the earlier scheme is made by the linking up of benefit and hospital treatment and rehabilitation. Under Workmen's Compensation no interest was taken in the physical condition of the injured workman except in so far as it entitled him to a cash allowance.

Under the present scheme the workman will be encouraged and assisted to take full advantage of available treatment and plans for restoration to employability which may be made under the Disabled Persons (Employment) Act. A grant may be made from the Industrial Injuries Fund "in order to ensure that persons injured in industrial accidents have the full facilities for training and for sheltered employment provided under that Act." (The Minister of National Insurance in the House of Commons speaking in the Debate on the Second Reading of the Bill.)

Finally, the new Act provides benefits higher than those awarded under Workmen's Compensation and does not, as at present and as recommended by Sir William Beveridge, relate them to the workers' earnings. There is, as the Government spokesman in the Debate admitted, a wide gap between the benefits received under the Industrial Injuries side of the National Insurance Scheme and those drawn under the ordinary sickness side of the same scheme. Is this fair? Should a man who is injured working in a factory draw considerably more than another who perhaps sustains precisely similar injuries just outside the same factory? There is certainly a difficulty here, but it cannot be resolved by lowering the benefits for industrial injury. Apart from considerations of adequacy, the level of benefit now awarded under Workmen's Compensation would make this course impossible. Would it be feasible to raise the level of sickness benefit? This would presumably necessitate raising the level of other allowances given under the insurance scheme, and, as the Minister has said, would not be practicable at present in view of the effect on contributions.

Taking it as a whole, however, there is no doubt that the new scheme does remove many of the disadvantages of its predecessors and gives the injured workman a fairer deal and greater encouragement and help towards recovery than he has ever had before.

Chapter III

NATIONAL HEALTH INSURANCE

By JOAN SIMEON CLARKE

NATIONAL Health Insurance has been in operation in this country for thirty years. Lloyd George's "ninepence for fourpence" National Health Insurance Act of 1911 came into force on 15th July 1912, against bitter opposition. The doctors said it interfered with their professional status and freedom, Trade Unions and Friendly Societies said it trespassed into their preserves, the Insurance Companies disliked the State dabbling in insurance anyhow, and certain far-seeing Socialists, notably Keir Hardie and Philip Snowden, deplored the introduction of quasi-insurance social services based on contributions; they preferred the State to provide these for the whole community out of taxation. Today, when National Health Insurance is doomed to be abolished, the position is reversed in every case. The doctors, through the British Medical Association, put out suggestions for reforming National Health Insurance but did not want to see it scrapped; the Friendly Societies and the Insurance Companies became, with few exceptions, a vested interest on the side of National Health Insurance. Thirty years after the first one, another controversy, perhaps more bitter, broke out about the merits and defects of National Health Insurance. The interests, attitudes and principles involved cannot be discussed clearly without a knowledge of the intricacies of the National Health Insurance system. This knowledge is not easily acquired. It has been said with some truth that there are two chief marvels about National Health Insurance: first, that the human brain was able to invent such complicated administrative machinery, and second, that the system actually does work. The following description begins with an outline of the principles embodied in the National Health Insurance Act, 1936—the latest consolidating Act. The outline is then filled in with as much detail as space allows, with discussion of the major principles involved and of the controversies centring round them.

General Outline

The next few paragraphs are meant to give a sketch which the reader, it is hoped, can hold in his mind during the more detailed description which then follows. In violation of the custom of National Health Insurance legal documents, they are written without "buts," "ifs" and caveats; these come later. First, it is necessary to set out as clearly as possible the general pattern of the scheme, but those familiar with this pattern will do well to skip the next few pages and to begin their reading at page 92.

Entry into insurance is simple; for all manual workers, and for non-manual workers earning up to a rate of £420, in the majority of occupations it is compulsory, provided they are engaged under a Contract of Service. Contributions are paid both by worker and employer, and it is the latter who buys stamps from the Post Office and sticks them on to the employee's card.

Weekly Contribution Rates for National Health Insurance [1]

	Employer.	Employee.	Total.
Men	5½d.	5½d.	11d.
Women . . .	5½d.	5d.	10½d.
Juveniles (up to 16) .	2d.	2d.	4d.

National Health Insurance offers to insured persons three types of benefit: cash, medical and maternity.

Sickness benefit is payable for 26 weeks of illness, beginning on the fourth day. If illness lasts longer than 26 weeks, sickness benefit is replaced by disablement benefit at a lower rate, which continues indefinitely until the age of 65 (Women, 60). Unlike medical benefit, to which people are entitled from the payment of the first contribution, sickness, disablement and maternity benefit are conditional on both a minimum period of insurance and a minimum number of contributions having been paid.

[1] These contributions are paid jointly with Pensions Insurance contributions (*v.* p. 171). The total contributions are, therefore : employer and employee, 2/- each for men and 1/8d. for women.

RATES OF SICKNESS AND DISABLEMENT BENEFIT UNDER NATIONAL HEALTH INSURANCE

	Men.	Spinsters and Widows.	Married Women.[1]
Sickness Benefit:			
After 26 weeks of insurance and payment of 26 contributions .	12/-	10/6	10/6
After 104 weeks of insurance and 104 contributions paid .	18/-	15/-	13/-
Disablement Benefit:			
After 104 weeks of insurance and 104 contributions paid .	10/6	9/-	8/-

Medical benefit entitles the insured persons to free medical treatment such as would normally be within the competence of a general practitioner, and to the free supply of such drugs, medicines and appliances as he may prescribe, subject to regulations made by the Minister of Health. The statutory benefits do not include specialist or hospital treatment or convalescence.

Maternity benefit entitles an insured woman or the wife of an insured man to £2 at her confinement. If both wife and husband are insured, double benefit, i.e. £4, can be paid. Qualification for maternity benefit is the payment of 42 contributions and a period of 42 weeks of insurance. A discussion of the efficacy of this and other benefits is postponed until the whole scheme has been briefly outlined.

Medical and cash benefits are separately administered. When somebody enters into insurance he sets in motion two parallel sets of intricate machinery, both geared, eventually, with the Ministry of Health. Even if the new entrant is superlatively healthy, the mere fact of his inclusion in insurance will keep the machinery revolving, for he will be constantly figuring in statistical and financial calculations. If he is ill, the machinery will run faster; but it will never absolutely stop.

[1] "Class K Married Women" are those who since marriage have ceased to be insurably employed but who are eligible for six weeks' sickness benefit and for one maternity benefit by right of their previous insurance within two years from the date of marriage. They do not figure in this Table.

The newly insured person is immediately faced with two decisions. He should choose a doctor, and it is in his interest to choose an Approved Society. He may find that his chosen doctor declines, for one of several reasons, to attend him, and he will then have to find another doctor willing to take him. Choosing an Approved Society is usually simplified by the individual's ignorance of the names of the 7,000-odd Societies and Branches in existence. He is likely to join the one to which his friend belongs, and to avoid the one with which his father quarrelled. He is unlikely to realise that his receipt or lack of additional benefits in cash and kind at some hypothetical future date will depend on his initial choice of a Society. The insured person has a good deal to do with his Approved Society. Its local agent may call upon him, the Society will send him the card which his employer stamps, and which once a year he must return to the Society. He will receive his cash benefit from his Society when he is ill.

This procedure is carried out for roughly 22,000,000 persons who are members of Approved Societies. The stamped cards are surrendered yearly to the Ministry of Health, the Societies receiving sums of money in proportion to the total number of contributions paid by their members. These funds are available for the payment of benefit and for administration. No money is paid direct to the Approved Society by the insured person; his money is paid into the Post Office from which the insurance stamps are bought. Part of the contributions then circulate via the Ministry of Health to the Approved Societies, and then eventually, as due, to the insured population in benefits.

The administration of medical benefit is separate but equally complex. Doctors wishing to take insured patients must notify their Insurance Committee, a representative committee set up in each county and county borough. The doctor's name is added to the list of insurance practitioners for the area, and the Insurance Committee keeps an index of all insured persons who have chosen to be on his panel. The Insurance Committee is also responsible for organising the supply of medicines, drugs and appliances to insured persons, and it therefore must keep a list of chemists willing to dispense insurance prescriptions. Each Insurance Committee is advised on medical and pharmaceutical matters by local Medical and Pharmaceutical Committees respectively. It also has specially appointed Medical and Pharmaceutical Services Sub-Committees for investigating complaints about the services rendered to insured persons. Every detail of the administration is either regulated by the Act itself, or by statutory Regulations, or by the rules formulated by each Insurance Committee and approved by the Minister of Health. The tightness of these instructions is among the remarkable features of medical benefit administration.

Payments to doctors and chemists are made by Insurance Committees out of the sums allocated to them by the Ministry of Health; just as one part of insured persons' contributions goes via the Ministry of Health to the Approved Societies, so another part goes to the Insurance Committees. The proportions in which the money is distributed between these Committees is decided by the Medical and Pharmaceutical Distribution Committees which are appointed by the Minister. Sometimes an Insurance Committee receives a sum less than that which should have been due to it. This is an ingenious device for making doctors and chemists conform to National Health Insurance standards. If they are considered guilty of one of a number of offences ranging from negligent treatment to over-prescribing, they may be arbitrarily fined—that is to say, the Minister,[1] guided by a special Advisory Committee, may withhold a sum of money from the relevant Insurance Committee, which in turn deducts this amount from the moneys normally due to the doctor or chemist in question. The Minister is also the final authority for deciding whether doctors and chemists should be disallowed from doing further insurance work; here again he is guided by special committees. Referees appointed by the Minister decide disputes arising between insured persons and Insurance Committees, or between the latter and Approved Societies. The multiplicity of provisions for deciding disputes is almost as great as the multiplicity of committees and of funds.

Insured Persons

We now begin to examine in some detail the system which has just been briefly and generally described. National Health Insurance is not national in the sense that our education is

[1] For fuller analysis of the judicial powers of the Minister see W. A. Robson, *Justice and Administrative Law* (Macmillan, 1928), p. 111 *et seq.*

national; it is not available to the whole nation. It is not even available to all persons in the lower income groups. Its benefits are very strictly limited to insured persons, that is, to all manual workers and to non-manual workers earning not more than £420 yearly, other than those in excepted employment.[1] There were in 1938 approximately 17,000,000 insured persons in National Health Insurance. Yet it is estimated that about 35,000,000 people were then in families where the chief wage-earner earned £250 or less yearly;[2] therefore half the people in these lower income groups were not insured in National Health Insurance. The extra numbers included in National Health Insurance since January 1942 are those non-manual workers earning between £250 and £420 yearly, so the lower income groups are not affected. Yet it is in these groups, living at a low standard, that the incidence of sickness is highest. There are rational explanations for the limitations of the scheme, which is restricted to employed persons, for whom their employers contribute. It is logical to ask an employer to contribute towards sickness provisions for his own employees—it is likely to be in his interest to do so—but it is not logical to ask that employer to increase his contribution so that the sick wives and children of his workpeople could share these provisions. Workpeople themselves are already paying out too much in insurance contributions to be able to stand the entire cost of an extension of the scheme, and those without dependants would probably object to having their contributions increased so that the families of their workmates could be assisted. The only way to finance the inclusion of dependants would be for the State's contribution to be greatly increased. This would mean the end of the façade of "insurance"; we should have increasingly a State-supported system. But even if the dependants of insured persons were included, and this is sometimes advocated as a panacea by those who seek to preserve the National Health Insurance at the cost of some concessions to its critics, there would still remain outside the scheme all those small income-earners who work under no

[1] Excepted employment is mainly that where provision is made for employees "on the whole not less favourable than benefits conferred by this (1936) Act," and it includes teachers, railway men, civil servants, and local government employees, and those in the Armed Forces (National Health Insurance Act, 1936, First Schedule, Part II).

[2] W. S. Crawford, *The People's Food* (Heinemann, 1938), p. 28.

contract of service and so are ineligible for insurance. This group includes costers and stall-holders, crofters, small shopkeepers, independent workmen (sweeps, window-cleaners, repairing tailors), and the wives and families who work with them in partnership. When the original Act was passed in 1911, provision was made for persons with incomes not exceeding £160 yearly, gainfully occupied but not insurably employed, to come into the scheme voluntarily. The response was meagre, partly because such persons had to pay the whole contribution normally shared between workman and employer, and, probably, partly because entry into voluntary insurance necessitates an understanding of the possibility and also the initiative and energy required to take the proper steps. As long as title to benefit depends on a record of contributions paid, and these are shared between employees and employers, there seems no way by which all those in the lower income groups can be included without extra cost to the self-employed.

The scheme is, of course, primarily designed for the industrial population. It may be argued that it is unjust criticism to undervalue it for not including those for whom it is not intended. That is probably true. But it is important, before analysing the provisions for those whom the Act reaches, to see the system against the background of the national life as a whole. This is particularly true of medical benefit, where the whole community has a vested interest in the health of each constituent member. Medical benefit is presumably included in the Act to prevent sickness and to promote health; to give people free doctoring is a valuable aid. But the wives and families of insured workers, as well as those of workers in excepted employment, cannot normally get free doctoring, nor can self-employed persons and their families. The only domiciliary medical service publicly provided other than National Health Insurance is available through the Poor Law. Quite apart from the common aversion to any form of "relief," many sick persons in the lower income groups who find it difficult to pay for a doctor would still not be poor enough to qualify for inclusion in the Public Assistance Medical Relief List. It seems illogical, considered from the standpoint of the nation's health, that, for example, we should take the trouble to provide a free doctor for the greengrocer's roundsman, but not for the man who keeps a fruit stall round the corner, and not for the family of either man, although, of course, any of these excluded persons can see the Poor Law doctor if they will first get themselves near-destitute so that they can qualify. But what usually happens is that they postpone the expense of a doctor as long as possible, to the detriment of their own health, and, if their illness is infectious, to the jeopardy of their neighbours. However good the medical services provided under the National Health Insurance Act may be—and we shall come to that later—it is absolutely fallacious to suppose they constitute a comprehensive and adequate health service for the whole nation.

Benefits under the Act

1. *Medical Benefit.*—Medical benefit is administered by the *Insurance Committees* of counties and county boroughs. These are statutory committees of from twenty to forty persons, appointed in fixed proportions by Approved Societies (three-fifths), the local Council, the local Medical Committee and the Minister of Health. When these Committees were first set up in 1911 they were supposed to study the causes of ill-health in their districts and to be the means of diagnosing social defects, but they have no access to the relevant information. Doctors' medical certificates go not to the Insurance Committees but to the Approved Societies, and the latter often have their members scattered all over the country, so that National Health Insurance provides no basis for local or even regional health statistics. Secondly, the Insurance Committees originally organised sanatorium benefit for tuberculosis, a function which, modified and no longer connected with National Health Insurance, has passed to the local Councils. The main job which the Committees now do is the organisation and administration of medical benefit, including the pricing of prescriptions to ascertain the amounts payable to dispensing chemists. They also administer cash benefits to Deposit Contributors, and are empowered to undertake health propaganda.

The health propaganda work is steadily diminishing. It is generally thought to be more properly a function of the local health authorities. A few Committees arrange for doctors' lectures, but there do not seem to be any current programmes of comparable vitality, for example, to that of the West Riding

Insurance Committee, which did excellent work until 1934, when it stopped for lack of funds. The Committee organised Health Weeks; it prepared skeleton notes for speakers; arranged lectures and film shows; distributed health leaflets and held annual competitions in the schools for Health Essays and Posters. Insurance Committees are increasingly concerned with routine and arbitration, and decreasingly with constructive work calling for imaginative zest among their members.

The inside of an Insurance Committee's building is a gigantic filing system. In London's large Insurance House room after room is lined from floor to ceiling with index files. Every insured person is indexed both according to his doctor and according to his Approved Society; even though some Society may only have one member in the whole of London, it will have its index section with the one member's card reposing in it. Similarly, one can see at a glance the size of any doctor's panel. The clerical work is prodigious, especially in a city like London where there are frequent changes of address, often involving change of doctor within the Committee's area. Changes of doctor give endless trouble to the staff. Not only must all the records be altered, but at the next quarter Doctor A, who has lost a patient, must be allocated correspondingly less money, and Doctor B, who has gained a patient, must have more. In Manchester, for example, although only 5·7 of the insured population changed their doctors in 1941, this amounted to 17,800 transfers. In addition, there were 19,000 removals from and into Manchester of insured persons, 8,000 notices of transfer of practices were sent to the insured, and 126,000 notices were sent to doctors of changes in their lists. In the same year 17,000 letters were sent off and the staff also dealt with 10,000 personal enquiries. These labours are multiplied for Committees in all the counties and county boroughs in the country. It is no slight on the activities of all those who as staff or committee members work for Insurance Committees to say that the machinery is cumbersome and, as more persons are included in National Health Insurance, will become more difficult to operate. The whole system depends, among other things, on, first, the recording of every change of address for insured persons, and that in a community where industrial, and therefore, geographical, mobility is increasingly desirable. Secondly, it depends on the allocation of every insured person to the list of a reasonably accessible doctor; and thirdly, on pricing each prescription for insured persons dispensed by insurance chemists. It is relevant to ask whether this intricate clerical machinery really contributes to the actual quality of the services rendered to insured persons, or even to the solvency of the Health Insurance system.

Insurance Doctors.—Insured persons have a good deal of freedom to choose and change their doctors. If they do not choose a doctor they are liable to be assigned to the list of one by the Allocation Sub-Committee, and if the doctor of their choice refuses to take them they may apply for assignment to the lists of another doctor. But if a doctor refuses a patient he is still required to give any immediate treatment needed, and he must give him the names of other local insurance practitioners and also tell the Insurance Committee that he has himself refused to accept him. When an insured person wants to change his doctor he can either get permission both from the old doctor and the new one and change immediately, or, if he shirks telling his old doctor that he wants a change, he may give notice to the Insurance Committee a month before the end of one quarter and attend the new doctor from the beginning of the next quarter. If he removes from his doctor's district he is entitled to apply for acceptance by a doctor near his new home at once, and if his doctor's practice is sold or transferred he may tell the Insurance Committee within one month that he declines treatment from the succeeding doctor; the Committee is bound to notify him of any such change. On the whole, insured persons change their doctors little. It is generally accepted that they change more in urban areas where there is more choice of doctor. Available figures for the second year of the war show that the percentage of insured persons on doctors' lists who changed their doctors were: Gloucestershire, 5%; West Riding of Yorkshire, 4%; Manchester, 4·3%. Urban war-time statistics of change are inflated by blitz and blackout (London changes are thought to have been increased from 1% to nearly 3%), but even so it seems likely that the higher urban figures more accurately represent the insured population's demand for change of doctor than the lower rural ones, which are controlled by scarcity of doctors and greater distances. Doctors, also, are at liberty to have patients removed from their lists; they must give notice to the Insurance

Committee, which will instruct the insured person to seek acceptance by another doctor. The patient's name is then removed from the original doctor's list as soon as he has found another doctor, or, in any case, within not more than fourteen days from the Committee's receipt of the notification. However, if the patient is actually under treatment and unable to work (unless he is a chronic patient), his doctor cannot have him transferred for the duration of the illness and for a fortnight after the patient has been declared fit to work.

Every doctor must be paid a quarterly instalment of a *per capita* fee (15/- per annum at present) for every patient on his list. To this payment will be added that for any approved claims the doctor may make for attendance on temporary residents, and for emergency treatment to insured persons not on their lists; the scale of such payments is stipulated in the Distribution Scheme prepared by each Insurance Committee and approved by the Minister of Health. The doctor will also receive payment for drugs, etc., administered for immediate use at the rate, usually, of 1/3 per annum for every hundred insured persons on his list; for those patients to whom he is required by the Committee to supply all drugs, etc. (because they are remote from a chemist), he may receive a capitation fee of 3/- yearly for each such patient, or he may be paid at a prescribed rate for all drugs, etc., actually supplied. After all this individual accounting, the doctor must still be paid his proper share from the Mileage Fund. This fund, to which the Minister of Health makes an annual grant from the Central Mileage Fund, is distributed to doctors on the basis of their returns showing the number of patients living far from the surgery or in places difficult of access. The Insurance Committees issue regulations defining when payments from the fund may be made. Surrey, for example, includes in its scheme payment in respect of patients whose homes must be reached on foot, and gives credit for "each half-mile or part of half-mile of walking." The West Riding Committee provides in this way financial compensation to doctors in respect of those of their patients who live along "gated roads"; doctors send in returns of the number of gates they must alight from their cars to open when visiting these patients. These details may seem trifling, but they are the content of National Health administration. They show, too, the doctor's relationship to the whole scheme. However skilled he be, and however interested in the practice of medicine, his relationship with the State service is mainly one of cash payment.

Insurance practice cannot be discussed separately from ordinary general practice in this country. The National Health Insurance scheme is interwoven with the whole pattern of our medical services. Most general practitioners have both private and insurance patients, treating them in the same surgeries and incurring the same overhead expenses in regard to both. The difference is, of course, that insurance patients, provided that the doctors can attract and keep enough of them, bring in a fixed income steadily even if the patients are not ill. This is a great help to young doctors just beginning general practice. On the other hand, the *per capita* fee for insurance patients is maximal and cannot be increased, either if the patients receive much attention or if the doctor's growing reputation enables him to charge high fees to private patients. It is therefore financially advisable for a doctor to start general practice with a large panel of insurance patients and then to reduce this gradually when he is able to build up his income through private practice. Intellectually this is also an advantage, for not until he can maintain or increase his income while decreasing the number of his patients can a doctor have either the leisure or the money to do medical research or even by reading to keep abreast of current scientific knowledge. However, the immediate concern of a young general practitioner without private means is to pay the high overhead expenditure on premises and equipment generally expected by his patients. At the same time he may be paying off a heavy debt incurred in the purchase of his practice. Money must concern him more than science. These problems are inherent both in private and insurance practice. However, unlike private practice, insurance practice is subsidised by public funds and carries with it the State's guarantee of satisfactory service to the patients. But for this qualification it is indistinguishable in principle and organisation from ordinary private practice. Therefore, although this chapter is concerned with National Health Insurance only, it is necessary to consider briefly the position of general practice for insured and uninsured alike, both to evaluate the quality of the service given, with Government backing, to the insured, and to determine whether the extension of the present form of insurance practice is progress in the right direction.

The Limitations of General Practice.—The limitations of general practice—and these are becoming increasingly apparent—result partly from the speed of scientific advance. Knowledge learned ten years ago may be already superseded. It is increasingly important but extremely difficult for doctors to keep up to date. A newly qualified doctor going into general practice will find it almost impossible to continue satisfactorily his medical education. There are two main reasons for this. First, he must work so hard and so long [1] that he will have little time for learning; second, even if he can find the time there is no recognised way for general practitioners to keep currently informed other than the perusal of medical journals. There is no way, for example, for the average practitioner to learn to administer any of the new life-saving drugs except by reading the instructions printed on the label by the manufacturing chemists; yet these drugs are difficult to use, and their effects are still unpredictable and often frightening; nor is there any way for doctors to learn to treat varicose veins by injection. Reading is not enough. A doctor wants to see new types of treatment carried out and to have instruction himself by experts. But he has no normal chance of this; when he first goes into general practice he will find himself remote, if not in mileage, in effect, from the big hospitals. He may become connected with a small "cottage hospital," but there he will have little chance of learning more than he and his colleagues put into the work. When he refers his patients to the big hospitals he will have little chance to see them treated or to discuss their symptoms with the specialists.

Post-graduate courses are an attempt to counteract the practitioner's isolation. In 1937 the Ministry of Health arranged courses for insurance doctors, who were able to attend recognised medical schools free of charge, a locum tenens being provided meanwhile to look after their practices. It is early to judge how successful these might have been if not interrupted by the war.

[1] Further, a N.H.I. doctor has a considerable amount of clerical work for which he must either reduce his income by paying a secretary or reduce his leisure by doing it himself. Apart from any special queries, he must make returns of the following: Refusal to add persons to his list, acceptance of insured persons, patients in respect of whom he claims from the Mileage Fund, claims of drugs supplied direct.

Certainly the first comments were unfavourable, doctors complaining that lecturers did not give instruction relevant to general practice. But curricula could have been improved with experience. In 1939 courses were to have been provided for about 1,200 doctors, or about 7% of all insurance doctors. A further experiment was planned in the provision of an eleven weeks' course at the British Post-graduate Medical School which doctors could attend on two afternoons weekly. But these courses, however good, will not be as good as facilities for doctors, once qualified, to remain in organic contact with medical progress. Short *ad hoc* courses cannot take the place of easy access, all the time, to a first-class hospital, with opportunity to observe modern methods of treatment. The insurance doctor is in a particularly anomalous position, for he is hedged about, and rightly, with penalties for "failure to exercise reasonable skill." But there is, and can be, no definition of "reasonable skill." The elderly doctor, with the best intentions, may exercise skill which would have been considered reasonable thirty years ago but which has been long superseded. If we want to build a healthy nation we must somehow see that our doctors are constantly versed in current medical knowledge. Tuition and demonstration must be available for them throughout their professional lives.

The insurance doctor cannot increase his lists beyond 2,500 patients, he may not charge or accept fees other than those paid him by the Insurance Committee, and if he wants to limit the size of his panel by refusing to have new patients allocated to him he may only do so with the consent of the Allocation Sub-Committee of the Insurance Committee; the moneys payable to him will then be reduced by a percentage fixed by the Sub-Committee. Most doctors, therefore, have both private and insurance patients. The latter, provided he keeps them, furnish an irreducible nucleus income; the former give the financial elasticity through which he hopes to better his position. Although about 84% of all doctors in the country have insurance practices, the majority of them run private practices as well. In the last year before the war the numbers of insured persons in the country worked out at roughly 1,000 per insurance doctor. In July 1941 there was an average of about 1,100 insurance patients per Manchester insurance doctor. In Gloucestershire at the same date the average was 680,[1] and the distribution of insurance patients among doctors is shown below.

PERCENTAGE OF INSURANCE PATIENTS PER DOCTOR IN GLOUCESTERSHIRE, OCTOBER 1941

Insurance Patients per Doctor.[1]	Percentage of Insurance Doctors.
2,000 and over	5·8
1,000 to 1,999	27·5
500 to 999	15·0
100 to 499	19·9
50 to 99	7·5
Less than 50	24·3
	100·0

This table shows that 52% of the Gloucestershire doctors had less than 500 patients on their panels within the county. So, from capitation fees, exclusive of mileage and emergency payments, 52% of the Gloucestershire doctors received less than £243 15/- per annum, the sum due for 500 insurance patients. Doctors all over the country with small panel practices look to their private patients to augment their incomes. It is in their interest to attract more and richer private patients. However scrupulously high-minded doctors attend to their insurance patients, it is clearly richer private patients who are profitable, and doctors are so placed that they have to think in terms of cash. The financial aspect of general practice must be clearly understood. Those who believe that medicine is a vocation and that the practice of medicine is a high form of service to the community would do well to recognise that general practice today is a commercial proposition. Many doctors buy their practices and thenceforward struggle both to pay off the debts frequently incurred and to equip themselves as conventionally expected. Increased capitation grants from National Health Insurance might give the doctors more security and might enhance the position of the insured persons *vis-à-vis* the private patients—(some doctors still provide separate waiting-rooms and

[1] Plus a few out-county patients for doctors living near the county border.

entrances for panel patients). But this would not alter the basic emphasis on cash rather than on excellence of service. Doctors would still be weighed down with the burden of debts and of expensive overheads. They would not have that security and that freedom to concentrate their whole energies on healing which they would have if their premises were publicly provided and if they were salaried servants of the State. Health is a vital national asset; medical practice is a vital national service. Health and medicine should be thought of nationally, and the whole resources of medical knowledge should be available to any sick citizen. National Health Insurance is inadequate not only because it is limited to one section of the community but because it is integrated in a medical system based on obsolescent methods and values.

Thirty years ago, when National Health Insurance was introduced, it was reasonable that it should be based on doctors' private surgeries. Diagnosis and treatment were likely to be satisfactory according to contemporary standards. Today modern medicine calls for elaboration of equipment which few private doctors have either the money to buy or the space to instal. How many general practitioners possess an X-ray apparatus or a fluoroscope? How many of them could use these instruments if they had them? Treatment by diathermy, iron lung, blood transfusion, all need specialised application and specialised equipment. The doctor sitting in his surgery or carrying his bag into the patient's home can no longer diagnose or treat to the standards demanded by modern medical technique. Frequently he needs help, advice or apparatus which he can only procure by reference to clinic, hospital, or Harley Street. His isolation handicaps him and affects his patients. These are the factors which have led to the new Act's requirement that Local Authorities shall establish Health Centres from which those general practitioners so desiring can see their patients instead of using private surgeries. The new idea here is the public provision of facilities for general practice, rather than Health Centres, which, with limited functions, have already been experimentally established by a few Councils. Also the development of Maternity and Child Welfare Centres, of Tuberculosis Clinics and Sanatoria, of the School Medical Service, of Adult Clinic Services provided under the permissive sections of the Public

Health Acts, and of Public Hospitals, are drawing patients away from general practice. Teamwork in hospitals and clinics is valued increasingly both by doctors and patients, and this seems to be the future way of medicine if the resources of modern medical knowledge are to be fully used. It is not the general practitioner who is obsolescent—he is the pivot of medical practice —but his isolation from specialised colleagues, his lack of apparatus and his struggle to make money.

Complaints against Insurance Doctors.—Complaints against insurance doctors may arise in various ways. The most threatening to the doctor is a complaint of negligence made by (or on behalf of, or in respect of the treatment of) an insured person. He may be accused of failure to attend a patient, of faulty diagnosis, careless prescribing, slap-dash examinations, or the issue of improper certificates. The case will be heard by the Medical Services Sub-Committee of the Insurance Committee, consisting of an equal number of doctors and of so-called representatives of insured persons (i.e. of Approved Societies), with an impartial chairman. Both the doctor and the complainant are invited to attend, and they may each bring a friend to help present the case, provided they do not pay a legal man to come. The Sub-Committees take a great deal of trouble to sift the evidence and to give fair decisions. Insurance doctors say that the machinery works extremely well, and that they have confidence in the judgment of the Sub-Committee. Reading through reports, one gets the impression that decisions favour doctors more frequently than patients, but the complaints of the latter are often extremely tenuous. This is especially so when a patient has died and the relatives complain; they seem to tax the doctor with past anecdotes and snatches of conversation of which they would have taken no notice if the patient had lived. There may be an element of the psychological projection of guilt here, relatives, particularly widows, seeking escape from their own real or fancied neglect of the patient by using the doctor as a scapegoat. Experience of many such cases may predispose Sub-Committees to take the doctor's part; one is certainly astonished sometimes, after reading attentively a case in which the doctor seems to blame, to find at the end a decision in his favour. But here, again, the Committee with its expert knowledge may think it hopeless to expect all doctors to maintain a first-class service all the time, especially that minority of doctors who have a full panel practice plus a large cash practice of relatives of the insured. For example, a doctor was recently cautioned for issuing two medical certificates without visiting a patient who sent for him; in defence the doctor said that—

> "at the time in question he was very busy, and from day to day was having to put off visits which he could not possibly make, although he was working from 9 a.m. to 9 p.m. with only short intervals for meals."

Working as hard and as long as they do, it is remarkable that more doctors do not get into these difficulties. But the interests of the patients would be better served by an alteration of the system than by "ex post facto" investigation.

If the findings of the Medical Service Sub-Committee go against the doctor he may appeal to the Minister, who will appoint three people to hear the case. When the case is substantiated, the Insurance Committee, acting on the advice of the Sub-Committee, may, first, "caution him," i.e. do nothing but warn him—this happened to the doctor just mentioned, who was found to have issued two certificates without seeing the patient, and to have refused to visit him during two separate short periods of illness. Or, secondly, the Committee may limit the number of patients which the doctor has on his list, on the grounds that he has too many to be able to attend to them all properly. This, as we have seen, means cutting his income. Thirdly, the doctor may be required to pay any reasonable expenses incurred by the complainants. (But if the doctor wins the case he does not get any expenses at all.) These are punishments which the Committee can inflict on its own authority. A more serious penalty is a report to the Minister that the doctor has been guilty of a breach of the terms of service; the Committee then confesses that, through the peccancy of the doctor, it has not fulfilled the conditions on which it receives money for the provision of medical benefit. If the Minister agrees, he may withhold money from the Committee, which in turn withholds it from the doctor. In plain language, the doctor may be heavily fined. There is no scale of such fines. They are fixed each time by an Advisory Committee appointed by the Minister and consisting of the Chief Medical Officer of Health, two other doctors from the Ministry and three insurance doctors. Finally, the Committee may make a "representation" to the Minister that the doctor should no longer be authorised to have insurance patients. The Minister then sets up an Enquiry Committee of a barrister or solicitor in actual practice and two doctors, and both the complainants and the doctor may be represented before this Committee by solicitors. The complainants are obliged to give beforehand a list of all documents they want to use as evidence, and the doctor is sent both a copy of their statement and a list of such documents, all of which he may inspect before the enquiry is held.

Although the Act and its Regulations contain these provisions for drastic measures against the doctor, they are rarely used. The fear of them does not hang over the average doctor any more than the fear of prison hangs over the average layman. They are penal measures designed to punish malpractice. Nowhere in the Act nor in its administration is there any provision for the encouragement of positively good practice. Each doctor sets his own standard, and his only index of efficiency is the number of his patients. One of the drawbacks of the National Health Insurance administration is this lack of constructive drive towards excellence in medical service.

Other complaints which may be brought against the doctor are heard by the local Panel Committee (the committee representing insurance practitioners for an area). Doctors may appeal against the decisions of the Panel Committee. The Minister then refers the appeal to three or fewer persons for decision. The penalty in every case is a fine, described as the "withholding of money from the Committee." Among complaints settled by the Panel Committee is excessive prescribing, when the doctor is in effect accused of wasting the money of the Fund by prescribing unnecessary or unnecessarily costly drugs. Actually this prohibition is rarely used, but doctors are supposed whenever practicable to prescribe drugs in their cheaper form rather than order costly proprietary medicines; but if a doctor can give a sensible reason for wishing to prescribe expensive drugs or branded goods he is usually allowed to do so.

Also, a doctor may be blamed for improper record-keeping. Under his terms of service he is required to keep a record of the diseases of his patients and of his treatment of them.

Actually the records of an insurance doctor are extremely sketchy, and would not normally be of much help to a consulting clinician; but there is a column for little ticks to be made whenever the patient is seen. These ticks are carefully counted when the doctor's records are inspected. Doctors feel that the ticks are more important to the Ministry than either treatment or disease.

Or, a doctor may be accused of improper certification. He is provided with various blanks for issuing initial, intermediate, final and monthly certificates, and he must be careful not only to date them on the dates when he sees the patient, but to see that the whole period of continuous illness is covered by dated certificates. This is not always as easy as it sounds, for if a patient is due to have another certificate on Wednesday, and arrives to see him not on Wednesday but on Friday, the doctor is in a quandary about the dating of the certificate. Patients literally demand certificates from their doctors when they consider they should stay off work. If the doctor seems to them hard-hearted in refusing such a certificate, the patients sometimes change doctors, taking their whole families with them. In the words of an experienced insurance doctor, "Certification is a ramp. We are absolutely in the hands of the patients."

A curious check on certification is provided by the sick visitors who are employed by Approved Societies to visit workers ill in their homes. The large Societies employ whole-time visitors, others have part-time workers only, still others, where the agent or secretary of a small branch is a woman, call her the sick visitor but in fact dispense with visiting. But the big Societies, especially those sponsored by industrial Assurance Companies, visit assiduously; insured persons object to this practice, feeling they are spied upon. Indeed, when a worker who is in receipt of benefit, but is not confined to bed, hastens home in the evening in a panic in case "they" catch him away from home after stipulated hours, one has the feeling of a small Gestapo. Theoretically, of course, sick visitors call to see that the doctor's orders are being carried out and that home conditions will accelerate recovery. In fact, their job is to see that insured persons do not malinger on the funds of the Society. Recently one of the leading Industrial Assurance Companies advertised for a sick visitor for its Approved Society in a country area. A woman answered the advertisement, emphasising her experience in welfare work. The secretary of the Company replied saying that welfare knowledge was irrelevant, as the object of the work was to prevent fraudulent claims. There is no reason why we should make a moral judgment here. It is reasonable to prevent fraudulent claims. But it is also important to give sick persons an idea that we want them to recover, not as an economy measure but because the community needs each one of them to be as fit as possible. The lack of any positive and constructive drive towards good health is clearly exemplified by the activities of the sick visitor.

Approved Societies in conflict with doctors over particular patients may refer them for examination to the Regional Medical Officers, who are full-time salaried officers employed by the Ministry. They have usually had long experience of general practice and are not "specialists." Doctors themselves may refer patients also, but do so considerably less. In 1938, of a total of 421,660 references, 420,010 came from Approved Societies and 1,650 from insurance doctors. Of the total referred, 65% were women, and as many as 28% received a final certificate before the date fixed for examination. Only 38% (and the same percentage the previous year) of those referred attended for examination and were found to be incapable of work. Even allowing for some patients receiving final certificates before the examination in the ordinary course of events, for other patients relapsing and being too ill to attend for examination, and for the Regional Medical Officer making some mistakes, there seems to be too high a proportion of patients whose cases were dubious enough for referral but who, for one reason or another, did not have their own doctor's judgment confirmed. We may see here a reflection of the difficulties of insurance practice: the doctor's economic fear of losing patients, the tremendous pressure of his work and his professional isolation. The atmosphere of pull-devil-pull-baker tussle over certification is deplorable, and bad in all ways for the patients; it does seem to be one of the inherent faults of the National Health Insurance system as it is now organised and administered.

2. *Cash Benefit.*—Criticisms of the present cash benefits are so well known and so generally agreed that it is only necessary here to give a résumé for the sake of completeness. First, *sickness*

benefit is entirely insufficient to maintain the recipient, let alone his dependants. If when he is sick he has no savings, or no membership of Sick Club, Slate Club, Friendly Society or Trade Union nor other source of income, he must apply to the Public Assistance Committee for help. He or his wife must face investigation, anxiety and assessment at the moment when domestic disorganisation and personal distress may be at their height. Second, when he has been ill six months, and his standard of living is probably depressed by his illness, and his psychological condition in need of stimulus rather than discouragement, his National Health Insurance benefit is arbitrarily reduced. The injustice and foolishness of this arrangement show the total lack of any constructive social policy underlying National Health Insurance. At the point when we should take a firm grip on the problem and review the whole situation of the sick person with a view to returning him to the community as a healthy person as soon as possible, we push him down one stage further by reducing his income. Further, it is nobody's business to enquire after the well-being of the sick man.

Disablement benefit (which follows sickness benefit after 26 weeks of payment) carries with it no ancillary service of occupational therapy or rehabilitation. Nothing whatsoever is done to explore the potential capacity of the sick man, who, after all, may be crippled or chronically sick but nevertheless capable of sharing in the life of the community and contributing to it within his physical limitations. Nothing is done to alleviate the isolation of invalidity.

Lastly, *maternity benefit* is wasteful, inequitable, unconstructive. It is supposed to be administered "in the interests of the mother and child in cash or otherwise by the Approved Society." But the Societies employ no trained staff who will judge what is the interest of each mother and child. There is no provision for co-operation between the Approved Societies and the Maternity and Child Welfare Centres. In practice, the cash benefit is paid out by the Societies and no questions are asked or stipulations made. The sum paid, £2 where the husband only is insured, £4 where either the wife only or both husband and wife are insured, is an arbitrary sum unrelated to any of the needs of pregnancy or childbirth. What is it for? Is it compensation for the loss of the wife's hypothetical earnings, given whether she goes to work or not? It is too small a sum for this, and in fact the pregnant woman who normally earns may suffer real financial hardship. She may find her employment suspended or terminated on account of pregnancy, and yet her doctor will not give her (or her Approved Society will not accept) a certificate for sickness benefit because pregnancy is not technically regarded as sickness. If she asks the Employment Exchange for work when she is pregnant or when she is feeding her baby, she may find that the officials do not consider her "capable of and available for work," and she will thus find herself short of a great deal more than the £2 or £4 of her maternity benefit—a hardship increased by the legal provision that women shall not go to work for 4 weeks after their confinement. Alternatively, is the benefit intended, not for maintenance, but for the purchase of layette, etc.? If so, why should it be £4 for one woman and £2 for another? Or is it for the actual cost of the confinement? If so, why is there no interlocking of National Health Insurance and local authority services? The discrepancy of charge for services at confinement is very wide between one authority and another. There is similar variation of charges for home helps. Maternity benefit might be for any of these expenses, but it does not seem particularly geared to any of them. It is an anomalous payment of £4 for some mothers, £2 for others, paid without any constructive aim at all. This is the more remarkable as subsidisation of childbirth bears not only on the physical and mental well-being of the mother, but on the increasingly important population problem. It is reasonable that we should do everything possible to ease the economic deterrent to child-bearing, and that the community should provide medical and nursing services for every mother as a service in kind. The present incidence of maternity benefit is unequal; one insured married woman gets £4, another £2, but the unmarried mother gets £2 only if she herself is insured—not a penny comes to her from her lover's insurance, even though she may have more difficulty than a married woman in maintaining her health and nutrition, and thereby the child's. This is one of the major injustices of National Health Insurance; it is also one of its greatest mistakes. Moreover, everything already said about the limited incidence of medical benefit applies to the limited incidence of maternity benefit; the case for giving financial help to insured mothers applies equally strongly to all mothers. If the State wants children it should do everything possible to encourage motherhood.

Coverage and Qualifications.—The majority of insured persons (91% of those entitled to benefit in 1938) are in Approved Societies. Since the passing of a special Act in 1937,[1] young children between the school-leaving age and 16 who are in insurable employment have also been brought into the scheme. They are entitled to medical benefit from date of entry into insurable employment, but they are not entitled to any other benefit. However, they are allowed to join Approved Societies, and this period of membership counts towards qualification for any additional treatment benefits provided by their respective Societies. An interesting section of the Act authorises any doctor having the care of an insured juvenile to ask the local Education Authority for confidential information from the child's school medical card.[2] This is an improvement on the previous arrangements, which left children without any State-provided doctor in the interval between leaving school and being eligible to enter insurance. But young people still have no continuity of medical care;[3] routine medical examinations cease when they leave school, and they are unlikely to go to a doctor again until they are actually ill, and then the doctor is unlikely to seek out previous medical information unless there is something markedly abnormal. It is also deplorable that children are ineligible for dental or vision treatment, even if their Societies provide this, until they have been insured at least 2 years.

If persons have been engaged in insurable employment for not less than 104 weeks and then cease to be so employed, they are entitled to become Voluntary Contributors on payment of a weekly sum equal to the employer's and the employee's contribution added together. They are allowed to choose whether they will become voluntary contributors for Health Insurance or for Pensions or for both. Their Approved Societies will continue to administer Health Insurance, but the Ministry of Health will itself look after

[1] National Health Insurance (Juvenile Contributors and Young Persons) Act, 1937.

[2] The L.C.C. received between 4th April and 31st December 1938, 1,739 of such applications from medical practitioners, analysed as follows:

Child's record not traced	288
Clear of defect at last school medical inspection	427
Minor defects ,, ,, ,, ,,	860
Major ,, ,, ,, ,, ,,	164

[3] Except, in certain circumstances, a routine examination by the Factory Certifying Surgeon.

their Pensions insurance. Provisions for "free" and "extended" insurance periods are the same for Health Insurance as for Pensions Insurance for insured contributors, and are explained in the chapter on the latter.[1]

Contributions are "deemed to have been paid" for weeks of genuine sickness and unemployment, otherwise members falling into arrears are allowed to make a lump sum payment to their Societies in cancellation of these arrears, and so become ordinarily eligible for normal benefits during the following year; failing this, cash benefits will be suspended or reduced. Cash and additional benefit provisions are administered by the Approved Societies, with whom, and not with any Government Department, their members have to communicate.

Approved Societies.—Persons entering insurance may choose between applying for admission to an Approved Society or becoming Deposit Contributors. If they do the latter, their contributions are held by the Ministry of Health and they receive benefits only in proportion to their own contributions paid, so that the insurance principle does not apply to them at all. They do not have the advantage of joining a large insurance pool, from which persons who have qualified for benefit may draw out much larger sums than they have paid in. Approved Societies may refuse to accept persons with a record of such chronic ill-health or disability that they are likely to be abnormally burdensome on the funds. For example, sufferers from goitre, duodenal ulcers or asthma are likely to be rejected. All such persons may become Deposit Insurance Contributors and be entitled to full benefits under the Act other than additional benefits. They are looked after by the Deposit Contributors Insurance Section of the Ministry of Health, which is financed not only by contributions but by interest on the Deposit Contributors Fund and by sums standing to the credit of Deposit Contributors who die or leave the country. Benefits for Deposit and Deposit Insurance Contributors are paid out by the Insurance Committees.[2]

[1] *v.* p. 172.

[2] Members of the Armed Forces who belong to Approved Societies have a weekly contribution paid for them by their respective services, but maternity benefit for their wives is the only benefit which they may have while actually serving. The Navy, Army and Air Force Insurance Fund has been created to stand in place of an Approved Society to men who had not joined one when they joined the forces. Seamen who are not members of Approved Societies are entitled to join the Seamen's National Insurance Society.

Any body of persons may band themselves together into an Approved Society in order to administer the money benefits under the Act, provided the organisation is not carried on for profit and that the affairs of the Society are under the absolute control of the members, i.e. the insured persons, or their delegates, subject to the approval of the Minister of Health. Actually, the Minister, or rather the National Health Insurance Joint Committee, exercises strict control. For example, in 1937 the Joint Committee asked a Society to submit draft amendments of their rules. The draft was approved by the Committee but rejected by the Annual General Meeting of the Society. The Committee then made an order amending the Society's rules in accordance with the draft amendments. In the same year the Committee appointed a manager to take charge of another Society. However, these contretemps are rare.

Approved Societies are of diverse types. The majority are sponsored by other bodies which run Approved Societies as separate sections of existing organisations, e.g. Friendly Societies, Trade Unions, Employers' Provident Funds, Co-operative Societies and Industrial Assurance Societies. For a general history of the development of Approved Societies and a detailed account of their administration, readers should see the able and lucid account in the P.E.P. Report,[1] which cannot be bettered.

In the controversy which is likely to arise soon about the Approved Societies we should remember that Societies vary so greatly both in outlook, in financial position, composition and size (100 to 1,000,000 members), that one cannot reasonably generalise about them. All Societies are bound to pay sickness, disablement and maternity benefit, to comply with the Act and subsequent Regulations, to submit to Treasury audit, and to have their funds valued by the Government Valuer every five years. Beyond that they vary. The Secretary and staff of a small Friendly Society or the local secretary of a Trade Union Approved Society will get to know the members, will supplement the official letter-forms with friendly notes, or will even write, on their own initiative, explanatory letters to a member who is impairing his position by obvious misunderstanding of the rules. They will know the members by name. An Industrial Assurance

[1] Political and Economic Planning, Report on the British Health Services, 1937, Chap. VII.

Company's Approved Society, or even a large Benefit Society, knows the members only as numbers. The administration is impersonal. If, for example, a member writes a letter about dental benefit, it will be dealt with among a pile of similar letters; it may be only related subsequently to any previous history of, or correspondence with, that member. This may not matter, but the secretary of a small Society who troubles to look up previous correspondence, or who happens to remember the member personally, may frame his answer much more helpfully for that particular case. This is done so rarely that it is cause for pride when it is achieved.

However, the insured person who is tempted to join the Society whose secretary is locally known as a helpful and interested fellow may forfeit substantial advantages. That Society may give few or no additional benefits. At the last Quinquennial Valuation it may have had either little or no "disposable surplus." That is to say, the payment of the general statutory benefits may have absorbed all its available resources.

3. *Additional Benefits.*—Additional benefits may be provided within a fixed range by any Society found, at the Quinquennial Valuation, to have "a disposable surplus." This means that the actuary estimates that there will be an excess of future income (from contributions, interest, State grants) over liabilities, which are estimated future cost of statutory benefits and administration.[1] Members must have belonged to the Societies for two or more years before becoming eligible for additional benefits, but otherwise the receipt or lack of such benefits is independent of any action or qualification on the part of the members. If a Society happens to have a high average age and a high rate of sickness it will tend to use up more money on statutory benefits and to have less to spare for additional benefits. An insured person who joined a Society giving high additional benefits might find that after the next Valuation it gave considerably less. For example, a member of a certain Society who, ten years ago, received £7, the full cost of extensive dental treatment, would now receive, from the same Society, only half the cost of similar treatment. From the beneficiaries' point of view this is a great weakness. Each Society is responsible for financing its own additional benefits; members of different Societies, therefore,

[1] After taking into account its accumulated Benefit Fund.

not only get different benefits for a uniform contribution, but they may even be entitled to less additional benefit after a long period of insurance than was due to them after a relatively short period. As far as the individual members are concerned, the whole thing is a question of luck. Societies with a preponderance of members who are in dangerous trades or in occupations giving rise to sickness naturally spend more money on sickness and disablement benefit and have less available for additional benefits. Also, Societies whose members have a high rate of unemployment have proportionately smaller Benefit Funds. Although the Act makes provision for the Societies' income to be supplemented from the Unemployment Arrears Fund in proportion to their members' unemployment, this is done at a rate lower than the rate for actually contributing members. Thus the Societies whose members most need additional benefits are likely to be least able to give them. It is heartbreaking for keen secretaries of small Societies, eager to do the best for their membership, to find that they can give little or nothing of what members of other Societies get for the same contribution.

There is a further point about additional benefits. They are dependent on a surplus of income over expenditure. Societies tend to gain in prestige, and thence, as we shall see, in membership, if they have a reputation for giving good additional benefits. So they have an incentive to economise on statutory benefits. In other words, the sooner they can get their sick members back to work, the better for their funds. The dilemma in which many Societies thus find themselves is sadly illustrated by a letter sent out by a certain Society when it found itself unable to give any additional benefits:

> "As members of the Society, we feel sure you will agree that, whilst we have to administer the payment of benefits with very great care, a surplus to allow of increased benefits being paid could only have been obtained by being harsh in the administration, and we feel confident that you will endorse the action of the Management Committee, in dealing with all benefit claims in a sympathetic manner.
>
> No one regrets the enforced withdrawal of Additional Non-Cash benefits more than (the Committee), but those who have knowledge of the National Health Insurance procedure

. . . will recognise that the present position is a matter outside their control."

Actually, the factors governing the provision of additional benefits are not generally known among contributors; for example, a recent experiment showed that of twenty women clerks only one knew that variations in additional benefits were not the result of the "meanness" of some Societies! It is not really surprising that the majority of Societies do strongly press sick members "to get well," i.e. "off the panel." As an objective fact this is desirable, but the motivation, considered socially or psychologically, is wrong. Sick persons are pressed to get well by a body which is inherently uninterested in that person's physical or mental well-being as such; they are pressed to get well because they are an expense when they are ill. There is no hint in the administration which might tell the sick that the whole community is interested in their recovery so that they may once more be able to play an active part in the national life. There is nothing constructive in National Health administration. The sick are told, negatively, that they are required not to be sick; they are never told that they are needed,

PROVISIONS FOR TREATMENT ADDITIONAL BENEFIT, 1939 [1]

Name of Benefit and Statutory Number.	Number of Schemes.	Approximate Membership covered.	Annual Amount allocated.
Dental . . . (No. 9)	4,834	11,786,000	£2,265,854
Ophthalmic . . (No. 14)	4,821	10,050,000	564,223
Convalescent Homes (No. 11)	2,603	10,796,000	216,640
Medical and surgical appliances . . (No. 13)	3,968	11,348,000	203,207
Hospitals . . (No. 10)	2,246	1,606,000	90,892
Want or distress . (No. 5)	728	6,160,000	37,060
Approved Charitable Institutions . . (No. 16)	393	7,533,000	33,748
Nursing . . . (No. 15)	643	6,396,000	31,273
Convalescent home premises . . (No. 12)	20	614,000	28,589
Infection . . (No. 6)	92	3,875,000	5,570
Convalescent Allowances . . . (No. 4)	53	433,000	2,340
		Total .	£3,479,396

[1] Ministry of Health, Annual Report, 1938-39, Cmd. 6089, p. 149.

positively, to be healthy, alert, co-operative members of the State.

Additional benefits are classified as Cash or Treatment benefits. The former may be supplementation of sickness, disablement or maternity benefit, or the payment of sickness benefit from the first instead of the fourth day of incapacity. Treatment benefits are those which are shown in the table on page 116. Approved Societies choose how they will use their disposable surplus for additional benefits within the permitted range, so that there are wide divergencies of practice, some Societies paying generously on a few benefits, others making provision for some assistance throughout the range, but not lavishly. As the P.E.P. Report,[1] which deals admirably with this whole question, emphasises, benefit is not transferable, and an insured person who wants to change his Society, or Branch, when he moves to another district, will have to qualify all over again in the new unit.

In 1939, 72% of members of Approved Societies were entitled to cash additional benefits, and 91% to treatment additional benefits.

The following table, which supplements a similar, but earlier, one in the P.E.P. Report, shows the disparity between typical Societies:

ADDITIONAL BENEFIT ARRANGEMENTS, 1942

BENEFITS.	SOCIETIES.				
(Quoted here for men only.)	Trade Union (Skilled). 24,900 Members.	Trade Union (Unskilled). 69,300 Members.	Trade Union (Sedentary). 7,000 Members.	Local Friendly. 10,300 Members.	Collecting. 387,900 [2] Members.
Sickness increase	Nil	Nil	5/–	2/–	3/–
Disablement increase	Nil	Nil	2/6	1/–	1/6
Maternity increase	Nil	Nil	£1	4/–	6/–
Paid from first day	—	—	Yes	—	—
Dental	Nil	Nil	75% of cost	50% of cost	50% of cost
Ophthalmic	Nil	Nil	Full cost of treatment and appliances	Treatment to 3 gns.	Treatment to 3 gns. Appliances by Society's scale
Want or Distress	Nil	Nil	Yes	Yes	Yes
Convalescent home	Nil	Nil	Travelling and Maintenance to 30/– p.w.	Nil	Maintenance Travelling to 20/–
Hospital	Nil	Nil	Maintenance, Treatment, Travelling to 3 gns. p.w.	Nil	Nil
Medical and Surgical Appliances	Nil	Nil	Full cost	Nil	Cost to £1, Full cost; above, one-half, max. £2 10
Nursing	Nil	Nil	Full cost	Nil	Full cost
Infection	Nil	Nil	Nil	Nil	Yes
Charitable Institutions	Nil	Nil	Yes	Yes	Yes

[1] Political and Economic Planning, *op. cit.*, p. 207.

[2] Membership at Fourth Valuation.

Dental and Ophthalmic Benefit.—Those additional benefits most frequently provided are both administered by Approved Societies in conjunction with specially appointed bodies — the Dental Benefit Council and the Ophthalmic Benefit Approved Committee. Maximum fees for dental treatment to insured persons are laid down by the Regulations, but it is important to note that dental benefit may only be provided by Approved Societies whose surplus funds permit of the payment of not less than 50% of the total cost of treatment. Members of Societies with insufficient surplus are entitled to no dental treatment. But even among those who are entitled to treatment many fail to procure it, for the majority of Societies expect their members to pay half the cost. The British Dental Association [1] quotes a pre-war enquiry in sample industrial districts which showed that "from 5 to 50% of insured persons applying and eligible for Dental Benefit are unable to proceed with treatment owing to their inability to pay their proportion of the cost." These defects in the insurance provisions contribute to the general dental neglect among adults, and it is not surprising that the Association reports an unduly high proportion of dentures and extractions among insurance patients when these do eventually reach the dentist's chair. All the circumstances of insurance dental treatment discourages first-class work: the patient obtains a Dental Letter from his Approved Society on which the dental surgeon must fill in details of all treatment required. The Society then states how much grant it will make towards the treatment indicated. The dentist must make his estimate before he does any work in the mouth at all, and rely on the patient's good sense to return quickly for treatment to begin; only very rarely can Approved Societies be persuaded to pay for (or to permit the member to pay for) X-ray examination for help in initial diagnosis.

The Ophthalmic Benefit Approved Committee is composed of representatives of organisations of Approved Societies and of opticians. It was set up in 1937, and then prepared, and now keeps current, a list of about 10,800 optical firms and opticians through whom insured persons entitled to ophthalmic benefit may procure glasses. This is a great advantage, as there is no

[1] British Dental Association: Memorandum to the Interdepartmental Committee on Social Insurance and Allied Services, 1942.

professional organisation or State registration of opticians as of dentists, and it is extremely difficult for members of the public to know whether a self-styled optician is genuine or bogus. Approved Societies must adopt a scale of charges drawn up by the Committee, and are not allowed to make any grant towards the cost of glasses if it exceeds that scale. Spectacle frames so supplied must conform to standards laid down by the Committee, and will then be marked "O.A.B.C."; they may only be manufactured under licence from the Committee when the pattern has been passed by its technical sub-committee. In 1938, samples manufactured by 85 firms were passed. Of course, obtaining glasses is the final process in the treatment of bad sight; examination, treatment, prescription, come first. The Regulations allow of a routine vision test by the optician, but examination by an oculist is only permitted on medical recommendation. It is extraordinary that when, for example, the London School Medical Service frowns upon parents who buy their children spectacles from opticians and encourages them to consult an oculist, National Health Insurance, into which the children pass when they go to work, provides a service of opticians only, except for special cases. Insured persons obtain ophthalmic benefit in the same way as dental treatment—they verify their title to benefit and procure an estimate from the optician; the Societies then tell the optician how much they will contribute towards the cost.

Other additional benefits are provided less frequently than dental and ophthalmic. Convalescent benefit is generally paid as a cash contribution towards the cost of maintenance in a convalescent home, but Societies are also allowed to build and maintain their own convalescent premises, and to make special out-of-pocket allowances to persons convalescing. These allowances, those to insured persons unable to go to work because they are in quarantine, and discretionary grants to members in want or distress, are paid direct to the member in cash. The other so-called treatment benefits are contributions towards the cost of specific treatment or appliances, but do not involve actual provision of these services by the Approved Societies except in the rare case of the building and maintenance of a convalescent home. There is no way for insured persons to obtain specialist treatment under the Act other than that of dental and ophthalmic surgeons. It is true that, one way and another, through voluntary or municipal hospitals, citizens, whether insured or not, can eventually be seen by relevant specialists, but there is no co-ordinated system for the provision of specialist services. Somebody with, for example, a diseased leg may be referred to a hospital by his insurance doctor. The hospital will assess him for cost of maintenance and treatment; perhaps his Society will pay this; if his leg is amputated he may find that his Approved Society may or may not help him with an artificial leg. If it does not, he will have to raise the money himself or hope to get it through the Surgical Aid Society, the Family Welfare Association or from the Samaritan Fund of the Hospital. The hit-or-miss administration of additional benefits is one of the worst aspects of the Act.

Membership of Approved Societies.—At the Valuation, Approved Societies are classified as having a Disposable Surplus, a Non-Disposable Surplus, Equality of Assets and Liabilities, and Deficiency. The total membership of Societies in the three latter categories has dropped; that of the former has increased. If the same trend continues, as it logically should, the Fifth Valuation, when it is completed, is likely to show continuing concentration of membership in Societies able to provide more additional benefits.

CHANGES OF MEMBERSHIP BETWEEN THIRD AND FOURTH VALUATION [1]

Position of Societies at 4th Valuation.	Total Membership.		Increase or Decrease.
	3rd Valuation.	4th Valuation.	
Disposable Surplus	11,588,144	19,811,266	+ 8,223,122
Non-Disposable Surplus . .	704,011	681,019	− 22,992
Equality of Assets and Liabilities .	733,999	694,401	− 39,598
Deficiency . .	759,231	642,324	− 116,907

The conditions which were formerly thought to be the main advantages of the Approved Society system are disappearing.

[1] Report of Government Actuary on the Fourth Valuation . . . of Approved Societies, Cmd. 5496, pp. 26 to 38.

Large centralised Societies no longer give opportunities for comradeship among the members; the whole insurance business is much too technical for the man-in-the-street to organise and control. Meanwhile, members increasingly resent getting unequal rights to additional benefits for the same contributions. Democratic partnership of members in each Society is extinct, and we have a machine which is impersonal, inflexible and inequitable in its operations. Originally Lloyd George was persuaded to initiate this extraordinary method of administering a public service by the pressure of the Trade Unions and the Friendly Societies, which claimed that the introduction of Health Insurance would cut at the root of the benefit arrangements which they themselves were operating.[1] He could hardly have foreseen that twenty years later the Assurance and Collecting Societies would have a greater total of members than any of the other groups of Societies, and that they would use their contacts with Approved Society members to further the interests of their Industrial Assurance sections. Anyone doubting the strength of this indictment should read Chapter XI on Industrial Assurance for confirmation.

Latterly there has also been a drift of insured persons towards the larger Societies, although, paradoxically, these have a lower *average* disposable surplus per head than the smaller Societies.[2] (At the Fourth Valuation Industrial Assurance and Collecting Societies had an average disposable surplus of £1.9.6. per member compared with the Trade Unions Societies' £3. 9. 2. This is thought to result from the generally better employment records of Trade Unionists compared with the rest of the population, and, possibly, to the stricter selectivity of their Approved

[1] In spite of Health Insurance Benefits, the private side of Friendly Societies flourish, and do not bear out the contention that a dissolution of Approved Societies would wreck their private work; e.g. Total membership of the 33 constituent Societies in the National Union of Holloway Friendly Societies on 31/12/40 was: Private side, 546,785; State side, 461,222.

[2] Administrative expenses do not make any difference to amounts of disposable surplus, as sums for the former are allotted to Societies annually on a *per capita* basis (5/- for ordinary members, 2/6 for members in H.M. Forces, 1/11 for juveniles, plus a proportionate sum for the administration of additional benefits as payable). If a society's expense account shows a deficiency it may, incredibly, be required by the Ministry to impose a levy on its members, non-payment of which will disqualify them from the receipt of statutory benefit in the next insurance year. Small societies run into deficiency more frequently than the larger, because they tend to have a higher salary expense per head of the membership, employing proportionately more executives and less junior clerks.

Societies.) The Report on the Fourth Valuation gives the following particulars of Approved Society membership:

COMPOSITION OF APPROVED SOCIETIES AT FOURTH VALUATION

Group of Approved Societies (Men only).	Number of Valuations (Societies and Branches).	Total Membership.	Changes since Third Valuation.	Maximum Age Concentration per 1,000 Members.	Deaths per 1,000 Members.	Attained 65 per 1,000 Members.
Friendly Societies with Branches .	5524	2,326,164	+ ·4%	25-35	7	12
Friendly Societies without Branches	689	3,125,029	+ 7·4%	16-25	7	9
Industrial Assur. and Collecting Societies . .	26	4,461,729	+ 6·0%	16-25	7	7
Trade Unions .	129	1,177,042	− 3·5%	45-55	10	12
Employers' Provident Funds .	67	80,131	− ·9%	45-55	8	12

The move is away from the small intimate Society and towards the big undertaking run on impersonal business lines. Although under the Act the control of the Societies must be entirely in the hands of the members, the membership shows itself decreasingly inclined to bother. Even small Friendly Societies with their members living close to the office find it difficult to get people to come to the Annual General Meeting. Clearly, insurance is one of the things which is so technical that the average man in the street is willing to leave its administration to the expert; the principle of self-government for Approved Societies sounded all right in 1911 as a means of preserving the companionable homogeneity of small Friendly Societies and Trade Unions, and of curbing the rapacious tendencies of the Industrial Assurance Companies, but it is no longer practicable, nor is it desired by the membership. One of the arguments for maintaining the diversity of size and type of Society was that the members liked it that way, even though greater centralisation might be more efficient. Statistics now show that this contention is out of date. The younger people are in the centralised Assurance and Friendly Societies already, and both the local Branches and the Trade Union Societies have an older average age. Higher average ages and higher death-rates imply more sickness among the membership, hence greater expenditure of funds on statutory benefit, less disposable surplus at the next Valuation for additional benefits[1] —and loss of membership to Societies able to give more. The tendency to concentration, once begun, will go on cumulatively.

Résumé

National Health Insurance attempts to deal with two separate but related problems—the healing of the sick and their maintenance during sickness. Working through the incredibly clumsy dual mechanism of the Approved Societies and the Insurance Committees, it provides the limited numbers of the insured with sums insufficient to maintain them during sickness, and it furnishes a medical service which stops short at specialist treatment. Cash benefits are administered by some 7,000 Approved Societies and Branches ranging in size from 100 to 1,000,000 and giving none, some, or all, of the possible additional benefits at varying rates. Among Approved Societies are those sponsored by Industrial Assurance and Collecting Societies, which are more efficient, because larger, than the majority of other Societies, but which can and do canvass their members for Industrial Assurance policies, with results which are described elsewhere. Sickness benefit takes no account of the dependants of the insured sick person, and when sickness has lasted six months it is automatically reduced to disablement benefit at a rate insufficient even to cover the cost of one man's food. Maternity benefit, at £4 for some women and £2 for others, seems unrelated to any of the normal needs of pregnancy and childbirth.

Medical benefit does not provide a full medical service for the whole nation. Wives and children of the insured, as well as all the uninsured at all income-levels, are excluded from the scheme. The scheme suffers because it is geared to the obsolescent organisation of general practice in this country; doctors work in professional isolation in which they have little incentive to maintain high quality skill; because of the large practices they need in order to make a living, and because of the long hours they must work to look after all these patients, they have little energy or leisure to keep abreast of modern medicine. Even if they can summon energy and find time,

[1] This is mitigated by the operation of the Reserve Values.

they cannot easily study new techniques, for they have normally no chance to observe treatment in hospitals and the insurance system makes no provision for medical team-work, co-operation or research. There are no general arrangements for the co-ordination of municipal health services with the work of insurance doctors, nor, a serious lack, is there any provision under the Act for the rehabilitation of those who have been sick or injured. The Approved Societies are keen to have their members rendered "capable of work"; it is nobody's business to carry through the whole treatment process constructively until the former patient is happily reinstated in work which he can do. Medical care is a basic human need; a healthful community is a basic social need. The present system gives medical care to less than half the population, and it gives it under conditions which militate against a first-class service.

The scheme which was remarkably progressive thirty years ago has not moved forward with the times and is now obsolete. Health Insurance has served its turn.

Chapter IV

UNEMPLOYMENT INSURANCE

By CLARA D. RACKHAM

It was in the year 1911 that, for the first time, some security against the disaster of unemployment was provided by Act of Parliament. It is true that the security did not go far. The weekly benefit was 7/- payable for not more than 15 weeks in the year, and the scheme only applied to a few selected trades covering about 2½ million workers. In the thirty-six years which have passed since those early beginnings, frequent changes and extensions have taken place, but the basic principle of weekly contributions from both employers and workpeople has remained throughout. It is interesting to note that with unemployment insurance (as with so many other of the British social services) voluntary effort was the first in the field. A few Trade Unions in skilled occupations had provided benefit for their unemployed members. The benefits were conditional on the previous payment of contributions; they were small in amount and paid for only a limited period. These schemes covered about a million and a half out of a total of two and a half million Trade Unionists.

It is impossible here to trace the history of Unemployment Insurance in this country, instructive though it is, but one conclusion at least may be drawn from it. It is clear that it presents a problem far more complex than does insurance against sickness or widowhood or old age. In the case of these three contingencies it is far easier to predict the number of persons who will in due course claim their benefits. The number cannot, of course, be predicted with accuracy and epidemics do occur, but the variations will be within limits. The fluctuations in the numbers of the unemployed have been startling and incalculable. Between 1921 and 1931 the percentage of unemployment varied between 8·6 and 23, and the numbers of unemployed varied between 1,075,000 and 2,900,000. Prolonged or chronic unemployment was also a feature of the post-war years, and regulations which had been framed to suit persons who only experienced brief spells of unemployment were called upon to meet the needs of those who had no work for years. And the proof of unemployment is more difficult to obtain than is the proof of sickness or old age or widowhood. It is true that complaints are made that medical certificates are sometimes too easily obtained, but this is a very minor trouble and can be overcome. The whole story of contribution conditions, the genuinely seeking work clause, and the means test, shows how severe has been the struggle to arrive at a satisfactory proof of genuine unemployment. It is no doubt for this reason that, whereas voluntary insurance has, through the Friendly Societies, insured millions of persons against sickness, and commercial insurance has done the same for widowhood and old age, it is only the State that has attempted to insure the workers against unemployment, if we except the small and inadequate Trade Union schemes mentioned above.

Before the passing of the National Insurance Act, 1946, there were about 15 million persons compulsorily insured against unemployment. Certain weekly wage earners were excluded as being in excepted employments, namely, private domestic servants, hospital nurses, members of the Armed Forces, civil servants, local government employees, police, teachers, non-manual (that is, "black-coated") workers earning more than £420 a year, and also the employees of railways and public utilities whose employment was permanent in character. These workers were regarded as being, generally speaking, in regular employment, and were thus in the happy position of neither suffering at any time from loss of wages nor from any deductions from their wages as contributions to the Insurance Fund. It will readily be seen that thus to exclude the "good" lives and to carry the "bad" ones was not a sound basis for an insurance scheme.

The whole scope of the scheme has been altered by the National Insurance Act, 1946. By this Act, insurance against unemployment has been merged in a general insurance scheme which covers sickness, old age and widowhood as well as unemployment. And it is hardly an exaggeration to say that everybody from school-leaving age to the age of 65 for men and 60 for women is insured. For, subject to certain exceptions, the Act brings in every person living in Great Britain, rich or poor, employer or employed, working for himself or not working at all, and everyone coming under the Act continues throughout his or her life to be insured. The exceptions are, persons who are not permanently resident in Great Britain and persons whose incomes are so small that a contribution cannot be demanded from them. Married women are dealt with under special regulations as will be described later. But, though the Act is thus completely comprehensive, it is only with one category of insured persons that we are concerned in this chapter. That is, the category of employed persons, defined as persons who are gainfully employed in Great Britain under a contract of service. This class will include nearly two-thirds of all insured persons, 19¼ million out of 32 million. The remaining one-third of insured persons are either self-employed or not employed at all: they are entitled to other benefits under the Act but not to unemployment benefit.

In future, no insured person will have more than one card to be stamped: there will not be separate cards for health and unemployment insurance as hitherto. The same stamp on the same card will cover all forms of insurance including the contribution which employed persons will have to pay to entitle them to benefits under the new Industrial Injuries Act. These benefits (which used to be termed "workmen's compensation") will, of course, be confined to employed persons. The employer will stamp the book each week when wages are paid, and he is entitled to deduct the employee's contribution from his wages. Special arrangements are to be considered for large employers to make bulk payments by cheque so as to save the labour of stamping so many cards. Regulations may be made to exempt from payment of contributions persons whose employment is of a casual or subsidiary nature or in which the insured person is engaged only to an inconsiderable extent. Contributions are as a rule payable by all persons over school-leaving age and up to pensionable age: that is, 65 for men and 60 for women. The exceptions are, that young persons who continue in full-time education or full-time unpaid apprenticeship may be excused from liability to contribute, while men who continue to work after the age of 65 do pay contributions up to the age of 70, the corresponding ages for women being 60 and 65. Nor are contributions payable by any insured person during weeks of unemployment or of incapacity for work due to sickness or industrial injury. Their contributions are credited to them during these periods.

Rates of contributions for employed persons are as follows (those under the Industrial Injuries Act are not included):

	Employee.	Employer.	State.	Total.
Men . . .	4/7	3/10	2/1	10/6
Women . . .	3/7	3/-	1/7	8/2
Boys (under 18) .	2/8	2/3	1/2	6/1
Girls (under 18) .	2/2	1/9	11d.	4/10

At the end of 5 years these rates will be increased by 4d. a week: 2d. each for employees and employers.

The foregoing are the normal rates. But in the case of low-paid adult workers, where the wages are less than 30/- a week, the employer must pay 1/11 per week of the employee's contribution (man) in addition to his own, making the employer's total 5/9, or in the case of a woman 1/5, making the total 4/5. This does not apply where the employee gets board and lodging in addition to his wages. It is as well to repeat here that the above contribution covers all benefits receivable under the Act including benefits payable to married women through the contributions of their husbands: these will be dealt with later.

When an insured person falls out of work, he receives his card from his employer, lodges it at the Employment Exchange, and puts in his claim for benefit. He must fulfil certain conditions if he is to make good his claim. He must have paid not less than 26 contributions since his entry into insurance and not less than 50 contributions must have been paid by or credited to him (i.e. in periods of unemployment or sickness) during the preceding contribution year. He must be genuinely unemployed—that is, he must do no work except a part-time job such as evening work which can be done by a person who is also in full-time employment. He must be capable of and available for work and he must attend a course of training if required to do so.

The expression "capable of and available for work" requires some further explanation. "Capable of" refers to the physical capacity of the worker, not his capability in terms of efficiency or competence. A claimant need not be capable of work in the particular occupation he has previously followed, but he must be capable of doing work of a kind he is reasonably likely to get, and of doing it in the ordinary way and under ordinary conditions. He may be called upon to produce a medical certificate to this effect. A blind person may be regarded as capable of work if he has had insurable employment since he became blind. It is difficult to define exactly what is meant by availability for work, but, briefly, a claimant must be prepared to accept at once any offer of suitable employment which is brought to his notice. If a woman claimant has made no arrangements for the care of her children, she may be regarded as not available and disallowed benefit. A person who is absent from home may be allowed benefit if he makes arrangements for his immediate recall in the event of an offer of work. If a claimant is refused benefit under this condition, his application can be reviewed from time to time at intervals of not less than six weeks.

The claimant has to wait three days before he becomes entitled to benefit. In the case of a very short spell of unemployment, these three days are not paid for, but if there is a duration of twelve days or more of unemployment, the three waiting days are paid for. Odd single days of unemployment are not paid for. But any two days or more falling within a week count for benefit as part of a spell of unemployment and are treated as "linked up" if within 13 weeks of the first day of unemployment in that spell. Days of unemployment within a 13-week period will be "linked up" with days of sickness in the same period and *vice versa*. The rates of benefit are 26/- a week for a man, or a woman, or a person under 18 with dependants, and in addition 16/- for an adult dependant and 7/6 for the first child. The children after the first will, of course, receive the family allowance of 5/- a week. The above rate does not apply to married women. A person under 18 who has no dependants receives 15/- a week. The amount receivable by a married man with two children will therefore be 54/6 a week.

The rules defining what is meant by "dependants" are elaborate and regulations under the Act will probably follow much the same lines. The following are regarded as dependants of a claimant: a wife, a husband if he is incapable of supporting himself, a female housekeeper who has the care of the claimant's dependant children, a widowed mother or stepmother, an unmarried mother, a mother whose husband is incapable of supporting her, a father or stepfather unable to support himself and living with the claimant, children still at school or unable to go to school because of some infirmity. In every case the claimant must show that the dependant is being wholly or mainly maintained by him; except that when a claimant and his wife live together it is immaterial whether or not this is the case. The term "child" includes illegitimate children, stepchildren, brothers and sisters, half and step brothers and sisters and adopted children —adopted not being used in the strict legal sense but meaning a child whose parent has transferred his rights to the claimant. No benefit is payable in respect of a dependant who is in receipt of Unemployment Insurance benefit or in regular wage-earning employment or in an occupation ordinarily carried on for profit. A claimant must show that a dependant is wholly or mainly maintained by him, and a man cannot claim dependant's benefit for his wife if she is in regular wage-earning employment or is engaged in any gainful occupation and earning more than 20/- a week.

Benefit is paid to claimants weekly at the Employment Exchange; claimants are required to sign on at the Exchange on fixed days and at fixed times each week. This is to signify that they are available for work. The normal duration of benefit is seven months (180 working days), and, at the end of this period, an unemployed person ceases to be entitled to benefit subject, however, to two important qualifications: the first is that, if his or her previous employment record has been good, a certain number of added days is allowed in addition to the 180 days. These added days will be calculated in accordance with regulations and may amount to a further 130 days as a maximum, bringing the total duration of benefit up to 310 working days maximum. The second qualification is that, if the insured person is still unemployed at the expiry of this total of days, he will go before a local tribunal, and, on the recommendation of the tribunal, the Minister may allow a further period of benefit. There will be no means test applied by the tribunal. An insured person who has exhausted his right to benefit will re-qualify in full when he has been back at work and has paid contributions again for 13 weeks.

There are certain disqualifications for benefit, such as loss of employment due to a trade dispute, or where the claimant lost his work through misconduct or voluntary leaving, or where he does not accept a suitable offer of employment or fails to carry out reasonable directions given him at the Exchange. A trade dispute is defined as any dispute between employers and employees or between employees and employees connected with the employment of any persons. There must as a rule (though not universally) be concerted action by the employees; for example, a dispute between an employee and his employer as to the price to be paid for a particular job was held not to be a trade dispute. The General Strike of 1926 was held not to be a trade dispute in the meaning of the Act as it was not a dispute between employees and employers but between the Trades Union Congress General Council and the Government. A sympathetic strike is a trade dispute. There are certain modifications of the disqualification. It does not apply if the claimant can show that the stoppage of work was not due to a trade dispute at the premises at which he was employed. Under certain conditions different departments on the same premises may be treated as different premises. Difficulty often arises in determining what is a separate department, and each case is considered on its merits. Another modification is that if the claimant during the stoppage of work gets employment elsewhere in his own occupation or becomes regularly engaged in some other occupation, he is not disqualified from drawing benefit if he again becomes unemployed. There is no provision as to the period of employment required: benefit was allowed to a locomotive driver who lost his employment in a colliery owing to a trade dispute and subsequently got employment lasting five days with a railway company. Relief is also afforded to persons who become accidentally involved in a dispute in which they have no real concern. A claimant must prove that he is not himself participating in or financing or directly interested in the dispute, and that the persons who are so doing do not include members of his own grade or class of workers.

"Misconduct" is a question of fact depending on a variety of circumstances. The main causes of disallowance under this head have been absence without leave, refusal to do certain work or to comply with shop rules, bad time-keeping, personal conduct resulting in neglect of duty. A repetition of mistakes or acts of negligence may amount to misconduct. Misconduct outside working hours may cause a disallowance if it renders the worker unsuitable for his employment; for example, a conviction of theft might be taken as evidence that the worker was not to be trusted, though the theft was not committed at the place of employment. A claimant who loses his employment through misconduct or voluntarily leaves his employment without just cause is disqualified from benefit for a period not exceeding six weeks. The main grounds on which a plea of just cause may be based are breach of contract of service, unfavourable conditions and personal circumstances. A claimant before leaving his employment is expected to make an effort to remedy his grievances through an appropriate channel. It is a just cause if an employee leaves his work because of changes in rates or hours making his conditions less favourable than he had enjoyed or than those enjoyed by similar workers in the district. But it is not regarded as a just cause that a member of a union is required to work with a non-member, or that women are employed on work regarded by the union as men's work, or that the claimant thought that the men with whom he was required to work were not qualified.

A "suitable" offer of employment is carefully defined. Employment is not regarded as suitable if it is available owing to a trade dispute or if it is offered on terms less favourable than the applicant might reasonably expect to obtain. Employment is not regarded as unsuitable merely because it is in an occupation other than the applicant's usual occupation. Considerations of the applicant's age, skill and period of unemployment all come into play. Cases of personal objection to a particular employment on grounds of conscience or of some infirmity are taken on their merits. An unemployed person is disqualified from receiving benefit while he is in receipt of sickness or disablement benefit under National Health Insurance.

The new Act makes great changes in the position of married women. If a woman ceases to be an "employed person" after her marriage, she ceases to pay any contributions and she receives benefits through her husband's contribution. These do not, of course, include unemployment benefit. If a woman continues to be employed after marriage, she can, if she chooses, contract out of the scheme and pay no further contributions. She can, however, continue her full insurance as an employed person and she will then be entitled to unemployment benefit but at a reduced rate, namely, 20/- a week instead of the 26/- to which she would have been entitled as a single woman. If she is not living with and not supported or assisted by her husband she will get the normal rate of 26/-. The married woman who is herself insured as an employed person is also entitled to a maternity allowance which she can claim for 13 weeks—6 weeks before the expected date of confinement and then another 7 weeks afterwards. This is a payment of 36/- a week and is conditional on her not returning to her employment while the benefit is in payment. This allowance is, of course, in addition to the Maternity Grant of £4 which is payable to her as a married mother.

It is clear that no insurance scheme which is bound by fixed rules as to benefit conditions can possibly cover all "hard cases" which may occur among 32 million people. There are some people who are not in the scheme at all because of their poverty; some will fall out of benefit or be disqualified; some will have special needs not covered by their unemployment pay. For these the Assistance Board is to some extent responsible while part of the field is at present covered by the Public Assistance Committee. The Minister of National Insurance has promised to introduce a Bill at an early date which will provide a National system of Assistance in place of Public Assistance. This will supplement the Insurance code in such a way as to provide a real safeguard against poverty and destitution.

Considering the great complexity of the insurance scheme, the Act is not a long one. This is due to the fact that a great many detailed administrative provisions are left to be dealt with by regulations. The Minister has himself said that, in something like 100 matters, he is given power to "legislate" in this way. Such things as the methods of claiming and paying benefit and the administrative machinery to be set up are included in the hundred. The meaning to be attached to various words used in the Act which has been discussed in previous pages may be modified by regulation. There is no doubt that this very extensive manufacture by the Executive of regulations which have the force of law is open to criticism and needs to be carefully safeguarded. The Act sets out to disarm such criticism in two ways. A new statutory body is to be set up, known as the National Insurance Advisory Committee. It will be appointed by the

Minister and will consist of a Chairman and from four to eight members of whom at least one must be a woman. These members will represent workers and employers and Friendly Societies and will be appointed in consultation with these bodies. Besides its general duty of advising and assisting the Minister, this body will have very important work in connection with the making of regulations. In all except a very few special cases the draft of any proposed regulation must first of all be submitted to the Committee. It will be the duty of the Committee to publish the draft and invite comments from the interested parties. Its report and recommendations will be made to the Minister, and he must, in his turn, lay the report before Parliament together with the proposed regulations. And he must inform Parliament of his reasons for differing from the suggestions of the Committee if in any case he does so differ. It is hoped that in this way Parliament may be made aware of the points at issue and will be able to come to an informed decision.

A second safeguard is that regulations will not be allowed to slip through Parliament because no member opposes them. All the more vital regulations are to be the subject of affirmative Resolutions of the House, which is thus required to give its deliberate authority before any regulations can become effective.

A very important matter to be dealt with by regulation is the establishment of the local tribunals which will decide all questions as to whether an unemployed person is or is not entitled to benefit. The Minister has indicated the lines on which the tribunals will be set up and they follow fairly closely the existing system. The Chairman of the tribunal will usually be a lawyer, and he will sit with two other members—one drawn from the employers' side and one from the workers'. These will be chosen as having experience of industrial life, and, if the claimant is a woman, one of them must be a woman. According to the present arrangement, decisions are made by a majority vote. The claimant has a right to bring with him to the Court a personal friend or his trade union representative but not a solicitor or a barrister. Under the new Act an appeal will lie from the decision of the tribunal to a judicial officer to be known as the National Insurance Commissioner: he will constitute the final arbiter on all disputes as to claims to benefit. He takes the place of the Umpire who fulfilled this function under the preceding Act.

The Central Office for the administration of the Act is at Newcastle and there will be Regional offices in each of the nine Regions. There will also be local offices and local advisory Committees. These latter will represent the insured persons in each locality and will have the duty of reporting to the Minister anything that may be wrong in the local machinery and of making suggestions for its improvement. As was stated above, unemployment benefit will be dealt with at the Employment Exchanges and not at the local insurance office.

The new scheme of National Insurance starts with a large capital sum to be called the National Insurance (Reserve) Fund. This consists of the capital balances of the present Health Insurance, Unemployment and Pension Funds, and will probably amount to nearly £800 million when the new scheme comes into operation. Of this sum, £100 million will be at once transferred to the National Insurance Fund from which benefits will be paid. This Fund will consist of the contributions of the employers, workpeople and the State, and also of the annual interest accruing from the Reserve Fund. The State contributes to the Fund in two ways. There is, of course, the State contribution paid weekly on behalf of each insured person as described above. The State also pays a lump sum every year into the Fund to equal the amount by which the income of the Fund falls short of the amount required to pay out the benefits and also to finance the administration. The State will also pay the whole cost of National Assistance which will be needed to supplement benefit or to assist those who, for one reason or another, have no claims for benefit.

It remains to note two new provisions in connection with finance. Five years after the Act comes into full operation, there is to be a review of the whole scheme and a report to Parliament. And the same procedure every five years afterwards. In this way the working of the Act will be kept under observation and any changes which are thought desirable can be made. The review will be made by the Government Actuary and, if necessary, he can be called upon by the Treasury to make it at any earlier date. This provision makes it possible to change the rates of contribution and benefit in the light of any change that may have taken place in the cost of living. The second new provision is an attempt to use the rates of contribution as a factor in maintaining a stable level of employment and thus keeping level the amount that has to be paid out in unemployment benefit. At a time of threatened slump, the Treasury is empowered to reduce the contribution rate and thus leave more purchasing power in the hands of the people. This would stimulate the demand for consumer goods and tend to increase employment. It is calculated that a reduction of one penny a week in contributions would mean that £4 million in a year would be liberated for spending, and, though this is a small sum in relation to the annual expenditure of the country, yet the device is a useful one and would make its contribution towards the task of preventing unemployment.

There is no fixed date on which the Act will come into force. The Minister will fix an "appointed day," and different days will be appointed on which different parts of the scheme will come into force. It is hoped that the scheme may be in full effect at some time in 1948.

To conclude with some general comments:—

(1) That part of the new scheme which deals with insurance against unemployment shows much less startling changes than the parts dealing with sickness benefit and with retirement pensions. The biggest change is that all employed persons are now insured against unemployment and not only a section. The rates of unemployment benefit are increased but not to a great extent in view of the increased cost of living. In 1941 the benefit for a man, wife and three children was 41/- a week; it will now be 59/6. It is obvious that there will still be need for personal savings if the family's standard of life is not to be considerably reduced when the breadwinner is unemployed. And the old limitation of insurance benefit to a certain number of weeks, though the insured person may still be unemployed at the end of the period, still remains. And this in spite of the fact that, in the new scheme, sickness benefit may continue to be drawn up to pensionable age without any limit of time as long as the sick person remains incapable of work. It is true that, when an insured person has exhausted his unemployment benefit, he can go before a local tribunal and get his benefit extended, the cost being paid as State Assistance and not from the Insurance Fund. As the Minister has stated that the tribunal will not apply a Means Test, there is a danger that the applicant will be asked to show that he is "genuinely seeking work," and past experience

has shown what very undesirable results may follow from this. Nor can it be regarded as altogether satisfactory that the number of weeks for which an insured person can draw benefit should depend on whether his previous employment record has been good. This may be a matter entirely beyond the control of the insured person, and it does not seem right that he should be penalised by an earlier termination of his benefit because periods of unemployment have come to him through changes in national policy or the ups and downs of local trade.

(2) The position of women in the new scheme is more satisfactory than under the previous Act. Women and girls pay smaller contributions than men and boys, presumably on the grounds that their earnings are less. They receive the same benefits respectively as do men and boys, presumably on the grounds that their needs are the same. That is to say, single women receive the same benefits. Married women who are themselves insured receive only 20/- benefit, their dependants' rate being the same. This is in place of the 26/- a week that a single woman receives, presumably on the grounds that the needs of the married woman are less. But married and single pay the same contribution. As against this must be set the welcome fact that the Anomalies Regulations which applied special and onerous conditions to married women who claimed unemployment benefit have been swept away, and married women who remain in insurance will not in future have to satisfy any conditions which do not apply to men.

(3) The old criticism remains that the scheme cannot be described as insurance in the commonly accepted use of the term as there is not and never has been any attempt to make the contributions cover the benefits, and the words solvent or insolvent as applied to the scheme have little or no meaning. Besides the weekly State contribution which has constantly varied in amount and in relation to the other contributions, the State pays into the Fund a large annual sum which is regulated by the amount required to keep the balance between contributions and benefits, and solvency can be created by this means. However, the contributory system has come to stay and logic was never a characteristic of the British social services.

Chapter V

THE ASSISTANCE BOARD

By JOAN SIMEON CLARKE

THE Assistance Board (formerly the Unemployment Assistance Board) is one of the major social experiments of the century. It is, in plain terms, a nation-wide relief agency administering needs payments according to uniform scales. It was originally designed to assist the long-term unemployed, the burden of whom, spread unevenly over the country, local rates were unable to support. The two underlying principles were that there should be national rather than local responsibility for the victims of national disaster, and uniformity of treatment of such victims. Since the Board was formed, a second national calamity, worse than the slump, has swept over the country—war. Many citizens have been reduced to penury. It was logical that the same principles should also apply to them, and that the Board should be specially empowered to administer the scheme for the prevention and relief of distress arising as a result of war. Although formerly the Board was an agency specialising in the assistance of the unemployed, it now deals with other categories, including the aged. As a swift-working, well-organised, centrally controlled body, the Board is the obvious choice when the Government is looking for an agency to administer or to enquire into the need for payments to fresh groups of citizens. The Board can be relied upon to undertake new work quickly, and to act uniformly throughout the land. So important is the Board today that there can be no informed discussion of the reconstruction of the social services without an understanding of the functions, organisation, achievements and deficiencies of the Assistance Board.

CREATION OF THE UNEMPLOYMENT ASSISTANCE BOARD

Before the Board was formed in 1934, the long-term unemployed had been receiving assistance under what was known as the Transitional Payments scheme, administered according to their diverse standards by the local authorities. Unemployment

Insurance had not been designed to support large numbers of workers for long periods, its Fund had already been supplemented by the Exchequer and the benefit period extended, but even so the scheme was plainly useless for coping with the unemployment problem of the slump unless it was radically altered. The Transitional Payments scheme was brought into being by an Order in Council made in the autumn of 1931, and introduced the means test as a principle in the relief of poverty due to long-period unemployment. It directed local authorities to make payments in accordance with their Public Assistance scales to unemployed whose right to benefit had been exhausted. The maximum scale was the prevailing rate of Unemployment Insurance Benefit. The Exchequer financed the scheme. In practice, few local authorities restricted payment to their Public Assistance scale and there came into being Transitional Payment scales which generally approximated to the benefit rate. Durham County Council refused to operate the scheme at all, and Transitional Payment Commissioners were appointed for that county; other local authorities were occasionally threatened with supersession.

In 1930 the Royal Commission on Unemployment Insurance was set up, to make recommendations with regard to:

(1) the future scope of the Unemployment Insurance scheme, "the provisions which it should contain and the means by which it may be made solvent and self-supporting"; and

(2) "the arrangements which should be made outside the scheme for the unemployed who are capable of and available for work."

The second of the terms of reference of the Commission was thus based on the assumption that certain unemployed workers would be outside the scope of the Insurance scheme. The Majority Report accepts this assumption and recommends that those outside the scope of Insurance should be maintained from national moneys administered under the control of the Ministry of Labour by *ad hoc* Committees of the local authorities according to a national standard. It also states that for these persons maintenance should be in accordance with needs, i.e. it accepts the principle of the means test for those who have run out of benefit. The Minority Report rejects the assumption implied in the terms of reference:

> "The conception is one of an Insurance scheme limited in scope and paying benefit for a fixed number of weeks, and ceasing to pay it to those who are still unemployed at the end of that time. Such a scheme divides the unemployed into two classes, one drawing benefit as of right, and the other denied any right and compelled to seek relief in some form outside the scheme." [1]

> "Such a division of the unemployed, based on the amount of their unemployment, has no basis in any real difference among them and must always appear inequitable to the unemployed themselves." [2]

The proposals of the Minority Report are for a scheme financed by employers, employees and the Exchequer, but not by local authorities.

> "It would continue to pay benefit at a fixed rate to the unemployed worker for as long as he remained unemployed and free from disqualification and disallowance. There is no reason for the imposition of a means test at the end of a specified period."

These proposals of the Minority Report were ignored. They were in fundamental opposition to the fixed policy implied in the terms of reference of the Commission, and were signed by the two Socialist members of that Commission. Their proposals were for an unlimited extension of the benefit period, involving heavy Exchequer subsidising of the Unemployment Fund. They were opposed to any difference of treatment of short- and long-time unemployed which might seem to discriminate against the latter, and held that, as long as employability was maintained, payments to the unemployed should be given uniformly, as of right, and without test of means. The principles of the Minority have been disregarded, but they represent a point of view applicable to other forms of social insurance—Health and Pensions—which is still heard, but which

[1] Royal Commission on Unemployment Insurance, Final Report, Cmd. 4185, Minority Report, p. 383.

[2] *ibid.*, p. 489.

reached maximum volume during the years of discussion about the unemployed. The question was: *Should social insurance rights be so limited that it is necessary to have an Assistance service to supplement and prolong benefit, or should participation in social insurance give title to full maintenance as long as necessary?*

The Assistance Board was created on the assumption that social insurance benefits must be limited both in amount and in duration, and that therefore it was necessary to have a net in which to catch those who had run out of benefit.[1] The Majority of the Royal Commission had agreed with this assumption. They had, however, stated definitely that a central body should not be set up for the administration of Unemployment Assistance, which should be administered by local authorities under the supervision of the Ministry of Labour and in close co-operation with the Employment Exchanges. They particularly emphasised that the Ministry of Labour should be the authority for supervising the Assistance administration, because—

> "The arrangements are intended for workers who are still clearly within the industrial field and for those alone. . . ."
>
> "No other department can properly accept this responsibility or attempt to undertake the task."[2]

The Majority took the trouble to be particularly explicit about this:

> "If the responsibility for this scheme of monetary assistance to unemployed industrial workers were placed under a central authority which is concerned mainly with the problems of need and destitution . . . and removed from daily contact with industry and employment, we believe that the object of the scheme would be lost."[3]

The Government received the reports of the Commission, ignored the Minority Report, and then proceeded to set up the Central Authority "concerned mainly with the problems of need and destitution" against which the Majority had warned them.

The Assistance Board is an *ad hoc* body consisting of chairman and deputy-chairman, full-time and appointed for seven and five years respectively, and three salaried part-time members appointed for three years each. The Board's spokesman in the

[1] And also those whose needs greatly exceeded their benefit money.
[2] Royal Commission, *op. cit.*, p. 154. [3] *ibid.*, p. 154.

House of Commons is the appropriate Minister,[1] to whom questions about the Board's activities are addressed; these are answered through the formula, "I am informed by the Assistance Board." The members of the Board are not allowed to sit in Parliament, and the Board's case is never, therefore, put to the House by somebody whose close concern it is. Opportunities for debate are available when the Annual Report is presented, and when the Board's Regulations are laid in draft before the Minister of Labour, who, if he approves of them, eventually lays them before Parliament as his own draft. If he disapproves he must state the reasons for his disapproval in a White Paper presented to Parliament simultaneously with the draft Regulations. There has been "no instance where the Board's draft has not been adopted." [2] During the passage of the Determination of Needs Act, 1941, the provisions of the Board's proposed Regulations were for the first time before Parliament during debate instead of being presented only after the enactment of the Bill. Collective action by the Board may be criticised in the House, but not the individual members of the Board. This procedure makes the Board seem rather remote and inflexible. Popular outcry may dislodge, or at least call to order, a democratically elected Minister, but the members of the Board are outside political life, and they serve their appointed terms irremovable by the protests of the community. There has rarely been more furious agitation than at the inception of the Board, and again in 1938 about the curtailment of Winter Allowances. On each occasion the Board did alter the policy which had given rise to the immediate disturbances, but the fact remains that

[1] The following Ministers answer questions about the Board :

Unemployment Assistance and P.R.D.	Ministry of National Insurance.
Supplementary Pensions (England and Wales)	Ministry of National Insurance.
Supplementary Pensions (Scotland)	Ministry of National Insurance.
Injury Allowances	Minister of Pensions.
War Service Grants (Hardship Allowances)	Minister of Pensions.
War Damage	President of Board of Trade.
Dependants' Allowances :	
Army	Secretary of State for War.
Navy	First Lord.
Air Force	Secretary of State for Air.
Overseas Evacuation	Under Secretary of State for the Dominions (Chairman of Children's Overseas Reception Board).

[2] Royal Commission on Workmen's Compensation, Minutes of Evidence, 2315, 28th April 1939.

indignation which would probably have wrecked a ministerial career left the Board still quietly ensconced in their headquarters at Thames House. The Board was originally put outside direct Parliamentary control so that it would be able to pursue a line of policy without being subjected to the shifts and pressure of political opinion. But public interest in its administration has never abated, with the twofold result that the Board has been forced to modify its policy, while the public has remembered its indignation rather than the Board's deference to its opinion. Fury about a Ministry usually abates after a scapegoat has been thrown out in the full light of public excitement; no scapegoat is thrown from the Board, and the public prowls round it unappeased. As a result, the good work for which credit is due (e.g. the speed with which the Board organised the payment of Supplementary Pensions) is ignored, and any lapses (e.g. the brusqueness of some of the staff to blitz victims) are magnified in the public mind. It is astonishing that the Board does not have a vigorous Public Relations Department. It has neither Public Relations nor Press Department. Its direct contact with the public is entirely through its Area Offices, the work of which will be discussed later, through infrequent speeches of its Chairman, and through its Advisory Committees and Appeal Tribunals in a more limited way. Members of the public have usually an anecdotal knowledge of the working of the Board based on their own experiences or on those of their friends; the broad lines of the Board's policy are not officially explained either by full and accurate Press reports or by frequent statements in the House. The Board is aloof. Paradoxically this aloof Board conducts an administration which not only intimately affects the domestic lives of well over a million persons, but which touches the core of major political principles. At least part of the anger which greeted the new Board was the anger of impotence. The Board seemed unassailable.

The Board opened its original 327 offices in 1935 and staffed them with 1,210 relatively senior officers, together with some 5,000 investigating clerks. Some of these officials were taken over from Public Assistance work, the rest were civil servants transferred from the Ministry of Labour and other branches of the service. No special training was given to those without experience of similar work; they all learned the Regulations as they went along. They were called upon to administer the household means test to persons who had previously been receiving transitional payment on Public Assistance assessments. These assessments varied all over the country, whereas the Board's standard was uniform. Many persons who had been receiving transitional payments were faced with reduced allowances or even with "nil determinations" from the Board; this was the cause of the first major outcry against the new administration, some of whose offices were picketed and windows broken. Under the "Standstill Order"—the Unemployment Assistance (Temporary Provisions) Act, 1935—this trouble was ameliorated when applicants were given the higher of the two assessments,[1] the "Liquidation of the Standstill" following in 1936 and involving the gradual reduction during a period of 18 months of higher Public Assistance assessments to the standard scale. The Board at first dealt only with those who had already been, or would have been, on transitional payment, i.e. those whose standard Unemployment Insurance benefit had already run out. On 1st April 1937 the Board took over unemployed persons who, though they were ineligible for Unemployment Insurance benefit, were or had been insured persons under the Widows', Orphans' and Old Age Contributory Pensions Acts. The scope of the Board for unemployed persons is thus wider than that of Unemployment Insurance. When the war came the Board was four and a half years old. It had passed through two severe storms, it had developed cohesion, and it had accustomed the public to the administration of Assistance by a nation-wide body on a uniform scale. It was still dealing exclusively with the unemployed.

At the outbreak of war many persons were suddenly impoverished; stall-holders in the Caledonian Market, music-teachers, landladies, became destitute. Instead of letting them go to the Public Assistance Committees, thus incurring Poor Law stigma (as it is thought) and becoming heavily chargeable to the rates in evacuation areas, the Government empowered the Assistance Board to help them under the Unemployment Assistance (Emergency Powers) Act, 1939. This Act extended the original Act to cover any citizen over 16 who could prove that he was in distress because on account of the war—

[1] i.e. during the standstill period all cases were assessed under two scales, Unemployment Assistance and the local temporary payments scale.

(1) "he has, or has been, moved from one area to another under or in pursuance of plans or directions for the transference of members of the civil population in the event of war or the imminence of war, prepared, approved or given by His Majesty's Government"; or

(2) "he or some other person on whom he is normally dependent for support has lost his employment or is unable to follow his normal occupation or has been otherwise deprived entirely or to a substantial extent of his normal means of livelihood."

"P.R.D.," as this scheme was called, covered also assistance to Government evacuees, foreign refugees and Channel Islanders (if their distress was due to the war), dependants of interned aliens and the dependants of persons interned by the enemy. In addition, the Board now acts as the agent of other Government Departments where it has no statutory responsibility; during the war it acted for the Ministry of Pensions in paying Injury Allowances to members of the public injured by enemy action and to Civil Defence workers injured on duty; also for the Board of Trade in making advances for immediate needs arising from war damage. Where necessary, the Board still investigates the home circumstances of Servicemen claiming Dependants' Allowances, and for the War Service Grants Advisory Committee it investigates applications for special Hardship Allowances; similarly, the Board investigates on behalf of the Dominion Governments Dominion soldiers' claims for allowances for dependants resident in this country. Under the P.R.D. scheme the Board assists refugee workers of insurable status who, when sick or unemployed, are not eligible for Insurance benefit. The Board has also recently acquired two additional delegated functions; it visits on behalf of the Ministry of Food when citizens ask for free welfare foods (cod-liver oil, orange juice, vitamin tablets); secondly, it pays home visits if asked to do so by the Ministry of National Insurance.

The greater part of the Board's work is now concerned with the administration of old age pensions. This is fully described in the following chapter, but it is interesting to note how the Board is gradually swallowing up the functions of the Poor Law. Under Part II of the Old Age and Widows' Pensions Act, 1940, the Board was empowered to grant Supplementary Pensions to persons over 60 years of age who were already in receipt of Old

Age or Widows' Pensions. Early in 1943 the Board was further directed to grant Supplementary Pensions to those widows who had dependent children and who were in receipt of a contributory widow's pension plus children's allowances under the Old Age and Widows' Pensions Acts. In this way a large group of old age pensioners, with a smaller number of widows, received their supplementation from the Board in the form of National Assistance instead of obtaining it from the Public Assistance Committees as Poor Law relief. Further, as from April 1947, the Board has been responsible for the administration of non-contributory old age pensions which have, since 1908, been in charge of the Department of Customs and Excise. It is therefore clear that, whatever miscellaneous functions and delegated duties the Board may acquire, its future work for several years will be predominantly concerned with the aged.[1] Only if there is an abnormally heavy incidence of long-term unemployment will the Board's original function (of assistance to those suffering prolonged unemployment) be of major importance. Should this ever happen, the Board would need to improve its administration in this respect as much as it has improved the quality of its work for the aged in particular, and for the public in general.

Since the war the Board has been charged with the assistance of new categories entirely different from its original charge, the unemployed. Meanwhile the numbers of unemployed persons on its books have dwindled. The situation is curious; the Board was created to deal exclusively with the industrial worker, to maintain his employability, and to support him till he returned to work. The object was to treat these persons as an industrial problem rather than as primarily a problem of poverty. We now find the Board dealing with very few unemployed persons, but with large numbers of pensioners who are altogether outside the industrial field, and with a varied assortment of other persons who are referred to the Board by other government departments for financial enquiries. In fact, the Board has become a national Assistance agency. It is no longer specialised. It is doing on a nation-wide scale what otherwise Public Assistance Committees would have been doing locally.

In 1945 the Board was paying, on the average, 27,000 Un-

[1] Especially if it contrives to manage contributory pensions as agent of the Ministry of National Insurance.

employment Assistance payments, 1,300,000 Supplementary old age pensions, and 39,000 Supplementary pensions to widows under 60 who were in receipt of children's allowances. Also, from 1940 to the end of 1945 the Board made about 3,750,000 war damage payments, and from 1939 to the end of 1945 its officers made some 6,000,000 visits concerning the payment of allowances to dependants of members of the Armed Forces. This tremendous shift of emphasis from the long-term unemployed to a wide variety of other persons of whom the most stable and the numerically largest group is that of old age pensioners, is not perhaps sufficiently reflected in this chapter, which now is a revision of that written for the first edition of this book before the redistribution of the Board's functions was so marked as it now is. This chapter should therefore be read in conjunction with Chapter VI, in which the new material about the administration of old age pensions has been collected.

Administration

The structure of the Assistance Board, like that of any other Government Department, is hierarchical. Instead of a Minister we have the Board itself, working through the Secretary of the Board and the Headquarters staff. As liaisons between Headquarters and the Districts come Regional Officers, and below them are District Officers, who are the authority immediately over the Area Officers, who, at fourth remove, translate the Boards policy into practice. The Area Officers are responsible for the actual day-to-day administration of Assistance, as well as for maintaining contacts both with local leaders of the community and with other relevant statutory and voluntary bodies. The whole of this organisation is controlled from Headquarters, which issues both general instructions and, as necessary, individual decisions. The Area Officers, when confronted by a problem which no rule seems to cover, consult their District Officers. The more difficult of these problems, transmitted upwards, serve to inform Headquarters of situations for which new rulings are required, such situations often being discussed eventually by the members of the Board themselves. Instructions multiply rapidly this way, and Area Officers have back numbers bound into thick volumes.

The Assistance Board has been much criticised in the past (and in earlier editions of this book) for allotting home visiting to those officers in the lower grades of its employment. The status of visiting is now raised to the extent that it will be undertaken by Clerical Officers who are the Board's senior employees within the clerical grade, and whose salaries are, for men, £350 in London and £320 in the provinces. It is perhaps unfortunate that home visiting is not further promoted by the Board so that it could be entrusted to Executive Officers; these officers do not enter the Civil Service until they are between the ages of 18 and 21, and they may thus have already acquired experience or even training which would fit them specifically for social work; further, officers at this higher level are expected not only to be able to collect data, but to draw deductions from it, whereas the work required from those in the clerical grades is primarily the ascertainment and collation and recording of facts. It seems unlikely that home visiting will be really satisfactory unless the visitor's obvious and inescapable responsibility for deduction is recognised by appointing for the work persons of such a status that they are supposed to be competent to *think* about the facts which they collect. Also, as the volume of the Board's welfare visiting increases (under the revised methods of old age pensions administration it will increase) there is a strong argument in favour of allotting this work to selected officers, who would thus have the opportunity of specialising in home visiting. Such a development of specialisation would, however, involve a change in the Board's policy. At present office staff are expected to know all the work of their grade in the office and to be interchangeable. The Board aims at keeping its staff fluid and interchangeable. The advantages of this, and the advantage of having a unified national system of record-keeping and administration, were seen both in the blitz and in the rapid expansion for the introduction of Supplementary Pensions. The Board was able to transfer staff about the country to ease local pressure, and found that such staff were very quickly able to be helpful. On the other hand, there is a difference between having staff acquainted with all sides of the work so that they can substitute for each other in emergencies, and having them so unspecialised that there is no official attempt made to match the type of work to the abilities of the worker, or, conversely, to train selected staff for special jobs. The broad line of demarcation in the Board's work should be between dealing with people and doing office work. Some persons are, by nature, very good at clerical work, others have a flair for getting on with people; the friendly and successful interviewer often means a slow, untidy clerk—the competent, clear-headed clerk is sometimes brusque and tactless when confronted with a human problem. The Board does not recognise this. The visiting officers are supposed to be equally available for clerical or interviewing work. This is not just a matter of expediency. It is a reflection of the Board's implicit attitude towards the work it has to do, an attitude conditioned apparently by several related considerations.

The Assistance Board is a Civil Service Department, and civil servants like to make things work. They are responsible for the startling rapidity with which the Board was created all ready to function. The Board is administered with the same high standard of efficiency as are, say, the Post Office or the Board of Trade; but whereas these Departments deal primarily with things, the Board deals primarily with people. It is impossible for the outside observer not to wonder whether in emphasising efficiency and smooth running the Board may not lose sight of the ends of its administration, and lay insufficient stress on its duty of service to its clients. The visit to a client's home is treated as a routine, like the selling of a postal order or the granting of a licence. When the visitor goes to the home, he or she fills up a form in the client's presence which the client signs as correct. The investigator is not in a position to discuss the client's difficulties or to give advice on any point, however desirable this may be (although "the Officer" is often thought to have an omniscience which encourages people to consult him), because, first, he is insufficiently trained and experienced, and secondly, he has no time, for he is supposed to do some twenty-five visits a day, including stair-climbing and report-writing. Lastly, the investigator has no authority to speak for the Board. He is only required to bring back a written statement of the family circumstances, to which he may add a further note. Assessment is authorised by a higher officer. The investigator is not told what the determination is, nor will he normally have cause to visit the home again until, should he still be doing the same street, he calls for a routine check-up. Even then he will not be told the original determination. The interview is not evaluated by the Board as the dynamic force in the client/Board relationship. It is one move in the smooth-working administrative pattern. Although the Board administers a service highly personal in its results, it discounts the effect of personal contact.

There is another reason for this peculiarly impersonal administration of a personal service. The Board is anxious not to become or seem like a State charity. Its administrators are determined to avoid anything reminiscent of the old-style parochial philanthropy—good works and kind words; they abhor the thought of meddling. This view is one with which everybody must agree. It would be intolerable if every one of the Board's clients were submitted to the patronising attentions of pitying persons. As an alternative to this treatment the Board therefore minimises the importance of the interview. The argument here is that the Board is the counterpart of the social insurances; application for Insurance benefit is by routine and impersonal form-filling, and so application for Assistance should be similar. The difference is, of course, that the social insurance claim consists of the relatively straightforward establishment of eligibility, and that thereafter benefit, or a pension, is paid as of right. Payment does not depend on immediate domestic exigencies of the claimant. It is also easy, from external evidence, to check falsification. But Assistance as administered by the Board depends on a number of domestic factors about which falsification, intentional or accidental, is easy, and subsequently rather difficult to check. For this reason it would probably be unsatisfactory to send the Board's forms to applicants by post. Secondly, the Board's final determination, including the exercise of discretion, is based to some extent on the report of the interviewer. The Board's payments are flexible, whereas those from the social insurances are not. It is, therefore, an advantage to the Board to send a visitor to the home as a check against falsification, and it is an advantage to the clients, as it may lead to the exercise of discretion in their favour.

Functions

By the Unemployment Act of 1934, Part II, the Assistance Board is charged with—

"the assistance of persons to whom this Part of the Act applies who are in need of work and the promotion of their welfare, and, in particular, the making of provision for the improvement and establishment of such persons with a view to their being in all respects fit for entry into or return to regular employment, and the grant and issue to such persons of unemployment allowances in accordance with the provisions of this Part of the Act."

The Board is thus charged with two duties towards unemployed persons coming under its auspices, (1) cash assistance, (2) welfare, with the aim of maintaining the employability of the claimant. The Board's scales are fairly frequently adjusted, and since the first edition of this book appeared in 1943 the basis of assessment has been greatly simplified. At the time of preparing the third edition of this book the Board is paying assistance on the following scales:

Assistance Board Scales—January 1944

1. *Amounts to be allowed for needs other than rent.*

	Unemployment Assistance.	Supplementary Pension.
(*a*) For a Married Couple . .	31/-	35/-
(*b*) Where the above rate does not apply:		
(i) For an applicant who is living alone or is a householder, and, as such, is directly responsible for rent and household necessaries .	18/-	20/-
(ii) For any other applicant (except where rule 4 applies):		
If aged 21 or over .	15/6	17/6
If under 21 years . .	12/6	—

2. *Allowance for Rent.*

To the amounts provided by the above table add the appropriate rent allowance as follows:

(*a*) If the applicant or the applicant's wife or husband is the householder, or if the applicant is living alone, add the net rent payable so far as is reasonable in view of the general level of rents in the locality.

(*b*) In any other case (unless there are special circumstances or the applicant is under 18 years of age) add a reasonable share of the rent payable by the person with whom the applicant is living, but not less than 2/6 nor more than 7/-.

3. *Allowances for Dependants other than wife or husband.*

If such dependants are living with the applicant add:

	Unemployment Assistance.	Supplementary Pension.
If aged 21 years or over . . .	15/-	15/-
If aged 16 years or over but less than 21	12/6	12/6
" 11 " " " 16	9/-	9/-
" 8 " " " 11	7/6	7/6
" under 8 years . . .	6/-	6/-

4. If the applicant (having no one dependent on him) is living in a household of which his father, mother, son or daughter is the householder and the householder's income amounts to £6 a week or other appropriate amount, the foregoing scales do not apply. In these cases the Unemployment Assistance rate is 7/6 and no supplementary pension is payable.

These regulations are much more simple in form than those they supplant. Regulation 4 is the last trace of the Household Means Test said to have been "abolished" by Determination of Needs Act, 1941. The only income now taken into account under the "personal means test" for aggregation is that of the applicant, his wife and dependants, and even here a part of the resource (except Old Age or Widow's Pension) is usually disregarded. Non-dependent members of the household are assumed to make a contribution towards the household expenses of 7/- from wages of 55/- or over, 5/- from wages between 30/- and 55/-, 2/6 from wages between 20/- and 30/- and nothing from wages below 20/-.

One should remember that the figure calculated on the above principles is not necessarily the sum payable to the family. There may be discretionary payments for special circumstances made in addition. Also, in the case of Unemployment Assistance cases the father's normal wage, which may have been low when he was in work, would operate to reduce his determination. The Board's officers might then get round this difficulty by finding good reason for adding a discretionary payment which would have the effect of making good the deficiency caused by the operation of the wages stop. Both discretionary payments and the wage stop are discussed in some detail later. They are mentioned here to show that the Board's allowances are subject to various modifications, and that there is no hard-and-fast method by which one can be sure what allowance should or would be made in a given case.

The following tables show for a number of typical cases the effect of these 1944 regulations. Various rents, arbitrarily chosen, have been assumed. From the amounts stated the basic pensions and any other available resources the pensioner may have will, of course, have to be deducted.

SUPPLEMENTARY PENSIONS

	Rates from 17th January 1944.
Pensioner living alone and paying 5/– rent	20/–+5/– Rent Allowance=25/–
Married couple paying 6/– rent: both pensioners; one not a pensioner	35/–+6/– Rent Allowance=41/–
Married couple living with son and daughter-in-law whose rent is 12/–	35/–+6/– Rent Allowance=41/–
Pensioner living with son and daughter-in-law whose rent is 12/–: Man; Woman	17/6+4/– Rent Allowance=21/6
Widow paying 8/– rent with one child aged 5	26/–+8/– Rent Allowance=34/–
with two children aged 14 and 11	38/–+8/– Rent Allowance=46/–
Widow living with parents whose rent is 14/– with one child aged 5	23/6+6/– Rent Allowance=29/6
with two children aged 14 and 11	35/6+7/– Rent Allowance=42/6

UNEMPLOYMENT ASSISTANCE

	New Rates from 17th January 1944.
Applicant living alone and paying 5/– rent . . .	18/–+5/– Rent Allowance=23/–
Married couple paying 6/6 rent	31/–+6/6 Rent Allowance=37/6
Married couple with two children aged 7 and 10 paying 10/– rent	44/6+10/– Rent Allowance=54/6
Adult applicant living with father and mother whose rent is 12/–:	
Man . . . . } Woman . . . }	15/6+4/– Rent Allowance=19/6

The Area Officer is able to make discretionary additions, above the scale rate plus rent allowance, to meet "special circumstances." This includes the provision of weekly allowances for extra nourishment for a member of the household on a medical certificate, and similar needs. Such discretionary payments are generally limited to 5/- weekly for any single cause, but more than one such payment might be made to any one family in one week if the need for it were established. The use made by Area Officers of these discretionary powers varies considerably, depending in part on the attitude of their District Officers, on their own ability to argue a case successfully with the Auditor if necessary, and, generally, on their own courage, initiative and sagacity. Often the decisions Area Officers have to make about the exercise of discretion are extremely difficult, for although a clear case may be made out for the exercise of discretion, a precedent may be created which would cause difficulty later. For example, an East London pensioner was going to an old people's outing. In her excitement she sent her shoes to be mended first; 4/6 was charged. She went to the Board, which refused a grant and told her to pay weekly by instalments, waiting meanwhile for her only walking shoes. No shoes, no outing. The old lady's predicament became known to her fellow-pensioners, who happened, in that area, to be organised, and immense harm was done to the reputation of the Board. On the other hand, once the Board started paying for running repairs which the allowances are supposed to cover, it would have to do so on every application. Thus the Area Officer is continually trying to square human needs with the Board's low scales and with the Board's emphasis on uniformity of treatment. He is further handicapped because he is largely dependent for his knowledge of cases on the judgment of his subordinates in bringing cases to his notice for the exercise of discretion. It is widely known among workers in other branches of social services that if contact is made direct with the Area Officer about a client whose special circumstances call for obvious attention something is done, even though the client himself may already have made repeated application to the office staff without result. The Area Officer may also make cash grants for "exceptional needs." During 1938, 20,141 such grants were made. These are intended for what may be called capital replacement, e.g. of furniture or bedding. The Board's allowances are supposed to defray normal costs of maintaining a home, and the exceptional needs grants are designed chiefly for the re-establishment of families who had previously been "subsisting on sums substantially less than the Board's ordinary allowances." [1]

The "Wages Stop"

The Board's task of maintaining its applicants at a reasonable standard is greatly complicated by the "provision of the Regulations which requires that, in the absence of special circumstances or exceptional needs, the assessment of an applicant's needs shall be less than the amount which would ordinarily be available for the support of his household out of his wages and those of his dependants if they were following their normal occupations." [2] Thus, because of the "wages stop," a family may have to be given an allowance which is less than its assessment according to the Board's scale. Naturally the families which suffer most from this provision are the large families where there are a number of dependants; because such families would have to live at a standard below the Board's minimum were the wage-earner in work, they are kept at the same level by the State when receiving Unemployment Assistance. This follows logically from the assumption that it is unsound to make it more profitable

[1] Annual Report of the Unemployment Assistance Board, 1938, p. 17.
[2] *ibid.*, p. 10.

for a man to be idle than in work. The Board, as it points out in both its 1937 and 1938 Reports, is thus in a quandary; it must in certain cases penalise children by underfeeding them because, in other circumstances, those children would again be underfed. The problem can hardly be tackled from the Assistance end. It needs tackling when the man is in work. If his income then, from whatever source, industry or the State, bears some relevance not only to his skill as a worker but also to the size of his family, he can be provided with a reasonable income when he is out of work without alteration of the wages stop provision. A further difficulty in the operation of the wages stop is the estimation of a man's potential wage rate: "A married man with dependants who has not worked since he was a youth, and then at a youth's wage, cannot as an adult be assessed on the basis of the wage he earned as a juvenile. On the other hand, it is no longer reasonable to regard a wage once earned by a man . . . as available to him today when through age, circumstances or disabilities he has lost his former skill or his skill has been rendered obsolete by changed methods of production." [1] If the Board gives its client the benefit of the doubt and overestimates his earning power, it is piling up trouble not only for itself but for the Exchange, which might eventually offer the man a job at his economic, and lower, wage rate. It is questionable in those circumstances whether the Tribunal would consider a man ineligible for continued assistance if he refused work at a rate below his Assistance rate. By a too lenient and humane administration of the wages stop provision the Board may get into serious difficulties. The Board's determinations are intended to be based on needs; but the wages stop may force the Board to disregard some part of a family's needs. Thus of two men, one skilled and the other unskilled, having families of the same sizes with similar-aged children, and paying the same rent, the unskilled man may, on account of the wages stop, receive a lower allowance from the Board than the skilled man. The final determination in such a case is based not, as is usual, on needs, but on the industrial status of the wage-earner. It is true that the Area Officer may use his discretion to give allowances on account of special circumstances which put the total above the amount prescribed

[1] Annual Report of the Unemployment Assistance Board, 1938, pp. 10-11.

by wages stop calculation, but too free a use of this power might easily lead to difficulties later.

Penalties

The 1934 Act (Part II, Section 40) permits the Board to penalise applicants in any of four stipulated ways if they are "cases of special difficulty." The Board must first have "regard to all the circumstances of the case, and, in particular, to the question whether the applicant has failed to avail himself of opportunities of employment or training and to the question whether there is any necessity for protecting the interests of the applicant or of persons depending on him." Where the officer of the Board (or the Appeal Tribunal) is convinced that a case is one of special difficulty, he may do one or more of the following:

(*a*) Pay the whole or part of the allowance to a member of the household other than the applicant. This penalty is chiefly used against drunkards and gamblers, the allowance being paid to the wife after a proper explanation to the applicant himself.

(*b*) Issue the allowance otherwise than in cash, i.e. in food and other tickets; both this penalty and the one above are sometimes used to indicate disapproval of an applicant's refusal to accept or to stay in suitable employment without good reason. Otherwise a man might be disqualified from receiving benefit and receive instead a comparable allowance from the Board.

(*c*) Grant the allowance only on condition that the applicant attends at a work centre provided for the purpose or at one maintained by a Public Assistance authority. This clause has been little used, ostensibly for lack of available centres. Actually, the extreme unpopularity of any sort of relief work is likely to have influenced the Board against enforcing it. However, before the war Advisory Committees reviewed all cases of persons under 30 on the Board's registers, and most of these Committees, according to the 1938 Report of the Board,[1] advised "that where there was evidence that a man was unemployed of his own will the Board's powers under Section 40 of the Act should be exercised." Accordingly, the Board began to make arrangements with local authorities for the use of their centres, and also to set

[1] Annual Report of the Unemployment Assistance Board, 1938, p. 47.

up such centres of its own. The war has, however, obviated the need for this. In 1938, 75 cases were so treated.[1]

(*d*) Grant the allowance only on condition that the applicant becomes an inmate of a Public Assistance institution, the allowance then being paid partly to the local authority towards the cost of his maintenance, and partly to a member of his household while he is away in the institution. This penalty, also, is very rarely used, and is chiefly useful for cases in which there is need for the protection of the interests of the applicant or his dependants. Its success would depend very much on the institution and on the attitude of its master. In 1938, 164 determinations were made conditional on institutional treatment.

The last two conditions are not operated without previous consultation with the Advisory Committee, and applicants on whom such conditions are imposed may appeal to the Tribunal without the leave normally necessary. In 1938, of 80 such appeals, 78 were decided in favour of the conditional determination.[2]

Appeal Tribunals

Appeal Tribunals consist of a Chairman and two other members, and operate over an area or a district. The Chairman is appointed by the Minister of Labour, "and of the two other members . . . one shall be selected by the Unemployment Assistance Board from a panel of persons nominated by the Minister to represent workpeople and shall be appointed by the Board, and the other shall be appointed by the Board to represent the Board." The Board thus has the selection and appointment of the workpeople's representative, provided that his name was on the panel originally compiled by the Minister. It is not suggested that this arrangement is in any way abused by the Board's staff, but it is easy to imagine situations in which the Tribunal might, on occasion, be unduly weighted on the Board's side, and that without any infringement of the law. One can imagine, also, that there might be persons on the Minister's panel whom the Board might prefer not to appoint to Tribunals in certain districts. There is no guarantee that

[1] Annual Report of the Unemployment Assistance Board, 1938, p. 22.

[2] Appeals about "scope," i.e. concerning an individual's eligibility to be dealt with by the Board, are settled by the Chairman alone, and leave to appeal is unnecessary. The Chairman's permission must also be obtained for leave to withdraw an appeal.

persons on the panel as workpeople's representatives will, in fact, ever be called to serve. No appeal may be made to the Tribunal (except under the last two clauses of Section 40) without previous permission from the Chairman, who must satisfy himself that "there is reason to doubt" either that the applicant has been rightly dealt with under the appropriate Regulations, or that there are not special circumstances affecting the case. In 1938, allowances were increased in 19% of the 42,000 cases heard by the 139 Appeal Tribunals.

Advisory Committees

Advisory Committees are an integral part of the Board's structure, so much so that instructions for their establishment come right at the beginning of Part II of the Act, next after a description of the basic functions of the Board. These Committees are composed of persons having knowledge of local conditions and of the social services. Members may be paid travelling expenses and other allowances "including compensation for loss of remunerative time." There is no ruling about the frequency of meeting, and practice varies over the country as a whole; some Advisory Committees are often consulted and are regarded as an indispensable complement to the work of the office, others meet seldom and count for very little. In general, apart from rent questions, they operate on the welfare side of the Board's work, advising not only in "cases of special difficulty," but also in cases which are for some reason puzzling or bothering the Board's staff. Unfortunately this excellent provision appears to militate against immediate welfare action being taken where necessary; a good many problems are either left over for the Advisory Committee or are not detected until the Committee sees the applicant in question. This position was described by one of the Board's senior officers:

> "One of the functions of the Advisory Committee is seeing individual applicants who are in difficulties of some kind. . . . We often find that an applicant has some difficulty in finding employment . . . or he is suffering from some optical or medical defect, or there is something rather unusual about the man." [1]

[1] Royal Commission on Workmen's Compensation, Minutes of Evidence, 2437-8, 28th April 1939.

This seems hardly satisfactory. If a man has defective vision, which is easiest, to tell him when and how to go to the nearest Vision session at a hospital, or to get committee members to tell him the same thing? Then, if "there is something unusual" about a person, if, say, he stammers, or is emotionally inhibited in some direction, or is unadjusted to his domestic situation, will he find it as helpful to discuss himself with a committee as he would in private interview with one person in whom he had confidence? For certain situations and for general discussion the Advisory Committees are obviously most useful, but they should not be the chief means of doing constructive work for the Board's clients. That the Advisory Committees do, in fact, give a good deal of individual welfare advice is an indictment of the Board's methods; its staff make little attempt to, it seems, deal with even quite straightforward difficulties. In 1938 the Advisory Committees interviewed some 40,000 of the Board's applicants aged 30 or less. Of these persons it was estimated that "from eight to nine per cent. were suffering from mental or physical defects that seriously impaired their employability." One might suppose that the Board's staff had already taken every step to have such defects diagnosed and treated, and had brought the sufferers before the Committee in the hope of finding new and appropriate advice. But this does not seem to have been the case, for the 1938 Report continues: "In about a quarter of these cases the defect was of dental, optical or other character that appeared to be remediable. . . . In some cases the applicant was advised to apply to his Approved Society under the Health Insurance Acts. . . ." It is extraordinary that these defects, impairing, as the Report says, the employability of the applicants, should have remained unknown to the Board. It is also extraordinary that advice so elementary as that the applicant should apply to his Approved Society should have to be concocted by a committee and be thought worthy of mention as a creditable piece of work in the Annual Report. This is just one example of inefficiency arising from the employment of unsuitable staff for the maintenance of personal contact between the Board and its clientele. All kinds of odds and ends which should be cleared up in the ordinary work of the Board are left until the Advisory Committee comes along.

Criticism of the work which is left for the Advisory Committees does not imply criticism of these Committees themselves. They are frequently composed of able persons with excellent knowledge of local conditions and opinion, whose advice and co-operation is of real value to the Board. They provide for the Board's officers those local ties which the Board, being a national organisation and nowhere locally indigenous, lacks. When the Board was faced with the tricky "Liquidation of the Standstill" in 1936, it especially urged its officers to convene, and to pay attention to, Advisory Committees:

> "The Board proposes to associate local opinion with this process of establishing the standard of assistance, and it is therefore provided that . . . officers of the Board . . . shall give consideration to the recommendation of Advisory Committees as to the manner in which progressive adjustments should be made in their respective Areas." [1]

The Advisory Committees are particularly important, as the Board's officers move round the country changing offices rather frequently and they find in the Advisory Committees a body of well-disposed and well-informed persons who can tell them about their new areas and advise them about local problems. The Committees also help to find local solutions to general problems, such as "the Liquidation of the Standstill, adjustment of allowances in rural areas, the application of the wages stop, the enquiry regarding applicants aged 30 and under." [2] Most Advisory Committees work through sub-committees and interviewing panels, and the members collectively give much time to the problems of the Board. This naturally varies according to the amount of work which the Board's staff put before them; there is no doubt that the Advisory Committees are a valuable part of the Board's organisation.

Rehabilitation

The Board's powers and activities for "the re-establishment" of the workless are now of historical rather than topical interest. All methods which the Board tried before the war covered only a small percentage of the Board's applicants. The Minister

[1] Cmd. 5229. Explanatory memorandum 53, July 1936.
[2] Annual Report of the Unemployment Assistance Board, 1938, p. 112.

of Labour's figures show that on 14th November 1938, of those in receipt of unemployment allowances 16·2% had been unemployed for periods of 6 months or more (but under 12 months) and that 45·3%, or 248,380 persons, had been unemployed for 12 months or more. The following table is obtained by relating this figure to approximate figures for the Board's applicants admitted to the various types of centre in 1938: [1]

Recipients of Unemployment Assistance Trained in Official Centres in 1938

Centre.	Recipients of Unemployment Assistance.	
	(1) Approximate Number admitted to Centres in 1938.	(2) Figures in col. (1) expressed as percentage of those unemployed more than 12 months.
Government Training . .	5,900	2·3
Instructional . . .	20,236	8·1
Local Training . . .	2,628 *	1·5
	28,764	11·9

* Exclusive of those later proceeding to Training or Instructional Centres.

Admission to all these types of centre was voluntary, and no employment was guaranteed at the end of training. The Board is empowered to make arrangements with local authorities, subject to the approval of the Treasury, for persons who have had a course of training to be employed for periods not exceeding three months upon work for the authorities. Very little has been done in this way, but had the war not started it is likely that arrangements would have been made with local authorities on the advice of the many Advisory Committees who interviewed the under-30 unemployed. The Board also has arrangements with voluntary bodies to which it makes payments on a *per capita* basis for any of its applicants trained or rehabilitated by them. These are the Central Association for Young Wayfarers Hostels, the Land Settlement Association, the Central Council

[1] Annual Report of the Unemployment Assistance Board, 1938, pp. 25-28.

for the Care of Cripples, and the British Legion (Metropolitan Area) Taxicab Drivers' Training School; for women the Board co-operates with the Central Committee on Women's Training and Employment. According to the 1938 Report of the Board, these agencies dealt with 1,339 men[1] and 812 women during 1938. In 1938, therefore, a total of 30,915 persons were given official training or were dealt with by a voluntary organisation. This figure represents 9·2% of the 336,280 recipients of Unemployment Assistance in 1938 who had been unemployed for 6 months or longer in November 1938. Whether or not the Board could have done more within the framework of our national economy at that time, it is impossible to regard its results as any kind of model for the future. The unemployment problem cannot be solved by the rehabilitation of small samples of the unemployed. But the Board must take some blame for the smallness of the samples.

Statutory Limitations of the Board

The Board is not allowed to provide for the medical needs of its clients. This is an important difference between the scope of the Board and of Public Assistance Committees, who can pay for any kind of medical treatment. Arrangements are made for those of the Board's clients and their families who have no Insurance doctor to see the Public Assistance doctor, but this is no solution to the whole problem, for the Board is not empowered to pay for any treatment, medicaments or specialist services, and as soon as these are advised, from whatever source, the problem of payment arises. It is true, as the Under-30 Enquiry showed, that the Board is much too slow in discovering the need for medical and surgical advice among its clientele, some of whom are adequately covered by Insurance, but it is also true that when that need is known the Board often has great difficulty in arranging for payment. It is reasonable that the Board shall not duplicate specialist services already provided by other authorities, but it is not reasonable that the Board shall be unable to pay for the use of such services when lack of payment hinders proper treatment. The Board itself

[1] Excluding the numbers of those in the Distressed Areas and elsewhere working on Group Holdings provided by the Land Settlement Association.

writes strongly of these difficulties, for the solution of which it is obliged to depend on the goodwill of other bodies:

> "There are, however, local authorities who are not in a position or are unwilling to co-operate fully. The Board feel bound to draw attention to this state of affairs and the regrettable consequences to which it leads." [1]

The Board is able to provide extra nourishment allowances on medical certificates, but only where it is established that it is food, not medicine, which is recommended. Thus Virol is considered a medicine, but cod-liver oil a food, and "when you have to go to a different authority to get the Virol you need, it can be a source of irritation in practice. . . ." [2]

The Law of Liability which can be invoked by Public Assistance authorities cannot be invoked by the Board. It is unable to recover from relatives the cost of maintenance of any of its applicants, even if children or parents of the applicant are known to be relatively wealthy. The Board's only power of recovery is from applicants themselves when overpayment of allowances has been made because of mis-statements of the applicant. The Board may then take proceedings for the summary recovery of such sums, as civil debts. The Board is not empowered to lend money to its clients, or to enter into any arrangement with them by which sums advanced by the Board may be repaid gradually. The Board can only make an outright grant or nothing. If, for example, somebody urgently needed to make a long journey to see a dangerously sick relative, he would, if being supported by the Board, be dependent on the discretion of the Area Officer for his journey money. There would be no way by which the sum could be advanced and repaid later either by a relative or friend or in small amounts from the recipient's weekly allowance. On the other hand, the Board is never in the difficult position of having to recover debts from applicants or former applicants.

Summing up, one can say that since the war the Board has shown the great value to the community of a nation-wide relief

[1] Annual Report of the Unemployment Assistance Board, 1938, p. 26.

[2] Royal Commission on Workmen's Compensation, Minutes of Evidence, 2434, 2435, 28th April 1939.

organisation which can act immediately. On the other hand, it has convinced nobody that national uniformity of scales is separable from administrative rigidity. The public has shown no confidence in the Board members collectively, who have seemed aloof and unassailable and have given the impression that they seclude themselves from the cries of those for whom they are responsible. None of the Board's members are great national figures, and the public has been baffled by its inability to pin its anger on to any well-known name. It was clearly a mistake to suppose originally that the public would lose interest in the administration of an intimate domestic service if this were "taken out of politics." On the other hand, the Board has won, chiefly through its war-time work for blitzed persons, general recognition as an essential and integrated part of our social administration. The quality of its staff has improved throughout, and home visiting is no longer the duty of the notorious temporary clerk, a grade which is now abolished; the Board's Area Officers have grown in confidence and therefore dare to show a reasonable flexibility; the scale provides increased purchasing power, and the hated household means test is abolished; welfare visits have become a recognised part of the Board's work as distinct from visits only for investigation; the Board is operating an embryonic internal staff training scheme. It is pleasant to list these improvements which have made it possible to delete much of the criticism which stood in the first (1943) edition of this book. Indeed, the speed at which the Board has travelled suggests that it may successfully survive the strains which will be put on it when the National Insurance Act first begins to operate. For not only will the Board have to carry a complicated legacy of destitution cases left it by the Poor Law, but it will be called on to supplement the various types of insurance payment and to maintain those necessitous persons not now insured who have not yet accumulated insurance rights under the new Act. The Board will have the great responsibility for acting as a shock-absorber when the public becomes aware both of the scope and the limitations of the National Insurance scheme. It will be the active and indispensable partner of the new Ministry, and its activities may well determine whether the new Act wins popular support or not.

Chapter VI

WIDOWS', ORPHANS' AND OLD AGE PENSIONS

By JOAN SIMEON CLARKE

"We have, therefore, been irresistibly forced to advocate that the means limit be abolished altogether, and that the Old Age Pension be given to all citizens. We are of the opinion that no other course will remove the very serious objections to the present system."

This is an extract from the Report of the Departmental Committee on Old Age Pensions issued in 1919. The arguments with which the Committee fortified this piece of advice have not been refuted; they have been shelved, so that twenty years later, in the year ending 31st March 1939, there were still 576,072 old age pensioners, 32% of all such pensioners, whose pensions were paid only after an investigation of the claimant's means. The remaining 68% were pensioned by right of insurance, and still other impecunious aged persons, being ineligible for any sort of pension, were supported by their local Public Assistance Committees. Had the 1919 Committee's advice been taken, it would have paved the way for a single and unified Old Age Pensions administration in this country. But after the provision of Supplementary Pensions we had a triple system. Non-Contributory Old Age Pensions were administered by the Customs and Excise to persons over 70, subject to various qualifications, including an income limit; Contributory Old Age Pensions for women over 60 and men over 65 (together with their uninsured wives over 60 [1]) were administered by the Ministry of Health under the Widows', Orphans' and Old Age Contributory Pensions Act; lastly, Supplementary Pensions can be paid to any old age pensioner after an investigation of means and needs carried out by the

[1] Also Widows' and Orphans' Pensions.

Assistance Board.[1] Three different Government Departments, operating under three different sets of rules, were, therefore, concerned with the financial support of the pensionable aged. The effect of these diverse ministrations will be discussed later, but first it is useful to look at the development of Old Age Pension legislation,[2] and to see how this legislation reflects the changing sense of community responsibility towards the aged.

The Old Age Pensions Act of 1908, which first introduced the payment of Non-Contributory Old Age Pensions, had been preceded in Great Britain by some twenty-three years of public discussion; six different bodies had wrestled with the problem of what to do about the aged poor.[3] Controversy raged fiercely over the relation of pensions to thrift. It was feared that the poor would no longer have sufficient incentive to save if they were assured of State-paid Old Age Pensions. The Treasury Committee on Old Age Pensions, 1896-98, postulated that "State aid cannot be justified unless it is limited to aiding the individual when circumstances beyond his control make it practically impossible for him to save from his own earnings an adequate provision for old age."

The Act of 1908 was strongly moralistic, reflecting the strict nonconformist backing of the dominant Liberal Party. It expressly declared that nobody was eligible for a pension if he had previously "failed to work according to his ability, opportunity, and need, for the maintenance of himself and those legally dependent on him" (Section III*b*). But a person should not be disqualified under this clause if he had, for the past ten years, made "provision against old age, sickness, infirmity, or want or loss of employment." Pensions, at 5/- a week, were meant to be supplementary to the resources of the righteous

[1] The Board now renews both Non-Contributory Old Age and Supplementary Pensions where these are both payable, issuing one book for the 2 pensions. However, responsibility for assessment and re-assessment of Non-Contributory Old Age Pensions still rests with Customs and Excise.

[2] For elaboration see Wilson and Mackay, *Old Age Pensions* (Oxford University Press, 1941).

[3] 1885-87. Select Committee on National Provident Insurance.
1893-95. Royal Commission on the Aged Poor.
1895-96. Treasury Committee on Old Age Pensions.
1899. Select Committee of the House of Commons on Aged Deserving Poor.
1899-1900. Departmental Committee on the Aged Deserving Poor.
1903. Select Committee of the House of Commons on Aged Pensioners' Bill.

man. They were to be the reward of virtuous living rather than any token of communal responsibility for the well-being of the enfeebled citizens. Further disqualifications for pensions were imprisonment without option of a fine, and detention orders made under the Inebriates Act; these disqualifications lasted for ten years from release from prison or the date of a detention order, the latter at the discretion of the Court. Also a pension was not payable to a person who was "being maintained in any place as a pauper or criminal lunatic."

The 1908 Act holds the balance between the past and the future of social policy. The nineteenth-century abhorrence of pauperism permits contemptuous references to "a pauper or criminal lunatic"; indigence is still an offence against society. On the other hand, it is with this Act that the twentieth-century idea of collective responsibility for individual members of the State first gets a foot in the door. It is expressly provided that "the receipt of an Old Age Pension . . . shall not deprive the pensioner of any franchise, right or privilege, or subject him to any disability." For the first time Parliament sanctioned the expenditure of public funds as cash grants to citizens without the stigma of pauperism. A man might receive a State pension without loss of respectability. Henceforth society's punitive attitude towards the poor diminished, while its sense of liability increased.

The stringent residence and nationality qualifications of the 1908 Act were amended in 1919, and these Acts, with less important ones of 1911 and 1924, were consolidated in the Old Age Pensions Act, 1936. This Act is still in force. To qualify for a Non-Contributory Pension today a person must be not less than 70 years of age, he must have had at least twelve years' aggregate residence in the United Kingdom since attaining the age of 50, and he must have been at least ten years a British subject. There are certain disqualifications which are common to Contributory Pensions also, and are discussed later. Pensions are inalienable and may not be distrained upon for debt.

The means qualification stipulates that pensions are payable on a sliding scale from 26/- per head (or 16/- for married women) downwards to 2/-:

INCOME LIMITS FOR NON-CONTRIBUTORY OLD AGE PENSIONS

Maximum Unearned Income.[1]	Earned Income.	Pension Payable Weekly.
£39 plus	£26 5 0 maximum	26/-
	£31 10 0 ,,	24/-
	£36 15 0 ,,	22/-
	£42 0 0 ,,	20/-
	£47 5 0 ,,	18/-
	£49 17 6 ,,	16/-
	£52 10 0 ,,	16/-
	£57 15 0 ,,	14/-
	£63 0 0 ,,	12/-
	£68 5 0 ,,	10/-
	£73 10 0 ,,	8/-
	£78 15 0 ,,	6/-
	£84 0 0 ,,	4/-
	£89 5 0 ,,	2/-

The Act provides that three months' income from National Health Insurance, Friendly Society or Trade Union, received by either the pensioner or husband or wife of the pensioner, shall be disregarded in any one year. For two pensioners living together, the figures in the table above are doubled. If the pensioner is one of a married couple of which the other one is not pensionable, he or she is assessed on one-half of their joint income. Unfortunately no account is taken of housekeepers, so that if, for example, an old man has a grown-up daughter to keep house for him after the death of his non-pensionable wife, his total resources are taken into account instead of only one-half of them as when his wife was alive. Pensioners also feel it to be unfair that earned income is taken more heavily into account than unearned. As soon as they earn more than 10/- a week they reduce their pension by the amount of their weekly earnings over this sum, until it vanishes altogether. Until April 1947 non-contributory old age pensions were administered by the Department of Customs and Excise, an anachronism dating from the 1908 Act. As a recent minor rationalisation those pensioners claiming supplementary pensions had subsequent assessments for their non-contributory pensions handled by the Assistance Board, thus eliminating duplicate

[1] This includes the estimated yearly value of houses not personally occupied, of investments, and other property not personally used or enjoyed.

visiting by two Departments. Now, as a step towards the full implementation of the National Insurance Act, the Assistance Board has responsibility for administering all non-contributory pensions, irrespective of claims for supplementation. The Pensions Officers formerly employed by the Department of Customs and Excise have therefore been superseded by Pensions Officers appointed by the Treasury from the local staffs of the Assistance Board. Recommendations of these officers are put before Local Pensions Committees, whose functions are derived from the 1908 Act.

Pensions Committees are appointed by Municipal Boroughs and Urban Districts of over 20,000 population and by County Boroughs and County Councils, and consist partly or entirely of co-opted members. In the Civil Estimates for the year ending 31st March 1942, £30,000 was allocated for the expenses of Pensions Committees, clerks, office accommodation, etc. The Committee decides whether or not claimants are entitled to pensions, and if so at what rates. If either the Pensions Officer or the claimant disagrees with the Committee there is right of appeal within seven days to the Minister of Health, whose decision is final. In the year ending 31st March 1939 there were 3,526 appeals:[1]

By Pensions Officers .	1,199 appeals.	45% allowed.
By Claimants and Pensioners .	2,737 appeals.	42% allowed.

Contributory Pensions

Pensions insurance is compulsory for all persons earning at a rate of remuneration not exceeding £420 per annum, and all persons employed by way of manual labour, other than those in excepted employment (i.e. that making comparable provision for its employees). Pensions stamps are combined with those for National Health Insurance, the employer and the insured person each bearing part of the cost of contributions. Persons claiming pensions[2] send their completed forms direct to the Ministry of

[1] Annual Report of the Ministry of Health, 1939, Appendix XL, p. 281.

[2] Contributory Pensions in payment in England on 31st December 1938:

Widows' Pensions	686,025	payable.
Children's Allowances and Orphans' Pensions . .	226,804	,,
Old Age Pensions (Ages 65-70)	708,750	,,
Old Age Pensions after 70, payable in right of insurance .	1,061,814	,,
	2,683,393	,,

Health, whence they are forwarded to the relevant local office of the Ministry. Here eligibility for pensions is determined, contributions are checked with the records of the claimants' Approved Societies, birth, marriage and death certificates are scrutinised (and actually obtained if the claimant has been unable to do this), and sometimes the claimants are interviewed. Every effort is apparently made to help claimants to establish their pension rights. Eventually pension books are sent by post and, like Non-Contributory Old Age Pensions, weekly sums are drawn from the Post Office. Old Age Pensions are also payable to uninsured wives over 60 whose husbands are in receipt of Old Age Pensions.

WEEKLY PENSIONS PAYMENTS

Type of Pension.	Weekly Payment.
Old Age	26/–
Widows' (under 60) . .	10/–
" (over 60) . .	26/–
Childrens' Allowances:	
Eldest child . . .	5/–
Other children . . .	3/–
Orphans'	7/6

WEEKLY CONTRIBUTION RATES FOR WIDOWS', ORPHANS' AND OLD AGE CONTRIBUTORY PENSIONS

Status of Insured Person.	Men.		Total.	Women.		Total.
	Employer.	Employee.		Employer.	Employee.	
Ordinary Contributor (over 18) .	1/6½	1/6½	3/1	1/2½	1/3	2/5½
Persons over 65 years of age[1]. .	2/–	Nil	2/–	1/8	Nil	1/8
Exempt persons .	1/6½	5½d.	2/–	1/2½	Nil	1/2½

[1] These contributions are the total payments made by the employer in respect of both Health and Pensions.

The 1946 Act embodies two conflicting principles concerning the paid employment of persons over pensionable age. Recognising that, in an ageing community, the output of every available worker is needed both to increase the national income and to provide for the considerable redistribution of this income which is effected by the National Insurance scheme, the Act stipulates that every worker postponing retirement beyond pensionable age shall receive an additional 1/- weekly on his postponed pension for every complete period of six months for which he has remained at work without claiming it. This is an undoubted incentive to the able-bodied to continue working. However, a different and contradictory philosophy appears in the legal provisions which deal with the earnings of a worker once he gives notice of retirement and begins to draw his pension. Henceforward his pension will be reduced shilling for shilling of his earnings in excess of 20/- weekly. This means that, from the worker's point of view, it is "not worth while" to earn more than £1 in any one week, unless he can put his earnings comfortably over £2. 16/-, i.e. above the total of pension plus permitted earnings. Thus the old person who has been bribed to continue his output as long as possible, finds himself penalised if, having retired, he attempts to maximise whatever productivity still remains to him. Of these contradictory provisions, the bonus on deferred pension claims is inoperative until the full application of the new Act, but the embargo on earnings operates at once. Curiously, too, this embargo does not apply to persons over 70, who, if they are contributory pensioners, are free to earn whatever they may get. The effect of the earning disqualification is therefore to reduce the output of those active and potentially productive persons between 65 (60 for women) and 70, many of whom are both able and happy to continue at work.

Contributory Old Age Pensions are paid on fulfilment of three statutory conditions (subject to certain disqualifications which will be discussed later). First, men contributors must have reached the age of 65, women 60, and they must have been continuously insured for the five years immediately preceding this date. If on reaching that age they have been insured for a shorter period, title to pension may arise on the expiration of five years from date of entry into insurance. It is possible to be insured without being continuously in insurable occupation. When employment ceases a free insurance period averaging two years is given, which may be extended by a period of sickness occurring at the beginning or at the date when it is due to cease. Moreover, if there has been ten years' insurance at the date when employment ceased an " extended insurance period" of one year follows the free insurance period if the employee proves genuine unemployment (except when incapacitated). These extended insurance periods are renewable indefinitely so long as genuine unemployment is proved. Re-entry into insurable employment during a free insurance period gives title to a new free insurance period on cessation of such employment however short, but if an extended insurance period has begun before re-entry into employment a new free insurance period cannot be given until there has been at least 26 weeks' employment within a period of two consecutive years. The effect of these provisions is that a person who has been insured for ten years and then falls out of employment can remain in insurance indefinitely even though illness or unemployment prevent the payment of further contributions.

For the second statutory condition a minimum of 104 weeks must have elapsed and 104 contributions must have been paid since the date of last entry into insurance. This is an absolute condition and there is no way round it. However, provided the insurance has not been actually broken, contributions paid any number of years ago can be counted towards the total, even if they were paid during numerous disconnected spasms of insurable employment. An insurance period is broken when, for reasons other than sickness and genuine unemployment, the insured person quits insurable employment and fails to return to it within the period of free insurance. This would happen when there is a rise in wages or salary putting the recipient outside the insured income groups, or when, for example, he leaves his employment to set up on his own. There is no surrender value of such lapsed insurances, but persons who, after two years' insurance, cease to be insurably employed, may voluntarily continue their pensions insurances, paying the full contribution which is normally shared between employer and employed. Pension rates are the same as those for ordinary contributors, if an average of 50 contributions have been paid yearly throughout the insurance. Contributions may be excused for that part of an illness exceeding thirteen weeks, otherwise there is no credit for weeks of illness or unemployment. A sliding scale of pension rates entitles contributors with lower averages of contributions to receive pensions and allowances at reduced rates.

The third statutory condition stipulates that an average of at least 39 contributions shall have been paid, or shall be deemed to have been paid, in the three contribution years immediately before the insured person reached the age of 65 (or 60 for women). For this purpose contributions are deemed to have been paid for weeks of notified sickness and genuine unemployment. This condition is waived altogether for persons who, on reaching the age of 60, have been continuously insured for ten years. The explanation of the average test is that it ensures that a considerable number of contributions shall have been paid in recent years prior to that in which the claim matures.

Widows' Pensions

Widows' Pensions are normally payable from the date of the husband's death, provided that he was insured at the time of his death. He must have been insured for at least two years, and must have paid 104 contributions. Also, if four or more years have elapsed since his last entry into insurance, he must have averaged 26 contributions in each of the three contribution years preceding his death, but this average test is waived in respect of men who had been continuously insured for ten years on reaching the age of 60 or who have been entitled to an Old Age Pension between the ages of 65 and 70. And, as in the case of Old Age Pensions, contributions are for the purpose of this condition deemed to have been paid in respect of weeks of notified sickness or genuine unemployment, so that the widow of a man who died at the end of a long illness is not disqualified if the other conditions are satisfied. The full pension of 26/- is payable to widows who were over 60 on 30th September 1946, and who were already receiving a contributory Widow's Pension of 10/-, and who have retired. This pension is subject to reduction according to earnings as if it were an Old Age Pension; however, no such reduction is made in respect of the earnings of widows who were over 65 on the same date and were then receiving a 10/- Widow's Pension.

When first introduced, the Act was particularly hard on the "pre-Act widow" whose husband died before 4th January 1926; she, and the widow of the man who was over 70 on this date and died subsequently, were not entitled to pensions until they became 55 unless they had children, and even then their pensions ceased when their children were 16 in one case and 14 in the other. A greater hardship is that women are entitled to Widows' Pensions by right *only* of their husband's insurances. If, for example, a man and wife were both working and supporting a family, but the wife was in insurable work, say as a cleaner, while the husband, who might be a window-cleaner working on his own, was uninsured, the widow, if the husband died, would be entitled to no Widow's Pension and to no Children's Allowances. However, should she herself die leaving the children orphaned, they would at once be eligible for Orphans' Pensions in respect of her own insurance.

A woman previously divorced is ineligible for a Widow's Pension in respect of the death of her former husband, and a pensioned widow who remarries also forfeits her former pension rights. A widow is also disqualified from receiving a pension while she is cohabiting with a man as his wife. However, these disqualifications do not apply to the children, who continue to receive Children's Allowances provided that they are under 14 years of age, or, if between 14 and 16, are under full-time instruction in a day school. If the widow dies, these Children's Allowances turn into Orphans' Pensions. When the eldest child passes the pensionable age, the next child, if there is one, becomes entitled to the higher rate. The word "child" includes a step-child, "and in relation to a man an illegitimate child, whether his or his wife's, who was living with him at the time of his death . . . in relation to a widow it includes her illegitimate child who was living with her at the time of her death." There is thus no provision for illegitimate children not living with a parent, even though in such cases the parent frequently is under obligation to contribute to their maintenance. A man's illegitimate child who continues to live with his widow becomes eligible, in company with his half-brothers, for an Orphan's Pension after the widow's death. Widows' Pensions are not payable if the husband was over 60 at the date of marriage, even though all his insurance qualifications are in order, unless there is or has been a child of the marriage, or three years have elapsed between the date of the marriage and the date of the husband's death, or the widow was, or but for the disqualification would have been, in receipt of a Widow's Pension before her marriage. This disqualification is obviously intended to thwart people who "marry an old man for his money," in this case a pension. On the other hand, it robs the husband of title to a pension to which he has established a right by virtue of his contributions.

Beside these disqualifications for Widows' and Orphans' Pensions, others are common to all pensions, contributory and non-contributory alike. First, inmates of any Poor Law institution are disqualified unless they were admitted for medical or surgical treatment, and then they are only eligible for a pension so long as the actual treatment lasts. Thus, if they are not admitted in order to have treatment, but subsequently need it, they are still ineligible for a pension. This whole question is discussed at length with great indignation by Sir Arnold Wilson,[1] who points out that even patients admitted for treatment are liable to have pressure put on them by local authorities to appoint one of the Council's officers as the agent to collect the pension, the greater part of which is then absorbed by the authority, the residue being spent on "comforts" for the patient. Secondly, Non-Contributory Old Age Pensions are not paid to persons while they are in a mental hospital, or are being maintained as "rate-aided persons of unsound mind," and no pensions are paid to persons being maintained as criminal lunatics, or undergoing imprisonment without the option of a fine. These disqualifications ignore the fact that persons detained for any of the above reasons may have dependants, and that they may have to have rent paid for them during their absence or "lose their homes." Disqualification during imprisonment means that after the law has inflicted punishment the pension authorities inflict a second one.

"Black-coated Workers"

The Widows', Orphans' and Old Age Contributory Pensions (Voluntary Contributors) Act of 1937 is commonly called the Black-coated Workers' Act. This special provision applies to persons not in insurable employment, or who, although in

[1] Wilson and Mackay, *op. cit.*, p. 158 *et seq.*

insurable employment, had not previously, on account of higher salaries, had the opportunity to enter insurance. Such persons may voluntarily insure for pensions subject to a total income of £400 per annum maximum for men, for which not more than £200 must be unearned (women £250 and £125). Incomes of married couples living together are aggregated and treated as the income of the potential contributor.* Entrants must be under 40 years of age, although contributors admitted to insurance before 3rd January 1939, and called "initial entrants," could be under 55. Contributors must be resident in Great Britain at the date of application, and must then have been continuously resident in Great Britain or Northern Ireland for a period of ten years. For a Widow's or Orphan's Pension at least two years must have elapsed since the date of entry into insurance, and at least 104 contributions must have been paid; for an Old Age Pension there must have been continuous insurance for ten years immediately before reaching the age of 65, and at least 260 contributions must have been paid. Credit for those weeks of incapacitating illness exceeding thirteen may be obtained by contributors normally engaged in gainful occupation and who have already paid 104 contributions. The number of contributions to be credited depends on his average number of contributions during preceding years. The Ministry of Health keep individual accounts for each voluntary contributor.

Full pension rates for voluntary contributors are the same as for compulsory contributors, provided that an average of at least 50 contributions have been paid yearly over the whole period of insurance. For lesser averages there is provision for lesser pensions according to a fixed scale. There is also provision for benefits on lapse in the form of reduced pensions. Absence abroad for periods not exceeding, totally, six years, is permissible; also persons removing to British Dominions and possessions, may continue to pay their contributions and may have their pension paid to them there.

The Act of 1941, operating from 5th January 1942, raises the income limit for compulsory insurance to £420 per annum, a sum exceeding the income limit for Black-coated Workers. A certain number of these workers will now be drawn into the compulsory scheme, provided that they are in insurable employment, but many others (e.g. small shopkeepers) will remain outside it still and continue in voluntary insurance. Other voluntary contributors have been enabled, under provisions previously described, to maintain voluntarily insurance which would have been broken when they quitted insurable employment. Some of these people left compulsory insurance because their incomes rose above the then maximum, and they will now re-enter compulsory insurance; others ceased to be employed altogether, and for them voluntary insurance will still be available.

Appeals

Claimants of Contributory Old Age Pensions may appeal against the decision of the Minister of Health to Referees appointed from a panel by the National Health Insurance Joint Committee. These Referees are barristers, the Senior Referees being two K.C.s who deal with the most important cases. Claims may be heard by one or more Referees, but are usually taken, latterly, by one Referee sitting alone. The Minister provides a Registrar who presents the cases and supervises the clerical work. Most of the claims are decided from written statements, but the Referees may have an oral hearing when they wish, the claimant appearing personally or being represented by a solicitor. The Referee may make an order for costs, and such orders are invariably in favour of the claimant, who would not be required to pay the costs of the Minister; travelling and subsistence allowances are usually made to claimants attending for oral hearings. A great deal of trouble is taken about these hearings, which are often complicated by the inability of aged claimants to prove that they are over 65. In the year ending 31st March 1939, of 3,004 appeals to the Referees only 14·6% were allowed; the low percentage of successful appeals is attributed to the previous care taken by the Minister in making decisions.

Machinery is also required under the 1946 Act to decide questions of earnings and retirement which introduce a new and complicating factor into pensions administration. Although technically not subject to a means test and "paid as of right," the new high rate pensions will involve close scrutiny of individual cases. Until the Act is completely operating, therefore, the machinery of Unemployment Insurance is being used. Initial decisions will be taken by the Minister, an officer of the Assistance Board first investigating doubtful cases. Appeals from the Minister's decision will be heard by the Court of Referees, with a further right of appeal to the Umpire.[1]

SUPPLEMENTARY PENSIONS

The new 26/- pension is a great advance on the 10/- which was previously payable to old age pensioners, but this, like the former rate, will be supplemented, where appropriate, by the Assistance Board. Until the Old Age and Widows' Pensions Act was passed in 1940, pensioners who could not supplement their pensions in any other way went to Public Assistance for help. This was generally felt to be humiliating, and large numbers of pensioners struggled to live without recourse to relief. The 1940 Act therefore established a tradition of self-respecting supplementation, which will be carried over into the operation of the new Act. Two points of criticism stand out here: first, the new pension rates appear munificent only when compared with the old rates; they have cleverly been introduced with publicity suggesting that they are an increase on existing pensions rather than the triumphant entry of the new Act; this is good psychology, but, the second point, for the majority of those without other resources the new rates do not represent an increase in total income, but only a shift in the proportion of their income which is derived from the supplementary pension. Thus a couple receiving a joint pension of 42/- will gain from the new rates only if their rent is less than 7/- weekly, because the Assistance Board's scale for a married couple is, at the time of writing, 35/- exclusive of rent. The new rates represent a real gain to those contributory pensioners with other resources, but there is no gain for those who are entirely dependent on their pensions.

Pensioners may appeal against the determinations of the Board to the Tribunal, but whereas unemployed persons must attend in person, pensioners need not do so. In fact, infirm pensioners need never journey to the Board's offices; they are visited in their homes by the Board's staff, and their pension books are sent to them by post. They are then entitled to

[1] See p. 130 in second edition.

appoint somebody else to collect their pensions at the Post Office of their choice just as ordinary Old Age Pensions may be fetched by a nominee when necessary.

The Assistance Board has recently improved its welfare services. It is now the sole public authority responsible for the care of the aged, and it plans to take this work seriously. Already, before the passage of the 1946 Act, the Board was making a routine "welfare visit" to all supplementary pensioners once a year, and was increasing the frequency of these visits as necessary in individual cases. Although some of those former supplementary pensioners receiving additional welfare visits will now cease to be eligible for supplementation, the Board will continue to visit them as formerly. Secondly, when, in April 1947, the Board administered non-contributory pensions, it visited recipients on the same basis as supplementary pensioners; it plans to make welfare visits on a 52-week cycle. The Board plans eventually to increase the frequency of these welfare visits so that the routine visit, as distinct from additional welfare visits, will occur twice yearly. Thirdly, the new leaflet for old age pensioners obtainable from the Post Office tells them that they may ask the Board's officers to visit them and to advise them on welfare problems; this facility applies alike to those who have and to those who have not a Supplementary Pension, and, further, all old age pensioners are entitled to call at the Board's office to talk over any problem or to seek any information. It is too early yet to evaluate these services in action. The framework and potentialities are obviously very good. A possible weakness in the scheme is the use of personnel trained thoroughly in the Board's methods of financial investigation, but with neither training nor qualifications as social workers. Nor is there any guarantee that old persons will see a second time (even less a third time) officers who are familiar to them. We do not yet know to what extent effective welfare work depends on continuity of personal contact, but, unless the Board's officers are to keep records as full as those of practising case-workers (which they are not trained to do) it would appear that much of the warmth essential to satisfactory welfare visiting will evaporate between one call and the next. Future development might, therefore, suitably include the delegation of welfare visiting to a specially selected corps of the Board's officers, fitted, both by personality and by training, to be the friends and counsellers of old and lonely persons. Forms and formulas, facts, and figures, should not be allowed to obscure the simple needs of the old for the amenities of civilised living. The *New Survey*,[1] in its mass of research material, says, "The old people have a passion for flowers." For many pensioners longevity is penalised today by lack of every source of personal enrichment. Among other things, old people need the opportunity of occupation, friendship and maximum contact with the community around them. The success of the administrative foundations now being laid will be judged by the measure of individual happiness and satisfaction among our pensioners in years to come.

[1] *New Survey of London Life and Labour* (1932), vol. iii. p. 209.

Chapter VII

BLIND WELFARE IN ENGLAND AND WALES

By W. McG. EAGAR

THE existing system of Blind Welfare is an elaboration of many local voluntary efforts which have been gradually extended into a national system. From 1791, when the first Institute for the Blind in Great Britain was established by Edward Rushton in Liverpool, to the passing of the Blind Persons Act in 1920, the system of welfare, though widely extended, was necessarily partial and incomplete. With the passing of the Blind Persons Act the system became for the first time "comprehensive," in the sense that a purposeful attempt could thenceforward be made to provide for all the needs of the blind from infancy to old age. By this Act the Blind were, *inter alia*, brought prematurely within the scope of the Old Age Pensions Acts, and County Councils and County Borough Councils had imposed on them the duty of providing a minimum scheme of welfare for all blind persons ordinarily resident within their area. Some of the provisions of the principal Act were extended and re-enacted by the Blind Persons Act of 1938, which, in particular, completed the long flight of the blind from the Poor Law by providing that, in general, all relief given to them should be exclusively by virtue of the Blind Persons Act and not by way of Public Assistance.

As compared with any other group of handicapped persons, the blind are placed in a unique position by the Blind Persons Acts. The system of welfare which has developed in the last twenty years is comprehensive, and also specific in the sense that it is devised to compensate the actual handicap of blindness at each point where it occurs: in education and training, in economic and industrial position, and in social and cultural life. It is probably true that the welfare service of the blind is more costly than that of any other group of handicapped persons in this country. According to the most recent available information the cost of providing for the 75,897 persons registered as blind in England and Wales, at 31st March 1946, is approximately £5,650,000.

A considerable amount is spent by the Treasury each year in providing Old Age Pensions (which under Section I of the Blind Persons Act, 1938, are payable to the blind on a means test basis at the age of 40) and War Disability Pensions for the Blind. In 1945-46 the cost of providing pensions for 21,091 blind old age pensioners aged 40 to 70 was £553,000. To this must be added pensions paid to blind persons over 70 years of age, the amount of which for, say, 25,000 persons may be estimated at £650,000. The estimated cost in 1946-47 of providing War Disability Pensions for 2,419 ex-service men and civilians, blinded in the two World Wars and still surviving, is £442,000.

The expenditure upon blind welfare of County Councils and County Borough Councils, which are the local authorities responsible under the Blind Persons Act, has grown rapidly during the last twenty-five years. At 31st March 1941 the expenditure of local authorities under the Blind Persons Act was stated to be £2,461,846. To this must be added payments by L.E.A.'s, estimated, for the year 1945-46, at £225,000, for the education of blind children aged 5-16, and at £125,000 for the training of blind adolescents aged 16-21.

Cost of Blind Welfare to Public Funds

(a) *Counties*

Expenditure of selected Local Authorities in England and Wales under the Blind Persons Acts, 1920 and 1938, for the year ended 31st March 1939.

Counties.	Expenditure.	Rate in the £.	Number of Registered Blind Persons.	Rate Expenditure per Head.
	£	*Pence.*		£
Yorkshire, West Riding	97,315	3·4	2,975	33
Brecon	3,462	3·3	193	18
Durham	42,212	3·2	1,851	23
Sussex (East)	6,024	0·5	511	12
Berkshire	3,272	0·5	303	11
Hampshire	7,457	0·5	728	10
Rutland	213	0·6	36	6
62 Counties	*1,003,487*	*1·17 (average)*	*47,153*	*21 (average)*

(b) *County Boroughs*

County Boroughs.	Expenditure.	Rate in the £.	Number of Registered Blind Persons.	Rate Expenditure per Head.
	£	*Pence*		£
Merthyr Tydfil .	7,046	8·68	309	23
Bradford . .	34,020	4·28	681	50
South Shields .	11,128	5·27	361	31
Coventry . .	3,422	0·60	220	16
Bournemouth .	3,204	0·40	183	18
Eastbourne .	1,220	0·34	77	16
Worcester . .	1,220	0·83	99	12
84 County Boroughs .	*858,445*	*2·03 (average)*	*47,153*	*21 (average)*

Since 1939 the amount of Local Authority grants has greatly increased. Wide variations still remain. The following table shows highest, lowest and average rates to which Local Authorities in 1945 made up the basic weekly incomes of "unemployable" blind persons under their domiciliary assistance arrangements.

(*N.B.*—A few exceptionally high and exceptionally low rates are excluded as unrepresentative.)

Domiciliary Assistance Scales 1945

	Highest Rate.	Lowest Rate.	Average Rate.
Single person . . .	37/-	27/6	32/-
Married couple, one blind .	54/-	41/-	45/6
Married couple, both blind .	60/-	45/-	53/-

The total annual expenditure by voluntary organisations for the blind has recently been estimated at £1,178,000. With the exception of grants paid from Blind Pension Societies, a total estimated for the year 1944-45 at approximately £48,000, the voluntary expenditure represents not cash payments but the cost of services providing for education, training, employment and general welfare of the blind.

The foregoing statistics, in themselves, give but little idea of the role of voluntaryism in blind welfare, and of the complicated and interesting partnership which, in recent years, has been developed between the voluntary and statutory authorities. In the areas of most County Councils and County Borough Councils there are voluntary societies which in a varying degree are subsidised by the local authority in respect of work which is left in their hands or delegated to them. In addition to these local voluntary societies there are a number of institutions, providing employment and education, which serve areas larger than local but smaller than national. These more-than-local areas are defined purely by convenience and historical accident: they may, and in fact do, overlap. There are also societies of national character and scope serving the blind, and other agencies for the blind, in all parts of the country.

The pattern of service in different areas varies greatly. In one area the service may be performed by a voluntary agency or agencies which provide education, training and employment in Workshops and Home Workers schemes, are responsible for the Home Teaching service, and act as paymasters of domiciliary assistance on behalf of the local authority or local authorities. In another all the services may be performed by the local authority direct, the voluntary agency having been superseded or, if still in existence, being ignored. Few local government areas are fully equipped to provide all services; one may have a school but not a workshop; another a workshop, not a school; many have neither and are compelled to send children to other areas for their education; similarly, trainees, whether adolescent or adult, have to be sent "abroad," and blind persons seeking employment in workshops have to go where such employment can be found.

Voluntary societies providing educational, training, employment and social welfare services receive fees from local authorities, and some of them other financial assistance. Local authorities secure their interests and safeguard their expenditure by representation, to varying degrees, on the governing bodies of the voluntary agencies concerned.

In the middle part of the 1920-39 period there was a tendency on the part of local authorities to take all services of the blind under their direct administration. Just prior to the war there was a slackening of this tendency, and even a reversal in a few areas.

The largest of the national societies, the National Institute for the Blind, is under the government of a council upon which are fully represented the interests both of the local authorities and of other voluntary societies. Its function is to provide those services which can most economically and effectively be provided on a national scale and are not already being provided. Other national societies are: the National Library for the Blind, St. Dunstan's Organisation for Blinded Soldiers, Sailors and Airmen, and a small number of other societies which serve specific needs.

The Ministry of Health, with the Ministry of Education and the Ministry of Labour and National Service in their own spheres, is responsible to Parliament for the welfare of the blind. The Local Government Act of 1929 made a considerable transfer of detailed responsibility for the welfare of the blind from the Ministry of Health to the County and County Borough Councils. The Blind Persons Act of 1938 relieved the local authorities of the duty of submitting their schemes of blind welfare for the Ministry's approval. The Ministry now retains a general advisory function, with ultimate power of enforcement which can be exercised by reducing the block grant, payable under the Local Government Act, in the case of any local authority deemed not to be fulfilling its responsibility to the blind. In addition, the Ministry has the function of revising for each fixed-grant period the payments to be made by local authorities to voluntary associations in virtue of the services recognised by the 1929 Act; and, in the event of a dispute between any local authority and voluntary agency in this matter, it acts as the Court of Appeal.

The Education Act of 1944 limited the responsibility of the Ministry of Education for training blind persons to those under 21, and the Disabled Persons (Employment) Act, 1944, transferred responsibility for the training and employment of the adult blind from the Ministry of Health to the Ministry of Labour. A further transference in respect of cash payments to the blind, from the Ministry of Health to the Assistance Board, is anticipated under the National Assistance Legislation. The extent to which these rearrangements of central responsibility will affect the responsibility of local authorities, and their relationship to voluntary agencies, is yet uncertain, but changes in local machinery are implied in the general trend of legislation.

Such, in brief outline, is the complex administrative machine that has been built upon the basis of the Blind Persons Acts. The effectiveness of combined voluntary and official action in this social service has now been tested by twenty-five years' experience, and that experience may be thought sufficient to justify proposals for further development in blind welfare, and possibly for analogous public-voluntary co-operation in other branches of social service. Blind welfare must essentially be considered in the environment of related systems of social welfare, and, indeed, many of the anomalies of the system at the present day result from the application to the blind of schemes which have a wider and more general scope. That is not a plea for administrative isolationism but rather for rational integration. In the words of Sir William Beveridge (Report, paragraph 169), blindness "is a special problem, to be dealt with within the general framework by methods appropriate to the special conditions of the blind."

As things stand at present the income of a blind person is derived from many sources: numerous Departments of State and local authorities administer the moneys he receives. The Blind Old Age Pension is administered by the Board of Customs and Excise; the Disability Pension through the regional offices of the Ministry of Pensions; the War Injury Allowance through the Assistance Board, acting as general agent for the Ministry of Pensions.

Payments from rate funds may be administered by several different committees of local authorities. In some instances the machinery of Public Assistance is actually used to administer domiciliary assistance, although one of the principles of the Blind Persons Acts, and of the Local Government Act, 1929, was to dissociate blind welfare from the Poor Law. Moreover, different authorities may, in respect of the same blind person, have different bases of assessing his means, with consequent multiplication of vexatious enquiries.

When, in 1920, the Pensions provisions of the Blind Persons Act were being debated during the Committee stage in the House of Commons, an effort was made to establish principles which were specifically referable to the blind. Parliament, however, preferred to abide by an existing pattern, and gave the blind an Old Age Pension at the age of 50. The 1938 Act, by lowering to 40 the age at which a blind person should be entitled to the Old Age Pension, made the anomaly even more preposterous.

One of the reasons given for this reduction of age was that at 40 a blind person can seldom be trained to earn a real livelihood. This argument is not true in all cases, and it conveys an implication contrary to the fundamental principle of blind welfare, that every blind person should be given the maximum opportunity and inducement to earn his livelihood.[1]

The real motive of the provision was revealed by the Parliamentary Secretary to the Ministry of Health, in charge of the Bill, when he said that, by reason of the devolution effected by the Local Government Act and of the increase in cost of blind welfare, the local authorities would be bearing more than their share of the burden. The object in view was, in fact, not attained, for the costs to local authorities of blind welfare have risen enormously since 1938. No further amendment of the Old Age Pensions Act, even if it were logically defensible, could give further relief to the local authorities. It seems, therefore, that if further relief is desired, some quite different expedient must be devised, and it may be added, with some relevance, that the exclusion of blind persons from Supplementary Old Age Pensions implies that the blind are not in fact regarded by the law as old age pensioners from the age of 40 onwards.

Section II of the Blind Persons Act, 1938, applies the rules contained in Section XXXVIII (3) of the Unemployment Act, 1934, requiring certain assets to be disregarded in determining the need of a blind person and his dependants. The Old Age Pensions Act, 1936, the provisions of which govern the Blind Old Age Pension, does not allow them to be disregarded. It frequently happens, therefore, that when a blind person receiving domiciliary assistance applies for an Old Age Pension at the age of 40 he loses the benefit of the statutory disregards.

For similar reasons, namely, that a different basis of assessment is used, reduction of a blind man's income will normally

[1] A substantial number of "unemployable" blind persons, whose training was not considered worth while, have, during the last five years, found remunerative employment in unsheltered industry.

result when he becomes entitled, at the age of 65, to a Contributory Pension instead of National Health Insurance.

It is evident from this bare recital of facts that the attempt to stretch the Old Age Pensions Acts to cover blindness is as inconvenient as it is illogical. Its continuance under the National Insurance and National Assistance Legislation could be justified only as a temporary makeshift.

The enactment that each local authority should frame a minimum scheme of blind welfare has, not unnaturally, led to local inequality in the amount of domiciliary assistance given. The amount spent per head on the blind by County Councils varied in the year 1939 from £6 to £33, and by County Borough Councils from £12 to £50. With the possible exception of rent, the cost of living is much the same for the blind everywhere. There is no rational defence for a system under which the amount of financial assistance given is governed not only by considerations properly taken into account in judging the needs of individuals, but also by such extraneous factors as the political complexion of the Local Council, the rateable value of the area, and even the efficiency in agitation of the blind in the area.

With the anomaly of local variations in domiciliary assistance is closely associated the problem of local chargeability. The responsibility fixed on local authorities, by Section II of the Blind Persons Act of 1920, is for all registered blind persons "ordinarily resident" within their area. Many difficulties were encountered in administering this provision. Workshops for the blind, almost all of which are situated in county boroughs, attracted a certain number of employable blind persons to become "ordinarily resident" in their vicinity, so that the county boroughs became to an increasing extent chargeable for the employable blind. Moreover, differences in scales of domiciliary assistance offered an inducement to blind persons to migrate to areas of greatest benefit, so that authorities with generous schemes had to bear a heavier burden than those who interpreted their obligation in less generous terms.

Section III of the Blind Persons Act, 1938, was designed, *inter alia*, to meet these difficulties. The area into which a blind person has moved is now allowed, within a certain period of time, to recover the cost of any assistance given to him from the area in which he previously resided. In practice, however, the later Act has failed to solve the difficulty, and the spectre of chargeability not only renders blind labour undesirably immobile, but puts formidable difficulties in the way of young blind persons receiving the most appropriate training in workshop occupations. The mere fact of wide variation between the basic rates of domiciliary assistance in different areas creates insurmountable problems of settlement and chargeability.

From the point of view of the employable blind these difficulties would not be so great were it not for the unsystematic distribution of workshops and home workers schemes. Workshops for the blind generally are situated where accidents of local goodwill or local need brought into being a voluntary agency which established itself, and in the course of time accumulated buildings, endowments and tradition. The fifty-four workshops for the blind in this country employed 3,327 blind persons in 1945-46. They vary in size from 7 to 230 workers. Only nine of them employ more than 120 persons, and twenty-nine have accommodation for fewer than 40. It is obvious that most of them are too small to be economic units of production. Managerial and supervisory expenses are multiplied over and over again. Specialisation is virtually impossible, and the proportion of sighted help per blind worker is at its maximum in the smallest shops. Some degree of co-operation in buying and selling has been effected, but there is still an undesirable amount of poaching, and unfair competition in tendering, in retail selling between neighbouring workshops.

Home workers schemes, according to the latest return, employed 1,527 blind workers in England and Wales. They enable blind workers to carry on trades in their homes, buying their material and, to some extent, selling it. The uneven distribution of home workers schemes may be illustrated by the fact that more than a third of the total of home workers in England and Wales are in the two schemes which serve the Home Counties south and north of the Thames. In many parts of the country the number of home workers is small and their earnings are low, although it has been proved that with effective management such schemes provide a practical alternative to workshop employment, of particular value to blind persons who want to continue their own home life in country places or their home town.

In the matter of training for manual occupations, too, there is some ground for criticism. The great majority of blind persons are unemployable, for blindness is predominantly an incident of old age. It is significant, however, that the total of blind persons classified as unemployable, 63,595, exceeds the total of blind persons over the age of 50. There is, in fact, among them a considerable number of comparatively young people. Some of the younger blind have other defects, mental or physical, which make them beyond doubt unemployable; but there is a temptation for public bodies to take the easiest way out of the difficulty presented by the loss of sight, and to have regard only to the prevention of destitution. They pay the cash and let the training go.

For the unemployable blind, domiciliary assistance and home visiting are services of outstanding importance. For home visiting, the majority of local agencies engage home teachers who have taken the Certificate of the College of Teachers of the Blind, which demands knowledge of Braille, Moon and handcrafts. In practice, the home teachers are seldom able to give much time to teaching. They are predominantly social workers rather than teachers. A war-time return from a South of England county showed that 95% of the visits paid by home teachers were purely social, a percentage somewhat exaggerated by the evacuation problem but fairly representative of ordinary conditions in many places. Nearly everywhere the number of teachers is small in relation to the number of blind people who need visiting. The attention given in recent years to the peculiarly hard lot of the deaf-blind has emphasised that home teachers with, say, 120 blind people on their books cannot possibly give all their charges anything like the attention they require. They do their best under considerable difficulties. Their salaries on the whole are low; but their work is both skilful and devoted. They themselves are the first to lament the inadequacy of their numbers. The cost of their service is, practically always nowadays, met from public funds, for even those voluntary societies which direct the work of the local home teachers receive grants for the purpose from the local authorities. It is the local authorities which are responsible in the long run for the adequacy, or inadequacy, of the service.

Before any moral is drawn from the facts and considerations

set out above, it is necessary to emphasise that blindness in itself adds to the cost of living. Every blind person labours under an economic handicap. It costs a man more to live if he is blind than if he can see. A blind man may be able to produce as much as a seeing person working alongside of him, but his skill and energy would have given him a larger output if he had his sight. A blind business man or administrator must have a reader or secretary; the blind professional man cannot drive his own car; the blind housewife must have domestic help; an old blind man cannot play his part in running the home; aged blind people in general must pay guides to take them about and, generally, the attention and amusement they require is a constant charge. In any scheme of financial assistance, therefore, it must be recognised that the subsistence level of the blind is higher than that of the sighted.

The function of this chapter is not to make proposals for reorganisation, but to outline the system of blind welfare as it exists today. From an administrative point of view it has been seen that the blind individually depend largely upon local administration; that local machinery is in most areas a complex of voluntary and official action, and that many of the services of blind welfare can best be administered not locally but regionally or nationally. It is evident that blind welfare cannot revert to the partial effectiveness of unsupported voluntaryism; and that under purely public administration it might too easily become stereotyped and static. Neither voluntaryism nor public administration by itself is enough. The comprehensiveness which follows from local authority responsibility, having once been established, cannot be dispensed with. The local authorities have in fact accepted their responsibility generously and with great goodwill. They cannot, however, move far in advance of public opinion or incur expenditure on experiments. Experimentation, research, pioneer work and new enterprise generally must be undertaken by voluntary agencies, or at least by bodies inspired with the voluntary spirit. The needs of the blind develop with the changing needs of the population at large. New inventions are constantly bringing new compensations for blindness within reach. The search for new devices and new methods of service must be incessant. Blind welfare, as we now understand it, must be both comprehensive and dynamic.

Whatever form social administration may take, and however the burden of social service is distributed between local and national resources, there must, in fact, be in every part of the country an authority responsible for ensuring that something is done for every blind person. That authority must be actuated by the ideal that the function of blind welfare is not only to enable the blind to keep body and soul together, but to encourage them, as far as possible, to take their place as self-respecting, contributive citizens.

Chapter VIII

WAR PENSIONS

By BARBARA CASTLE, M.P.

A NEW generation of dead has modernised Remembrance Day. The second World War has caught up with the first and placed on the shoulders of the Ministry of Pensions a new and gigantic task while it is still winding up its original responsibilities.

In March 1939, 877,400 pensioners of the 1914-18 war, and dependants of pensioners, were still on the payroll of the Ministry of Pensions. The total cost of war pensions since 1914, together with administrative costs, had, by that date, amounted to £1,315,000,000. In the 1939-45 war something like a miracle happened. It was a total war and we had every right to expect that those who would be dependent on the Ministry of Pensions for support and assistance as a result of it would reach "an all-time high." Yet the casualties and their dependants have never reached the 1914-18 figure. From 1939 to 1945 the number of those killed, whether civilians, members of the Armed Forces, Women's Auxiliary Services, Home Guard, Merchant Navy or fishing fleet, totalled 357,116. Another 369,267 in these various classes had been injured.[1] In addition there were still, in February 1946, over 178,000 prisoners of war and internees with potential claims in respect of their disabilities due to war service. All these casualties were bad enough but they were less than we had any right to expect in the light of those suffered in World War I. By December 1946, although the Ministry was admitting about 80% of the cases applying for pension in respect of the 1939 war, it was only paying pensions to about 1,130,000 persons compared with 3,000,000 in 1922.

But the fact that war today engulfs everybody has led to radical changes in our conception of the State's duty to the casualties of war. War pensions today form one of the major branches of social security. It was not so in 1914-18. The Ministry's field was narrower then. The civilian element hardly entered into it at all, and the provision for the women auxiliaries was so hap-

[1] "Strength and Casualties of the Armed Forces and the Auxiliary Services of the United Kingdom, 1939-1945." Cmd. 6832.

hazard that, apart from nurses and others covered by the Officers Warrant of 1920, the injured women had to secure what assistance they could under the Workmen's Compensation Act or the Injuries in War (Compensation) Acts. Today, the Ministry of Pensions has gathered into its fold not only the officers and men of the three Fighting Services, but their women members, the Merchant Navy, the fishing fleet, the Home Guard, all the civil defence organisations and the civilian population.

The Ministry has indeed travelled a long way in its short but crowded history. From 1916, when it first saw the light of Whitehall, its scope has been extended and its ideas progressively humanised. Some of the most important changes have taken place during the recent war. In 1939 the Ministry was still working on the basis of policies crystallised out of the experience of World War I. As the new total war unfolded, new Royal Warrants were introduced to amend and improve rates and conditions of grants and to provide new benefits. But the process of adapting the old system to the new needs was slow and, despite important concessions made in July 1943 and April 1944, was still woefully incomplete by V.E. Day. Some of the most valuable changes were not made until after July 1945.

At every stage developments in pensions policy have reflected the effect of modern war on the community's idea of social justice. The setting up of the Ministry in 1916 was in itself a radical departure from pre-1914 methods, necessary to meet the problems of a new type of war. At the outset of the Great War an attempt had been made to make the previous pensions machinery work. The Army, with its satellite body the Commissioners of Chelsea Hospital, continued for a year and a half to administer Army pensions, and the Admiralty continued to administer those of the Navy. The Mercantile Marine was the responsibility of the Board of Trade. The flood of casualties soon proved too much for a system adapted only to the needs of the small regular forces of normal times, with an average discharge rate of some 4,000 a year. The system lacked, for one thing, an adequate local organisation to give cases the individual attention that was essential. It was only made to work at all thanks to the influx of voluntary funds and voluntary labour.

Voluntary help was, in fact, given administrative powers for a time under the War Pensions Act of 1915, which created, under the Central Statutory War Pensions Committee, a network of over a thousand war pensions committees representing all sides of local life. The Statutory War Pensions Committee was empowered to give supplementary assistance to the pensioner, and even to grant a pension in cases of hardship. It had also to provide medical treatment in hospital and vocational training for the disabled.

The voluntary funds on which at first the war pensions committees subsisted were later supplemented by the grant of £1,000,000 from Parliament, but this confused the situation rather than helped it. A half-hearted attempt was made to solve the difficulties by setting up a Joint Pensions Board of the Service Departments. By December 1916, however, the need for a single Department, under a Minister responsible to Parliament, was irresistibly apparent and was met by the creation of the Ministry of Pensions.

The Statutory War Pensions Committee was dissolved the following year. Its administrative functions in connection with the provision of medical treatment and training were transferred to the new Ministry, and its powers for giving supplementary assistance were transferred to a new body, the Special Grants Committee, appointed by the Minister and financed by his Annual Vote.

The local committees continued for the time being in their old form, but the need to bring them, too, under central control was recognised in the War Pensions Act of 1921. The existing 1,200 bodies gave way to some 166 new ones covering larger areas and acting only in an advisory capacity. The administrative functions of the old committees were transferred to Area Offices of the Ministry.

In October 1921 the administration of pensions for members of the Regular Forces and their dependants reverted to the Service Departments concerned under the provisions of new peace-time Warrants. The Ministry of Pensions was left to care for the victims of enemy action in the period 4th August 1914 to 30th September 1921, the official date of termination of the Great War (1914-18). This did not mean that no new cases were admitted to compensation after that date. The effects of the 1914 War are in fact still coming to light, and in 1945, 27 years after the Armistice, the Ministry of Pensions admitted liability for over 100 cases of disablement arising for the first time.

From 3rd September 1939 the Ministry of Pensions has again taken over responsibility for the "retired pay and pensions of, and other grants for, members of our Military Forces disabled, and the widows, children and dependants of such members deceased." This responsibility will continue until Parliament revokes the powers.

The Ministry works in close conjunction with the Service Departments, which continue the service pension of a re-employed officer or pensioner who returns to active service. They only do so, however, until he is disabled by war service. In such an event he is awarded, in place of his service pension, a disability pension consisting of his existing service award together with a disability element, and this new pension is administered by the Ministry. The Service Department concerned ceases to have responsibility for the man, and the cost of the pension falls in its entirety on the Pensions Vote.

The Ministry's responsibility for members of the Armed Forces is, however, further conditioned by the fact that the death or disability in respect of which assistance is claimed must be attributable to or aggravated by war service. If this condition is not fulfilled, a service man who is invalided out is referred to other agencies for assistance. The grounds on which men are accepted or rejected as eligible for war pension have been the subject of some of the fiercest of all the battles over war pensions. Concessions were made during the war itself, but the most important change was made as a result of a new ruling in 1946. This will be dealt with later.

Compensation is also payable to merchant seamen for disablement which is directly attributable to a war injury, war risk injury or to detention. Broadly speaking, war risk injury is one sustained on board ship at sea owing to abnormal conditions prevailing in time of war.

The Ministry's responsibility for civilians is confined to the effects of war injuries or war service injuries. A war injury is a physical injury to an ordinary civilian caused by the enemy or in combating the enemy. A war service injury is a physical injury to a civil defence volunteer "arising out of and in the course of the performance by the volunteer of his duties as a member of the civil defence organisation to which he belonged at the time the injury was sustained." It therefore includes any injury incurred while on duty and is not limited to the effects of enemy action. The Civilians Scheme also provides for the dependants of those suffering qualifying injuries.

The creation of the Ministry of Pensions in 1916 laid the foundations of the administrative machinery which operates today.[1] After the 1914 war it was found necessary to create for a time local microcosms of the Ministry in the form of Regional Offices which embodied the counterpart of the several sections of the central Ministry. The bulk of the work was decentralised on to these regional offices, leaving to the central office the powers of regulation, control and payment of pensions. This arrangement brought the Ministry into closer touch with local opinion. After the peak year of 1919, however, the claims for pensions fell sharply, and one by one the regional offices were closed. Area offices continued in operation until 1939, when their functions were extended and they were described as regional offices.

For the war period the administrative machinery consisted of a regional office in every civil defence region, usually in the same town in which the regional commissioner had his headquarters. In some parts of the country the work of the regional offices is supplemented by that of district offices, working under their control and along very similar lines. The number of part-time offices which handle interviews and medical examinations and limb-fitting work has been greatly increased to meet the pressure of war needs.

The creation of the Ministry of Pensions in 1916 was not only an important administrative advance, it meant that the whole problem of war pensions was approached from a wider viewpoint. An exhaustive re-examination of the principles governing the fixing of rates and the grant of pensions was begun at once. The Select Committee on Pensions of 1919 made recommendations which led to important changes, and keen scrutiny of the pensions schemes has continued to be made by successive Parliaments.

Disability Pensions

The disability pensions which operate today vary widely, both in amount and in type, from those operating in the early days of the 1914 war. The principle of the pre-1914 Warrants was soon

[1] Nineteenth Annual Report of Minister of Pensions, 1935-36, Part II.

found inapplicable to a civilian army; the rates of pensions were obviously inadequate. Increases in the rates were at first linked with the disabled man's capacity to work, and the pension of a partially disabled man took the form of bringing the amount he might be able to earn up to the figure for total disablement. This penalised the man who struggled to hold down a job, and a principle so unsound was abandoned by the new Ministry in its first Warrant.

In 1917 the present basis of assessment for disablement was adopted. Disablement is measured in degrees which represent the extent of incapacity by comparison with "the condition of a normal healthy person of the same age and sex, without taking into account the earning capacity of that member in his own or any other specific trade or occupation and without taking into account the effect of any individual factors or extraneous circumstances." The Select Committee on Pensions of 1919 advocated that incapacity should be measured by reference to industrial conditions as a whole and not to loss of individual earnings. A rise in the general level of wages would be relevant, but not the conditions in the individual disabled man's pre-war occupation. That principle is embodied in the current Warrant in the form quoted above, and in the Mercantile Marine and Civilian Schemes.

Like naval and military pay, the money value of the disability pension in operation in 1914 had remained practically unchanged for the best part of a century. For the needs of a civilian army it was quite inadequate. With the criterion of "loss of earnings" at first in mind, the Government took steps to relate the rates to the rapid rise in wages. The maximum pension of 17/6 per week for the private soldier (100% disablement) was raised first to 25/-, then to 27/6 in March 1917, and to 33/- in November 1918. The pension was put on a firm basis in 1919 as a result of the researches of the Select Committee, which faced the issue of the pension as a maintenance grant in relation to the existing cost of living. The maximum rate for the lowest rank was fixed at 40/-. An allowance of 10/- a week for the wife was added for the first time in history. Children's allowances had been granted by the Royal Warrant of May 1915.

The continuance of these pension rates was intended to be conditional on the maintenance of the cost of living figure, but subsequent Governments dared not venture to reduce the rates, despite the fall in prices from the 1919 level. In 1928 a pledge was given in the House of Commons that the existing rates would not be reduced but that, on the contrary, if the cost of living rose by 5% or more of 215 (the 1919 figure), consideration would be given to adjusting the rates accordingly.

In fixing the rates for the 1939 war, however, the Government at first created a lower pension level, justifying its action by reference to the lower cost of living figure. The Royal Warrant and Orders of 1940 [1] established maximum disability pay for the lowest rank of 34/2, with a wife's allowance of 8/4. The distinction between the pensioners of the first and second World Wars created a good deal of dissatisfaction which no argument about cost of living figures was able to dispel.

The cost of living figure of 181 in June 1940 was eventually admitted by the Ministry to be unrepresentative, and in February 1942 the rates were adjusted to correspond to a figure of 200.[2]

This improvement did not go far enough, however, to satisfy the growing feeling that the Forces were not getting a square deal and the agitation for higher pensions continued. In July 1943, therefore, the Government announced [3] that the then existing war rates were to be "assimilated broadly to those payable for the last War," and in February 1946 the rates for men for both wars were further increased.[4]

RATES OF 100% DISABILITY (MEN)

Navy.	Army.	Air Force.	Weekly Rate.
Sergt.-Major R.M.	W.O. Cl. I .	Warrant Officer .	61/8
—	Class I .	W.O. Class II .	58/4
Chief Petty Officer	Class II .	Flight-Sergeant .	55/–
Petty Officer .	Class III .	Sergeant . .	51/8
Leading Rating .	Class IV .	Corporal . .	48/4
Other men (and boys).	Class V . .	L/Aircraftman and Aircraftman.	45/–

[1] Cmd. 6205, H.M.S.O. (Army), S.R. & O. 1940; No. 1469 H.M.S.O. (Navy and Marines); Order by His Majesty, 23rd October 1940, H.M.S.O. (Air Force).
[2] Cmd. 6342, H.M.S.O. [3] Cmd. 6459.
[4] Cmd. 6714.

RATES OF 100% DISABILITY (OFFICERS)

Navy.	Army.	Air Force.	Annual Rate.
Rear-Admiral .	Major-General	Air Vice-Marshal	£420
Commodore .	Brigadier .	Air-Commodore .	£375
Captain . .	Colonel . .	Group Captain .	£330
Commander .	Lieut.-Colonel	Wing-Commander	£300
Lieut.-Commander	Major . .	Squadron Leader	£270
Lieutenant . .	Captain .	Flight-Lieutenant	£240
Sub-Lieutenant .	Subaltern .	Flying Officer or Pilot Officer.	£210
Midshipman or Warrant Officer .	—	—	£180

FAMILY ALLOWANCES FOR 100% DISABLEMENT PENSIONERS

	Officers (Annually).	Men (Weekly).
For a wife . .	£36	10/–
For each child . .	£30	7/6

Family allowances for disabled officers were originally subject to establishment of "pecuniary need," but in July 1943 this qualification was abolished. It has never applied in the case of men of the ranks.

The 100% rate of disablement is not restricted to those totally disabled in the ordinary sense of the word. Total loss of sight, for instance, or the loss of two limbs, is valued at 100%, as well as total paralysis or lunacy. A 100% pensioner who requires regular attendance because of his disabled condition may be given an attendance allowance of from 10/- to 20/- a week. In exceptional cases of very severe disablement the allowance is 40/- a week.

A degree of disablement of less than 100% is medically assessed on the merits of each particular case. Experience has helped to achieve uniformity of assessment; in addition, certain specific disabilities have been recognised to rank at a given degree.

The children's allowances normally terminate at 18 in the

case of officers' children and 16 in the case of other ranks. They may, however, be continued after that age if the child is an apprentice, or is being given higher education, or if it is incapable of self-support.

Where the family's financial position warrants it, the Minister may at his discretion award an education allowance to the child of a disabled man or officer provided he is satisfied "that the child would have been likely, having regard to the ability of the child and the circumstances of the family," to have received an education of the same type had the father not been disabled. The amount for one child in any one year may not exceed £80.

Women members of the Forces receive disability pensions at the following rates:

Rates of 100% Disability Pension for Women Members of other than Officer Status

Navy.	Army.	Air Force.	Weekly Rate.
Member with status	equivalent to tha	t of:	
—	W.O. Cl. I .	Warrant Officer .	53/4
—	Class I . .	W.O. Cl. II .	51/8
Chief Petty Officer	Class II .	Flight-Sergeant .	50/–
Petty Officer .	Class III .	Sergeant . .	48/4
Leading Rating .	Class IV .	Corporal . .	46/8
Able Seaman .	Class V . .	L/Aircraftman and Aircraftman .	45/–

Family Allowances

	Maximum Rates for 100%	
	Member with Officer Status.	Other Members.
For a dependent husband . .	£36 p.a.	10/– p.w.
For each child	£30 p.a.	7/6 p.w.

RATES OF 100% DISABILITY RETIRED PAY FOR NURSES AND WOMEN OFFICERS

Navy.	Army.	Air Force.	Annual Rate.
Member with status above that of Commander	Member with status above that of Lieut.-Col.	Member with status above that of Wing Commander	£270
Member with status of Commander	Member with status of Lieut.-Col.	Member with status of Wing Commander	£235
Member with status of Lieut.-Commander	Member with status of Major	Member with status of Squadron Leader	£205
Member with other commissioned officer status	Member with other officer status	Member with other officer status	£175
Member with status of Warrant Officer	—	—	£150

Family allowances are only payable to a woman member's dependants if she is in pecuniary need. The husband must, to qualify for an allowance, be physically or mentally incapable of self-support and have been dependent on her. Their children only qualify for allowances if the husband is himself eligible for allowance. If she is a widow, her children qualify for allowance at a higher rate. If she has children of qualifying age other than those by her husband, the Minister may grant them allowances at his discretion.

MEDICAL TREATMENT

An important part of the provision for disablement takes the form of medical treatment. The Ministry of Pensions only takes over this work, as far as the Forces are concerned, after discharge from the Services has taken place. If a disabled man is to be invalided out of the Service while still under treatment, the Ministry takes responsibility for the treatment while the decision is being reached on whether the disability is attributable to war service. Treatment allowances are granted until the decision is reached.

A man for whose disability the Ministry accepts responsibility may be required, if necessary, to undergo medical or surgical treatment in an institution or otherwise. In such a case he may be granted, under such conditions as the Minister may determine, an allowance at the rate appropriate in his case for the highest degree of disablement, in lieu of his current award, for as long as the treatment continues. No deduction is made from the allowances on the grounds that home expenditure is reduced as a result of being maintained in hospital, except where a patient is a permanent inmate. Family allowances at the appropriate rates are also payable during treatment and the allowance for a dependent wife is raised from 10/- to 16/- a week.

In a case where only part-time treatment is necessary, involving occasional absences from work, an allowance may be granted, graded according to the time lost, but not exceeding 21/- in respect of any one day subject to a maximum allowance of 30/- for any one week provided that the allowance together with pension does not exceed the amount of treatment allowances which would have been payable if the person were on full-time treatment.

Ministry's Medical Services.—The medical work of the Ministry is one of its most important functions. It relies for its execution in the first place on the medical staff attached to headquarters and the regional offices. In addition, the Ministry employs sessional medical officers and specialists on whose services it can call at need. This medical organisation carries out the boarding and other forms of medical examination necessary to determine title to pension and assessment of disablement; also the certification of all forms of treatment, including the supply of appliances and the medical examinations necessitated thereby.

A man may be brought in the first instance before a general board, which, after examining him, may refer him to a specialist or, if his case is clearly a specialised one, he may be referred immediately to a specialised board—for example, in the case of an eye injury. In cases of serious doubt or difficulty the case may be referred to one or more of a panel of independent medical practitioners nominated by the Presidents of the Royal College of Physicians and the Royal College of Surgeons respectively.

During the first twenty years of the Ministry's history some five million medical examinations took place, three million of which were held during the three years immediately following demobilisation after the 1914-18 war.

An attempt has been made to secure uniformity of assessment in case of disability, and it has been necessary to give guidance to the numerous medical boards working separately and dealing with a very wide range of disabilities. The first step was taken in the Schedule to the Royal Warrant of 1919,[1] which laid down standard assessments for certain specific injuries. For example,

[1] Cmd. 457, H.M.S.O. 9d.

amputation of the right arm through the shoulder was held to rank as 90% disablement; total loss of speech, 80%; total deafness, 70%; and so on. A further step was taken by the establishment in 1919 of a "Disability Committee" manned by eminent men, including the Presidents of the Royal Colleges of Physicians and Surgeons. With the aid of specialist sub-committees, this committee has from time to time devised standard, though elastic, criteria of assessment for certain disabilities.

In addition, trained medical officers from the headquarters of the Ministry exercise supervision over the work of the Medical Boards and help to ensure uniformity, though it is stressed that this should not unduly fetter their judgment based on the individual circumstances of the claimant.

In providing medical treatment for war disabilities the Ministry's function has been to supplement existing agencies. A disabled man requiring treatment which can be given in the home is expected to procure that treatment, if possible, through the facilities of the Health Insurance Acts. In-patient and out-patient treatment is organised for pensioners by the Ministry, partly through civil and general hospitals and partly in its own institutions.

At the peak period of treatment of claims from World War I the Ministry had set up an extensive hospital and out-patient service of its own. In 1921 there were 67 hospitals with over 13,000 beds maintained and controlled by the Ministry, in addition to the 5,000 beds reserved for Ministry cases in other institutions. In the second World War the Ministry's own hospitals were only 14 in number. The Ministry prefers to have surgical cases directly under its own care because of the need for close co-ordination between the work of amputation and the work of limb-fitting. The correct amputation of a limb is essential to the successful fitting of an artificial one. The need for more extensive provision for medical and surgical cases led the Ministry, at the outbreak of war, to turn over to this work two of its hospitals formerly reserved for neurological cases.

The Civilians Scheme

The Civilians Scheme is a security development of the 1939 war. The threat of bombing necessitated provision to meet a situation in which civilians were brought into the front line of battle as extensively as members of the Armed Forces. All members of the community ran the risk of injury or death by enemy action, and all had to be provided for.

The Personal Injuries (Civilians) Scheme, 1941,[1] the third scheme approved by the Government, forms the basis of the provision to meet this need. The scheme divides the community into four main groups: civil defence volunteers, gainfully occupied persons, non-gainfully occupied persons and children under 15. The latter are not pensionable until they reach 15. Non-gainfully occupied persons were originally pensionable at a lower rate than those gainfully occupied. This has been partially adjusted so that the personal disablement pension is now the same, but the provision still remains that if their injury results in death their widows and dependants do not qualify for pensions unless they are in need. Civil defence volunteers injured while on duty are eligible for the same scale of compensation as gainfully occupied persons. If they sustained a war injury while not on duty, they are eligible for compensation as ordinary civilians.

Civilian Injuries and Disablement.—Provision for disablement falls into two classes. During the period immediately following injury, injury allowances were payable in respect of certified periods of incapacity for work, which lasted for seven consecutive days, and they were not normally payable for more than twenty-six weeks from the date of injury. At the end of that period if the injured person had not recovered an award of injury pension was made.

Civil defence volunteers include both those paid and those unpaid. Qualifying civil defence organisations are listed in the schedule to the scheme. Professional firemen and policemen and special constables are provided for under their own pension schemes.

Certain civil defence organisations listed in the schedule are limited to "members who are unpaid." For example, in the Billeting Service only unpaid billeting officers, assisting local authorities, were held to be civil defence volunteers. Regular local authority employees are eligible for compensation in respect of war injuries as gainfully occupied persons, but are covered for other injuries sustained on duty by the ordinary arrangements applicable to their employment, e.g. Workmen's Compensation.

[1] S.R. & O., 1941, No. 226, H.M.S.O. 9d.

The personal rate of injury allowance was 45/- a week but, unless married, three-quarter rates were payable to persons who had attained the age of 17 but were not yet 18 and half-rates to children of 15 or 16 years of age.

In the case of gainfully occupied persons who sustained war injuries and civil defence volunteers who suffered war service injury, the injury allowance was increased by 7/6 a week in respect of the first child and by 5/- a week in respect of each other dependent child. The injury allowance was also increased by from 10/- to 16/- a week in respect of a wife.

The weekly rates of pension for 100% disablement are as follows:

Class of Injury.	Aged 18 and over.	Aged 17.[1]	Aged 15[1] or 16.
(*a*) War service injuries: war injuries sustained by gainfully occupied persons and by students and apprentices aged 15 or over . .	45/-	33/9	22/6
(*b*) War injuries sustained by non-gainfully occupied persons	45/-	33/9	22/6

[1] Married persons under 18 are treated as if 18 and over.

A person in class (*a*) is granted an allowance of 10/- for his wife and 7/6 for each child. If no wife's allowance is payable the allowance for the first child is 10/-. The allowance for a child ordinarily ceases at 15 but may be continued after that date on the same conditions as are outlined above.

Education allowances may also be granted to the children of injured or disabled civil defence workers or gainfully occupied civilians on the same terms as for the children of ex-Service personnel.

It will be seen that, under the Civilians Scheme, the rate for a man or woman of over 18 is the same as for the lowest rank of the Armed Forces. Under the Civilians Scheme there is no allowance for rank, not even in the case of civil defence volunteers.

The degree of disablement sustained by a civilian is determined by a Medical Board appointed by the Ministry of Pensions. The same principles of assessment apply as in the case of the Armed Forces.

WIDOWS' AND DEPENDANTS' PENSIONS

Widows' Pensions.

Widows' pensions are payable without means test to the widows of deceased officers and other ranks of the Armed Forces and, under the Civilians Scheme, in the case of gainfully occupied persons and civil defence volunteers.

A widow under 40 and without children receives less than a widow with children or over 40 years of age, presumably because it is assumed that she is more likely to be able to earn her own living.

A widow who was separated from her husband at the date of his death may receive the same pension which she would have received had they not been separated, provided he was contributing that amount to her support.

Pensions to widows of officers and men in the Armed Forces are payable at the following rates [1]:

ANNUAL PENSIONS FOR WIDOWS OF OFFICERS

Navy.	Army.	Air Force.	Widow over 40; or with eligible Children or incapable of self-support.	Widow under 40; without eligible Children and capable of self-support.
Admiral of Fleet	Field Marshal	Marshal	£700	—
Admiral	General	Air Chief Marshal	£540	—
Vice-Admiral	Lieut.-General	Air-Marshal	£440	—
Rear-Admiral	Major-General	Air Vice-Marshal	£350	—
Commodore	Brigadier	Air-Commodore	£290	—
Captain	Colonel	Group Captain	£230	—
Commander	Lieut.-Colonel	Wing-Commander	£210	—
Lieut.-Commander	Major	Squadron Leader	£180	£170
Lieutenant	Captain	Flight-Lieutenant	£165	£150
Sub-Lieutenant	Subaltern	Flying Officer or Pilot Officer	£150	£130
Warrant Officer	—	—	£125	£105

[1] Cmd. 6459 and Cmd. 6521.

Pensions for Unmarried Dependants who have lived as Wives of Officers Deceased

Annual rate where there are children eligible for allowances £95

Pensions for Widows of Men

Navy.	Army.	Air Force.	Widow over 40; or with eligible Children or incapable of self-support.	Widow under 40; without eligible Children and capable of self-support.
Sergt.-Major, R.M.	W.O. Cl. I .	Warrant Officer .	40/-	28/4
—	Class I .	W.O. Cl. II .	39/-	26/8
Chief Petty Officer	Class II .	Flight-Sergeant .	38/-	25/-
Petty Officer .	Class III .	Sergeant . .	37/-	23/4
Leading Rating .	Class IV .	Corporal . .	36/-	21/8
Other men . .	Class V .	L/Aircraftman and Aircraftman .	35/-	20/-

Pensions for Unmarried Dependants who have lived as Wives of Men Deceased

Weekly rate where there are children eligible for allowances 27/6

Children's Pensions.

Allowances for Children of Deceased Officers

Children maintained by widow, separated wife or unmarried dependant living as wife:—

Commissioned Officers . . . . £36 per annum
Warrant Officers, R.N. . . . . £30 " "

Motherless child:—

Commissioned Officers . . . . £60 " "
Warrant Officers, R.N. . . . . £45 " "

Allowances for Children of Deceased Men

Children maintained by widow, separated wife or unmarried dependant living as wife:—

For each child . . . . . . 11/- per week
Motherless child . . . . . 13/6 " "
to the age of 15, thereafter 20/- a week, and 26/- at 18 if extènded on grounds of infirmity.

O

Here again the pension rates of the last war have only recently been brought up to the level of the 1919-20 peak. The pre-1914 Warrants made scanty provision for a fighting man's widow, and both the scope and the rates of widows' pensions were steadily increased during and after the Great War. Within a few months of the outbreak of World War I the pension for the widow of a Class V soldier, for example, was raised from 5/- to 10/- a week. It was again raised to 13/9 in 1917; there was a further rise in 1918, and finally, following the Report of the Select Committee in 1919, it was stabilised at 20/- a week—one-half of the maximum disability pension—for a widow under 40 or without children, or 26/8—two-thirds of the maximum disability pension—for a widow with children or over 40 years of age. In the same way the pensions rates for officers' widows rose rapidly. But in the 1939 war the rates did not climb back to the 1920 peak, despite the small increase on the 1940 figure made in 1942 to meet the increased cost of living, until August 1943. In April 1944 [1] they passed that peak and in 1946 further increases were made.

So great had been the feeling in favour of better treatment of the Serviceman's widow that the new concession included provision to supplement the 1920 rate still further in certain cases. Widows of "other ranks" with children are now [2] paid supplementary allowances to a sum equivalent to the amount paid by them in respect of rent and rates over 8/- a week. Thus if a private's widow with one child is paying 15/- a week rent she receives 53/- per week instead of 36/2; if her rent is 17/- she receives 55/-. The maximum amount of supplementary allowance is 15/- per week, payable when the rent reaches 23/-.

Before any widow's pension is payable, the attributability of the man's death to a wound, injury or disease of service origin or aggravation by war service must be established. Up to May 1947 it was provided that death must have occurred within seven years of the receipt of the wound or the onset of the fatal complaint, but this now only applies to cases where the pensioner died before September 1939.[3] Death must not have been due to a man's own serious negligence or misconduct.

Education and additional allowances for children are payable on the same conditions as in a case of disablement. In addition,

[1] Cmd. 6521. [2] Cmd. 6459. [3] Cmd. 7124.

where a pension has been continued over the age of 16 to the motherless child of a deceased member of the Forces on the grounds of mental or physical incapacity to earn a living, the pension may be continued even beyond the age of 21 if the pensioner is certified to be totally and permanently incapable of earning a living. Thus the invalid motherless child of a deceased soldier receives 13/6 a week up to the age of 15, 20/- a week up to the age of 18 and thereafter 26/- a week indefinitely.

Civilians Scheme.

Pensions are payable to the widows of civil defence volunteers who die as a result of a war service injury and of gainfully occupied civilians who die as a result of a war injury at the rates applicable to the lowest ranks of the Armed Forces and on the same conditions. Supplementary allowances are also payable to widows with children whose rent and rates exceed 8/- per week.

Women Members of the Forces.

The husband of a deceased woman member of the Forces may be granted a pension if he was dependent on his wife and is, in whole or in part, incapable of self-support. The rate varies with the husband's circumstances. Pensions and children's allowances are as follows:

PENSIONS FOR DEPENDENT HUSBANDS OF DECEASED WOMEN MEMBERS

	Maximum Rate.
Members of officer status . .	£95 a year
Other members	35/- a week

A woman member's children are eligible for allowances only if a pension is in issue to her husband, save that, if she has other children than his, the Minister may, at his discretion, pension them as orphans.

The same conditions for the extension of children's allowances beyond 16 and 18, for the grant of education allowances, and for the indefinite continuance beyond the age of 21 of the allowance to an incapable orphan child, apply as in the case of male members.

Women Civilians.

Provision is made under the Civilians Scheme for husbands who were dependent on their wives and whose wives have been killed, leaving them in need. Provision is, also, made for the children of a deceased woman civil defence volunteer or gainfully occupied woman if they were dependent on her and if it is not possible "for means of support for that child to be obtained from any individual liable to contribute to the support of that child." Such children are pensioned at the same rate as the motherless children of a deceased soldier.

Parents and Other Dependants.

The present scheme of parents' pensions has travelled a long way from its first beginnings. In the early days of the 1914 war two types of pension were in payment—the flat rate of 5/- a week pension payable automatically to all parents who lost a son, and the "pre-war dependence" pension, based on the amount of support the son was giving up to the time of his enlistment. The Select Committee of 1919 condemned the flat rate of compensation, and this type of pension was not issued after 1922. It was not revived in the second World War although parents who drew it in respect of losses before 1922 still continue to do so. The current conception is that parents' pensions should be based on need "arising from old age, or from infirmity or other adverse conditions not merely of a temporary character," and also on the extent to which the deceased son or daughter would have been likely to have contributed to their parents' support if they had lived.

The interpretation of need has broadened during the 1939 war and particularly since the advent of the Labour Government. The Ministry of Pensions stress that in making an assumption as to the amount of contribution a son might have given if he had lived, no regard is paid to the possibility that he might have married and been unable to support his parents. They also emphatically deny the often-repeated allegation that "a parent must be practically penniless to qualify for a pension." The formula on which need is assessed is rather complicated, but briefly it provides that the basic means limit is 40/- a week where there is one parent and 60/- a week where there are two, and they are eligible for pension if their income does not reach this figure. This basic sum is increased by that amount in excess of 15/-, which it is felt that the son would have contributed to his parents' upkeep if he had lived. Where the son was living at home on enlistment, it is estimated that 10/- a week of any contribution he had been making would have been in respect of his own board and lodging. Thus, for example, if a son on enlistment was paying 30/- a week while living at his parents' home, he would be regarded as having contributed 10/- for his own upkeep and 20/- to his parents' support. This means that the basic means limit of 40/- (one parent) or 60/- (two parents) would be increased in this case by 5/-, or the excess over 15/- of the boy's net contribution. Although, under this formula, the parents' income can in certain cases be supplemented by pension to reasonable sums, the present provision has still left a sense of hardship in other cases. In addition, of course, a strong campaign still continues for the payment of a flat rate pension as of right without means test to all parents who have lost an unmarried son.

Pensions are also payable, under the Civilians Scheme, to the parents of a civil defence volunteer who dies as a result of a war service injury, or of a gainfully occupied person who dies as a result of a war injury, with the qualification that the support given by the son or daughter must normally have been actual in the form of a regular contribution for the period of 6 months preceding death.

The rates of pension are varied in each case according to need, the maximum rates being as follows:

Pensions for Parents of Deceased Officers

Maximum annual rates vary according to the rank of deceased officer.

Maximum annual rates for officers below the rank of Lieutenant-Commander, Major or Squadron Leader are:—

Commissioned Officers:		
One parent	£75	In exceptional cases these rates may be increased by an amount not exceeding £20 a year.
Two parents	£100	
Warrant Officers, R.N.:		
One parent	£60	
Two parents	£85	

Pensions for Parents of Other Ranks

Maximum weekly rates:		
One parent	. 20/-	In exceptional cases these rates may be increased by an amount not exceeding 7/6 a week for one parent and 12/6 for two parents.
Two parents	. 27/6	

Pensions for parents of deceased women members, civil defence volunteers and gainfully occupied civilians, who die as a result of a qualifying injury, are the same as for "other ranks" in the fighting services.

Funerals

A military funeral without cost to the relatives may be arranged by the naval, military or air force authorities, as appropriate, in the case of a member of His Majesty's Forces who dies whilst still serving. Similarly, in the case of a civilian or civil defence volunteer during the war, the Government arranged with local authorities, through the Ministry of Health and Department of Health for Scotland, that State burials free of cost to the relatives should be accorded to persons who died as the result of war injuries or war service injuries.

The Government was also prepared to make a grant of £10 towards the cost of privately arranged funerals in the case of a civil defence volunteer killed on duty, or in the case of a gainfully occupied person who died as a result of a war injury, where the arrangements had been made by the widow or by a wholly dependent relative whom the deceased was regularly maintaining in his or her own home.

A similar grant is payable in respect of the death of disablement pensioners of the Forces who die while undergoing treatment in an institution to which they have been admitted for a course of treatment, or where death occurs at home and the cause of death is certified to be the same as the pensionable disability. If the relatives so desire the Ministry will carry out the funeral free of cost.

Welfare Work of the Ministry

In addition to the grant of pensions the Ministry does a great deal of welfare work for the different classes of pensioners and for their dependants. The Ministry is, in the first place, committed to much supervisory work by the terms of the pensions schemes themselves. The Royal Warrants, for example, empower the Minister, at his discretion, to decide whether, in order to secure the proper care of a child on behalf of whom an allowance is payable, the pension should be paid to the parent or guardian or "administered under such conditions as the Minister may determine."

The Minister's powers in connection with the care of war orphans of the recent war are derived from the War Orphans Act of 1942. This is, in fact, a re-assumption of the obligation placed on the Minister under the War Pensions Act of 1918 to take under his care all children of men killed in the war who, being motherless or for other reasons, were found to be suffering neglect. Some 5,000 children of the first World War passed wholly into the Ministry's care, homes were found for them and their education supervised, and nearly a quarter of a million pounds was spent on the welfare of these "neglected children." This special welfare work was carried on mainly through the agency of the Special Grants Committee and the Local War Pensions Committees, with the combined aid of State and voluntary funds.

The effect of World War 1914 on the children of soldiers was severe and far reaching. In the peak year one and a quarter million children, the majority in the care of their mothers, were in receipt of pensions or allowances and some one hundred and thirty-two million pounds had been spent on this account by 1936.

The effects of the World War 1939 extended to children of civilians also. Bombs, in many cases, killed the parents in the towns, leaving as orphans the children evacuated to the country. The number of children on the Ministry's books as under care or supervision up to January 1947 was 4,666, most of them in the care of relatives. Because of war-time developments in legislation affecting children, and the consequential problems arising, the Ministry appointed specially selected women officers in every Region who visit and look after the welfare of all World War 1939 war orphans and take such steps as are necessary to ensure their well-being. This work has received the emphatic approval of the Curtis Report on the "Care of Homeless Children."

The administration of the education allowances and of the extended maintenance allowances to children receiving higher or technical education involved the Ministry in a good deal of supervisory work after the 1914 war, and this responsibility is again placed on the Ministry under current Schemes.

The education allowances are to enable pensioned war orphans to receive such education as their father would have provided, unless it can be provided under other State schemes. Extended pension allowances are granted after pension would normally have ceased so long as the child is undergoing an approved course of full-time education. Extended pension allowances are also granted, on a similar basis, where a child is an apprentice or the like or is unable to work because of infirmity which existed before pension was normally due to cease.

The Local War Pensions Committees have been tireless in alleviating the lot of adult pensioners in many ways—by organising comforts and entertainment for disabled men in hospital and in their own homes; by visiting seriously disabled pensioners in their own homes; by campaigning for free travelling facilities from local authorities for seriously disabled men; by keeping the Ministry and the public alive to the claims of pensioners in a number of ways.

One of the most important forms of assistance for ex-Servicemen after the World War 1914 was the scheme for giving preference in employment to disabled men in the period of acute unemployment, a scheme supported by the Government, by Local Authorities and by large firms and Corporations.

This principle has been developed both during World War 1939 and, following the cessation of hostilities, by the institution of special schemes of rehabilitation for industry which operate while the disabled are still in hospital; the passing of the Disabled Persons (Employment) Act, 1944, which lays down that employers must employ a quota of disabled persons; the setting up of training centres and an arrangement whereby every disabled ex-Serviceman is seen by a representative of the Ministry of Labour, whilst still in hospital, to discuss post-discharge employment or training. In addition, schemes are being developed whereby very seriously disabled men, e.g. paraplegics, can follow remunerative occupations in their own homes or in bed, e.g. boot repairing, clock assembly.

Administration

One of the biggest tests of a Government Department is the speed with which it can act in a human emergency. When a family is in distress, delay in meeting its need is almost as cruel as not meeting it at all. At the beginning of the 1939 war a good deal of unnecessary suffering was caused by red tape, but under the pressure of "blitzes," Government Departments learned to act quickly. The Ministry of Pensions, to its credit, learned this lesson early. It soon rivalled the efficiency of the Assistance Board in dealing rapidly with the effects of heavy raids. In fact the Departments worked closely together in dealing with civilian casualties, and soon both earned a good name for themselves. When an area was heavily raided the Ministry of Pensions moved in and, if it had not a local office of its own, billetted itself on the Assistance Board. Where casualties were less heavy a single pensions officer would visit the area after a raid and, with the help of the local authority, get in touch with civilians likely to have claims. Widows of air-raid casualties were interviewed by these officers among the ruins of their own homes and handed on the spot the special temporary allowance of 50/- a week to which they were entitled pending the settlement of their claim to a pension. The pensions man was as much in evidence the morning after the raid as was the food convoy or the field kitchen.

Efforts were also made to relieve the widows of deceased Servicemen of financial worries in the hour of their bereavement. Full Service allowances, including war service grants, were continued for thirteen weeks after the husband's death, and, as soon as the death was confirmed, the Service Department arranged for the widow to fill up the necessary forms. The completed forms were referred automatically to the Ministry of Pensions and in the normal way a widow's pension was in issue by the end of the thirteen weeks. Similar provisions operate today, though their fullest value was obviously felt at the height of the war, when one anxiety seemed to pile upon another.

When a disabled Serviceman is to be invalided out of the Service he is given 8 weeks' furlough plus any overseas leave to which he is entitled, dating from the day of the decision that he is to be invalided out. If he is undergoing medical or rehabilitative treatment, invaliding is deferred for at least 8 months where the disability is not connected with service, or until medical or surgical finality is reached (subject to an overriding limit of 2½ years) where the disability is accepted as attributable to or aggravated by service. In either case he remains on Service pay for the period of treatment plus the period of terminal leave to which he is entitled. When it is decided that he is to be invalided, the Service documents are transferred to the Ministry of Pensions at the earliest possible moment and the Ministry is able, in the majority of cases where the disablement is due to service, to get a disablement pension in payment before the end of the terminal leave. If the man is unfit for work he may draw national health insurance benefit, and if he is fit for work but no suitable employment is available for him he may draw unemployment benefit or possibly be eligible for training under one of the training schemes of the Ministry of Labour and National Service.

Concessions and Controversies

During the war the struggle to remedy grave faults in the pensions scheme was persistent and, on some issues, bitter. Considerable improvements were won, but by the time the worst of the fighting was over substantial grievances still remained. The Labour Government, in fulfilment of promises made during the election, has remedied the bulk of these: though it must in honesty be admitted that one of the most important concessions, under which the claimant gets the benefit of any reasonable doubt, was forced on the Ministry as the result of a High Court ruling.[1] Whatever the reason for it, this concession removed the last important source of grievance, and today the emphasis of complaint has turned largely from policy to minor details of administration, as any issue of the *British Legion Journal*, for example, will show.

The first major concession since the General Election has been the improvement in rates of benefit. Not only has the basic rate of pension for 100% disability been raised to 45/- but the additional benefits payable in cases of very severe injury have also been increased. As a result, the attack by Conservative critics on the 45/- pension as "totally inadequate" does not reflect any real agitation throughout the country. As the Minister has pointed out, the man suffering from 100% disability is not

[1] See footnote p. 221.

necessarily unable to work and many are helped to find employment—which does not, of course, affect the pension. The pensioner who, though only partially disabled, has to take a less well-paid job because of his disability, can be granted a special hardship allowance of 11/3 a week, and by December 1946 nearly one thousand of these allowances had been awarded. If a man is unemployable as a result of his war injury (whether or not he is 100% disabled) he qualifies for an unemployability supplement of 20/- a week which is not prejudiced by earnings of up to 20/- a week. Should he be so badly disabled as to require special attention, he may receive a constant attendance allowance ranging from 10/- to a new maximum of 40/-. In addition, it must be remembered that the war pensioner is an exception to the general ban on "duplication of benefits," so that he receives family allowance for his eligible children in addition to their children's allowance of 7/6 a week. By all these provisions the needs of even the most tragic cases of disablement are, therefore, reasonably well met. Under them a private soldier, disabled to the point of helplessness, could receive for himself, wife and two children £7, 1/- a week, plus a special clothing allowance of up to £5 a year for wear and tear of clothing due to the wearing of an artificial limb.

Although, therefore, the Government would like to see every disabled man even more comfortably placed, it can fairly claim that he is receiving a not unreasonable share of the country's existing resources.

Equally welcome was the Ministry's decision in Febraury 1946 to admit for benefit the wives and children of men who married after their disablement. Protracted efforts to win this concession during the war were met by the argument that a man could not be "entitled to increase the public charge arising from his service and the disablement due to it by any obligations he may voluntarily incur after his service." In taking this attitude the British Government lagged behind those of France, the United States, Australia and New Zealand. Public opinion revolted at the idea of young men conscripted at 18 and injured before they had reached full manhood, being denied for the rest of their lives assistance in maintaining a wife and family. But it revolted in vain until the General Election. Even then the new Minister hesitated to make a complete change. At first the concession was limited to cases where marriage took place not later than ten years after the end of war service. But so many obvious injustices were created by this distinction that the Minister finally abandoned all restrictions and from 1st January 1947 allowances have been payable irrespective of the date of marriage.

One of the biggest pension campaigns during the war was waged round the slogan "Fit for Service, Fit for Pension." This claim had all the attraction of simplicity. It reflected the resentment against the ruthlessness of the military machine which drew millions of men into its maw without any fine regard for the niceties of individual needs. If a man is passed A1 on going into the Services, ran the argument, and is later "scrapped" as unfit, the only fair thing is to assume that his disability has some connection with his war service. In the face of this barrage of public opinion the Ministry of Pensions gradually retreated from its original position that death or disability, to be pensionable, must be "directly" attributable to war service or to a wound, injury or disease which was aggravated by war service "to a material extent." The first victory came in July 1941, when the Minister announced a new ruling in the House. He had "come to the conclusion that, where in such cases effective service is found to have caused a degree of aggravation in a previously existing condition, the fact of discharge would justify me . . . in regarding the aggravation as material and thus bringing the case within the scope of the Royal Warrant."

Members of the House still continued to protest that the new principle did not go far enough. In his review of pensions provisions in July 1943 [1] the Minister resisted this demand as "inconsistent with the principle, which obtained in regard to the war of 1914-18 and has since been maintained, that there must be causal connection between disablement and war service to enable a pension to be awarded." Acceptance of the demand would, he argued, make him automatically responsible for every disability which a Serviceman developed at any time after the commencement of war service, whether the latter had anything to do with it or not, and this would abolish the qualification of "causal connection," which forms the basis of the war pensions scheme.

At the same time the Minister bowed to the storm to the

[1] Cmd. 6459.

extent of agreeing to the removal from the Royal Warrant of two unpopular words: aggravation of a disability by war service need no longer be "material"; disablement or death no longer "directly" attributable to war service. It is also made clear in the Warrant that there is no onus of proof on the claimant that the conditions have been fulfilled.

Despite this important admission, pensioners continued to complain that they were not being given "the benefit of any reasonable doubt." Cases still arose in which the medical experts confessed themselves ignorant of the origin or causes of a disease but found against the claimant on the grounds that there was no reason of which they were aware to suppose it was caused or encouraged by war service. Early in 1946 one of these unsuccessful claimants whose case had been rejected by the pensions appeal tribunal appealed to the High Court on the grounds that the terms of the Royal Warrant were not being observed. The High Court ruled in his favour[1] and, by so doing, brought into question the validity of the findings in hundreds of similar cases which had previously been rejected. A later verdict in the Court of Session in Scotland reinforced Mr. Justice Denning's findings in the High Court.[2]

To meet this situation the Minister announced in July 1946 that those persons who, having had their appeals disallowed previously, were of the opinion that their claims would have succeeded if they had been heard after the promulgation of the High Court and Court of Session decisions, could have their cases re-examined. The response to this offer has been considerable and the percentage of cases admitted for pension after re-examination has been high. Applications are first considered by the Ministry and, if still rejected, are referred to a non-statutory Tribunal, known as the War Pensions (Special Review) Tribunal, whose decisions are final. The new ruling and the re-examination procedure have finally taken the sting out of the "Fit for Service, Fit for Pension" claim.

Another milestone was reached in July 1946 when Section 5 of the Pensions Appeal Tribunals Act, 1943, at last came into operation. Until this date a pensioner had no appeal against the degree of disability at which he was assessed, only against the

[1] *Rowing* v. *Minister of Pensions*.
[2] All England Law Reports, Vol. I, p. 664.

decision on eligibility. Section 5 takes from the Minister the right to have the last word on assessment and gives it instead to an independent statutory tribunal.

Almost the only point of policy about which there is still organised agitation is the parent's pension. In certain parts of the country the claim for a flat rate of pension for the loss of an unmarried son is still strong. The Minister has considerable support for his reply that it is better to concentrate on giving effective help where it is needed than to broadcast a small sum to all bereaved parents regardless of their circumstances. But the effectiveness of this argument is rather weakened in practice by the stringency of the means test at present applied. The income which is considered adequate without pension is too low. Too little regard is had to the way in which members of working-class families stand by one another so that a son, even if he marries, is always a potential refuge in hard times. The treatment of widowed mothers in particular, left all alone by the death of a son, is too harsh. Even if they have only the 10/- a week widow's pension to live on they cannot draw more than the maximum parent's pension of 27/6 a week, and if they go out to work to supplement this, they risk losing it altogether. None the less it must be admitted that the new administration of these pensions has been more generous than the old and in its issue of February 1947 the *British Legion Journal* noted that 9,200 parents had had their pensions raised. By this date over 40,000 such pensions were in issue.

Future of Ministry of Pensions

British pensions policy has always had regard to the general background of the country's social life, and, in particular, to the existence of other agencies of assistance in the form of our social services. For this reason, specific assistance for the ex-Serviceman, able-bodied as well as disabled, has tended in the past to be smaller than in other countries, such as the United States, where general social services were slower to develop. The existence in this country of widespread health services, of unemployment insurance schemes and of contributory pensions schemes has modified the nature of the provision specifically made for members of the Forces and their dependants.

Since the Labour Government came into power two things

have happened. In the first place there have been marked advances in the provisions for war pensions, but in addition there has also been a review of all other social services to bring them up to a level consistent with the conception of a nation-wide social security scheme. Although, therefore, the conditions for war pensioners have improved, this has not been done at the expense of other members of the community. The provision for men disabled in industry, for example, has been brought, under the Industrial Injuries Act, up to the level of the provision for the man disabled by war. The basic pension for the 100% pensioner is the same and so are the additional allowances, with the sole exception that the war pensioner receives the State family allowance in addition to the allocation he gets for his child from the Ministry of Pensions, while the industrially disabled only draw the family allowance and nothing else for every child beyond the first. Even about this distinction the Labour Movement is uneasy. Opinion within the Movement is increasingly in favour of ironing out distinctions between the war pensioner and other persons in need of State help; of bringing everybody within the scope of one adequate all-embracing social security scheme. It is indeed doubtful whether it will be possible, once the social security scheme is in full operation, to justify the existence of a separate Ministry of Pensions to deal with only one section of the State beneficiaries. Once the idea is firmly rooted that social security means more than cash payments, that it means welfare work, sympathy and imaginative help in every direction, it is more than possible that we shall see the Ministry of Pensions "wither away" as having fulfilled its function and as having been superseded.

Chapter IX

FINANCE OF THE SOCIAL SERVICES

By GERTRUDE WILLIAMS

THE finances of the various services that have been described in the previous chapters fall into two categories. Some of the services, such as Unemployment Insurance, National Health Insurance, and Widows', Orphans' and Contributory Old Age Pensions, have an actuarial basis; on the other hand, Unemployment Assistance, Public Assistance, State Old Age Pensions and Supplementary Pensions are paid entirely from public funds. The present chapter gives a brief outline of the financial arrangements of these forms of social provision and discusses some of the problems to which they have given rise.

The basis of insurance is the making of collective provision for an individual risk. Of a group of persons each individual may incur a particular risk, but no one of them knows for certain whether he himself will incur it and, if he does, what its incidence will be. Yet experience leads us to expect that only a certain proportion will fall victim to it over a period of time. If each person is left to his own devices he must set aside a sum to cover the costs of a risk that may never eventuate, and is thus bound to make what may be a very real sacrifice at the moment, which later proves to have been unnecessary. If the income is small, the sacrifice may be so great as to make it impossible for the individual to bear it, and if later he proves to be the unfortunate person on whom the calamity falls, he has no provision to meet it. If all band together, the collective amount required is less than the sum of the individual amounts, since only a proportion will, in fact, be affected, and consequently the contribution that each makes is less than he would have needed to save on his own account. How much less depends, of course, on the incidence of the risk. If normally it falls on only 5% of those liable, he need contribute only 5% of the amount he would have needed to have saved on his own account in order to get the same degree of security.

Certain things follow from this: firstly, whilst there is no need for benefits and premiums to balance each week, month or year, it is essential that they should do so over a definite period of time if the scheme is to remain solvent and the provision for the sake of which the contributions have been made is to be actually forthcoming when the risk is incurred. Secondly, a risk is insurable to the extent that it is calculable; that is, it must be possible to base one's anticipations of the future on the experience of the past with reasonable assurance that what happens in the future will not be very different from what has happened in the past, or that the divergencies arise from circumstances which can themselves be foreseen and the effects calculated. Unless this is so, it is impossible to estimate the amount of contribution that each should make to build a fund large enough to meet the claims made on it. Thirdly, either the risk that is run by each participant in the scheme must be, roughly speaking, the same, or else it must be possible to grade the contributions according to the risk run by the particular contributor.

In a voluntary insurance system this third condition is not of serious importance. As people have a choice as to whether they will insure or not, those who feel that their risk is so slight as to be negligible, or that they can meet it from their own resources, remain outside the scheme, and it is necessary for the company to charge different premiums in relation to different degrees of risk in order to attract the others. The voluntary method is, however, inapplicable to the type of risk which is discussed in this book. Most wage-earners have such small and irregular incomes that it is almost impossible to maintain regular contributions, and just those large sections of the community whose own resources are least adequate to meet the vicissitudes of life are the ones who are unable to enter insurance voluntarily. Compulsion at once introduces an entirely new character. The classes to be included, the premiums to be paid, the benefits to be drawn and the conditions on which claims can be made, are laid down by law; and provided they appear to be just in general, they can continue to operate without consideration of whether they fulfil actuarial criteria. In fact, as the various insurance schemes get lopped and changed, added to here and trimmed off there, according to the exigencies of the political and economic situation, they travel so far from the actuarial framework into which they were originally built that the question quite naturally arises whether it is worth while to retain even the semblance of insurance. It has often been suggested that the payments should be made to persons needing them, when the various emergencies arise, out of public funds and without the bother and paraphernalia of maintaining the fiction of an insurance scheme. The proposal has the attraction of simplicity, since it cuts away with one movement the regulations and restrictions which are an inevitable concomitant of a scheme which is tethered, however loosely, to an actuarial base. If the individual drew his support from a common fund, irrespective both of his own contribution and of the causes from which his necessity arose, administration could work with greater ease, efficiency and speed. The insurance method has, however, one outstanding advantage. It does away with any necessity for a means test, since the beneficiary claims his benefit in respect of his position as an insured contributor who has paid the requisite number of premiums and not because of his lack of financial resources. It is, of course, possible to maintain that no means test is required even without an insurance scheme, but that the individual should have a right to certain payments from public funds if he is unemployed or sick or whatever it may be, irrespective of his needs. This is not the place to argue the rights and wrongs of such a contention. It is enough in explaining the finances of our present social services to point out that they have been based on the belief that the alternatives lie between a system in which payment of benefit is a statutory right depending on payment of contributions and without regard to other resources, and one in which there is payment of allowances which takes into account the other means at the disposal of the applicant. The whole trend of social service development has been towards providing aid to the individual without the need to enquire into his personal means; and the social insurance systems are the result.

There are good reasons for this apart from the natural dislike of the individual to the searching enquiries of the investigator. A means test tends to penalise thrift, since the man who has saved to meet a period of difficulty finds himself unable to get help, whilst the more happy-go-lucky person is able to demand assistance immediately. But there are two other more important considerations. A benefit which is paid irrespective of other resources enables the individual to maintain his standard of living nearer to its previous level instead of being forced first to exhaust the savings which form the foundation on which that standard depends. A standard once broken is extraordinarily difficult to build up again, so many psychological values are involved. It is important to prevent it from dropping by more than the slight amount from which human elasticity will allow it to recover. The second consideration is also a psychological one. The misery caused by the common vicissitudes of life is not confined to the period of their activity; the fear that they will happen, bringing their consequent train of poverty, throws a shadow over life. The sense of security that is provided by the confidence that financial aid will be forthcoming without question when the unfortunate happening occurs is a very real addition to the well-being of people during the times that they are earning their living in the normal way.

Insurance has, therefore, come to be accepted as the recognised framework wherever it can be established. From the first it has been based on a tripartite contribution, i.e. premiums have been paid not only by the wage-earner himself but by his employer and the State. The funds are collected by the sale of special stamps. It is the duty of the employer to buy a stamp corresponding in value to the joint contribution of himself and the worker, and he has the right to deduct the employee's share of the cost from his wages before paying them. The State grant is proportionate to the contributions of employers and employed. But this is about the only characteristic that the social insurance systems have in common. In practically all other important matters they are widely differentiated from one another, and it will be best, therefore, to deal with them separately.

UNEMPLOYMENT INSURANCE

The Unemployment Insurance system has been subject to more changes and more criticism than any other of the forms of social provision. The details of the scheme at present in operation are given in the chapter by Mrs. Rackham;[1] she

[1] See Chap. IV, p. 125.

discusses the Unemployment Insurance Statutory Committee which was appointed by the Act of 1934 to supervise the finances of the Unemployment Insurance Fund. The Fund is made up of all the contributions of employers, employed and the State subsidy (fixed by the Act at half the joint sum contributed by the other two parties), and out of it are paid all benefits, costs of administration and such grants as those to the Junior Instruction Centres. If the Fund is unable to meet its obligations the Treasury may advance the necessary sums, and interest is then paid on these loans. During the severe and prolonged unemployment of the 'twenties which culminated in the unprecedented depression of the early 'thirties the Fund was forced to borrow very largely, so that in 1934, when the new Act was passed, it found itself with a debt outstanding of £105,780,000. By the Act an annual sum of £5,000,000 had to be set aside out of the Fund in order to meet the interest on this amount and to repay a part of the capital every year, and by this means it was reckoned that the whole of the debt could be got rid of by 1971.

It is the duty of the Unemployment Insurance Statutory Committee to take care that the Fund never again gets seriously into debt. Its obligation is to report at least once a year on the Fund's financial situation, and if it believes that the Fund "is likely to become, and is likely to continue to be, insufficient to discharge its liabilities, or is, and is likely to continue to be, more than reasonably sufficient to discharge its liabilities," it has the duty of recommending changes and of estimating the cost of its proposals. The fulfilment of this obligation is by no means as simple as it sounds. Reductions in contributions or improvements in benefits or in conditions which, on the recommendation of the Committee, are incorporated by the Government in the system cannot be lightly given up. They must remain in force for a reasonable period of time if the scheme is, in fact, to provide the sense of security for which it exists. This means that the Committee has to be concerned more with the future prospects of unemployment than with the situation at the moment of the report. It has been pointed out earlier that there is no need for benefits and premiums to balance in as short a period as one year. It is, however, essential to the Fund's solvency that it should do so over whatever period of time is accepted as constituting a unit of time in employment fluctuations.

There is real uncertainty in determining whether there is any such periodicity in the incidence of unemployment as would justify designating such a unit, but, as a working hypothesis, the Committee has, in general, agreed that it should aim at retaining solvency over a period of 8 years, i.e. it assumes that the cyclical fluctuations in employment make it reasonable to take 8 years as the unit within which good and bad years will have a chance to even themselves out. But in estimating the probable claims on the Fund it is not enough to prophesy merely the total number who are likely to be out of work. Benefits vary according to age and sex; the period for which benefit may be claimed depends on the claimant's previous industrial history; as no benefit is payable for the "waiting days," short-term unemployment is less burden on the Fund than long-term; on the other hand, the longer a man is out of work, the more likely he is to fall out of benefit and receive his allowance from the Assistance Board; family conditions vary from man to man, and so, accordingly, do dependants' allowances; if unemployment is concentrated among the older men the burden on the Fund will be less than if it is mainly among the younger married men with young dependent children; if an industry with a high birth-rate is depressed, such as coal-mining, the cost of benefit is greater than if the depression is in an industry with a low birth-rate, such as cotton, or one employing a high proportion of women. The composition of the unemployed group is, therefore, as important to determine as their total number if the future solvency of the Fund or the cost of any proposed change is to be calculated with any degree of precision.

Experience has shown that it is, in fact, exceedingly difficult to foretell the course of employment, even without analysing the composition of the unemployed. Every year the Unemployment Insurance Statutory Committee has carefully scanned the economic horizon in the attempt to foretell the economic weather. In every case its prognostications have proved incorrect, not because its arguments were unsound, but because it was impossible for it to foresee that certain events would happen and consequently it could not estimate their probable effects on the incidence of unemployment. The Committee has itself realised the impossibility of its task and has made its estimates only because of the need of having some working hypothesis on which to base its recommendations. It is not any criticism of the Committee's judgment if this hypothesis has not been borne out by the facts on account of some big change in the economic policy of this or some other Government which has vitally altered the course of trade; or because the deterioration in international relations so far increased apprehension as to set on foot a programme of rearmament with its consequent repercussions on munitions and allied trades. In the 1937 Report the Committee drew attention to this fact: "We draw conclusions as to the course of unemployment in the future only because without some conclusions of whatever character we cannot perform our statutory duty of reporting on the prospective relation between the income and expenditure of the Unemployment Fund and adjusting its finances. We only prophesy because we must."

In every year since the Committee was set up the actual unemployment has been considerably less than was anticipated, and it has, consequently, been possible for the Committee to report that the Fund was, and was likely to continue to be, more than able to meet its liabilities. The problem then arose of deciding the size of the disposable surplus and what to do with it. The Committee has rightly recognised that it is not within its competence to alter the basic principles embodied in the Insurance system; that is a matter for Parliament. It has, therefore, always avoided recommending such changes as, e.g., that the waiting period should be entirely abolished, or that the Anomalies Regulations should be fundamentally altered, even if the cost of such alterations could have been easily met out of the disposable surplus. It has concerned itself solely with financial considerations. In making its recommendations it has to keep clearly in mind the number of persons who are likely to be affected by any change that is made. There is always a demand on the part of both employers and employed that the contributions should be lowered, and on the part of the workers that the benefit should be increased. But it must be remembered that the first of these proposals covers everybody, the whole of the 15,000,000 persons who are insured, and that a reduction of contribution automatically reduces the State subsidy which is fixed at half the joint contribution of employers and employed. The effect of an increase in benefit is much more difficult to calculate, as it depends not only on the estimate of total unemployment but on the proportions of those unemployed who will qualify for benefits of varying amounts. Unless the surplus is very large, the recommended change must deal with matters on a less wholesale scale than this, and, in fact, the Committee has generally proposed such alterations as an increase in dependants' allowances, which has the double advantage of costing less than a general increase and at the same time affording help where the need is greatest.

The problem assumed a rather different character in the years in which the effect of the rearmament policy became visible in a rapid shrinking of the number of the unemployed. Such a factor could not be considered as part of the normal cycle of employment, and it was felt that any surplus of funds to which it gave rise must be taken as non-recurrent, particularly as there must be anticipated a later increase in unemployment as the rearmament programme neared completion. With the outbreak of war, however, this period was pushed further into the future and the Fund became extremely swollen from three sources: (1) As more and more people were drawn into employment the income from contributions rapidly expanded; (2) the 1940 Act raised the limit of remuneration for the inclusion of non-manual workers to £420 and thus brought the contributions of a new group into the Fund; (3) the reduction in unemployment cut down the drain on the Fund for the payment of benefit, particularly amongst the younger married workers who are most likely to claim dependants' allowances. How far the large surpluses that were thus created could be considered "disposable" is open to differences of opinion. The verdict depends largely on the view that is taken of the probable course of post-war employment. There was a general determination during the recent war that we could not permit as catastrophic a fall in employment as occurred in 1920, and that the Government must early undertake the task of preparing plans for immediate operation when the war programme ended. At the same time one must realise that a war of world-wide dimensions with its cataclysmic effect on life in general cannot slide into peace without any noticeable jolt. There is certain to be a period of dislocation, however carefully plans have been laid, because men and women cannot be taken from war industries and thrust into civilian occupations as if they were so many inanimate bits of movable furniture. One has only to remember the difficulties that were encountered in getting the war industries staffed to appreciate that fact. We must anticipate, then, a certain amount of post-war unemployment and remember that a much larger proportion of the community than normally have built up claims to benefit by the regularity of their war-time employment. The Fund must be prepared to meet these claims.

At the same time it is obviously absurd and uneconomic to keep in reserve an enormous surplus while the Fund is heavily in debt. The average interest on the debt is about 5%. The amount that can be earned by the Fund on its investments is much less than this, because it must invest in short-term securities which can be rapidly liquidated if claims for benefit increase. On the average, the interest it can earn is not more than 2%. The maintenance of an unduly large reserve thus costs the Fund about 3%. The Unemployment Insurance Act which funded the debt fixed the statutory annual charge at £5,000,000. Any surplus could, on the recommendation of the Committee, be applied to paying off a portion of the debt, but it had no effect on the requirement to continue to pay this annual charge in the following years. All it could do was to bring nearer the date at which the total debt would be extinguished. At the time the Act was passed there had been a good deal of criticism of making the debt a charge on the Fund at all. It had been contracted at a time of very severe depression and as a result of allowing to those who had been long unemployed rights to benefit which had not been part of their original contract and had not been taken into account when the amount of the premiums had been settled. These types of benefit were later accepted as a national responsibility to be borne on public funds. It was difficult to justify the retention of high rates of contribution from employers and workers in order to pay off a debt the burden of which should never have been placed on their shoulders and the reduction of which would affect not them but a later generation. If, however, the law allowed the annual debt charge to be reduced as the capital sum was paid off, i.e. leaving the period of time over which the debt was spread the same, it would be worth while to use a surplus for this purpose, as the resulting lower annual charge would provide a bigger fund out of which to pay present benefits. The Committee's recommendation that such a change should be made in the law was acted on in 1938, and the big surpluses due to war employment have since been used to pay off the whole of the debt. "At the beginning of our work in 1934," the Committee reported in 1941, "the debt of the Unemployment Fund stood at £105,780,000. It was calculated that by means of the debt charge of £5,000,000 a year the principal and interest of the whole should be repaid and the debt extinguished by 1971. Events have made it possible to anticipate this date by 30 years and to leave the debt and all the controversies that have centred round it behind us." The use of an exceptional surplus for this purpose has a dual advantage. It sets free the annual sum of £5,000,000, which can be used either to reduce contributions or to increase benefits, and it enables the Fund, in the event of later unemployment, to reborrow part of its repayments and thus to remain solvent without any drastic curtailment of benefit. Since the Committee last reported, unemployment has become even less than it was and still larger numbers have been drawn into employment. As long as contributions are kept at their present level, then, the Fund will get increasingly swollen, and as there is no longer any large capital item on which to spend, the question arises as to the steps that should be taken to deal with the disposable surplus. An increase of benefits would not have much effect. As, on the average, there are less than 200,000 people out of work at any one time, benefits would have to be phenomenally high in order to absorb the surplus millions. The only way in which a noticeable reduction could be achieved would be by an appreciable lowering of contributions. At first sight this seems a sensible line of attack, but there is much to be said against it. At no time since the war of 1914-18 have contributions borne so lightly on both employers and employed, and a decrease in the amount paid would bring little sense of relief to either party. Moreover, as the supply of civilian goods is being continually further restricted, there is less and less on which to spend wages. The retention of the high contributions can thus be justified as a form of compulsory saving. If, when the war is over, the difficulties of readjustment prove greater than we hope, the power to increase rates of benefit or to prolong the period during which benefit is payable will be of greater social value than a reduction in premiums now when employment is regular and earnings are high.

Health Insurance

With the exception of the tripartite basis, the financial arrangements of Health Insurance are widely different from those of Unemployment Insurance. The scheme was based on the organisation of the friendly societies with which so large a proportion of the wage-earning population were already familiar, and administration by "approved societies" was consequently established. The Post Office pays over the amount got from the sale of Health Insurance stamps to the respective approved societies, the sum due to each society being calculated when the insured person makes the half-yearly surrender of his card. The State grant is fixed at one-seventh of the expenditure on benefits for men and one-fifth of the expenditure on women's benefits, including the cost of their administration, payable on disbursement, i.e. payment of a benefit attracts a grant; and the whole of the cost of the Central administration is borne by public funds.

Not all the money contributed by its members and their employers is paid over directly to the approved society. There is always the danger that a particular society may have an unusually large number of claims to meet, owing, perhaps, to an epidemic or other incalculable occurrence. If it had been allowed to distribute all its surplus in some form or other of additional benefit it might find itself unable to meet its statutory obligations; and it is to prevent this that a form of re-insurance has been devised. A small part of the members' contribution is held back and credited to the society in a Contingencies Fund, which is, in effect, a subsection of its Benefit Fund. If the approved society has branches, the Contingencies Fund is common to the whole society, though each branch has its own Benefit Fund, and from this Contingencies Fund payments may be made to restore solvency if the Benefit Fund proves insufficient. Very small societies are subject to wider fluctuations than are normal for the bigger bodies, and in order to overcome the danger inherent in this, those societies with less than 1,000 members each are grouped together so that part of the Contingencies Fund of one is available to make up the deficiencies of another. A still further measure of security is provided for all societies, whatever their size, by the existence of the Central Fund. This is made up of not more than one-eighth of the contributions to the Contingencies Fund, with an additional annual Exchequer Grant. If, however, few calls are made on the Fund and societies' contributions are consequently cut down or suspended, the Exchequer Grant is proportionately reduced. There are thus a good many barriers between a society's immediate resources and insolvency, and there is little likelihood of an insured contributor being refused his legal rights because of the inadequacy of the funds of the society to which he belongs. In a very large number of cases, indeed, he will find himself able to claim a good deal more than his legal rights. Societies differ very materially from one another. Some are extremely large, with careful and efficient administration; there are others with few members and proportionately heavy overhead costs. As societies are often formed on the basis of occupational groups with similar health risks or from the inhabitants of a district whose health environment is the same, there are wide divergencies in the incidence of sickness between one body and another, and resources which are only just sufficient to meet the statutory obligation in the case of one society leave an ample margin in that of another. Every five years a valuation of the assets of societies is made by Treasury-approved valuers, whose duty it is to estimate the surplus likely to be disposable in the next few years. As the incidence of sickness is not so subject to rapid fluctuations as a result of external social and political factors as is that of unemployment, this is a very much simpler and more practicable estimate to make than the one that falls to the lot of the Unemployment Insurance Statutory Committee. On the basis of this estimated disposable surplus the society may submit a scheme for additional benefits for its members. These may take the form of dental or ophthalmic treatment, or other specialist medical care, or of further money payment extra to the statutory weekly benefit.

The result of administration through approved societies is, therefore, that members get very different benefits for the same compulsory contribution. The Royal Commission on National Health Insurance reported in 1926 that, after the first valuation, the difference in surplus was such that 1,880,630 got nothing extra, while, of the rest, those with the highest additional benefits received five times more than those with the lowest. In the last full year before the war 72% of members were drawing extra cash benefits, and 91% additional treatment benefits.

The original calculations of the point of balance between contributions and benefits rested on the assumption that the insured person would be paying premiums from the age of 16. It was anticipated that there would be comparatively few claims made by the average person during youth and the prime of life, but that the claims would increase as the individual grew older. As, however, everybody within the scope of the scheme came into it at the same moment, the large majority of newly insured contributors were older than 16 and approaching to a greater degree than the calculations had assumed the period when they would normally begin to make heavier claims. It was necessary to make financial provision for this, and the Central Department has done so by a system based on a calculation of reserve values. Part of the member's contribution is retained to meet any deficiency in the society's resources that arises on this account. As the age composition varies from society to society, each has a different liability in this respect, those with a larger proportion of older members being more likely to have to meet heavy claims, and the amount of assistance each society requires from the Central Fund varies according to the amount of extra liability it has to meet in view of the ages of its members.

Each person entering insurance after the age of 16 has been given a reserve value, which represents his society's liability with regard to him on account of his age. Interest at the rate of 3½% per annum is paid out of the retained income on this reserve value, and if anything is left over it is put to the society's credit to redeem the full reserve value eventually. It was originally estimated that all reserve values would be fully redeemed in 18½ years, but owing to various changes, as e.g. the creation of the Contingencies Fund (explained above), the amount of money available for redemption was reduced. It is now expected that the full period of redemption will be about thirty-five years.

The approved societies deal only with the money benefit. The control of medical and prescriptions benefit rests with the Insurance Committees of each county and county borough, to whom a sum of 14/6 is paid on account of each insured person.

From this money the Insurance Committee pays the doctors and chemists a *per capita* fee in respect of each name on the panel. In the last year before the war total expenditure on medical benefit was £10,326,800, for which sum about 16,840,000 persons were entitled to medical benefit from over 16,000 doctors and received drugs and appliances from over 12,000 chemists' shops.

The maintenance of rights to benefit in any system run on actuarial lines depends on the payment of premiums at prescribed intervals. It has not always been easy to maintain this regularity in the Health Insurance scheme, as the wage-earner cannot continue to make payments unless he is earning a wage. If the interruption to earning capacity is due to sickness he is, of course, not expected to pay premiums at the same time as he is drawing benefit. But if he has lost his employment and remains out of work for a considerable time he may find it quite impossible to maintain his Health Insurance rights. This became so serious and so general a problem during the great depression of the 'thirties that it was essential to make legislative provision for it. A person who is unemployed can now present his Health Insurance card at the Employment Exchange, where it is franked free in respect of every week of proved genuine unemployment. The funds for this are collected in the Unemployment Arrears Fund by a levy on all those still in employment (and until 1942 by an Exchequer Grant). The Government Actuary estimates the amount of the levy that is necessary for the following year. At the moment the levy is kept up so as to provide a reserve for the future, but it will presumably later be reduced as a consequence of the slight amount of unemployment. This levy enables the insured contributor to claim medical and maternity benefit and to retain his premium rights for so long as he can prove to be genuinely unemployed, i.e. still available for employment.

Public Assistance

The two schemes dealt with so far have an actuarial basis. Neither is true insurance, not because the funds are subsidised by the State, but because there is not the same degree of relationship between risk and premium as would satisfy actuarial criteria, and because the liability of premiums and benefits to constant legislative change render them only superficially the subject of a contractual obligation. In most of the remaining forms of social provision there is, however, no attempt to build an insurance framework. The allowances are paid out of public funds, on conditions of need, proved according to statutory enactment. They still present different features. Certain allowances, such as Unemployment Assistance and Old Age and Supplementary Pensions, come from funds provided by Parliament, and Public Assistance is paid out of money derived from local taxation, subsidised by State grants.

The rapid development of types of public provision outside the Poor Law has had financial as well as social causes. The Poor Law is financed principally out of local rates which are levied on the annual letting value of premises, so that if, for any reason, one particular locality has more than an average number of needy people to support, its local inhabitants will be taxed more heavily than those in other areas. Since the last war the severe unemployment which has characterised industry has been concentrated in the export trades. As these industries are highly localised, the cost of supporting those who, through prolonged unemployment, had lost their right to Unemployment Insurance benefit fell on the districts in which these industries were situated. This had many unfortunate effects. Firstly, the rates rose to great heights in just the areas in which an unprecedented depression had already hit incomes severely. Secondly, as the output of these trades was reduced owing to loss of markets, the high rates comprised a proportionately heavy overhead charge. Industrialists looking round for suitable sites for the establishment of new firms tended to shun the heavily rated areas, and the absorption of the unemployed into new occupations was consequently much delayed.

The maintenance of people in need by Poor Relief had another disadvantage. Until 1929, Poor Relief was administered by Boards of Guardians, and although the general principles of their work were laid down by law, a very wide margin of local discretion remained. The treatment of individuals in similar circumstances might, therefore, be substantially different according to the locality in which they happened to live, and these differences offended public ideas of justice. There has thus been a general tendency to provide for needs in such a way that individuals in like circumstances receive like treatment and that the necessary financial burden might be spread as evenly over the community as possible. Thus the newly established services such as Unemployment Allowances and Non-Contributory Pensions are financed out of national taxation and only Public Assistance remains as a practically local charge. But even here important changes have been introduced. At the same time as the Local Government Act, 1929, transferred the functions of the Boards of Guardians to County and County Borough Councils, the basis of calculation of the State grant to local expenditure was altered so as to enable more to be given to the needy districts and less to the wealthy. The State pays to the local authority a General Exchequer contribution which is assessed on a somewhat complicated formula. It is based on the size of the population "weighted" according to the rateable value per head of the property in the area, the number of children under 5 years of age, the road mileage in relation to the density of population, and the number of unemployed among insured men and women in the three years preceding the beginning of the grant period. The grant, once calculated, remains in force for five years and is then re-assessed to take account of any changes in these factors in the local situation. At the same time as the "block grant" was introduced, agricultural property was completely derated and industrial premises very largely so, with the result that the main burden of local rates now falls on commercial and residential property. This was a serious matter for the first few years following the change in law, but when in 1934 the maintenance of the unemployed was taken almost completely out of the province of Public Assistance, one of the causes of the different incidence of rates in different localities was removed.

Some such causes do, however, still remain. Public Assistance is largely a residual service, i.e. it deals with all those who do not fall within the scope of one of the specialist services or whose needs are inadequately met by such a service even if they do fall within its scope. For example, as National Health Insurance benefit takes no account of dependants, a married man with young children will probably need additional help if he falls sick. But a very large number of people are not insured at all, because they are not wage-earners, and such persons have no other body than Public Assistance to which to turn if they are sick or out of work. Now, largely owing to the development of cheap and quick transport, residential areas are much more class-specialised than they used to be. There are many districts which have practically no middle class but which are almost entirely inhabited by the small wage-earner or by the small employer (shopkeeper, jobbing carpenter, shoe-repairer, etc.) whose income falls within the same limits as that of the average wage-earner. The large employers and successful professional people live outside the area in which the workpeople reside, and come into their business each day by train or car. The result of this class segregation is that in certain districts there is a much larger proportion of the population that is likely to have to apply for Public Assistance, while the remainder not only have to bear a proportionately heavy burden but themselves have such small incomes as to feel this burden to be particularly onerous. The Local Government Act certainly extended the area of the local rating unit, but it did not extend it far enough, considering the social effects of modern transport; and despite the "weighted" block grant there are still wide discrepancies between the rates of different localities.

It is open to question indeed whether the local financial basis for Public Assistance has any longer any justification. It might be argued that it would be just as practicable to establish Public Assistance as a "national system" as Unemployment Assistance. The money for Unemployment Assistance comes entirely out of national taxation, and the local officials who administer the scheme are controlled by a Central Board which lays down detailed regulations for their guidance. But it is just here that, in practice, a good deal of difficulty is encountered. Men and women are not mechanical robots. Each individual differs from others in important respects, and the Assistance Board has found it no easy task to frame regulations which maintain a semblance of national uniformity whilst still taking account of local or individual differences. A residual service such as Public Assistance would have even greater difficulty in doing so, because it would have to deal with a whole variety of causes of loss of income instead of the single one with which the Unemployment Assistance officials are concerned. It would need, therefore, to give a much greater degree of local discretion if its assistance were to be of any real value. It is because of the necessity of maintaining local elasticity that so large a part of the financial burden is placed on local shoulders. It is a generally accepted fiscal axiom that financial responsibility must be linked to local discretion unless irresponsible extravagance is to be the result. The present problem is how to maintain the check on local expenditure and yet do away with both a narrow and soulless national uniformity and the injustice of an unequal incidence of financial burden. The answer might possibly be found in the conception of a wider local region which includes areas containing all social classes and income grades, but which is not so large as to make it impossible for local variations and individual differences to be taken properly into account.

The cost of Public Assistance varies not only in accordance with the numbers relieved but also according to the type of relief that is given. In the last year before the war the total expenditure on domiciliary relief was £17,973,193, which represents an average weekly cost per person assisted (including dependants) of 7/8½. The low average is due to the fact that a large proportion of those assisted were already drawing varying amounts from other sources, e.g. National Health Insurance, Old Age Pensions, etc. As other forms of special social provision have been devised and the amounts paid under them have been made more adequate to support life, the cost of outdoor relief has diminished. For example, the amount spent on relieving persons ordinarily engaged in some occupation fell from £8,307,000 in the year ending 31st March 1937 to £4,674,000 in the following year because the Second Appointed Day (see Chapter V) fell on 1st April 1937. Similarly, the cost of out-relief is likely to show a diminution as a result of the grant of Supplementary Old Age and Widows' Pensions.

But Public Assistance covers also expenditure on General Institutions, on Poor Law Hospitals and Children's Homes. The average cost here is much heavier, because a much larger part of the cost of maintaining the person necessarily falls on the Public Assistance authority. The person who is being relieved has no other resources and is not a member of a household from which he is drawing some part of his support, and those who are legally liable are rarely able to make a large contribution. The average weekly cost in the last year for which figures are available (ending 1938) was 28/5, 38/4 and 37/2 per person for the three categories mentioned. The development of special provision has reduced the number in receipt of institutional relief in the same way as of domiciliary. The Local Government Act, 1929, expressly laid upon the new Poor Law authorities the desirability of securing that all assistance which could lawfully be provided by other means than by way of Poor Relief should be so provided. As part of this general plan the treatment of the sick has come to be more and more provided under Public Health powers than under those of Public Assistance, those Public Assistance institutions which were suitable for the purpose having been appropriated for it. The total cost of indoor Public Assistance has therefore fallen considerably in recent years. As Public Health is, however, mainly a local expense, this transference has not lessened the financial burden on the local rates.

The Assistance Board

The establishment of Unemployment Assistance Allowances and Supplementary Pensions has relieved the local authorities of financial burdens that they were expected to bear when the Exchequer Grant was assessed. In respect of the first commitments, therefore, County Councils and County Borough Councils were compelled to pay to the Unemployment Assistance Fund amounts based on their estimated expenditure in 1935 on providing relief which would not have been provided if the Unemployment Assistance Act had been then in operation. This obligation ceased in 1937, the end of the third grant period, because after that date the reduced demands on the local authorities were taken into account in assessing the grant. Similarly, as the recipient of a Supplementary Pension cannot also get Public Assistance, part of the burden on which the current grant was calculated has been removed, and until re-assessment takes place local authorities are bound to pay £1,000,000 into the Fund from which pensions are paid.

The scale of Unemployment Allowances is laid down in the Regulations issued by the Assistance Board. The cost to public funds depends on the sex and family position of the applicant. Unemployment Allowances are concerned primarily with those who have been unemployed over a long period, and it is likely, therefore, that a large proportion of those assisted will be older men, i.e. they are probably married men whose children are no longer dependent. A sample enquiry in 1938 bears this out. Of the Board's applicants

54·3%	had	0	dependent	children.
15·1%	"	1	"	child.
11·6%	"	2	"	children.
8·0%	"	3	"	"
5·0%	"	4	"	"
2·9%	"	5	"	"
2·1%	"	more than 5		"

The cost varies also according to the amount of resources of the applicant and, until 1941, according to the resources of other members of the household. The Annual Report of 1939 shows that less than one-third of applicants had resources (either their own or their household's) which were sufficient to be taken into account. The exact proportion varies from year to year but has generally been of this nature. Since the passing of the Determination of Needs Act, 1941, this proportion is likely to be smaller. In the last year before the war the total cost of Unemployment Allowances was £34,740,000, which represents an average weekly allowance of 24/4.

Old Age Pensions

The cost of Public Assistance and Unemployment Allowances varies, apart from administrative changes, with the social and economic situation, and mirrors fairly faithfully the ups and downs in industrial and commercial activity. The future burden can be guessed at, but it cannot be foretold with any accuracy. On the other hand, the cost of Old Age Pensions depends on a quite different factor and can be estimated with a high degree of precision, because it depends mainly on the age composition of the population. The persons who qualify are (1) those who have been insured under the Contributory Pensions scheme and who at the age of 70 have already been drawing Contributory Old Age Pensions; and (2) those who have not been included in the National Health Insurance scheme and who, at the age of 70, have less than a certain prescribed income from their resources. The first group is capable of almost exact calculation. Knowing the death-rates at different ages, one can determine just how many persons who are drawing Contributory Pensions will reach the qualifying age at any date in the future, and, unless there is any extraordinary occurrence which violently and profoundly alters those death-rates, the estimate is very likely to be correct. With the second group there is a little more speculation involved. Changes in economic circumstances may affect the savings of the people in those sections of the population that normally apply for Old Age Pensions. But even here the changes are unlikely to be catastrophic and an estimate can be made within fairly narrow margins of error.

As a result of the general trends of birth- and death-rates, the age composition of the population has changed considerably during the time that Old Age Pensions have been in force. Birth-rates have been going down since 1876, and the birth-rate in the last year before the war was much less than half what it was in 1875. At the same time the expectation of life has increased as a corollary of higher standards of living, increased medical knowledge and care and the great development in public health, and more men and women now reach the age of 70 and over. The combined result of these two factors is that the proportion of the community that is old is now much larger than it used to be and is still growing. The cost of Old Age Pensions has therefore gone up, and will continue to go up, simply because of the larger number of persons in the qualifying age groups, and, quite irrespective of any further changes in the conditions or size of the pension, this tendency will continue for some time—how long depends, of course, on the birth- and death-rates of the future. When lowering the age of entry into the qualifying group of Old Age Pensions is under discussion, this fact must be borne in mind. On a conservative estimate, the proportion of the community that is 60 or over will be over 23% in 50 years' time as against less than 14% at the present. With this changing age composition in mind, it is no matter for surprise that the cost of Old Age Pensions has gone up so much during the last few decades. In the ten years from 1927 (when insured persons qualified automatically for State Pensions at the age of 70) the cost of Non-Contributory Pensions went up from £29,984,000 to £43,117,000.

In what has so far been said, Old Age Pensions have been classed with Unemployment Allowances and Public Assistance as types of social provision the money for which is derived solely from public funds. In so far as the Old Age Pensions that are paid to persons over 70 as a result of a means test, that classification is correct. But in so far as it refers to the pensions paid to people over 70 by virtue of their having drawn Contributory Old Age Pensions between 65 and 70, such a statement requires considerable modification. The position is by no means simple, because, although the money for paying such pensions does at present come principally from taxation, the scheme was planned on an actuarial foundation, and as time goes on, provided there are no further legislative changes, it will come to fit more and more closely into an insurance framework. The very fact that there are fewer incalculable factors to be taken into account than in other of the social insurance schemes has, indeed, made it possible for the Old Age Pensions to be designed more definitely as an actuarial system. At the same time, the scheme, as it exists at present, contains several features which have social rather than actuarial justification, or which have been admitted because they correspond with the general idea of what is fair.

Contributory Old Age Pensions, Non-Contributory Old Age Pensions by virtue of having been an insured pensioner, Widows' and Orphans' Pensions, were introduced as an omnibus measure in 1925. Several problems of a social rather than an actuarial character had to be tackled.

(1) The wage-earning population concerned in the new measure was of all ages in 1925—some just entering insurable employment, others on the point of retiring. Insurance for such an eventuality as old age is usually entered into early in life so that premiums and the interest earned on them can be built into a fund adequate to meet the claims. But in this instance the need for some provision for the elderly was considered to be of such social importance that it was out of the question to exclude from benefit those who were already approaching old age, even though there had been no opportunity to accumulate funds in respect of them in the past. The premiums were calculated on the basis that a contributor entered insurance at the age of 16 and remained in it until he reached the age of 65. In fact, however, only a negligible proportion of those at present in the system fulfil this condition. Nobody who was older than 16 in 1925 could possibly do so, and there is, consequently, a deficit in respect of the vast majority, which has to be made up by an Exchequer contribution.

(2) The majority of women marry, and when they marry, or shortly after, they cease to be employed in insurable occupations. This means that most women are compelled during the early part of their lives to pay contributions towards something from which they can never hope to benefit. On the other hand, wives of insured men, widows and orphans can draw pensions towards the cost of which they have made no contribution at all. The contribution of women workers is, in fact, a social compromise. The intention is to make provision for those women who *do* remain in the industrial world, and at the same time the premiums of those who retire from wage-earning before they qualify for pension are justified on the ground that it is these same contributors who become pensionable widows and wives of insured men. It cannot be pretended that any accurate actuarial calculation can be made of these relationships. Yet the present scheme does represent a reasonably just financial arrangement for attaining what it is in the social interest to achieve, i.e. that every woman who does remain in industry shall be provided for, and that those sections of the community that experience shows to be least capable of providing their own living, widows, orphans and elderly couples, shall have a statutory right to a minimum maintenance without recourse to Public Assistance.

(3) This line of reasoning, whilst it might justify the payment of pensions to widows and orphans out of a fund to which they had made no specific contribution, could not be equally well applied to provision out of the fund of pensions to those women who had been widowed before the passing of the Act, and in respect of whom, therefore, no contributions could possibly have been made, either by themselves during their youth as wage-earners or by their husbands. Yet to leave this group to Public Assistance, particularly when there were young children to be cared for, was felt to be lacking in humanity, and any such woman was allowed to claim a pension. After 1929 this group was enlarged to include widows without children when they reached the age of 55. Though such women derive their pensions through the machinery of the Pensions Act, the money is provided, in fact, from public funds.

So far, what has been said applies to the Contributory Pensions, whether they are truly contributory or only apparently so. But it is impossible to draw a hard-and-fast line between these and the Non-Contributory Pensions, which, in appearance at least, are entirely a charge on the Exchequer. When Contributory Pensions were first introduced in 1925 the scheme had two very real advantages. It reduced the age at which a pension could be obtained (a great asset in a world in which the strain of industrial work makes it difficult for a man to keep his employment after 65), and it did away with the much-disliked means test. In view of the changing age composition of the community, a measure which provided a pension as a right to all those over 70 years of age could result in a serious budgetary problem in the future, and it was felt that early provision ought to be made to raise the necessary funds. For this reason the original scheme provided for decennial increases in the contributions paid by the insured and their employers. The first decennial increase duly took place in 1936 and, unless future legislation intervenes, similar increases will be made in 1946 and 1956. Assuming that these increases take place as planned, it is calculated that the contributions paid in respect of a person entering insurance at the age of 16 after 1956 will be adequate to pay the whole of his Old Age Pension both between 65 and 70 and after 70. Meanwhile, however, the whole of the deficit is paid by the Exchequer.

It seems from this that a time will eventually arrive when the whole of the pensions being paid will come from contributions and no further charge is borne by the Treasury. Such a time, however, will never come. This is because the money paid in contributions is not accumulated in a separate fund, but the contributions of those who are paying in now are used to meet the claims for pensions made at the present moment by widows, orphans and the elderly. Thus not only must the Exchequer bridge the gap between present contributions and the pensions claimable in respect of them, but it will, in perpetuity, have to make a grant in respect of the interest that would have been accumulated on the premiums paid in by those who will have been paying contributions over a long period of time before qualifying to make a claim against those payments.

The actual machinery of the Exchequer grants is as follows:

(1) An annual grant is made to the Treasury Pensions Account out of which pensions up to 70 are paid. This sum is designed

to meet the deficiency due to the admission of persons above 16 and whose contributions had consequently not been paid over a sufficiently long period to provide for the benefit to which, nevertheless, they had been given a statutory right. It also makes good the interest that would have accrued on previously paid premiums if they had been allowed to accumulate at interest instead of being used for current payments. This grant was fixed by the Act at £4 millions, and increased to £9 millions for 1930-31, with provision for an annual increase of £1 million to a maximum of £21 millions in 1942-43 and thereafter as Parliament shall determine.

(2) Annual appropriations are made in respect of "over 70" pensions and depend on the growing number of old people who qualify either because they have been in receipt of a Contributory Pension or because of lack of means.

The administrative costs of the social services are rather difficult to compute. There are, of course, exact figures of the cost of the statutory machinery, but these do not take into account the work done by the employer in stamping the cards for all his employees and in calculating the appropriate deductions to be made from their wages. A small employer, with only a few workers, probably does this work himself and does not trouble to assess its value, but a large firm must employ a quite considerable clerical staff solely for this purpose. Again, the scheme of contributory compulsory pensions for widows, orphans and the aged is interlocked with that of Health Insurance, and it is not possible to say how much of the administrative charges is due to one and how much to the other. If, as is usual, the main cost is attributed to Health Insurance, it means that the pensions scheme gets its premiums collected for nothing.

In the latest year[1] for which complete returns have been published—1937—the total administrative cost of the Unemployment Insurance and Assistance schemes was just over £8,000,000 for an expenditure of over £73,000,000, i.e. slightly under 11%. For Health Insurance it was over £5,000,000 for a total expenditure of £35,500,000, i.e. over 14%. It would be wrong to draw from this the conclusion that Health Insurance

[1] Cmd. 5906 of 1938, pp. 6-7. Figures for 1938 and 1939 were given in the House of Commons on 5th February 1941, by Captain Crookshank, in answer to a question by Mr. R. Morgan, but they were not analysed to indicate the amount spent in administration (H. C. Debates, vol. 368, pp. 956-60).

is necessarily less efficiently and economically administered than the Unemployment schemes, because both contributions and benefits have remained on a lower level in the health scheme, and it is obvious that it costs no more administratively to pay out high benefit than low. If the Health Insurance benefit were the same as the Unemployment, a good deal of the difference in the percentage cost of administration would disappear. At the same time, the system of administration through approved societies in the case of Health Insurance undoubtedly leads to some increase in costs, since the overhead expenses of the smaller societies are proportionately much higher than those of the larger ones.

It is tempting to compare these costs with those of the commercial insurance companies, but this is hardly fair, as a great deal of the expense of the latter is incurred in persuading people to take out insurance policies and to continue to pay the premiums punctually. Compulsory social insurance is able to dispense with all such expenditure, and is obviously able, therefore, to use a much larger proportion of the money received in premiums in the payment of benefits.

Chapter X

SUPERANNUATION

By EMMELINE W. COHEN

OLD age is one of the most constant sources of economic insecurity and involves a combination of risks. To feel secure, a person needs to know that provision is made so that he will not be destitute in old age, and also that when he retires he will enjoy a standard of living related to that which he enjoyed when working. This is the simplest of his needs and is met by all superannuation schemes. Superannuation may be described as a retiring pension related by a defined scale to the recipient's length of service and rate of salary. Unlike other forms of pension, superannuation necessitates the keeping of individual records of all those covered.

The risks of old age involve a good deal more than the possibility of surviving the normal span of working life. There is the risk of dying just before retiring age and leaving a dependent spouse, child or parent. There is the risk of dying just after receiving a pension and leaving dependants unprovided for. There is the risk of breaking down in health and being forced to retire after long service but before reaching the normal pension age. The most comprehensive and satisfactory superannuation schemes make provision for all these risks, and thereby offer a substantial degree of security to those covered.

Superannuation schemes allow those undertakings which adopt them to enforce a retiring age for their employees without inflicting injustice on those who have grown old in their employ. They encourage continuity of service, and at the same time discourage dishonesty and unapproved forms of conduct. They also reduce the need for individual saving.

Satisfactory pension schemes were made possible by the growth of actuarial knowledge in the late eighteenth and early nineteenth centuries. From 1780, Royal Commissions advocated the payment of superannuation allowances to permanent civil servants on their retirement. An Act of 1810 put these recommendations into operation. In the course of the century railway companies, banks, insurance companies and similar undertakings introduced schemes to cover their salaried staffs. Elementary school teachers were covered, and so too were the employees of some local authorities. In 1905 the National Association of Local Government Officers opened a campaign, which only came to a successful conclusion in 1937, to secure compulsory superannuation for all officers and permanent servants of local authorities. Until the outbreak of the war the number of undertakings which had adopted schemes was continuously increasing. Two factors contributed to this increase. There was a growing recognition of the importance of offering this kind of security, particularly where life service was desired, and consequently there was a tendency amongst public utilities such as railways and building societies to offer "Civil Service conditions." On the other hand, the facilities offered by insurance companies have made it comparatively easy for firms to institute superannuation schemes for their salaried workers. These schemes are administered by the companies.

It is difficult to estimate with any degree of accuracy how many people are covered by superannuation schemes of one sort or another at the present time. A survey was published by the Ministry of Labour Gazette for 1938. This showed that in 1936 there were some 6,544 schemes in operation, covering 1,617,000 employees—803,000 administrative and salaried workers, clerical and sales assistants, and 814,000 wage-earners. The figures are not complete. They do not include local government employees, teachers or civil servants. In 1938 there were 370,000 permanent civil servants and about 145,800 teachers. In addition there were approximately 300,000 local government officers covered by the relevant superannuation Acts. Thus there were roughly 2,432,800 persons covered by superannuation schemes of one kind or another. Significant as are these figures, they represent but a small proportion of the total working population of the country. For the vast majority there is no superannuation. The only security for old age is that provided by Old Age and Contributory Pensions schemes, and the provision individuals make for themselves through insurance.

The most fundamental distinction between superannuation schemes is based in the methods by which they are financed, between contributory and non-contributory schemes. The funds for contributory schemes are jointly subscribed by employers and employed. The funds for non-contributory schemes are provided by employing bodies only. Clearly both types of scheme are designed to cover the same risks. The conditions they impose differ.

The most important non-contributory superannuation is that which covers all permanent civil servants. Although all permanent civil servants are covered by the provisions of the relevant Acts, no civil servant has an absolute right to a pension. The Treasury and the heads or principal officers of a Department have authority to dismiss any person from the public service without pension or compensation. Pensions are calculated on the basis of an eightieth of the annual salary enjoyed in the last three years' service, multiplied by the total number of years of service, with a maximum of forty-eightieths of the last three years' annual salary.[1] In addition officers receive a lump sum according to service up to a maximum equal to one and a half times the annual salary. Subject to certain conditions, such as proof of good health, those entitled to superannuation may allocate a part of their pension to a dependant by surrendering not more than one-third of the annual sum to which they would have been entitled. The conditions of allocation allow alternative options.

The Treasury has power to grant a gratuity to the legal representatives of a male officer who dies after five years' service or upwards, and also to the legal representative of an officer who dies so soon after retiring that he has received in superannuation less than the amount of his annual salary. There are also regulations under which officers receive pensions who retire before attaining the normal retiring age on account of ill health.

Thus the chief risks of age and infirmity appear to be well covered, and a civil servant who has established his claim to a pension seems adequately provided for. It must be remembered that those who enter the service have to pass a medical test.

The scale of salaries offered to civil servants is drawn up on the presumption that service will lead to superannuation. This assumption holds for a majority of men; but until recently the "marriage bar" enforced retirement for women on marriage in

[1] The basis of calculation for those who entered the Service before the passing of the Act of 1909 is somewhat different. The Superannuation Act, 1946, Section 2 makes provision for a higher rate of superannuation for late entrants to the service.

all but exceptional cases. It is too early as yet to say whether, now that the bar has been abrogated, a substantial proportion of women civil servants will in fact continue in the service to the normal retiring age and so qualify for superannuation. Those who resign on marriage after not less than six years' service are still entitled to a marriage gratuity (at the rate of one month's pay for each year of established service up to a maximum of twelve).

This is the only exception to the rule that those who resign the service before reaching pensionable age receive neither pension nor gratuity nor any other form of compensation for loss of pension "rights." This follows consistently from the non-contributory basis of the scheme, which was devised to encourage continuity of service, and to discourage experienced civil servants from leaving. Those dismissed for misconduct or breach of the undefined but none the less real Civil Service code receive no pension or compensation. The decision of the head of the Department is final, and there is no appeal. The term misconduct has no precise definition. The system sounds arbitrary. It must be remembered, however, that the political heads of the Departments may be questioned in the House of Commons.

As will be seen, the standard of pension compares favourably with other schemes. The disciplinary element in the conditions of qualification is intentional, and is in part the outcome of historical circumstance which it would not be relevant to discuss here.

Where non-contributory superannuation schemes operate, pensions are always granted at the discretion of the granting body; there is no right to a pension. Inevitably this may give rise to an element of arbitrariness in the conditions required for qualification. Thus a large and well-known insurance company which has a non-contributory scheme for its employees stipulates in its published prospectus that the Directors retain the right to stop the benefits of a pensioner who shall after retiring and without their consent engage in any business or concern which they deem to be adverse to the company's interest. Decision rests with the Directors of the company, and there is no machinery for arbitration or appeal.

A majority of superannuation schemes at present in operation are contributory; that is to say, the pensions are paid from funds subscribed jointly by employers and employed. The details of individual schemes differ considerably both as to rates of contribution, options, scope and methods of administration. There are some few large schemes, covering a considerable number of persons. Some have to be devised for those who normally enter the occupation early in their working life and remain within the same scheme normally until retirement. Others have to meet conditions where recruitment is at different ages. Some schemes meet the needs of a small number of persons, sometimes the employees of a single firm. There are contributory schemes controlled by statute, there are schemes administered by trusts, by committees, by insurance companies on behalf of firms and companies. Of the large statutory contributory schemes, the most important are those covering teachers and local government officers.

Before considering the kinds of benefit offered by different types of scheme it is well to discuss some general points. Where funds are provided on a contributory basis, contributors may reasonably consider that they have a right to that part of the funds which are derived from their salaries, and this whether they qualify for pension or leave without so qualifying. Consequently, equitable conditions of withdrawal should be an essential feature in all schemes. It is important also that funds shall be adequately safeguarded, and that administrative costs shall be kept as low as possible. With regard to withdrawal, it is important that the question of accrued interest on contributions shall be given proper consideration, and also that wherever possible it shall be made easy for persons to transfer from one contributory scheme to another. A satisfactory machinery for settling disputed claims should be a feature of all schemes.

To form an idea of the kind of security offered by contributory schemes, it will be sufficient to examine the main features of teachers' superannuation, the superannuation scheme for local government officers, and some of the larger and some of the small private schemes.

Acts of 1898, 1925 and 1937 regulate teachers' superannuation. Teachers contribute 5% of their salary, and employing bodies a matching sum. The allowance is one-eightieth of the teachers' salary during the last five years' service, multiplied by the total number of years of service, and with a maximum of forty-eightieths. Those with thirty or more years' service to their credit receive also a lump sum when they retire. By the provisions of the Act of 1937 a teacher entitled to superannuation on account of age and who is in good health may allocate up to a third of the annual allowance for the benefit of a spouse or dependant. There is a death gratuity for those dying in the service or just after retirement. There are special provisions to allow those who temporarily discontinue contributory service, and who during that period are engaged in certain approved kinds of service, to pay 10% of their salary to the fund and receive ultimate pension benefits as though no absence had taken place. This provision allows teachers to serve in the Dominions or abroad in approved circumstances. There is a short-service gratuity for those who break down in health. Those who leave the service without qualifying for pension have their contributions refunded with 3% compound interest. Teachers dismissed for misconduct are entitled to the return of their contributions. Where there are disputes over the qualification for superannuation or amounts payable or returnable, the final decision rests with the Board of Education.

The superannuation scheme for local government officers is somewhat similar to that for teachers, although the details differ. This is necessarily so, for the scheme covers a far less homogeneous group.

Before the passing of the Act of 1937 a number of authorities had schemes for their employees. The existing Act covers all authorities. Consequently there is nothing to discourage an officer from moving from a less responsible post under one authority to a more responsible one under another, for he takes his pension rights with him. Thus a valuable element of mobility has been introduced. There have had to be elaborate arrangements to cover late entrants and those transferred from previous schemes. But for our purpose the important question to consider is the conditions for new entrants to the local government service.

Both officers and servants of local authorities are covered. They pay 6% and 5% of their earnings respectively, and the authorities pay matching sums. Superannuation is based on one-sixtieth of the average remuneration for every completed year of contributory service, and the maximum pension payable is two-thirds of the average remuneration. The average remuneration is calculated on the earnings of the five years immediately preceding retirement. The Minister is empowered to make rules to enable contributory employees entitled to superannuation to allocate up to one-third of the allowance to provide a pension for a surviving spouse. Contributions with compound interest at 3% are returnable to those retiring for reasons other than voluntary resignation, dismissal for inefficiency or misconduct, and also to the representatives of employees dying in the service before becoming superannuable. Where an employee dies after becoming superannuable but before he has received an amount equal to his contributions and 3% compound interest upon them, the difference is paid to his legal representatives. Contributions are returnable without interest to employees who resign voluntarily or are dismissed for inefficiency or misconduct. Disputed claims are settled in the first instance by the local authority, but appeal may be made to the Minister of Health, whose decision is final.

These two contributory schemes have been described in some detail because they afford an interesting standard. Both schemes cover large numbers of individuals. The teachers' scheme covers a small range of occupation, but a great number of schools and educational bodies. A teacher, therefore, who does not change his profession has the opportunity of considerable changes of employer and varied experience without his benefits diminishing in value. Within the profession a satisfactory degree of mobility is provided for. The particular interest of the local government scheme is that it is designed to cover very varied forms of activity, and includes wage-earners as well as salaried officers. The machinery for settling disputes has the satisfactory feature that final decisions do not lie in the hands of the body which contributes to the pension and is therefore a financially interested party.

Turning to other schemes, it is necessary to draw attention to figures which have already been quoted. There are some 6,544 schemes in existence, covering approximately 1,617,000 persons. Clearly, a majority of these schemes are small schemes, covering small numbers of persons. When superannuation is considered, as we are now considering it, from the point of view of how far it provides security in old age, it is clear that the question of the size of the group is important. However satisfactory the conditions for refunding contributions with a satisfactory rate of interest, it is clear that withdrawal before the contributor reaches retiring age fails to produce the security the schemes should be designed to provide. For where there are withdrawals there is no provision that the sums withdrawn will not be used for current purposes. It is therefore important that where small schemes operate there should be means of effecting transfer from one scheme to another. Unfortunately there are not figures available to illustrate the usual rate of withdrawal of members from schemes prior to qualifying for pension. From the security point of view, the small scheme is only satisfactory for those workers who remain within it for the whole of their working life. It has to be remembered that any transfer which does not entail transferring employers' as well as workers' contributions leads to devaluation of the ultimate pensions received.

A large number of individual employers and group schemes are operated through insurance companies. The estimated figure for 1936 was 3,861. On the other hand, over four-fifths of the employees covered by superannuation schemes were at that date covered by schemes operated internally by the firms and groups concerned.

Insurance companies adapt their schemes to the needs of the firms for whom they operate schemes. Typical schemes provide a retirement pension at 65 based on the number of years' service in the different salary grades, and a benefit to the legal representatives of the contributor if he dies before reaching pensionable age. Arrangements for those withdrawing from the scheme voluntarily provide for the return of contributions.

Conditions and benefits vary considerably. For salaried staff, contributions range from 2 to 5½% of the salary, for male wage-earners from 1/- to 2/- a week, for women wage-earners from 6d. to 1/6 a week. There are a large variety of ways of calculating benefit. It is usually based on multiplying a given fraction of the average salary by the number of years' service.

Most schemes offer certain options as regards age of retirement and the form of the pension.

Clearly the scope of benefits that can be offered depend to a certain extent on the size of the scheme. As has already been pointed out, small independent schemes involve certain unavoidable difficulties, and chief amongst them their inability to provide means of mobility without contributors having to withdraw from the scheme or sacrifice the ultimate value of the pension. There is always the question of making special arrangements for late entrants, where contributors are likely to be taken on at a mature age. These difficulties are more acute where wage-earners are concerned than where clerks and other salaried officers are concerned, because their degree of mobility is usually higher.

One of the most interesting schemes at present in operation is the Federated Superannuation Scheme for Nurses and Hospital Officers, which makes arrangements so that a member who migrates to an institution which does not participate in the scheme may temporarily suspend payment or else pay a stipulated proportion of her remuneration to the fund, and in either case retain full membership. The scheme is also interesting in that it makes provision for arbitration in cases of dispute by a single arbiter nominated by the President of the Law Society. This recognition of the importance of impartial settlement of disputes is rare. It is usual in private schemes for decision to rest without appeal with the firm or trust which grants the pension.

In conclusion, it is necessary to consider the question of superannuation from a general point of view. The position is best assessed by consideration of the table on p. 259, which was published in the Ministry of Labour Gazette for May 1938 and described the position as it was in 1936.

The striking facts in this table are the large number of individual industries or services which operate schemes and the small number of manual workers covered. It is clear that the problem of providing security in old age for skilled manual workers has hardly been tackled. Nor does it seem probable that it will whilst the present popularity of small individual schemes persist.

The importance of security in old age has been recognised up to a point. The necessity for co-ordinating existing schemes and for working out a comprehensive plan which will cover all salaried and manual workers has not been recognised. Admittedly the task is prodigious. Individual records must be kept. American experience shows that such a task is not beyond the bounds of human and actuarial ingenuity. In that country,

Old Age and Survivors Insurance, which is their equivalent to our Contributory Pensions scheme, is based on individual wage records for each insured worker. The records are kept by the Social Security Board. Perhaps a study of American methods might suggest a solution to our own problem.

PRIVATE SUPERANNUATION SCHEMES 1936[1]

	Schemes operated by the Individual Firms or Undertakings (either directly or through Insurance Companies).	Group Schemes, each covering a Number of Firms or Undertakings.	Total.
Number of firms, undertakings, etc., with pension schemes at the end of 1936	2,580	4,144	6,544
Administrative, clerical, sales, etc., staffs:			
Males	597,099	40,335	637,434
Females	145,632	19,569	165,201
Total	742,731	59,904	802,635
Manual wage-earners:			
Males	633,142	11,449	644,591
Females	169,102	765	169,867
Total	802,244	12,214	814,458
All employees:			
Males	1,230,241	51,784	1,282,025
Females	314,734	20,334	335,068
Total—all employees	1,544,975	72,118	1,617,093

It is clear that superannuation should be greatly extended. It is not clear what form this extension should take. The arrangements of the local government superannuation scheme show that there are advantages in a scheme which covers large numbers, and that varied types of employees can be covered

[1] *Ministry of Labour Gazette*, vol. xlvi, No. 5 (May 1938), p. 172.

by one scheme. It seems probable that what is needed is a number of comprehensive schemes for various groups of employment or kinds of occupation. Certainly alternatives should be worked out in detail before further multiplication of the present types makes the task of co-ordination still more complex. Co-ordinated superannuation schemes, covering wide ranges of workers, should certainly figure in any social security plans. And when these schemes come to be drawn up, there is much useful experience which can be utilised. Some of the larger existing schemes offer excellent ranges of benefits and options. Some few have a satisfactory and just method of settling disputed claims. All these features need careful consideration, and new comprehensive superannuation schemes must be based on careful analysis of the social as well as the actuarial value of proposals.

Chapter XI

INDUSTRIAL LIFE ASSURANCE

By LOUIS GINSBURG

INDUSTRIAL Assurance has been defined by the Industrial Assurance Act of 1923. It is described as the business of effecting assurance on human lives, premiums in respect of which are payable at intervals of less than two months and are received by means of collectors. The principle of personal collection at the home of the assured distinguishes this from other life assurances. The system embraces the millions of policies for small amounts, seldom providing more than £30 each, effected by the wage-earning classes. The premiums are paid weekly, sometimes as little as 1d. only, infrequently more than 1/- on a single policy, to a collector who calls regularly for that purpose. In addition to policies on one's own life and on the life of one's wife, it is expressly permitted by statute to effect policies on the lives of one's children, parents, grandparents, brothers and sisters without reference to the question of insurable interest. An insurable interest is an "interest of a pecuniary nature . . . which would be prejudicially affected by the occurrence of the event insured against." Such an interest would have to exist before an ordinary insurance policy could be effected on the lives above. Ostensibly policies are intended to meet the cost of "reasonable" funeral expenses which one might expect to incur on the death of a relative within the permitted range.

The business of industrial assurance is now so widespread as to be almost universal. In 1938 no fewer than 11 million new policies were taken up, and at the end of the year there were over 100 million policies in all in existence. One hundred and sixty-four assurance undertakings are registered for the purpose of carrying on this business in the British Isles, and in 1938 they collected premiums worth £72 millions. This represented on the average about 2/9 per week from each of the 10 million families in which the total income from all sources did not exceed £5 per week, and from whom almost the whole of the industrial assurance premiums was derived. These include some in dire poverty and others in comparative comfort.

Origin of Insurance

Insurance is a contractual obligation to provide stated benefits on the occurrence of a given contingency. It is not charity, for charity depends on goodwill and does not involve a binding contract. The earliest insurance arrangements were co-operative, they were made for mutual protection between persons or parties subject to the same risks. The loss of a craftsman's tools by fire or theft was made good by his guild. The shipowner arranged with his competitors that tonnage lost at sea should be replaced out of common resources. Individuals meeting regularly for any purpose, business or pleasure, sooner or later arranged to provide each other with "decent" burial. And so on.

These arrangements were made for mutual protection. It was not until much later, about the end of the eighteenth century, that a new figure, the "underwriter," appeared. The nature of many hazards had become more clearly understood. Experience and statistics had accumulated from which reliable averages could be computed. Using this newly available information, the underwriter calculated the "premium" in exchange for which he was prepared to accept the liability for the risk. He naturally added a percentage to the calculated premium to allow himself a margin of profit. By carefully selecting his risks to exclude those which seemed unduly hazardous, and by closely studying the nature and statistics of the risks which he was prepared to assume, the underwriter was often in a position to charge smaller premiums than those charged their members by the mutual associations. He wanted insurance business because, if carefully managed, it was profitable, and went out of his way to find it. Gradually the older mutual insurance associations were left behind. In some fields they dropped out altogether; in others, burial insurance for instance, they adopted the methods of the underwriters and in due course prospered too.

The Development of Industrial Life Assurance

Against the contingencies of sickness, old age and death, insurance was an easily recognisable feature of the guild system. The guilds broke up in the seventeenth century, but their insurance activities were ultimately restored by the formation of small "friendly societies" in nearly every town and village. By the end of the eighteenth century they were numbered in tens of thousands. They insured their members for sickness, old age and burial benefits on a mutual basis just as the guilds had done. The old age benefit was soon dropped on the grounds of expense which only few members could afford.

The Industrial Revolution brought about a large-scale redistribution of the population, and to cope with the changing circumstances many of these small local friendly societies voluntarily amalgamated to form "affiliated orders." Some of these orders attained considerable size, constituent societies numbering hundreds and total membership many thousands. Because of their size they could afford to employ full-time salaried officials, and they did tend on the whole to have more careful and efficient managements than the small independent societies amongst whom insolvency and defalcation had been only too common. The largest of the affiliated orders, the Manchester Unity of Oddfellows, still flourishes and continues to provide sickness and burial insurance facilities for a large number of people.

The orders have retained many of their original features. They were formed by the voluntary amalgamations of small friendly societies. These societies, now called "branches" or "lodges" or "tents," have preserved their identity. They play an important part in the administration of the order, have some degree of autonomy and in certain restricted circumstances have even the right to secede. The order is controlled by the members through lodge delegates who attend the annual Grand Order meeting and elect an Executive Committee to govern the affairs of the concern for the following year. A bond of friendship and brotherhood is maintained between the members, and the lodges arrange social functions at which the members gather from time to time. Application for membership of a lodge is not merely a question of undertaking to pay insurance premiums. A prospective member has to be proposed and seconded by persons who are already members. Certain conditions have to be satisfied, character has to be vouched for, and there seems to be a general insistence that those who wish to join the lodge for financial gain alone had better take their insurance business elsewhere.

During the early part of the nineteenth century there was a firm public demand for sickness and burial assurances. To cater for those whom the affiliated orders were not interested in absorbing for reason of occupation, location or other conditions, friendly societies were formed which operated on a wholly centralised plan. They had neither branches nor lodges, and some of them employed full-time canvassers to procure new members. The members sent their contributions by post direct to the office of the concern. These friendly societies provided mutual insurance arrangements for sickness and burial benefits in the same sense as the affiliated orders did, but members were attracted on a purely financial basis, there were no social connections between one member and another as such. Control was vested in the membership as a whole through an Executive Committee elected by the members at an annual general meeting.

Sickness benefits are notoriously difficult to manage. Unless careful supervision is exercised, members are apt to "stay on the funds" long after they are really fit for work. Malingering may become so acute that the financial stability of the whole concern falls into jeopardy. In the early days, too, the statistical basis of the premiums was most uncertain, charges on the whole being too low. The centralised friendly societies, in which the members are animated more by monetary instinct than by considerations of brotherhood and in which there is no personal contact between members as in the affiliated orders, found payment of sickness claims an increasing strain on their resources. Various steps were taken to cope with this difficult position. As a result, some societies continued to prosper and still survive, but many decided in the 1840's to discourage or even terminate the sickness insurance and provide burial benefits alone. Here then, about the middle of the nineteenth century, organisations came into being whose sole or principal purpose was to provide burial insurance facilities on a mutual basis. In effect, this was the beginning of Industrial Life Assurance; and to distinguish their special purpose the friendly societies which chose to concentrate their activities on burial assurance later became known as "collecting societies." The other friendly societies and the affiliated orders fall outside the scope of Industrial Assurance proper. The provision of a death benefit is for the most part incidental to their main purpose, namely, sickness insurance. Their activities do not now resemble those of the collecting societies.

Through the progress of actuarial science insurance contingent on death had by the middle of the nineteenth century become a feasible and sound proposition. Statistics became available on which reliable mortality tables were constructed, so calculations of adequate premiums afforded little difficulty. Malingering proved a grave problem in the sickness insurance world, but it is no easy matter to simulate death in order to raise a few pounds on the burial money. The collecting societies were soon in a flourishing condition, and to many seeking fields for profitable investment the business showed distinct possibilities. Capital was put up, shares issued and companies formed in numbers for the sole purpose of providing burial assurance facilities for the "industrious" classes. These concerns became known as "industrial assurance companies." They are owned, controlled and operate for the profit of their shareholders in just the same way as any other commercial undertaking. Those who effect insurance with them, the "policyholders," have no say whatever in their management, as have the members in the management of a collecting society. The companies adopted vigorous selling methods, introduced house-to-house collection of premiums, and in due course outstripped the collecting societies in size and importance. Impressed perhaps with this "success," the Executive Committees of some collecting societies, committees which customarily are re-elected intact from year to year, arranged on behalf of the members as a whole to convert the mutual society into an insurance company. Shares were issued to the members in exchange for membership rights, but the advantages accruing to the body of members are not immediately obvious. On the contrary, the majority seem to have got a very poor bargain indeed. The story of one such conversion is given in detail in the Cohen Report,[1] from which the following facts are taken.

[1] Committee on Industrial Assurance under chairmanship of Sir Benjamin Cohen, K.C., appointed by the Chancellor of the Exchequer in April 1931, report published July 1933.

In the year 1913 the Blackburn Philanthropic Friendly Society converted itself into a company owned by shareholders. The shares were allocated to the 373,262 members on the books at 31st December 1912, in proportion to the contributions paid to the society. Since the sum which the society could assure on any one life was limited by statute to only £300, as between one member and another a relatively even distribution of shares must have taken place. No dividends were paid for many years, during which period a considerable change took place in the ownership of the shares. In 1932, 9 Directors and the Secretary held between them no less than 86,713 out of a total of nearly 800,000 shares, and 59 other officials of the company held another 58,659 shares. Of the balance, 446,723 shares were owned by 639 persons. Thus, while on conversion there were 373,262 shareholders, by 1932 75% of the shares were in the hands of only 708 persons, i.e. in the hands of only one-fifth of 1% of the former body of members. "How far this change of ownership took place before dividends were paid, and at what prices the changes were effected, are matters on which we have no information but on which certain inferences may reasonably be drawn. The company now pays a dividend of 3¼% free of tax on the authorised capital. This is on the face of it a modest rate, but when it is realised that no cash was subscribed and no liability imposed on the shareholders . . . it is easy to see that an apparently modest dividend may be a serious burden on the policyholders" (Cohen Report). Since the policyholders had at one time enjoyed full controlling rights as members of the erstwhile society, rights which they had parted with on letting the shares slip through their fingers, it could hardly have been for their benefit that the Executive Committee arranged the conversion.

By 1853 industrial assurance on a profit-making basis had come to stay. Ninety-six companies had been registered, but by amalgamation and occasional failure these were reduced by 1938 to 15 in number. During the year 1938 these 15 companies collected £58 millions in premiums, and at the end of that year no fewer than 76 million policies were on their books. Through rapid expansion of the business and because of the increasing longevity of the population, the profits realised by these companies soared beyond all the dreams of those who put up their original capital. As long ago as 1915 Mr. Sidney Webb[1] estimated that the cash capital of the largest of these companies amounted to only £5,839. On this sum an annual dividend of £600,000 was being paid to the fortunate shareholders. The aggregate of shares representing this cash investment of £5,839 was in 1915 worth about 10 millions sterling! Mr. Webb hastened to add that the magnitude of the profit was no indication that the policyholders were being badly treated. Generally speaking, the capital of an industrial assurance company which has actually been put up in cash represents only an insignificant fragment of the funds which have accumulated from the pennies paid each week by millions of policyholders. It is these funds which secure the ultimate payment of the burial moneys, the shareholders' capital is now of no real value to the policyholders. Correspondingly, payment of even the munificent profits which the shareholders have enjoyed has not in general imposed an intolerable burden on the assuring public. In 1938 some £2 millions was absorbed in dividends to shareholders compared with £58 millions collected in premiums. The profits have been none the less remarkable, the prosperity of the companies free for all to admire in the magnificence of the office buildings they have chosen to inhabit. In recent years most companies have given their policyholders a share in the annual profits in the form of a free addition to the sum assured. On the average, about two-thirds of the whole profits available are now being allocated to the policyholders in this way. The companies deserve a great deal of credit for voluntarily giving their clients these extra benefits without charge. The cynic might wonder whether, in view of the handsome profits they were making, public opinion in the long run would not have achieved a similar result!

The companies now transact all kinds of insurance business, fire, accident, theft and so on, but they are required by statute to maintain separate accounts and funds in respect of their industrial assurance business, which in effect therefore is completely self-contained. The industrial assurance funds at the end of 1938 amounted to £360 millions.

In 1853 there were many hundred collecting societies, but in 1938 only 149, of which all but 6 were of negligible size. During

[1] "The *New Statesman* Special Supplement on Industrial Assurance," by Sidney Webb, March 1915.

1938 these societies collected £14 millions in premiums, and at the end of that year there were 25 million policies on their books. Although ostensibly providing insurance facilities on a mutual basis, it is doubtful whether the control vested in the members of these societies is ever exercised. Through ignorance or indifference or both, rarely more than a handful of members or their delegates ever attend the meetings at which governing committees should be appointed by them. Some societies numbering their members in millions issue an open invitation to all to attend the annual general meeting, and then perhaps hire a single hall which could accommodate 5,000 at the most! Indubitably the Management would be surprised if every one of their million or more members tried to force a way in. In point of fact, the members have very little voice in the management of these societies, the effective control of which has "fallen into the hands of those whose relations to the society should be that of servants" (Cohen Report). The administrative officials and collectors pack these meetings with their own nominees (collectors are by statute debarred from attending in person) and generally manage to run the show in their own way. As a result, the policyholders in a mutual collecting society are little, if any, better off than those whose policies are insured in a company owned by shareholders. Where in the one dividends are paid, in the other, as we shall see later, the collectors and other officials have taken advantage of their position to secure higher remuneration for themselves. For better or worse, the members of these societies have evinced no desire at all to exercise their rights.

A number of collecting societies still maintain a small sickness insurance section, the funds for which are required by statute to be kept separate from the industrial assurance funds, which in effect therefore are completely self-contained. The industrial assurance funds at the end of 1938 amounted to £76 millions.

Since the early days of the friendly society movement, the State has admitted its responsibility for the safety of the savings and insurances of its workers. As long ago as 1793 a comprehensive Act was put on the Statute Book, as a result of which some restrictions and supervision could be exercised over the management of the friendly societies, amongst whom defalcation followed by winding up had become distressingly common. In return for these limitations the societies were given particularly advantageous terms for the investment of their funds in Government Securities. Since 1793 a succession of Acts, 1809, 1829, 1871, 1896, 1909, 1923, and 1929, has been carried through. The earlier Acts were concerned principally with the prevention of insolvency, first among the friendly societies and later among the rapidly growing insurance undertakings. The later Acts, in particular the 1923 Industrial Assurance Act, sought to reduce the abuses and malpractices which had become widespread as high-pressure salesmanship methods were inflicted on a population which lacked the knowledge thoroughly to understand what it was they were being induced to buy. The office of the Industrial Assurance Commissioner was set up to secure due observance of the 1923 Act, and the Commissioner adjudicates on any disputes which may be referred to him under that Act.

The industrial assurance companies and collecting societies play an important part in the administration of the National Health Insurance scheme. This is described in detail in another chapter of this book. It is sufficient to mention here that the National Health or "approved" sections of these concerns have no financial connection at all with their industrial assurance activities. Yet the industrial assurance and National Health activities are not wholly disconnected. The Cohen Committee commented on "the assistance in their canvassing activities which the collectors derived from the connections of their offices with the State system of National Health Insurance." Payment of National Health benefits, especially maternity benefit, was stated to be of great assistance when canvassing for new industrial assurance policies.

Industrial Assurance Organisation

The Agent.—The towering structure of the industrial assurance business rests on the activities of the individual, usually described as the agent, who is responsible for collection of premiums. The offices require him not only to collect premiums but even more to procure new business. The drive for new policyholders is the outstanding feature of the relations between the offices and their agents. Insurance business is peculiar in that constant expansion and ultimately bigger profits (or higher remuneration for the officials) may be obtained without much fresh capital expenditure. A vigorous and efficient sales organisation alone is necessary. No additional plant has to be set up, pressure on the agents is the only requirement, and since without exception the companies and societies wish to expand their activities, the pressure is intense and continuous.

The agent's remuneration depends on his success as a canvasser of new business, although primarily he is a collector of premiums. In some companies he retains as procuration fee the first 12 weeks' premiums paid under each new policy. In others, the procuration fee is a percentage of the net increase in his total collection week by week. Over and above the procuration fees, a renewal commission is paid amounting to 15 to 20% of his weekly collection. The largest industrial assurance company, a colossus controlling some 30% of the whole business, remunerates its agents by salary and bonus alone, although salary increases and promotion are dependent, among other things, on canvassing results. The collecting societies pay renewal commission at the standard rate of 25% of the weekly collection, and procuration fees absorb the first 13 to 16 weeks' premiums paid under each new policy. Further, the agent of a collecting society has what is known as a "book interest" in his collection. This is expressed as the right of the agent to nominate his successor; in other words, the right of the agent to sell his "book" or "collection." A "book" seems to change hands for as much as 30 times the weekly premiums for which it is responsible. So that a book charged with the collection of £20 per week, and worth to the agent holding it a wage of £5 per week, would sell for £600. By procuring new policies and increasing his collection the agent not only obtains substantial procuration fees but also increases the value of his "book." Without the control which the agents are able to exercise over these societies, it is difficult to see how this system of book interest could have arisen. Control brings them high rates of commission and security of employment. These have consequently acquired a marketable value.

Whatever the basis of his remuneration, an agent who over a period fails to produce a satisfactory stream of new business either endangers his job or causes the value of his book to depreciate. In any event, he incurs the extreme displeasure of his superior officers. By word of mouth or written communication, exhortation, threat and plea for new business descend incessantly on the agent. Childish devices are used to encourage him.

Special weeks, birthday weeks and so on. Pep talks and sales talks, *ad lib.* The agent is never allowed to forget that he must procure new business, more and more of it.

There are some 50,000 to 60,000 individuals employed full time as industrial assurance agents, the majority of whom earn between £3 and £5 per week. An exceptional few may make as much as £10 per week.

From the assured's point of view the agent is the company. The agent is responsible for advising the policyholder on the many points that can arise in connection with these policies. The office relies on him to smooth away contentions which if allowed to develop might lead to protracted correspondence. An office which numbers its clients in millions cannot afford to enter into correspondence over every point of explanation which may arise.

The agent customarily completes the form of proposal, the proposer merely signing his or her name in the appropriate places. The proposer has to rely on the agent to inform him what assurances he may effect on his relations and for what amounts. On discontinuing payment of premiums, the assured has certain statutory rights. These are set out in every premium receipt book which the assured holds, but in language incomprehensible to all but very few of the people who own these policies. Insurance is a financial transaction of a somewhat technical nature in which ignorance can easily lead one into monetary loss. Yet ignorance of the contract is almost universal among industrial assurance policyholders. On all issues the assured has to rely on the information and advice tendered by the agent. The offices make a big point of the service which the agent thus renders to his clients. They attempt on these grounds to justify the heavy expense of personal collection. One would therefore imagine that they select their agents bearing particularly in mind their suitability in this respect. Yet it is only an exceptional agent who does not receive his appointment on his potentialities as a successful canvasser alone. Where "book interest" exists, the vendor has not the slightest concern in the purchaser's suitability for the job.

A new agent is generally on the "road" after spending only a few days at the nearest branch office, where he is instructed in his clerical duties. From the pages of an instructions book issued by the Head Office and which he may or may not read, the new agent is supposed to learn something about the nature and legal aspects of insurance. More usually his understanding of the article he sells and services is acquired along the rough road of experience, trial and error. Even this would be tolerable if it were not that there are good reasons to believe that the labour turnover among agents is extraordinarily high. Statistics of turnover are not easy to come by. This is more than regrettable, for turnover is the ultimate criterion by which the worth of these agents may be measured. There is no doubt that thousands are as knowledgeable, hardworking and interested in their clients' welfare as Sir William Beveridge acknowledges, but the relative influence of these men of excellent type can only be estimated against labour turnover in their ranks as a whole. Data available for the insurance industry include withdrawals from all types of insurance work, clerical as well as sales staffs, "ordinary" as well as industrial insurance. Without a great deal of information which is not available, only a conservative guess is permissible. It has been suggested, however, that of the 21,000 persons who left the insurance industry in 1931, not less than 60 %, i.e. 12,000, had been full-time industrial assurance agents. This represents a labour turnover of 25 % per annum, and if within measure of the truth, means that only a minority of the agents remain long enough in the business to learn thoroughly what it is all about. While the offices measure their "progress" by the number of new policies they secure each year, a large labour turnover cannot be avoided. Whatever other functions the agent has to carry out, he remains in essence a door-to-door salesman; that is the basis of his relationship with his office. He is pressed continuously to obtain more and more new business, a large number fail to produce the results, and within a short time have to find other employment. The intensity of the effort may be gauged from the fact that some 10 million new policies have been secured every year for the past 25 years.

Over-insurance.—Pressure on the agents to procure new business dominates the whole system of industrial assurance. Subject to this insistent pressure, the agent in turn has to press his clients and employs all the arts of his trade to induce them to increase their assurances. His efforts have been crowned with extraordinary success. At the end of 1937 there were no less than 85 million industrial assurance policies in existence, assuring on the average a sum of £18 per policy. There were in addition some 13 million policies for which premiums had been discontinued and the policyholder granted a reduced "paid-up" assurance in lieu of what he had already paid. The sum assured by these policies averaged £4. Since the working-class population, who alone might be interested in these policies, did not exceed 40 millions, it seems that by the end of 1937 at latest the industrial assurance system had succeeded in providing a decent burial for all, with unavoidable expense for interested relations and a little to spare. Yet by the end of the next year, 1938, another million and three-quarter policies were being maintained, although the population increased during the year by less than 200,000. At the end of 1927 there were 70 million policies for which premiums were being paid; ten years later, 85 million, i.e. an increase of 15 million. During the same period the working-class population increased by less than 2 millions, from about 38 to 40 millions. So far as decent burial is concerned, saturation point seems long since to have been reached, yet there has been no diminution in the success of the agents' efforts to obtain new assurances.

The offices point out that while they are prepared to issue policies subject to a premium as low as 1d. per week, the number of policies in force is an index only of the extent to which people gradually augment their assurances by small amounts, and cannot by itself indicate gross over-insurance. That is true only so long as one fails to relate the number of policies to the average sum assured for new business. This has been as much as £18 per policy for many years despite the increasing incidence of Endowment Assurances at relatively much higher premiums. In 1933 the Cohen Committee concluded that the increase in the premium income of all offices from £36 millions in 1920 to £54 millions in 1930 was evidence of excessive pressure for increase and resulting over-insurance. The offices now [1] deny the validity of that argument on the grounds that (*a*) many policies were issued immediately after the last war which had in effect been postponed during the war period, (*b*) the improved economic status of the people provided a larger margin for savings, and (*c*) changes in money incomes reflected in the increased price level alone

[1] *Industrial Assurance Explained—a Reply to Criticisms.* Issued by the Industrial Life Offices, January 1944.

justified a steady increase in the premium income to the level actually attained in 1930. Superficially that reply seems convincing. But from 1929 to 1934 the premium income increased from £52 millions to £62 millions, and during that period (*a*) there were no postponement policies, (*b*) the economic status of the people suffered a marked deterioration, and (*c*) the price level, reflecting changes in money incomes, fell from 167 to 144 (official cost of living index figures). The logic of the offices' reply seems to have gone awry. It seems clear that, stimulated by intensive canvassing, a multiplicity of policies is being effected on relations within the permitted range which have only a remote connection with decent burial and unavoidable funeral expenses. The Cohen Committee reported that the moneys available from the policies "have facilitated the economic waste on expense of every kind in connection with death in working-class homes." A casual enquiry revealed that an undertaker would generally "do" a working-class funeral for anything between £15 and £40. One got the impression that the style of the funeral was as much dictated by what the undertaker could elicit about the amount of assurance moneys becoming available as by the expressed wishes of the bereaved. Naturally at such a time the bereaved would have little inclination to bargain.

Since the last war policies of Endowment Assurance have been taken up in increasing numbers. Under such a policy the sum assured is payable on survival to the end of a specified term of years (10, 15, 20 and so on) or on previous death. Endowment Assurances in force numbered 5 million in 1929 and some 10 million in 1938, when nearly one-third of all industrial assurance premiums was received under this head. It is claimed that these endowments combine the advantages of life assurance and savings. The savings, however, are tied up absolutely until the policy matures at the end of the agreed term, unless death intervenes, and if an emergency should arise in the meantime the money cannot be made available except by surrender at considerable loss. This disadvantage hopelessly invalidates the savings motive amongst working people, whose finances are almost invariably arranged on a precarious week-to-week basis. Even on maturity the sum suddenly made available, typically £25-£30, after saving 6d. a week for 25 years, may be devoted to purposes far removed from the originally thrifty intentions of the policyholder. The end often hardly seems to justify the effort. Burial benefit is the only socially valuable purpose that these assurances can be made to serve. The endowment is only a camouflage that may make them superficially attractive.

It is thus idle attempting [1] to create the illusion that because one-third of the premiums are received from these Endowment Assurances and one-third in respect of whole life assurances taken out by people on their own lives (or by a wife on her husband's life and vice versa), burial expense is a diminishing factor in the business. When an individual effects a policy for a small sum on his or her own life, or on the life of his or her spouse, it is only the funeral expense motive that makes the transaction worth while. It is only on this basis that the business could be sold, and out of the sums thus produced burial expenses are the first charge. A policy for £40, say, is a vastly different article from one for £400—the purpose is determined by the amount of the policy. The dividing line between funeral expenses and provision for dependants obviously cannot be fixed at a given sum, but it is certainly far in excess of what is secured by most industrial assurance policies. The sums normally available after meeting funeral expenses might provide for needy dependants at the most for a few weeks—an admitted advantage, but of such a temporary character that to it there cannot be ascribed the motive for an overwhelming number of own life or life of spouse policies. Funeral expenses is the only contingency against which policies for these very small sums provide complete protection, and that is the only justification for their existence.

The flow of new policies has been stimulated by the high-pressure salesmanship methods of the agents, but the procuration of 10 million new policies every year can hardly be ascribed to an artificially induced demand alone. The public want burial assurance. Dread of burial by the parish is widespread. Many believe that an expensive funeral is something of a passport to heaven for the deceased and the hallmark of respectability for the bereaved. These are natural and deep-rooted, even if illogical beliefs. They gave rise, as we saw, to the original schemes for mutual insurance, but the business today has left these simple beginnings far behind. To the natural desire of the population to obtain burial assurance facilities there has

[1] *Industrial Assurance Explained*, p. 5.

become closely attached a perhaps equally natural desire of shareholders to increase their profits, and agents to increase their earnings. The public created the demand, but the offices have fastened on it, exaggerated it and ultimately inflated it far beyond its simple, elementary purpose, namely, decent burial. As a result, for a working-class population of only 40 millions there are now 87 million policies assuring some £1,600 millions at a cost of over £70 millions per annum.

Why do they do it? Are the public so easily swayed by the solicitation and persuasiveness of the agents that in their millions they embark on financial commitments they can ill afford to maintain, and often abandon within a short time? Seemingly they are: perhaps through exaggerated fears, or ignorance or misunderstanding of what is involved—or perhaps simply to get rid of a persistent canvasser, especially as very often it is an already harassed housewife who has to deal with him.

The extraordinary success of the industrial assurance business may be compared with the dismal experience of the now defunct system of insurance through the Post Office. As long ago as 1882 facilities were provided through the Post Office for "members of the working classes to insure their lives with the advantage of Government security." The idea seems to have been conceived shortly after a number of insurance concerns had become insolvent and defaulted. Yet, however admirable the conception, the scheme never prospered. It was all but ignored by the public. At the end of 1927 there were only 10,000 policies in the Post Office scheme, compared with 70 million in the industrial assurance offices. No real effort was ever made to popularise the scheme, no inducements were offered to Post Office employees to bring the advantages of the scheme to the public notice. However real the demand for burial assurance, there is invariably some reluctance voluntarily to go out of one's way to obtain it. It is an axiom of industrial assurance that only persistent canvassing produces results. The Post Office scheme ignored the effect of sales resistance. It took no account, too, of the precarious way in which working-class finances are arranged. Payments had to be taken to the Post Office every week by the assured themselves. Yet it is a freely acknowledged fact by all connected with industrial assurance that without the regular and frequent collection of premiums at the assured's house, or without compulsory deduction from wages, the money would never be saved at all. The failure of the Post Office scheme shows how true this is. In January 1929 the scheme was wound up.

Lapse

Although 11 million new policies were taken out in 1938, there were in force at the end of that year only 1¾ million more paying policies and ¾ million paid-up policies than at the end of 1937. 8½ million policies were terminated in the year by de or maturity, or allowed to lapse voluntarily.

From figures made available to Sir William Beveridge by six of the largest offices whose experience it was assumed would be representative of the whole business, he deduces that outright forfeitures after payment of premiums average 3¼ million per annum. Sir William's assumption of complete representativeness, however, is not wholly valid. Statistics for all offices for the year 1929 were supplied to the Cohen Committee, and while the six that obliged Sir William then had a forfeiture rate of 46% of the new business done, the combined experience of all the others showed forfeitures at a rate of no less than 55%. Since 1929 these others have increased their share of the business from barely 30% to nearly 35%, an expansion hardly conducive to diminution of forfeitures. Even if they had succeeded in reducing forfeitures in the same ratio as the selected six had done during the decade, in 1938 they would still have been responsible for no less than 1½ million of them. The selected six had 2½ million forfeitures in 1938, so in all 4 million policies that year were forfeited by their owners after payment of premiums, that is ¾ million more than was estimated by Sir William Beveridge. As well as outright forfeitures there are also policies lapsed after at least one to two years' premiums have been paid, and for which a surrender value is given or a reduced assurance granted in lieu. Since these lapsed policies have had to bear their full share of the heavy initial expenses, and the cost of the temporary assurance cover too, the sum which can be paid out on surrender or applied to purchase a reduced assurance is, in the early years, only a fraction of what has been paid in. The loss suffered by the policyholder is no less than would have been the case if his policy had been forfeited outright in the first two years. As a result of the greater liberality of the offices' forfeiture provisions these assurances surrendered or paid-up each year have been increasing rapidly, from some 1½ million in 1929 to fully 3 million in 1938. A proportion of the policies which in 1929 would have been forfeited outright now have surrender value or paid-up assurance rights. Thus altogether, in 1938, 7 million policies were allowed to lapse by their owners after payment of premiums had commenced, 80%, i.e. 5·6 millions, of these (according to figures supplied to Beveridge) in the first two years. The experience of 1938 was not exceptional in any way. Of the odd 10 million new policies issued each year between the two wars, at least 5 million involved their owners in material financial loss within a short period, either by outright forfeiture, by surrender or conversion into paid-up assurance!

The offices state[1] that lapses have now been reduced by "nearly" two-thirds of their pre-war number. They fail to point out, however, that new business, too, has been substantially cut by the same wartime conditions, and this has an obvious bearing on the number of lapses experienced. Only 8·4 million new policies were written in 1940, 7·4 million in 1941 and 7·3 million in 1942, compared with the 10 million or so in the years before the war. Out of this much smaller volume of new business—and, of course, some too out of policies effected before the war—at least 2¾ million were lapsed in 1942 despite the greater economic security of the people interested. (War Service Grants are made towards industrial assurance premiums contracted more than 6 months before enlistment.) Under the abnormal conditions of total war the proportion of lapses to new policies, not an unfailing index while drastic changes are taking place in the volume of new business, has been reduced from 68% (1938) to 38% (1942). What evidence is there that this reflects a permanent improvement in the situation? The only reliable conclusion that may be drawn is that even when economic insecurity is largely removed, and despite the depletion of selling staffs on war service, lapses can still occur to the extent of 38% of the new business done, about one-half of them, according to the offices without supporting figures, and 80% according to Beveridge, within two years of the policy's having been taken up. These 2¾ million policies lapsed in 1942, therefore, represent the extent to which the business is being oversold (or overbought) and deny the offices'

[1] *Industrial Assurance Explained*, p. 12.

assertion that economic insecurity is the major and, by implication, the sole cause of lapsing, which is therefore beyond their control.

The offices have a gargantuan appetite for new business; to satisfy it they maintain countrywide sales organisations, and their relationship with the agents is based primarily on the necessity for procuring new policies. The agents scour the country for new business, not because they're anxious lest some unfortunate might otherwise have to lie in a pauper's grave, but because their livelihood depends on their satisfying their employers' demands for new assurances and more and more of them. As a result the agents secured a steady 10 million new policies every year between the two wars, depression and boom alike—but barely 50% of these were maintained for more than a few months. It seems only common sense to conclude that, subject to the intensive solicitation of the agents, millions are being persuaded to take out further policies without having the means or the interest to maintain them. These are the policies which lapse. If the offices are sincere in wishing to reduce lapses, they need only to cease measuring their "progress" by the amount of annual new business which the army of agents secures for them. It is indicative of the frailty of human nature that many who have lapsed an assurance are within a short time persuaded to try again. Where otherwise do the ten million new policies come from every year?

It is true, as the offices point out,[1] that a certain (unknown) proportion of these lapsees effect new assurances within a short time and have been, in fact, only "temporarily out of benefit." If, as is likely to be the case, one or more birthdays have passed since the original policy was effected, the sum assured, however, suffers a permanent reduction, e.g. for entry at age 30 from £23 : 14/- for 3d. a week to £22 : 19/- at age 31 and £22 : 4/- at age 32. On the other hand, there can be no guarantee that a replacement policy will be continuously maintained—it is just as likely to be lapsed as its predecessor. It is a slippery slope, and with lapses on such a gigantic scale, lapse and subsequent re-entry must occur several times with the assured temporarily out of benefit over and over again, while his original sum assured steadily decreases. On lapsing, the erstwhile policyholder doesn't ask himself how much he's going to save from the wreckage of his original policy by forthwith effecting another. He is much

[1] *Industrial Assurance Explained*, p. 14.

more interested in ascertaining how much he has got out of his assurance and how much has been lost. At age 30 he would pay 3d. a week for an assurance of £23, 14/-. Suppose he lapses nine months after entry, having paid in nine shillings. The office maintains his policy in full benefit for another three months after that, giving him twelve months' assurance cover for nine months' premiums. This cover costs them approximately 3/-, including some provision for policyholders in bad health who naturally don't lapse, and this is a measure of the true value of the lapsed assurance to the ex-holder. The balance of 6/- has been swallowed up in meeting costs of administration, including agents' commission, euphemistically described by the offices as the "home service." To a policyholder who has allowed his policy to lapse the home service has been of no value at all. It merely represents a machine through which he has been induced to embark on a long period of financial commitment which subsequent events proved he had neither the means nor the interest to fulfil. When forfeiture takes place within the first year or so the total loss is not great, in only a few cases exceeding 10 or 20 shillings. Even these small sums are considerable bearing in mind the nature of the households from which they are drawn. In their efforts to maintain these policies with inadequate means the owners have created for themselves a source of constant anxiety and aggravation.

Sinister motives have been attributed to the offices in connection with lapses out of which it is commonly supposed a very handsome profit is made. This is not so. Agents' commission is by far the largest item on the expenses' side, running away as it sometimes does with the first 12 weeks' premiums. When the agent is remunerated by net increase or by salary alone, the office from the premiums paid in the first few months creates a fund out of which it is able to pay its agents a living wage. That is a subtle point in insurance economics. If the public took out no more policies than they could afford to maintain continuously the living standards of the agents would crash. Either the offices would be forced to dispense with the services of a large number of them—and there is a limit beyond which rationalisation cannot be pushed in the tedious work of house-to-house weekly collection of small sums—or the agents' remuneration would have to be made up from the only other available source, viz. premium income. Thus in the long run a noticeable diminution in lapses must either cause unemployment amongst industrial assurance agents (in wartime "call-up" operates in the same direction) or force up premium rates and that portion of them absorbed in expenses. The offices do not make substantial profits out of lapses, but lapses provide the fuel which keeps this hopelessly uneconomic engine in motion.

Perturbed by the enormous number of lapses, some companies now pay procuration fees based only on net increase in amount of premiums collected. It was hoped that the agents would thus have an incentive to see that policies were maintained in force. Yet the companies which operate this scheme have never boasted that it has led to a noticeable diminution in lapsing. To the agent pressed by his company all except the obviously destitute are prospective policyholders irrespective of capacity or willingness to maintain the policy in force. So runs the psychology of salesmanship. Alas for the agents' hopes, payment of even half-a-dozen pennies for a few weeks is the acid test of the policyholders' intentions, and if the wherewithal is not available, payment simply has to cease, however glib and forceful the agent may be. It is one thing to persuade people to take out a policy, it is quite another matter to persuade them to maintain it after paying a few premiums. Despite "net increase" remuneration, lapsing goes on just the same.

Under the Industrial Assurance Act of 1923, the offices before lapsing a policy are required to give notice of the arrears of premium and to allow 28 days for payment. Rules are laid down for giving policyholders a reduced policy free from payment of further premiums in return for the payments already made. Steps, too, were taken to prevent lapse and re-entry (called "substitution") for the benefit of agents whose procuration fees absorb the first months' premiums.

Expenses

It has always been noticed that a large proportion of the industrial assurance premiums is absorbed in expenses of management (the "expense ratio"). Not long ago it was common to find that 50% of the premiums disappeared in this way. Considerable improvements have been made, and today most companies operate on an expense ratio of between 30 and 35%, and most societies 40 to 45%. The difference is due to the higher rates of commission paid to the agents of the societies. The expenses of most "ordinary" assurance companies by comparison absorb only 10 to 15% of their premium income.

The expense ratio calculated by Sir William Beveridge is not altogether sound. Through the skilled investment of the large funds in their hands, the offices have earned a rate of interest substantially higher than could have been earned if the business had been run by a Government Department which would have been required to invest the funds in Trustee Securities. A simple actuarial calculation shows that this additional interest has met all the dividends paid to shareholders together with the income tax thereon. It seems reasonable, therefore, to reject dividends and tax as items of expense (Beveridge includes them as such) for they have been a charge not on premiums but on interest from investments which wouldn't normally accrue to the people. Even on this basis the expense ratio of all companies in 1938 was 31%, 6/2 in £1 premiums, compared with Beveridge's estimate of 37%—7/6 in £1 premiums. This is the basis put forward by the offices themselves,[1] but they don't give an expense ratio for all companies combined. The only ratio they quote (25·6%) is for the Prudential, by far the largest of all these concerns and hardly representative of the business as a whole. The Prudential has brought the organisation of industrial assurance to a fine art, and so long as the business retains its present distinguishing features its expenses are hardly likely to exhibit still further reductions. The expense ratio of all companies, including the Prudential, was 35% in 1928, and ten years later had only been reduced to 31%, not very spectacular progress at a time when much comment was being made about high expense ratios. While considering expenses it is essential to distinguish between companies and collecting societies; the former operate as a group with a charge of 6/2 in the £1 for expenses, the latter (responsible for about one-fifth of the whole business) require no less than 8/- in the £1, even after allowing them a credit for the excess interest they manage to earn. It is a noteworthy fact that despite its success, within the limitations imposed by the nature of the business, the Prudential's share of new policies has been steadily decreasing for a number of years.

[1] *Industrial Assurance Explained*, p. 19.

It is not possible to pass from this aspect of expenses without dealing with a most amazing calculation in *Industrial Assurance Explained*, p. 20. Beveridge related premium income with outgoings that do not go to policyholders. These outgoings are purely and simply expenses met for the most part currently out of premiums as they are paid. To counter Beveridge the author of *Industrial Assurance Explained* decided to relate premium income with outgoings that do go to policyholders, despite the fact that about one-half of these outgoings is extracted from the Funds, i.e. from the accumulation of past premiums, and not from current premiums. He was thus able to create the impression that the policyholders of eight of the largest offices as a whole benefited in 1939 by nearly 18/2 for every £1 paid that year in premiums. A completely valueless and misleading figure which was widely publicised in the less well-informed Press. It was his misfortune that the calculation did not produce an immediate contradiction showing that the policyholders "benefited" by more than £1 for every £1 paid in premiums. This would be the case in an old-established office which had done a steady amount of new business for a long period. For example, in 1935 the policyholders of the Prudential "benefited" by nearly 25/- for every £1 paid in premiums that year!

The business of industrial assurance depends for its existence on the regular and frequent collection of premiums at the home of the assured. Without collection the premiums could never be saved at all. But collection at frequent intervals is laborious. There is a physical limit to the total amount in small sums (3d. to 1/- per week) which one man can collect in a limited time. Especially if he has to call more than once before receiving payment. The agent has to be given a living wage, and this must absorb a large proportion of the small sums he collects. Once the necessity for collection is admitted, heavy expenses are unavoidable. It is no reflection on the administration of the offices that at least 30% of what they receive in premiums should necessarily be absorbed in this way. The burden is none the less a heavy one, it is all the more regrettable that it has to be borne by those who can least afford it.

It would be interesting to compare the deal which the working man gets with his little policy with what the rather better off get with their larger policies. Valid comparisons unfortunately are not easy to make. The industrial assurance policyholder is accepted without medical examination and after only a brief enquiry as to health. In the ordinary branch, either a medical examination is required or a most searching enquiry is made into both personal and family medical history. Only "first-class" lives are acceptable for ordinary assurance, and a correspondingly lower premium can be charged. Then there is the question of "bonus" or share in profits [1] from which free additions are made to the sum assured. After several years these bonuses may make a very substantial difference to the amount paid out when a claim arises. They cannot be anticipated with certainty as a contractual benefit, yet on the other hand they should not be ignored when making comparisons. Fortunately there is a way out of our difficulty. There is an industrial assurance company with over 1 million policies on its books which has never given any but wholly negligible bonuses to its policyholders. There is also a collecting society assuring nearly 10 million policies in which members are not entitled to a share in surplus until after 20 years' membership. The terms given by these concerns may be compared with what a healthy working man would obtain in an ordinary assurance company assuming he could find one willing to accept a policy for a small sum. Our healthy working man would have to keep his 3d. a week by him for a whole year before paying over to the ordinary assurance company. The sums secured by a premium of 3d. a week (or its annual equivalent) are shown in the table below for various ages at commencement of the assurance. The last column shows what terms could be obtained in the Prudential, which has 27 million policies on its books, and in which the policyholders have enjoyed substantial bonuses of some 30/- per cent. per annum for many years. That is, a policy originally for £20 would after 5 years have increased to £21, 12/-, after 10 years to £23, after 20 years to £26, and after 30 years to £29. Assuming, of course, that future profits remain on the same scale as those in the past.

[1] Theoretically a collecting society makes no "profit." Owing to improving longevity and skilled investment of the funds "surplus" has accrued in many cases, represented by the difference between the actuarial valuation of the liabilities for claims and the assets available to meet these liabilities. This surplus is distributed to members in exactly the same way as the share of the profits is distributed to policyholders of an industrial assurance company. Needless to say, the officials and agents of the societies take a proportion of the surplus before it goes to the members.

SUMS ASSURED BY SAVING 3d. A WEEK

Age at Commencement.	Industrial Company with Negligible Bonuses.			Collecting Society. No Bonuses for 20 Years.			Ordinary Company. No Bonuses at all.			Industrial Company. Substantial Bonuses.		
	£	s.	d.	£	s.	d.	£	s.	d.	£	s.	d.
20	31	16	0	31	13	0	43	16	0	32	14	0
30	22	10	0	22	7	0	34	8	0	23	11	0
40	15	12	0	15	3	0	26	18	0	16	1	0
50	10	7	0	9	18	0	17	10	0	10	7	0

The advantage in favour of an ordinary policy ranges from 40% at age 20, 55% at age 30, to 75% at ages 40 and 50. At the higher ages, of course, the industrial assurance concerns take quite a proportion of people inacceptable for ordinary assurance on health grounds.

The similarity in the basic terms offered by the industrial assurance concerns is no mere accident. The pace has been set by the best-managed offices, and competition has forced the others to follow. The differences become obvious only when the respective profit-sharing schemes are compared. One company above gives substantial bonuses, the other practically none, while the society allocates bonuses only after 20 years' membership. In the long run there would be a substantial difference in the respective sums paid out on death. The working man may be capable of comparing what 3d. a week will bring him in different concerns, but the intricacies of relative shares in future profits mean next to nothing to him.

CONCLUSIONS

We have seen that payment of industrial assurance premiums figures in the finances of almost every working-class household in the country. On the average, about 2/9 has to be put aside every week for this purpose. The desire to secure a decent burial for close relations is a natural one, but compared with average weekly expenditure on essentials (food 21/6, rent 10/-, clothing 6/-, fuel 2/6 in the average family with 2 children [1])

[1] *Parenthood and Poverty*, L. Ginsburg : Fabian Society Research Series, No. 43, 1939.

the cost of providing for burial seems wholly out of proportion. Still, no one can cavil at that alone. The public want burial assurance and should be prepared to pay for it, but one is bound to enquire whether the demand couldn't be met for something considerably less than £72 millions per annum. Besides, our examination of the industrial assurance business has revealed many features which, to say the least, are disturbing, even if not outrageous.

In the first place, owing to the necessity for collecting premiums an industrial assurance policy is a very expensive article: 30 to 40% of the premiums are absorbed in expenses of management, and as a result the working man with his small policy is given a considerably poorer bargain than the well-to-do with their larger policies. If in some way collection could be eliminated, say by compulsory deduction from wages, a substantial reduction in premiums would be effected.

But mere reduction of premiums is not enough unless the problems of over-insurance are dealt with at the same time. As a result of the offices' all-powerful desire to expand their activities, they now assure no fewer than 87 million industrial assurance policies[1] for which £72 millions premiums are being paid each year. These policies provide an average sum of about £20 each, or about £36 on each life. The moneys are intended to cover reasonable funeral expenses, but what is reasonable has never been clearly defined.[2] A multiplicity of assurances is being effected which has created waste and extravagance in connection with death in working-class homes even if indirectly it has not led to increased burial costs. Respectable burial by all means, but ostentation seems both illogical and unnecessary when so much else may be in short supply. A simple yet decent burial seems to be the most effective tribute one can pay to the deceased. Re-direction of public tastes to this end would not be easy while the industrial assurance offices measure their progress by the increasing millions of policies they assure and press an army of agents to get the business for them.

This army, over 50,000 strong, secures from the working-class population over 10 million new policies every year. Every week

[1] There are also 15 million paid-up assurances.

[2] Except in the case of children's policies, which may not assure more than £6 on a child under 3 years of age, £10 between the ages of 3 and 6, and £15 between 6 and 10 (Industrial Assurance Act, 1923, and Friendly Societies Act, 1896).

over 100,000 households are persuaded to embark on fresh financial commitments the successful culmination of which depends absolutely on making continuous payments over a long period of years. Alas for the hopes and motives of the new policyholders! Some 50% for better or for worse let their policies lapse within a few months. The monetary loss on forfeiture is measured in hard-earned shillings. Of the aggravations and worry these policies cause their owners we can only guess.

A business exhibiting defects such as these and affecting the meagre resources of millions of the poorest among us cannot claim that there is no justification or need [1] for the State Funeral Benefit of £20 which Sir William Beveridge proposes together with conversion of the Industrial Assurance business into a Public Service. This Service, the Industrial Assurance Board, would honour all existing policies and "set out to encourage more economical methods of insurance and saving than are represented by industrial assurance." The offices are not convinced that the proposed Funeral Grant is as attractive as represented, having regard to the initial deficiency of £150 millions which would fall on the Exchequer as a result of making everyone eligible for benefit at its inception at the premium appropriate to entry at age 16. But the vast majority of those thus included at the beginning will have already made private arrangements for burial assurance, arrangements which it is intended to place under the aegis of the Industrial Assurance Board. Making these people eligible as well for the State Funeral Benefit would only serve to increase wasteful expenditure in connection with funerals, which it is a major object of the scheme to prevent. Alternatively these private insurances would be lapsed wholesale. There are adequate grounds therefore for removing the Funeral Grant from the benefits of those aged over 16 at the inception of the scheme, provided existing industrial assurance policies were taken over by an Industrial Assurance Board, when they would enjoy corresponding advantages reflected in increased bonuses or reduced premiums. The initial deficiency therefore need never arise, while on a cost for cost basis the State Funeral Benefit must prove 20-25% cheaper than the existing voluntary methods by the saving in expenses of administration alone. No comparisons can disguise that,[2] even by introducing the red herring of reversionary

[1] *Industrial Assurance Explained*, pp. 28-30. [2] *ibid.*, p. 31.

bonuses which not even the most optimistic office would care to guarantee at the relatively high pre-war rates for the expectation of life of a youth aged 16. By eliminating the 5 million lapses inseparably associated with industrial assurance each year before the war, and by confining burial assurance to what is reasonable and sufficient for funeral expenses, a State Funeral Grant would ultimately effect a total saving to the working classes measured in tens of millions sterling every year.

PART TWO

Chapter XII

THE BEVERIDGE REPORT AND AFTER

By R. W. B. CLARKE

THE impact of the war upon the social and economic structure has made permanent changes. The new society may be an improvement on the old; it may be worse. But it is certainly new and vastly different from the society of the 'thirties. One of its main characteristics is an insistence upon social security. This is becoming a symbol for a society which enables a man to live his life without fear of poverty and family disaster. Other things are as important as freedom from want. But a society that guards its members from want is likely to do its other tasks well. Social security has thus become a touchstone for the future. Herein lies the real significance of the Beveridge Plan.

The Beveridge Plan is a massive reconstruction and unification of the social insurance services, the purpose of which is to bring every man and woman in the country into a comprehensive scheme which would provide them, when unemployed, ill, aged, or widowed, with incomes at a rate adequate for maintenance, and which would provide special grants at the crises of marriage, maternity and burial. Linked with the Plan are three assumptions which round off the major needs for social security—children's allowances, a national health and rehabilitation service and reasonably full employment. The three assumptions are an integral part of the Plan; social insurance cannot be isolated from positive policies to develop health, to maintain employment and to assist parenthood. The Report stresses this repeatedly; one of its great merits is that it sees the social process in its entirety and not in compartments. In stressing this interdependence, however, we must not lose our sense of proportion. It is wholly untrue to assert, as some commentators have done, that the Plan cannot be carried into effect until we have abolished mass unemployment. It is equally unrealistic to argue that the

Plan requires that there should be a tremendous expansion of public ownership of industry. It is, of course, much easier to have proper social benefits in a dynamic and expanding economic system, planned to make full use of the nation's resources; indeed, if the nation's productive power were exerted in peace-time as effectively as it is developed under the pressure of war, the nation could take the Beveridge Plan in its stride. But even in the sluggish economy of the period between the world wars, the nation achieved a very striking improvement in the social services and in the standard of living generally, and the scale of the Beveridge Plan is such that it is well within the nation's capacity in any but a catastrophic post-war world. We need not be content with the Plan. It is only one part of the new society. But it is simply untrue to say that we cannot get it unless we get other things first.

Principles of Social Security

We shall return to these fundamental assumptions later. The Plan itself embodies six principles: comprehensiveness, unification of administrative responsibility, classification, adequate benefit, flat rate of contribution, flat rate of benefit. These principles are the backbone of the Plan. Their interpretation, however, presents certain difficulties, for some of them may in particular circumstances conflict with others. The weaknesses in the Plan are caused by misplaced emphasis in their interpretation rather than by inadequacy of the principles themselves. The Report is from time to time faced with awkward choices between these principles. Sir William Beveridge tends at such moments of choice to rank the principles of flat rate of contribution and benefit—and the implicit assumption that benefits must be mathematically linked to the contributions paid—ahead of the principles of comprehensiveness and adequacy of benefit. The result of this is that a number of unjustifiable anomalies are introduced into the Plan. These can easily be ironed out when the time comes for legislation; they appear in the detail rather than in the basic structure. But they are of considerable importance.

The principles of comprehensiveness, unification, classification and adequacy of benefit are paramount. Any social security scheme which is worth its salt must cover all citizens irrespective of means or occupation, and it must cover all universal risks. It must be one scheme, with one card and one contribution and one standard rate of benefit, and one office from which payments are made. It must provide adequate benefit, which will buy enough food to maintain good health, pay the rent, and buy sufficient clothing, fuel and other household necessities; it must provide these benefits for the entire duration of the contingency. It must classify the population and provide for the special needs of various sections of the community—the self-employer needs protection against loss of his livelihood, but not against unemployment in the ordinary sense; the married woman has a unique need for protection against widowhood. These are essentials; we should not override them unless a very powerful practical case can be made for doing so.

The two other principles—flat rate of contribution and flat rate of benefit—require more careful interpretation. We may reject at once the European and American systems which relate contributions and benefits to earnings. Besides being intolerably complex, such systems are out of place in a scheme designed to establish a national minimum standard of living below which no one should fall. If the higher-paid workers wish to receive higher benefits, they can arrange it by voluntary insurance, for which ample facilities exist in this country; surely nobody suggests that the State should subsidise benefits above the necessary minimum. It is soundly democratic to have flat rates paid by everybody and payable to everybody on an equal footing. Provided that the scheme embodies the principles of comprehensiveness and adequacy of benefit, moreover, it is useful to make benefits contingent upon the payment of contributions. The objections which are properly raised to the working of these conditions in the present social insurance schemes—which limit eligibility for benefit and duration of benefit according to wholly arbitrary relations to the number of contributions paid—fall to the ground when those other principles are applied. If the whole population pays contributions or is credited with them in all circumstances, and if the benefit lasts for the whole duration of loss of earning power, these absurdities can no longer exist. The contribution then becomes a reasonable means of registering the population and of determining to whom the benefits shall be paid. But it must be clearly understood that the principle of flat rate contribution linked with flat rate benefit may, under certain circumstances, conflict with the principles of comprehensiveness and adequacy. The rate of contribution may be so high that a minority of the population cannot afford it and so must be allowed to contract out or be compelled to undergo hardship by paying it; the scheme is then no longer comprehensive. High rates of contribution, moreover, have all the social disadvantages of regressive taxation. The principle of flat rate of benefit must likewise be modified to provide bigger benefits for people with dependants, and it should also be modified to provide for differences in rent obligation, for it is impossible to fix a flat rate benefit which is adequate equally for the Londoner and the agricultural worker. There is a danger that the contribution-benefit principles will be raised above the others, for they are established features of social insurance and have some traditional sanctity, whereas the others are new. It is the application of the four new principles that turns social insurance into social security.

The strength of the Beveridge Plan is that it puts these new principles on the map; its weakness is that on occasion it subordinates them to the old. It is comprehensive both in covering the whole population and in covering all universal risks. The qualification is simple.[1] But the contributions are high, and some people will be able to contract out [2] while others will suffer hardship in maintaining their payments. The Plan provides for complete unification of administrative responsibility in a Ministry of Social Security. Its standard benefit of 24/- a week for a single man or woman and 40/- for a married couple is adequate, subject to the very important qualification that the flat rate treatment of rent means that the benefits will certainly be inadequate for Londoners, will probably be inadequate for people with large families, and will be unnecessarily excessive for people with low rent obligations.[3]

[1] Twenty-six weeks' contributions in all for eligibility for unemployment and disability benefit; three years' contributions for disability lasting more than a year; somewhat more complex qualifications for pensions in the transition period. Report, paras. 366, 367.

[2] Report, para. 363. Self-employed and non-gainfully occupied persons with incomes less than £75 a year may contract out. The whole question of the appropriate level of contributions and the function of the contributory principle is discussed below, pp. 380-87.

[3] The problems arising in the treatment of rent are fully discussed below, pp. 348-54.

The application of the classification principle, by which the population is divided into six classes, each with its respective kinds of benefits, is admirably done.[1] Everybody is entitled to medical treatment, retirement pension and funeral benefit. Class I, which consists of all employees, is protected against unemployment, disability and industrial disability. Class II, the self-employed, receives disability benefit after 13 weeks' illness, and a maintenance benefit while training for a new job. Class III, the housewives, receives marriage grant, maternity grant and benefit, widow's and guardian benefit. Class IV, the non-occupied of working age, can receive training benefit. Class V, children below working age, receive children's allowances. Class VI, the retired aged, receive pensions. There are some possibilities of opting between classes—the gainfully occupied married woman may be in Class I, II or III, and will receive different benefits accordingly. The classification corresponds to real differences of need between various types of people, and the whole conception is original and powerful. Finally, the principles of flat rate contribution and benefit are, of course, carried out, even at the expense of the others. Strengthened by the amendments which we propose—in particular, the reduction of the contributions and the rational treatment of rent—the Plan stands the test of the guiding principles which Sir William Beveridge has formulated.

The Plan is a complete whole, but different considerations arise in the provision of each type of benefit. The handling of unemployment benefit raises altogether different problems from those of industrial disability and old age; at each point there are difficult questions of administrative principle and practice. We shall deal with the financial and quantitative aspects in the next chapter; here we are concerned with the administrative framework and with the various social considerations which emerge. The merit of the Plan is that it combines sweeping general principles with the most detailed and careful working out of the minutiae of administration; to assist in making the Plan a workable Act of Parliament, we must deal with the details as well as the principles.

[1] Report, p. 123.

Unemployment and Training

The Plan provides unemployment benefit for all normally employed persons without exception; [1] benefit is paid without means test for the whole duration of unemployment. The claimant must, of course, be ready to accept suitable work; after six months' benefit—or a shorter period for young people—he may be required to attend at a work or training centre as a condition for continued receipt of benefit.[2] This sweeps away the conception which has dominated British policy since 1931, that unemployed men can be made to seek work more effectively by the application of financial pressure through the means test. The qualification for benefit becomes willingness to work and willingness to re-train for other work, rather than financial need. This is entirely right. As the Report points out, it is wrong in principle to reduce a man's income because his unemployment has lasted 26 weeks; his need for income will grow rather than diminish. His financial position is in a sense irrelevant; what is necessary is that he should get work. If he is in a declining industry in which he cannot hope to regain employment, he must be re-trained for a new job, and he must be given facilities for moving to other places where there is more opportunity. This is clear. But the phrase "attendance at a work or training centre" smacks of a somewhat sordid past. The corollary of this method of treating unemployment benefit is the development of vigorous and effective re-training schemes designed to give people the skills which the community needs at the time. The whole conception is far removed from pre-war ideas of the scope of Government training; [3] it is a basic part of national employment policy, not a mere adjunct of unemployment administration. The Report stresses the importance of re-training as a means of ensuring industrial mobility and adaptation to change; it provides training benefit which will enable self-employed who

[1] Report, paras. 137-152. Special schemes for agriculture, banking and insurance are of course merged in the general scheme.

[2] Report, paras. 129-131, 326-329.

[3] The Charity Organisation Society, in its statement on the Beveridge Report (*Times*, 30th January 1943), makes the point very clearly: "Experience has shown that training schemes in the past have been mainly pretences at work in order to qualify for State assistance. The society suggests that a training scheme should only be brought into operation after a reasonable period of unemployment, lest it should be regarded as penal and become a political byword equally with the means test; and that real training could best be obtained in a factory alongside the wage-earner."

lose their means of livelihood and non-occupied people who wish to enter the labour market to maintain themselves while they are learning a new job.[1] But it fails to appreciate the vast increase in scope and change in spirit of Government training and placement organisation which is required.

Before the war, Government training facilities were practically non-existent. In 1938, the average number of men and women on the unemployment register was 1,800,000, of whom possibly 300,000 were a solid core who had been out of work for a year or more. During that year less than 14,000 completed training in Government training centres—and of these nearly 5,000 were serving soldiers. Some 27,000 passed through the Government instructional centres and local training centres, but of these only 2,653 passed out to employment, while more than one-half completed the course unplaced, and most of the remainder voluntarily gave up their training.[2] It is difficult in the throes of total war, in which trained man-power of all kinds has been the main bottleneck from the start, to understand why this lamentable record was allowed to stand without public outcry. Even the Unemployment Assistance Board, which might reasonably have been expected to do something about it, was moved plaintively to declare that it "would welcome increased opportunities of vocational training for men who had exhausted their benefit rights."[3] This ineptitude in the training field is an awful blot on the Ministry of Labour's record. It is the clearest proof that entirely new means of handling this problem must be devised.

There is no inherent difficulty in providing training facilities. They must be varied, to provide a wide range of skills. They must be plentiful, so that they are accessible without complicated removal problems. They must be linked with industry; the

[1] Report, paras. 122, 349. A minor point in connection with training benefit is not covered in the Report. A person in Class IV who wishes to learn an occupation applies for training and receives training benefit; at the end of training no job is available, or during training he falls ill; according to the strict letter of the Plan he would neither get unemployment benefit in the first instance nor disability benefit in the second, for he has not paid contributions in Class I and so does not qualify for benefit until he has worked for six months. This is clearly wrong; a person in receipt of training benefit should be eligible for disability benefit during training and should be eligible for unemployment or disability benefit immediately afterwards, without a further qualifying period.

[2] Ministry of Labour Annual Report, 1938, pp. 105-6.

[3] Unemployment Assistance Board Annual Report, 1938, p. 25.

training centre should have arrangements with local firms, in association with the trade unions which would be required to modify unduly restrictive control of entry. The training centre should also have arrangements with local training establishments, such as secretarial colleges; it should give grants to trainees for approved courses of specialised training. The people who come forward for training will include a tremendously wide range of men and women—unemployed who have been without work for six months, shopkeepers who have failed, widows without children, juveniles from blind-alley occupations and scores of people who are tired of their occupation and want to find another. There cannot be a single pattern of training; the arrangements must be varied as and flexible as the industrial system itself. It must be recognised that this is not ambulance work. It is the provision of industrial opportunity. The object is to enable ordinary people to find a better niche in society; it is to give opportunities, not penance. The same applies to the rather analogous work of rehabilitation of disabled persons; it is a job of fitting people into the right places in the industrial system—the places where they can use their capacities best. This clearly means that placement and training must be closely linked together; the work of training is incomplete if the trainee cannot get a job afterwards.

This is one of the key points at which society must plan. It is useless to provide training facilities unless people are trained to do the jobs that the community needs. In the war, the problem is easy. People are trained in engineering. Immediately after the war, building workers of various kinds will have to be trained in large numbers. But in the long view the decision will not be so simple. There must be a broad plan of national development which will show the major long-term trend which it is desired to achieve—the industries which will expand and the industries which will contract, and the regional distribution of this expansion and contraction. The placement and training agencies would guide people—especially the young—accordingly. This does not involve the planning of industry to the remotest detail; it does mean that we must have a long-term pattern of social priorities and a long-term picture of the shape of national economic activity. Just as in the war the broad lay-out of the labour resources of the community is determined in advance and the policy of all Government Departments is directed to secure that lay-out, so must there be in peace-time an advance lay-out of resources. It is not necessary in peace to employ the ruthless methods to carry out the Plan which are needed in war-time; the tempo is less urgent, and the size of the changes from year to year is very much less. The job of training and placement is greatly eased, of course, if there is reasonably full employment; with heavy unemployment it would be extremely difficult to carry out effective training policies. But full employment is not enough. Social goals are needed in order to provide the framework in which every man and woman can have the opportunity to learn and use the highest level of skill of which they are capable.

It is apparent from this that the administration of unemployment benefit must be intimately associated with training and placement. The Report leaves this question open, but tentatively suggests [1] that the first and last of these functions should be carried out by the Ministry of Social Security, and that training should be carried out by the Ministry of Labour. This suggestion is based upon a faulty conception of the problems of training and placement. Both must be in the same hands, and both must be controlled by the agency which is responsible for employment policy in the large—that is, the Ministry of Labour. If this is not done, people will be trained for jobs which do not exist, and the placement agency will fail to find people jobs and throw discredit upon the whole service. The Ministry of Social Security should no more have responsibility for placement than for running the public medical service or the public education system; nor should it be responsible for the rehabilitation of disabled people. Its job is to ensure that people who lose their earning power are properly maintained. There is a clear distinction between this work and the positive creation of health and employment. It is necessary, of course, that the administration of unemployment benefit should be very close to the employment service; the latter would have to keep the unemployment register and certify that the unemployed man satisfied the qualification of being available for work. The best way to achieve this, however, is for the Ministry of Labour employment service to be housed in the same building as the Social Security office; the man would go to the Ministry of Labour office first, receive a

[1] Report, para. 174.

chit showing his eligibility for benefit, and then proceed to the Social Security office, where the actual payment would be made. The closest co-operation between the two Ministries would be needed. But the ultimate responsibility for placement and training must be with the Ministry of Labour.

Ill-Health

The essence of the Plan is that free medical treatment is provided for everybody. The whole medical and disability provisions are based upon the assumption of a comprehensive national medical service.[1] This service could take an infinite number of shapes. It might be no more than an adaptation of the present system—but with all patients on the panel. It could likewise be a real public medical service. An attempt to graft free medical treatment for all on to the present National Health Insurance system would lead to serious difficulties, even if the complicated machinery of approved societies were replaced by simple direct administration. We have already seen [2] that many of the anomalies of our existing free medical treatment provision result from the structure of the medical service and not from the financial structure of the National Health Insurance. Purely financial change—the extension of the panel system to cover everybody—would not suffice to provide a satisfactory national medical service. An extension of the present system can hardly hope to develop the prevention of disease to an adequate standard of efficiency; in the curing of disease, there is good reason to believe that the collective system will yield superior results by making better specialist and hospital services available and by organising medical effort into the most effective channels. The existing atomised service cannot easily be adapted into a vigorous and positive social agency, exterminating disease and creating positive health.

If the medical service were centralised in each district, moreover, the work of rehabilitation could be much more easily achieved. The bulk of illness in the community is relatively long-term illness. From the point of view of the community as a whole, the greatest gains which are to be made are in the

[1] Report, paras. 426-437.
[2] See above, pp. 95-108.

reduction of chronic disability. As the Tomlinson Report [1] points out, the gain is twofold; we save the cost of prolonged benefit payments, and we regain the productive capacity of the rehabilitated. Conversely, each disabled worker causes double loss. Medical science should eventually reach the stage at which the chronic invalid or the totally dependent cripple will become as rare as smallpox patients. Already modern fracture treatment, manipulative and plastic surgery, psychiatry, remedial exercises and occupational therapy are restoring lost capacity. The Tomlinson Report makes valuable proposals for furthering this. But this national rehabilitation service must be closely linked with the national medical service, and if the latter is built round the hospital and the health centre, this link is much easier to forge than if the latter is dispersed among scores of individual doctors. Hospitals and health centres should be linked to rehabilitation centres; [2] the latter should provide a gymnasium, massage rooms, playing fields and sports track, swimming bath and workshops.[3] The rehabilitation centre is the point at which the cure is completed and the disabled person once more becomes able to return to his normal occupation.

The work of rehabilitation must be a joint one between the national medical service and the Ministry of Labour. As the Beveridge Report says: [4]

> "Rehabilitation is a continuous process by which disabled persons should be transferred from the state of being incapable under full medical care to the state of being producers and earners."

It will be possible to achieve complete restoration of function and return to normal occupation for some people; for others, it will be necessary to provide re-training for another occupation; some will be able to earn only in sheltered trades or workshops. This underlines the part that the Ministry of Labour

[1] Report of Inter-departmental Committee on the Rehabilitation and Re-settlement of Disabled Persons, 1943. Cmd. 6415, p. 7.

[2] Evidence of the Joint Committee of the T.U.C. and the B.M.A. to the Inter-departmental Committee on the rehabilitation of persons injured by accidents, November 1937.

[3] An interesting example of treatment is the bicycle for men with stiff leg joints, the crank is adjustable; at first only a tiny leg movement propels the machine; as full function of the limb returns, the crank is lengthened so that increasingly vigorous movement is required. Bicycle gymkhanas are popular at the R.A.F. Centres.

[4] Report, para. 438.

has to play. If the worker can get back to his previous occupation, finding him a job is the last stage in the cure. If the worker has to find a new occupation, he must be given one in which there are good employment opportunities. If he remains largely disabled, special provision must be made for him. Given good enough organisation, far more can be done than has ever been attempted in the past. The R.A.F. rehabilitation centres have achieved extraordinary successes; the centres for war-disabled have done well; in the industrial field, the centres at Crewe for railwaymen and at Mansfield for miners are outstanding examples. But the existing arrangements have only scratched the surface of the problem, both in the medical sense and even more in the absorption of disabled people into employment. A great extension of this type of facility—including not only the rehabilitation of crippled persons but also of people suffering from nervous diseases—is a necessary part of the national medical and employment services.

The health and rehabilitation services are related to disability benefit in very much the same way as the training and placement services are related to unemployment benefit. The Plan provides that benefit should be paid for as long as the claimant is ill; [1] the condition for the receipt of benefit is certification by the national medical service and willingness to accept treatment for the disability. The public must, of course, have the safeguard that malingering will not be tolerated. This should not create serious difficulties. The control of claims by certification and otherwise would be greatly simplified under a comprehensive national medical service; in those conditions, only medical considerations would have any weight in the doctor's mind, and it would also be much easier to arrange the necessary organisation of sick visitors. In the initial stages, the amount of notified sickness would probably rise, for the present sickness insurance benefits are so inadequate that people cannot afford to be ill. But when the national medical service got under way it

[1] Report, paras. 129-132. A peculiar anomaly in the Plan's disability benefit proposals is the exclusion of illnesses of less than 13 weeks for self-employers. The reason is stated as the difficulty of claim control for people working on their own account. This is hard to understand ; it would be no easier for a shopkeeper to get a medical certificate than for a shop assistant to get one, and he would need the benefit to replace lost earnings just as badly. To meet the objection in the Report it would surely suffice to lengthen the waiting time for Class II people from the normal three days to two weeks. Report, paras. 118-119.

would soon yield results in the prevention and speedier cure of illness.

The disability benefit can and should be administered directly by the State, without passing through the approved societies. The latter have no longer any useful role; the evidence adduced in the Report is conclusive.[1] The Report suggests that the friendly societies and trade unions should be allowed to continue to act as responsible agents for the administration of State benefit. From the point of view of tidiness and uniformity of administration, the complete supersession of all intermediaries between the Ministry of Social Security and the individual is necessary. The administration of benefit will be closely linked with the national medical service; the collection and analysis of the health insurance statistics will play an increasingly important part in the war against disease—the existence of the approved societies is the main reason why our health statistics are so vastly inferior to our unemployment statistics; people will be receiving their other benefits from the Social Security office, and payment of one type of benefit through a friendly society would complicate matters. The friendly societies have a contribution to make, and they have played a valuable role in the past; they are, moreover, reasonably efficient in their administration. But on balance the case for excluding them is much stronger than the case for leaving them in. As a matter of policy, it may be desirable to retain these non-profit-making intermediaries, and not much would be lost thereby. But it would be altogether simpler and tidier to exclude them.

Finally, we come to the treatment of the blind. This is, of course, a special case of disability benefit.[2] Blind persons, in so far as they had been contributors in the past, would automatically receive disability benefit. This would cover all people who became blind after the age of 18—and had thus paid the three years' contributions which are necessary to qualify for disability benefit lasting more than a year. Under the Plan, the tiny minority who were born blind would still have assistance only; the blind people who are now receiving non-contributory pension in respect of blindness would presumably, at the introduction of the Plan, receive the new rates of benefit. The blind have

[1] Report, paras. 48-76. See above, Chapter III.

[2] Report, paras 166-170. See above, Chapter VII.

greater needs than most other disabled persons, both for cash benefits and for special welfare arrangements. The proposal in the Plan is that the cash benefits should be provided by the Ministry of Social Security, while the provision of special facilities should be left with local authorities. The case for retaining the local authority is sound enough, provided that the unit of administration is large enough to provide all the most modern forms of treatment. This, like all other rehabilitation work, is well worth the expenditure of considerable resources; the blind have a real and positive function to perform in society, and the contribution which they are able to make depends upon the facilities which can be provided. The spirit in which disablement is treated, be the disabled people blind or crippled or afflicted with mental disease, must be constructive from start to finish. The disabled are not helpless liabilities of the community; they are potential producers and valuable citizens, and persistent effort must be exerted to assist them to attain or recover productive power.

Workmen's Compensation

Industrial disability benefit is brought within the Plan, but in rather a separate pattern. A worker disabled by an industrial accident or disease receives 13 weeks' benefit at the ordinary rate, and then passes to an industrial pension, which represents two-thirds of his normal earnings, subject to a maximum of £3 a week and a minimum of the ordinary rate of benefit.[1] The widow of the victim of an industrial accident or disease receives a lump sum in addition to ordinary widow's benefit. The Report accepts the traditional case for special treatment of industrial accidents or diseases and for extra payment of their victims. This case, indeed, cannot lightly be rejected. Men work to provide goods which the community needs; in doing this work they take risks; it is right that they should be protected against these risks. Logically, of course, this special treatment should be confined to those who work in abnormally dangerous occupations. A miner, who is likely in the course of his working life to be injured time after time, should receive compensation when this injury takes place. There is no obvious reason, however, why the clerk should get greater compensation for an accident in the

[1] Report, paras. 77-105. See above, Chapter II.

office than he gets if he is run over in the street; he is actually safer in the office than on the way to work. The logical plan would therefore be to provide special benefits for those who work in specially hazardous jobs, and to treat other forms of industrial disability on precisely the same lines as ordinary disability. This would be administratively difficult, for there are dangerous occupations in safe industries and it would be difficult to pick them out in detail. Moreover, as the Report points out, there are other arguments which justify the greater payment for all industrial disability: a bank clerk may be ordered to carry an unduly large load of ledgers, and fall and break his leg—the fact that his accident results from his employer's orders is significant. The traditionally separate arrangements for compensation for industrial accident or disease, continued in the Beveridge Plan, have much to commend them.[1]

The Report breaks with tradition in separating the short-term industrial disability, which accounts for 90% of all claims, from the long disability lasting more than 13 weeks. For the initial period, the ordinary disability rate is paid; the single man would fare somewhat worse in this period than he does at present, while the married man would fare better—such apparent anomalies are inevitable when a thoroughly tangled system of benefits is replaced by a comprehensive and logical scheme. The special industrial pension comes into operation when the claimant has been disabled for 13 weeks. It is a vast advance upon existing scales—the £3 maximum compares with a present maximum of 35/-, and the children's allowance is doubled. The increase after 13 weeks compensates the single man for the reduction in his benefit in the initial period. The Plan holds the balance rightly in providing the really substantial benefits for those who suffer serious industrial accident or disease. There is the added advantage, furthermore, that the claimant has free medical benefit like everybody else, and has the full use of the rehabilitation service. Moreover, it is very properly provided that the claims are settled by administrative procedure instead of by the existing method of lengthy and costly litigation.

[1] It is illogical, of course, to relate the industrial pension to earnings. The risky jobs are not well paid. The pension should, strictly speaking, vary according to risk and not according to earnings. But the industrial pension provided in the Plan is for the bulk of workers a flat rate of £3 per week, and this is quite a reasonable way of fixing the matter.

Until the present time, workmen's compensation has been a charge on the employer, on the traditional grounds that if the employer has to pay for accidents he will therefore adopt the proper safety measures. It has never worked like this. The employer was able to insure against employer's liability and so cover himself at trivial cost; there is no evidence whatever that the financial burden of workmen's compensation has induced any improvement in safety measures. We can therefore follow one of two courses. We can argue that safety measures can be completely dissociated from workmen's compensation, in which case the industrial disability benefits can properly be financed in the same way as other social security benefits. Or we can devise a scheme which will, in fact, provide a real financial incentive to stimulate the prevention of accidents. The Fabian evidence recommended the latter; [1] the State would take over all insurance against employer's liability, which would be made compulsory, although employers would have the right to contract out into mutual indemnity funds; the premium paid by each firm would be merit-rated according to the safety provision made, and not according to the accident record. Under this arrangement, a coal mine with the latest safety measures would pay less in premiums than, say, a department store with a dangerous escalator. This would provide the maximum incentive to prevention of accidents, for the cost in excess of the minimum premium for the best possible precautions would fall upon profits.

The Report rejects this plan, on the grounds that the merit-rating of each undertaking would be administratively impossible; it may also be argued that in relation to total production costs, the premiums would be so small that the scheme would have very little effect upon safety. The Beveridge Plan treats the provision of industrial disability benefit against ordinary industrial risks—that is, the degree of industrial risk in all but the most hazardous industries—on precisely the same lines as other risks; this means that it is covered by contributions from employers, workers and the State. Certain industries, employing about one-third of the total number of employees, are then scheduled as hazardous. Two-thirds of the excess cost of compensation in these industries over the non-hazardous level is financed by a levy on these industries, and the remaining one-

[1] Appendix, p. 442.

third from the central pool of employers', workers' and State contributions. The net effect of this arrangement is that of the total estimated annual cost of £15 millions, two-thirds would be met from the Social Security Fund—representing contributions from the three parties—and one-third from the special levy in hazardous industries.[1] This is not a particularly tidy arrangement; the Report admits that it is a compromise between irreconcilable views—neither the trade unions nor the employers' organisations could present a united front. The covering of the non-hazardous level of risk from the Social Security Fund is permissible; the controversial point is the treatment of the excess risk in hazardous industries, which is shared in the ratio of two to one between the hazardous industries and the whole Fund. The levy in the hazardous industries will be administered by statutory associations of employers and workers in each industry; these associations will be specially charged with the active development of safety measures. It would be possible in these industries for the levy to be made between the various firms on merit-rating lines; over the field of hazardous industry this would be administratively practicable, and, as we have seen, it would provide a definite financial incentive to support the work of the associations.

On the whole, the proposals in the Plan are ingenious and acceptable. The benefit provision is well balanced; the settlement of claims by litigation is abolished; the non-hazardous level of risk is treated financially like the other social security provisions; the excess risk in the hazardous industries is borne jointly by the hazardous industries themselves and by the Fund as a whole. The scheme is, in fact, a mixture of tradition and reform, and is reasonably simple in administration.

Retirement Pensions

Old age pensions present by far the greatest difficulty of all the social security provisions. There are so many aged. They are one in every five of the adult population. The State must therefore treat them well, for they are a powerful political influence. But it must not treat them extravagantly, for excessive provision may seriously jeopardise the whole financial basis of social security. To provide the full Beveridge pension at once for every man of 65 and woman of 60 would cost as much as the whole of the

[1] Report, pp. 190-3.

nation's medical services—public and private—the whole cost of disability benefits, and the whole cost of children's allowances under the Beveridge Plan. This gives a sense of scale. From the Budgetary point of view, it does not matter very much whether a child's allowance is 9/- or 8/-, or whether unemployment benefit is 20/- or 25/- a week. But the number of aged is so great—and it will be more—that each half-crown a week must be carefully weighed and calculated. Provision for the aged requires a nice balance of statistical factors. The facts and figures are set out in the next chapter.[1] The Report strikes a reasonable balance between impracticable extravagance and inadequacy of benefit. A number of amendments could usefully be made to the Plan. But the structure is sensible.

There are three principles in the Beveridge Plan for the aged, and these govern the statistics. The first is, that the old age pension must be conditional upon retirement. The second is, that people should be induced to work for as long as possible. The third is, that there must be a transitional period before a full maintenance retirement pension is paid to every aged person. The retirement condition and the inducement to work are clearly sound on general grounds. The purpose of paying a maintenance pension is to replace lost earning power; there is no justification for paying such a pension while the pensioner is still earning. At present the rate of pension is only 10/- and does not claim to be a maintenance pension; it is therefore reasonable that people should be able to continue to work and still receive the pension. But as soon as the pension becomes sufficient for maintenance, it must necessarily become a retirement pension and not an old age pension. This will be generally agreed.

The need to induce people to postpone retirement is less apparent to those who think in terms of a restricted labour market; in the past, arguments for better pensions have been supported by the claim that these pensions, by enabling aged people to retire from work, would "reduce unemployment." Such conceptions belong to the past. They have some substance in a society riddled with unemployment. But they have no place in a rational society in which resources are kept fairly fully employed. To the community as a whole, it is advantageous that the aged should continue to work for as long as possible;

[1] See below, pp. 360-67. Report, paras. 233-357.

by working, they contribute to the national income and to the State's revenue, whereas in retirement they contribute nothing and are a charge upon the financial resources of the rest of the community. This is especially true in an ageing community, and appears even more true when we bear in mind the need to lengthen the period of education at the other end of the age-scale. Some inducement to postpone retirement should therefore be given; the Beveridge Plan does this by increasing the pension for every year by which retirement is postponed; the Fabian evidence suggested the alternative plan of making a 10/- old age payment to everyone of pensionable age who continued to work—this would be some compensation for loss of earning power resulting from old age—with a full maintenance pension on retirement.[1] In the finance of the Plan, this is an important factor; the extent to which people remain at work may make a difference of 10% in the size of the pension which it is possible to provide.[2] The choice between the two methods of inducing the aged to postpone retirement requires further investigation; the Fabian idea seems likely to be much the more effective. This choice having been made, one of the most important tasks will be to determine methods by which special employment can be provided for the aged, suitable for their declining powers. Very little is known about the prospects of developing such work—there has been no incentive to research upon it—but there is good reason to believe that research and organisation expended in this way would yield valuable results, and might revolutionise the scale of the old age provision which would become possible for those who had eventually retired.

The aim of the Plan, therefore, is a retirement pension for every aged person at the full maintenance rate of 24/- single and 40/- for a married couple; this is a generous level, and it is adequate in the fullest sense of the term. But it is both impracticable and unnecessary to enact this immediately. The cost in 1945 would be some £280 millions, compared with a prospective cost of £151 millions of the existing provision for the aged under the Pensions Act of 1940, which itself is nearly double the pre-war expenditure. The difference is just about the same as the whole pre-war expenditure, national and local, on public edu-

[1] Appendix. p. 439.
[2] See below, pp. 363-67, for the explanation of this and other detailed figures.

cation, and it is a good deal more than the whole estimated expenditure on unemployment benefit. Such an increase is more than the community can afford at one blow. It is reasonable, therefore, to adopt the principle of a transition, and to introduce the full maintenance retirement pension gradually. This has the additional advantage of providing an interval in which existing superannuation schemes can be adjusted to the new arrangements, and in which people approaching old age can also adjust the provision they make. The basic reason for the transition is financial and economic, but there are other good arguments for it.

This transition can be made in an infinite number of ways. Firstly, the existing aged. About one-quarter of them would under the present arrangements obtain supplementary pensions; they need full maintenance from the State, and must have it. The Plan therefore provides for assistance pensions at a full maintenance rate for all who need it; these would be paid on a unified means test basis, instead of the present scheme by which aged persons are means-tested either by the Customs and Excise or by the Assistance Board or by the Public Assistance Committee, according to the particular category in which they come. Another large group—more than one-third of the whole—have contributory pensions of 10/- but do not apply for supplementary benefit; the Plan for them is to increase their pensions to 14/-, provided they have retired, and to step this up by 1/- every two years until the full rate of 24/- is reached in 1965. Most of the remainder—about one-quarter of the whole—receive no State pension of any kind, and are not in need; they are looked after by superannuation schemes and by their own savings. Under the Plan, they would continue in the same position, but would, of course, have full assistance pensions available to them in case of need. All the aged, like every other section of the community, would have free medical treatment—an important service for the old.

This pattern will remain until 1955. By then, the contributory pensioners will be receiving 19/-. Members of the present contributory class who retire during this period will receive the appropriate rate on the stepped-up scale, or more if they postpone their retirement. But no one else will automatically receive a pension. In 1955, however, the new contributory classes—

broadly, the whole present uninsured population, but primarily the self-employed and the non-gainfully occupied—will become eligible. A farmer reaching the age of 65 in 1955 will be able to retire and claim a pension of 14/-; his pension will not be stepped up, but people coming in later will come in at a higher rate—the coster who retires at 65 in 1960 will receive 19/-. So gradually as time passes, the whole aged population will be receiving the full maintenance pension as of right; in 1965 the great bulk of the aged will be getting it, and by 1975 the minority without pension will be less than 5%.

As a twenty-year transition this Plan has its merits. It takes account of the profound social fact that there is a large section of the aged whose need for a State pension certainly ranks far behind other vital claims upon the national resources. It is a balanced programme, in that the cost increases during the twenty years at much the same rate as the national income can reasonably be expected to increase. It brings in the new pensioners by an orderly method. If the provision of full maintenance pension for everybody in the initial stages has to be ruled out, then we have to decide somehow who is to be included and who excluded, and unless we do this by means-testing everybody, the test of contributory status is as good as any other, provided that the proper provision is made for those who need pensions. But, as the Report says, there is no sanctity about twenty years. We shall see in the next chapter, when the financial implications are discussed, that there is some margin in the total expenditure figure of the Plan which would permit some increase in the provision for the aged. This could either be done by a more universal pension from the start at a lower rate, as was recommended by the Fabian Society, which would give pensions to a good many people who in no sense need them, but which would be more in line with comprehensive social security. Or it would be possible to speed up the Beveridge transition, starting off at a higher rate for contributory pensioners and bringing in the new classes more quickly, aiming at reaching by 1955 the position which the Plan reaches in 1965. In determining old age pensions, it is best to err on the conservative side. But a somewhat shorter period of transition should be within the nation's financial capacity.

HOUSEWIFE'S POLICY

The introduction of the Housewife's Policy is one of the most imaginative features of the Plan.[1] For the first time the social position of the married woman is recognised and safeguarded. She is no longer a "dependant," but a member of a joint team; when her husband dies, she is not regarded as a person whose usefulness to the community is at an end, but as a person who will then contribute to society in another way. She has special needs at the crises of marriage, maternity and widowhood; the Plan aims at providing these needs. This is something like a charter for the married woman. The Plan stops short of the more radical proposal to treat the housewife as a gainfully occupied person in receipt of pay from her husband for the domestic work she performs, and thus entitled to disability benefit when she is ill and has to pay someone else to do the domestic work of the household. But even in this it provides in substance for the need, for it arranges for the supply of household help as a social service when the housewife must go to hospital, and this can be expanded as necessary to cover cases in which the housewife is ill at home. For married women, the Plan is a revolution in status. Such changes in status, of course, bring responsibilities as well as benefits. The treatment of widowhood, for example, is greatly changed; some women, firmly rooted in the last century, may consider that it is changed for the worse. But for younger women, there can be no question of the soundness of the Plan.

According to the Plan,[2] the widow gets 36/- a week in the first 13 weeks of her widowhood; this is designed to see her through the period of adjustment to her change in circumstances. If she has children, she then passes to guardian benefit at the rate of 24/- a week—which is incidentally too low.[3] If she has no dependent children, or when her last child ceases to be dependent, the benefit stops. The widow is no longer entitled to continue to receive a pension indefinitely just because she is a widow. She must have a good benefit during the first shock of widowhood; she must have an adequate benefit while she has dependent children to look after. But there the special responsibility of the

[1] Report, paras. 107-117, 339-348. See below, p. 367.
[2] Report, paras. 153-156.
[3] This arises directly from the treatment of rent. See below, p. 348 *et seq*.

State ceases. This is, of course, in direct conflict with the present scheme, which provides small pensions which are wholly insufficient for maintenance to those widows whose husbands happen to have been in the contributory classes. There is no doubt which is right. If a woman is regarded as a useful citizen in her own right, not to be burnt on the husband's funeral pyre, then after an appropriate interval for the adjustment of her position she must no longer rely upon the State to maintain her. The overwhelming weight of evidence submitted to the Beveridge Committee favoured this basic change of treatment.

This is undeniably right in principle. But there are practical difficulties. About one-half of the women who are widowed below the age of 60 are above the age of 50 when their husbands die; another one-third are between the ages of 40 and 50; the vast majority would be over 45 when their widow's or guardian benefit ceased. It is not altogether easy to absorb women of that age into the labour market after they have been a long time away from it. The Plan enables them to get training and to receive training benefit while they are receiving it; much depends upon the scope and spirit of this training, and upon the efficiency of the placement machinery. It would probably be necessary in practice to treat the period in receipt of training benefit as a qualification period for receipt of unemployment and disability benefit when the period of training comes to an end. It would probably be necessary, too, to have a system of percentage pension which would be applied to those who were only capable of light work or part-time work. Similar considerations admittedly apply to spinsters of this age, but it is probably easier for spinsters to maintain their position in the labour market than it is for married women who have lost the habit of industrial discipline. The difficulties of re-employment of widows must not be exaggerated; under pre-war conditions, a 10/- pension hardly released widows without other resources from the need to work, and only a very small proportion—almost all with dependent children—were in such poverty that they had to apply for public assistance; an even smaller proportion of the widows without pension applied for public assistance. The war record of women of this age shows that the difficulties can easily be magnified out of all proportion. They can certainly be overcome.

Maternity benefit presents no practical difficulty; the shocking thing is that the existing provision is so unsatisfactory.[1] For gainfully occupied married women, the position is clear. They must be made to leave work for 6 weeks before and after confinement, as stipulated by the Washington Convention of 1919, which Britain should immediately ratify. As compensation for loss of earnings, they should receive a substantial benefit—the Plan provides 36/- a week for 13 weeks, which is both adequate in itself and is in reasonable relation to women's wages. For the married woman who is not in a paid job, there is no need to provide a weekly benefit, for there is no loss of earnings. But household help should be available as a social service. Both classes of married women, however, require a special grant to cover the incidental expenses of maternity; the Report suggests £4, but this is altogether inadequate; a figure of £10 is much nearer what is reasonable—the cost of such grants is so small that no purely financial question arises; what is necessary is that the need should be generously covered.

The Plan suggests a marriage grant which would be proportionate to the number of contributions paid by the bride before marriage, subject to a maximum of £10. Here, too, a somewhat larger grant would be in order; the scale of Budgetary expenditure is small, and this is a point at which it would be possible very substantially to encourage earlier marriages, with correspondingly beneficial effects upon the population trend.

At each stage the married woman with a job is given a choice between being treated as a housewife and being treated as an employed person. In either case she receives maternity benefit and the universal widow's and guardian benefit, retirement pension and funeral benefit. If she chooses to be classified as a housewife, she pays no contributions and receives no other benefits. If she chooses to be an employed person, she is entitled to a retirement pension in her own right, whether her husband is working or not; she receives unemployment and disability benefit at a reduced rate of 16/- instead of 24/- —she is assumed to have no rent obligations; she pays the ordinary employed person's contribution. For the first time, in fact, the needs of the woman with a job find expression; the Housewife's Policy rights the anomalies of the Anomalies Regulations and provides appropriate benefits for housewives who have jobs and housewives with none.

[1] Appendix, p. 452.

FUNERALS AND INDUSTRIAL ASSURANCE

The Plan provides a funeral grant—better called death benefit—of £20 for an adult, with lower scales for children.[1] People aged 60 or more at the beginning of the scheme will not be eligible; otherwise the grant is universal. Britain has been far behind other countries in omitting funeral benefit from social insurance. Yet the British people are second to none in their determination to make voluntary provision for burial. So the vast industrial assurance business has been built up, trebling its scale in the last generation, employing an army of collectors in a continuous offensive to extract the last penny of weekly savings from the working people of the country. The abuses and inefficiencies of this business have been frequently exposed, both in official investigations and in the works of independent researchers; the Report sets out the facts with impressive clarity.[2] The cost figures alone are enough to justify the nationalisation of industrial assurance; of every 1/- paid by the policy-holder to the companies, only 7½d. goes to the assurance fund. But the statistics of lapses are even more spectacular; in the last years before the war, about 10 million policies were issued every year, and about 6¾ million ended prematurely; nearly one-half of this 6¾ million represented outright forfeitures after the policy had been taken up and premiums paid upon it; these are the consequences of high-pressure salesmanship. There is no need for us here to make the case against private industrial assurance; the Report is a crushing indictment. The remedy proposed is straightforward and simple—the establishment of an Industrial Assurance Board, a public corporation which would take over and operate the whole business. The Board would become the sole provider of the small man's life assurance, and would no doubt eventually become the main repository of working-class savings.[3] This

[1] Report, paras. 157-160.

[2] Report, paras. 181-192 and pp. 249-76. See also Chapter XI above, and Wilson and Levy, *Industrial Assurance.*

[3] The Board could, for example, institute a simple superannuation scheme to which people could contribute. In particular, employers who desired to supplement the State pension provision could be encouraged to make contributions on behalf of their employees instead of running individual schemes. The individual superannuation schemes are an important obstacle to industrial mobility, and they are probably more costly to run than a standard Industrial Assurance Board scheme would be. A contribution of 1/- a week paid regularly from the age of 20, or of 2/6 a week from 40, would purchase an annuity of 10/- a week at the age of 65. Appendix, p. 440.

solution of the problem is by far the easiest and most satisfactory; it may prove more satisfactory for insurance companies' shareholders than the alternative loss of business which would result from the introduction of the social security funeral grant; for insurance agents, it provides opportunity for new jobs with the new Board, and in any case adequate compensation.

Industrial assurance, however, is not the only obstacle to the proper and simple treatment of the problem of burial. The present cost is far too high.[1] The average working-class expenditure on a funeral, at 1942 prices, is about £18. In London, in April 1942, it was possible to get earth burial in a common grave, a hearse, coffin, one car and undertaker's services for £15, but the charge is sometimes as much as £30. In provincial cities, the cost is very little less. These figures are about double the true cost of the services provided; the Ministry of Health makes grants up to £7 10/- for funerals undertaken by local authorities, and this is the order of magnitude of the cost which must necessarily be incurred—this provides a funeral indistinguishable from the £15 one. This excess of prices over the cost of the services is remarkable. The main reason is that the prices are maintained by a network of trade associations;[2] they therefore correspond to the costs of the small undertaker whose overheads are high in relation to turnover. The large firms, with full employment of their capital, could do the service much more cheaply, but prefer to keep their charges high. Subsidiary reasons are the unnecessarily small-scale production of coffins and other funeral accessories, at excessive cost; there is also some element of financial risk-bearing in the cost, for the undertaker pays the interment fees before he gets his money.

The various fees, such as the cost of the grave, the fee for grave-digging, the fee for the clergyman, the fee for the verger and the fee for the tolling of the bell, vary widely from place to place—they vary not only according to the size of the grave to be dug, but also according to its location in the cemetery. In London these costs for burial in a common grave are about £1 10/-; for a private grave the cost is £5 to £10. Cremation costs are somewhat higher; the charges vary from £2 2/- to

[1] Appendix, p. 452. The standard work is Wilson and Levy, *Burial Costs and Funeral Reform*; the latest facts are given in *Fabian Quarterly*, January 1943.

[2] For particulars of these, see Levy, *Retail Trade Associations*, pp. 142-3, 188-90.

£8 8/-.[1] To this must be added the cost of the coffin and the funeral service as a whole, together with the fee of the second doctor—normally two guineas—whose certificate that death was from natural causes is required before the body may be cremated. The cost of cremation could be greatly reduced if more use were made of crematoria; practically the whole of the cost consists of overhead, the actual cost of the fuel being only a few shillings. In this respect, cremation is greatly preferable to burial in an earth grave; the crematorium works under conditions of decreasing cost, whereas the cemetery actually loses capital at each burial.

The whole process of burial is riddled with anomalies and petty instances of overcharging, as is inevitable when the natural delicacy of the public restrains the working of publicity. This can best be dealt with by municipal control. Local authorities should be required to make schemes for the regulation of charges, and in default of satisfactory co-operation from private firms should be required to provide municipal burial or cremation at a standard acceptable to the local *mores* at a reasonable price. The undertaking services will certainly expand in the coming years, and it is highly necessary to ensure that the community secures the fullest advantages of concentration of undertakers' concerns over large areas and the consequent quantity production of accessories without being subjected to the undertakers' associations' monopoly price policy. This would make certain that a suitable service was provided for all; it would tend to reduce the social competition in funerals; it would cut clean through the tangle of fees and charges, and provide a sane and reverent treatment of death. The Beveridge Plan institutes proper financial provision for death, by the introduction of funeral grant and the nationalisation of industrial assurance; to this must be added energetic and far-reaching funeral reform.

National Assistance

However complete the quasi-insurance provisions may be, there will always be some contingencies and some needs which cannot be fitted into a universal scheme. This is the field of

[1] *Fabian Quarterly*, January 1943, pp. 26-7, sets out the full breakdown of charges in different parts of the country; the £2 2/- figure is for the municipal crematorium at Hull; the £8 8/- is for private crematoria in Glasgow and Edinburgh.

national assistance.[1] This would cover the sort of emergencies represented by applications for Prevention and Relief of Distress assistance in war-time;[2] it would cover people outside the scheme, such as wives of men in prison or people of private means who had lost their incomes and could or would not apply for training benefit to reinstate themselves as active working members of the community, or people who failed to comply with the minimum contributory qualifications; it would cover the tiny minority who would disqualify themselves for unemployment or disability benefit by refusing to comply with the conditions; it would cover cases in which people were unable for justifiable reasons to maintain themselves upon the basis benefits provided. In the period of transition to the new universal retirement pension, there will be large numbers of people who require assistance pensions to supplement their contributory pensions to a full maintenance level. In this field, payment of benefits would, of course, only be made after full investigation of financial resources and other circumstances. In general, it would be desirable to allow local officers some degree of discretion in payment, for this is the point at which individual needs must be assessed and satisfied.

This field is now shared between the Assistance Board and the Public Assistance Committees.[3] The Plan provides rightly that it should all pass to the Ministry of Social Security. The various types of assistance which are required would, of course, be treated in different ways. The provision of assistance pensions can be made according to unified regulations, defining the kind of financial resources which should be ignored in the assessment of means, and the scale of payment which should be made. This is the most formalised part of the work of national assistance. At the other extreme, the treatment of people who voluntarily place themselves outside the scope of the scheme by failure to co-operate with the placement, training and rehabilitation services, or with the medical service, must be individual and elastic, and must be of a definitely deterrent nature. People who apply for special relief because of special needs—for example, disabled people with abnormal expenses resulting from their disability—must be treated sympathetically and rationally. The

[1] Report, paras. 161-165, 172, 369-374.
[2] See above, pp. 144, 145.
[3] See Chapters V and I above.

management of national assistance requires a far higher quality of trained staff than the straightforward payment of benefits. The bulk of the Ministry's work is reasonably simple—it consists of determination of whether people are eligible for benefit, and payment accordingly; the eligibility flows directly from the certification of the Ministry of Labour for unemployment benefit, and of the Medical Service for disability benefit. But in the assistance field, people have to be treated as individuals with individual problems, and a high standard of social purpose in administration and a high quality of personnel are accordingly necessary. The implications for staff training are discussed in a later chapter;[1] it must be appreciated from the start that social security here becomes social welfare, and the work must be organised on a welfare basis, with the aim of satisfying the need of the individual claimant, instead of on standardised formulas.

This represents the final and complete abolition of the Poor Law. There remains the question of the other functions fulfilled by the Public Assistance Committees of local authorities—in particular, the institutional treatment of the aged and the provision of special welfare facilities for the aged. The Report recommends that this work should remain under the control of local authorities; it is a field in which there are great opportunities for experimental work by advanced authorities, and the need for such services does differ from one locality to another. The old Public Assistance Committees, many renamed Social Welfare Committees, following the lead of the London County Council, would have a valuable and expanding scope for activity on these lines. The Ministry of Social Security would exercise some supervisory control of them, both in requiring minimum standards of service and in laying down standard principles upon which means tests would be applied. Co-operation between the Ministry and the local authorities would have to be intimate and permanent; the underlying principle is that the Ministry must be responsible for all cash payments, and the local authority for treatment and services of an institutional character.

[1] See Chapter XIV below.

Children's Allowances

The Plan provides for children's allowances for each child after the first, varying according to age, but at an average rate of 8/- per child.[1] It is hardly necessary, in 1943, to make the case for children's allowances; only those who are implacably opposed to a scientific treatment of social problems now raise any objection. About one-quarter of all poverty is due to the insufficiency of earnings to meet the needs of large families, and it is in any case desirable on population grounds to remove all financial obstacles to parenthood.

There appears to be something of a rhythm in the standard of living of the ordinary man. In childhood he has one chance in five of being below the poverty line. His position then improves rapidly. In the early twenties he is less likely to be in poverty than at any other time of his life—a chance of less than one in twenty-four. He gets married; by the time he is in his early thirties his danger of poverty is double what it was ten years before. His family obligations grow; by the late thirties there is one chance in eight that he will be below the poverty line. Then his children grow up; his position improves again; by the time he has passed fifty, the risk has fallen to one in fourteen. Then as his earning power declines his position gradually deteriorates, until after the age of seventy his danger of poverty is over one in eight.[2] It is hardly an exaggeration to say that to have children—certainly to have more than two children—is to court poverty. One-quarter of the families containing three children, and one-half of the families containing four children or more, are in conditions of poverty;[3] one child in every four is living in conditions of poverty. This state of affairs is clearly intolerable for a self-respecting community, and the best remedy is children's allowances. This having been agreed, there are only three major points at issue. First, should children's allowances be given in respect of every child in the family, and every family in the community? Second, should each child have the same allowance? Third, what should the allowance be?

[1] Report, paras. 410-445.

[2] *The Standard of Living in Bristol*, p. 37.

[3] In Bristol 6·5% of families containing one child were below the poverty line; 11·1% of families containing two children; 24·8% of families containing three children; and 51·3% of families containing four or more: *op. cit.*, p. 38.

There is no doubt that the allowances should be universal, in the sense that there should be no upper income limit nor contributory conditions. The income tax payer receives some allowance already in the form of tax relief, and this could, if necessary, be correspondingly reduced.[1] But every family should certainly be entitled to the allowance. The need for allowance for every child in the family is less clearly established; the possession of one child very rarely plunges a family into poverty, for earnings are normally adequate to provide for a married man with one child. People on social security benefit must, of course, receive an allowance for every child, but general provision for the first child is not a matter of urgent social priority. The Plan omits the first child.

The second question is more difficult. The cost of maintaining a child varies from, say, 6/6 per week, at current prices, for an under-5-year-old to 11/6 a week for a boy of 14. These costs are exclusive of rent. But against this there are already services in kind—free and cheap milk, school meals and so on. These vary also according to the child's age. There is evidently a good case for paying an allowance which varies with age, which will take in both the needs of that age and the services which are likely to be available. The Report decides in favour of this principle, but leaves open the actual scales; the determination of appropriate scales would be very difficult, for the social service provision differs widely from one locality to another, and may completely distort the assumptions upon which the scale would be based. This is one disadvantage, but there is a more profound objection. It is important to encourage people to have three or more children. This suggests that we should provide a larger allowance for the third child than for the second, and for the fourth child than the third—simple stepping up of allowances of this kind, which emphasises the importance of a large family, cannot be linked with a variation of allowance for age. It would be much too complicated. It would confuse the parents, who would miss the fundamental point, that the community intended to remove all financial obstacles to large families. The parent would not know where he stood. The proposal in the Plan to vary allowances according to age should therefore be rejected

[1] The complications of tax relief, together with the statistical and financial framework of children's allowances, are discussed in detail below, pp. 368-71.

—except possibly for social security benefits, which must be related closely to costs of maintenance. The general scheme should provide a stepping-up of allowance for each successive child.[1]

Thirdly, the size of allowance. The Plan proposes an average of 8/- per child. This compares with an average cost of maintenance, excluding rent, of 9/-; it is assumed that services in kind are available to the average extent of 1/- a week. For the children of parents on social security benefits, to whom the full cost of maintenance must clearly be allowed, the 8/- rate is probably adequate as modified by the appropriate variations according to the age of the children.[2] For the general scheme it is not necessary to link the allowances with maintenance costs. If allowance is paid for the first child, a rate of 6/- for each of the first two children, 7/- for the third, and 8/- for the fourth and subsequent children would be reasonable. If no allowance is made for the first child, rates of 7/- for the second, 8/- for the third, and 9/- for the subsequent children would be more appropriate than the Beveridge rate of 8/- per child, varied according to age. There is little difference in total cost between the stepped-up rate and the flat rate; the former would distribute the allowances where they were needed most. It is not to be expected, of course, that such a plan would immediately have a significant effect upon the willingness of people to have large families; not enough is yet known about the reasons underlying population movements to enable us to generalise about the effects of various policies. The basic optimism or pessimism expressed in the social system and social customs may well be the fundamental determinant of the birth-rate in an advanced community in which reliable birth control methods are available to the great mass of the population. In an expanding society, in which there are ample opportunities for young people, men and women will have families. Such a society will be confident of its future, and will put parenthood in the proper place in its social priorities. These basic conditions bear the same relationship to children's allow-

[1] The Beveridge Plan children's allowances can in one sense be regarded as being stepped up for each successive child; a family with one child receives no allowance; a family with two children an average of 4/- per child; a family with three, 5/4 per child, and so on. This rate of increase, however, is not nearly enough.

[2] If the social security benefits do not vary according to rent obligation, of course, the children's allowance should contain some element of provision for rent; to that extent, the Beveridge allowances are inadequate.

ances as employment opportunities and health bear to unemployment benefit and disability benefit. Cash allowances alone will not solve the population problem; they are only one of a score of expressions of the community's attitude to parenthood. But their immediate institution would not only strike at the root of much poverty, but would also be a sign of the nation's determination to put first things first in the post-war world.

War Pensions

War Pensions are outside the natural scope of a plan for social security. Injury or loss of life in war is an altogether different type of contingency from unemployment, disability and old age. The basic considerations which are involved in the determination of war pensions are different from those of the peace-time social security plan. Although these differences exist, however, the whole structure of war pensions is profoundly affected by the introduction of a social security plan. About 650,000 people are now receiving war pensions of various kinds from the war of 1914-18;[1] the number of members of the armed forces killed, missing, and wounded in the recent war exceeds 400,000, and nearly 30,000 merchant seamen have been killed; up to August 1944 nearly 60,000 civilians had been killed in air-raids and nearly 80,000 seriously injured.[2] These men and women and their dependants will have rights under the Beveridge Plan just the same as anyone else. It is clearly necessary that the payments which they receive in virtue of their war disability should bear some rational relationship to social security payments generally.

The problem is particularly difficult, for the war pension structure dates from the war of 1914-18, when the social services were in their infancy. The structure is antiquated and unscientific;[3] according to present-day criteria, it gives some people too much and others too little; compared with the streamline of the Beveridge Plan, its classification is unreal and outmoded. Nowhere in the jungle of Royal Warrants is there any trace of the purpose which war pensions are designed to achieve. Are they meant to provide maintenance? Are they meant to provide special compensation for the risks of service in the armed forces? Or are they meant to be a simple recognition of service to the

[1] Report, p. 244.

[2] *Economist*, 16th January 1943.

[3] See Chapter VIII above, which explains the whole structure.

nation? It is indeed difficult to say. In the past this has not mattered very much, for war pensions were far in excess of the benefits provided by the social services. But when we have real social security provision, the matter becomes extremely important, for we shall find some war pensioners on the present scale faring worse than people on social security benefit. The position has greatly improved since the big increases in war pensions of July 1943 and April 1944, which brought war pensions much more nearly into line with the standards laid down in the Beveridge Plan. But nevertheless it is necessary to straighten these matters out.

The first difficulty is to establish proper standards of comparison between war pensioners' benefits and social security benefits. We have to determine principles by which we can decide whether a class of pension is or is not anomalous. Is a war disability pension comparable with disability benefit under the Beveridge Plan or with industrial disability pension? Should the disabled soldier get more than the disabled coal-miner? Should the widow of a man killed in an air-raid get more than the widow of a man who is run over in the street? These are difficult questions, especially in the context of total war. Time and time again it is said that we are all in the front line together, and indeed in the first two years of war the enemy killed as many civilians as fighting men. If we were replanning the whole war pensions structure, we should have to find new principles to govern its relationship with the social security structure. It is too late to do this for the recent war. When the Beveridge Plan is enacted, the State will only have a one-way option in adjusting war pensions, for it can hardly take away pensions which it has already given; one cannot make major reforms on the basis of a one-way option. All we should do is to adjust glaring anomalies. If the Beveridge Plan were enacted as it stands, how significant would these anomalies be?

War disability pensions would be at least 7/6 a week too low. These pensions are fixed on the workmen's compensation pattern; they vary according to rank, which is equivalent to earnings. The disabled private gets a pension for 100% disability of 40/- a week; the flight-sergeant or chief petty officer 50/-. To this is added a wife's allowance of 10/- a week, which is not meant to cover the needs of a wife on the social security principle, but which is paid because a married soldier gets more pay than a single one, and is therefore entitled to a larger pension. It is by no means unreasonable to handle war disability pensions on the workmen's compensation principle; it means that the soldier's pension is calculated in much the same way as the industrial pension of the worker disabled in an explosives factory or coal mine. The soldier's disability pension must therefore be in line with that of the industrial worker of comparable status. This seems a sound basis of comparison. On the present workmen's compensation scale, with a maximum of 35/- a week, the soldier is the better off. But under the Beveridge Plan, most munition workers disabled in the war would receive the maximum industrial pension of 60/- a week and few would get less than 50/-. This would be well ahead of existing war disability pension scales. In the context of the Beveridge industrial pensions, therefore, it would be impossible to justify a basic war disability pension of less than 47/6 for a private and 57/6 for a senior N.C.O. plus the wife's allowance of 10/-. This means an over-all increase of 7/6 a week, which should, of course, apply to officers as well as to other ranks. The standard children's allowances must be increased from 7/6 a week, as at present, to 8/- a week. These rates of war disability pension must apply to merchant seamen, fishermen and full-time civil defence workers. Servicewomen's disability pensions at the minimum level of 40/- a week would be fairly in line with women munition workers' industrial disability pensions; a woman munition worker's earnings in 1944 averaged something over 60/- a week, which would provide a Beveridge industrial pension of 40/-.

According to the present arrangements, the war-disabled civilian is treated as if he were a private. This cannot be justified except on grounds of expediency. Civilian war disablement is entirely different from servicemen's disablement. All civilians must take equal risks during the war. All have to help in civil defence and fire-fighting; all have to take their chance. The industrial pension principle has no application here. The analogy is with ordinary disability benefit. The risks of disablement by enemy action must be pooled among civilians in just the same way as the risks of influenza. The company manager should receive the same benefit as the docker; a man should receive the same benefit as a woman. The rates of benefit should be higher than the normal disability benefit of the Beveridge Plan. The civilians are in the front line, and casualties must be well cared for. If we were starting from scratch, the simple plan would be to pay a civilian war disability pension of 50% more than the Beveridge normal disability benefit. This would provide 36/- a week for the gainfully occupied single man or woman, and 60/- for the married man. Housewives and non-gainfully occupied people could receive 18/-. There are two basic points. The man and the woman must receive equal pension, fixed in some relation to subsistence cost and not to earnings; the wife's allowance must be fixed in the same relation to subsistence cost. The present civilian scheme provides 40/- for a gainfully occupied single man; 40/- for a single woman; a wife's allowance of 10/-. This is anomalous at both points. There is no justification for sex discrimination; the wife's allowance is based not in relation to subsistence cost, but is just the figure that happens to be included in a private soldier's pension in virtue of the fact that a married soldier gets more pay than the unmarried. How should these anomalies be righted? We cannot change the whole thing, for this would involve a reduction in the single man's pension, which is impossible. But it would suffice to increase the gainfully occupied woman's pension up to the man's—and also the pension paid to the housewife, or Class IV woman, up to the Class IV man's—and to increase the pension to a married man from 50/- to, say, 55/-. The children's allowances would also have to be increased to the standard 8/- rate. This fairly simple adjustment would remove the anomaly and bring the pensions into reasonable relationship with normal disability benefit.

The treatment of widows is much more difficult, for the war pensions scheme follows principles which have no analogy in the social services of the past or the future. The best standard of comparison is between the war widow and the munition worker's widow.[1] The private's widow with children receives a pension of 32/6 a week; this is stepped up by a small amount for each rank. The widow of a munition worker killed in an industrial accident

[1] The comparison must be between the war widow's pension and the treatment of widows of munition workers killed in accidents during the war, not the treatment of new widows under the Plan.

in this war will have received a lump sum.[1] When the Beveridge Plan is introduced she will receive guardian benefit at the rate of 24/- a week—which is somewhat too low. On this comparison the pension of the war widow with children is adequate. The children's allowance, at 11/- per child, is of course far above that paid in respect of any other kinds of children. The childless war widow, moreover, fares appreciably better than the munition worker's widow. She receives 20/- a week if she is under 40, and 32/6 if she is over 40; whereas under the Beveridge Plan the childless munition worker's widow will have only the contributory widow's pension of 10/- in addition to her lump sum. It is reasonable, therefore, to leave the childless war widow's pension unchanged. The pensions of civilian war casualties' widows are on the same lines as war widows' pensions and require no adjustment to conform with the Beveridge Plan.

These illustrations show the extreme complexity of the problems which will arise in the adjustment of war pensions to the Beveridge Plan. Similar questions arise when war pension rates are compared with those of the White Paper. There must necessarily be a considerable process of rationalisation and removal of anomalies. As the new Plan approaches the Statute Book great pressure will very rightly be exerted upon the Ministry of Pensions to right these anomalies. This must be met, not by wild and extravagant increases, nor by cheese-paring resistance, but by vigorous action according to rational principles. It is very difficult to see how this situation can be adequately and equitably handled by a separate Ministry of Pensions. These problems will have to be solved at a very early stage, probably before the Ministry of Social Security has the Plan in full operation. This points clearly to the need for transferring the administration of war pensions from the Ministry of Pensions to the Ministry of Social Security as soon as the latter is formed; the Ministry of Pensions machinery should become a separate division of the Ministry of Social Security, with a special Parliamentary Secretary. On general grounds there is much to be said for this. It would be

[1] For most workers' widows this is £300; an addition is made to the lump sum in respect of children, varying according to their number and age, with a maximum of £600.

much easier for the pensioner; it would simplify administration and save staff; it would prevent uneconomic duplication of rehabilitation services. The only argument against the transfer is that the existence of a separate Ministry of Pensions ensures a just and sympathetic treatment of claims based upon war disabilities, and makes certain that the war pensioners will be heard. But this argument has no validity when there is a comprehensive social security plan; indeed, the interests of the war pensioners would be better protected under the new regime, for the Social Security Ministry will attract to itself the best staff, social workers, technical advisers and social administrators, and in such conditions a separate Ministry of Pensions would probably become rather a backwater. The Beveridge Report leaves this question open. It says very little about war pensions.[1] But there is no doubt whatever where the rights of the matter lie. Unless the Ministry of Pensions is assimilated into the Social Security Ministry, the extremely difficult and complicated problems involved in adjusting the position of the war pensioner to the new social security structure will never be equitably and effectively settled.

Administration

The administration of social security presents no serious difficulties. The creation of a Ministry of Social Security is not nearly as complicated and arduous a task as was the building of the Ministry of Supply or the Ministry of Food. In the initial stage, the problem is one of gathering together the various Departments which are concerned with the administration of the existing social insurance and assistance schemes—the Assistance Board, some of the Ministry of Health, some of the Ministry of Labour, part of Customs and Excise, part of the Home Office, the Ministry of Pensions, and much of the local authorities' Public Assistance organisation. This must be welded into one cohesive Ministry. The responsibility of the Ministry would in general cover the payment of benefits and the provision of the corresponding welfare facilities; the work of developing the

[1] Report, para. 387.

placement and training service would remain with the Ministry of Labour, the national medical service with the Ministry of Health, and the national rehabilitation service with the Ministries of Health and Labour jointly. This appears to be the rational division of function; health and employment policy go far beyond the scope of social security in the ordinary sense of the word.

The Ministry would, of course, operate through regional and local offices, shared by the Ministry of Labour for placement organisation. Much of the work would be simple and standardised, and would be hardly more than the checking and payment of claims for benefit. It is necessary, however, that the local offices should become an integral part of local community life, and in order to keep officers in touch with local opinion and affairs there should be local Advisory Committees.[1] These would have no executive powers, but they would provide facilities for the ventilation of complaints and for transmission to the officers of comments and suggestions. In such questions as the treatment of rent, the treatment of long-term unemployed in depressed communities, the development of welfare facilities or the linking of maternity grants with attendance at the clinic, these local contacts are of first-class importance. The success of the Ministry depends to a very large extent upon the positive co-operation which it can secure from the public, and the development of local and regional Advisory Committees plays an important part in this.

Part of the same problem is the attainment of proper standards of service to the individual. The record of Government Departments in this field is not impressive. This is partly a question of office accommodation—the Ministry will unfortunately inherit rather dingy local premises, and rebuilding would come rather low on the list of post-war priorities, but even the existing premises could be made much more attractive. It is also a question of standards of training and quality of staff—and this is discussed in detail later.[2] But it is mainly a question of the atmosphere of administration; if the Minister and his senior officials at headquarters and in the field regard their job as one of actively and positively advancing the public welfare and of

[1] Appendix, p. 444.
[2] See below, Chapter XIV.

destroying poverty, the right atmosphere will follow as a matter of course. The whole activity of a bank is directed towards attracting clients; the Ministry of Social Security must likewise be dominated by the idea of giving prompt and efficient service. An important element in this is the development of a proper public relations policy which would educate the public in what the Ministry was trying to do, and would show the Ministry the public reaction to its policies. The need for active public relations has been insufficiently appreciated in this field in the past; the result has been a failure of the public to take advantage of the services provided for it and—what is much worse—serious misunderstanding of official policies and the consequent growth of mistrust and suspicion of the service provided. The unwillingness of many poverty-stricken people to apply for assistance is a typical instance of the first of these; the trouble which attended the inception of the Assistance Board is a typical instance of the second. The public must be associated with the Ministry as far as possible. Otherwise much will be lost.

There is no reason to suppose that the development of properly trained staff and efficient and imaginative service will unduly increase the cost of administration. The Report goes into the problem of administrative cost in some detail,[1] and comes to the conclusion that the cost of administration will be very little higher than that of the present patchwork scheme, in spite of the introduction of a number of completely new services. The cost of administration of the present schemes is on the average about 6% of the benefits paid; the cost of the comprehensive scheme's administration will be about 4½% of the benefits paid, and will gradually fall through the transition period. The economies of central administration are likely to be so great, indeed, that they will be able to absorb quite easily a considerable improvement in the service provided without an increase of cost. In any case, efficiency of service is an absolute necessity for success, and if it costs more to provide it, that additional cost should be paid. A universal scheme covering the whole population must work with streamlined efficiency; otherwise the goodwill of the public will be lost and with it the opportunity of instilling a new spirit into the relations between the State and the community.

[1] Report, p. 202.

Social Accountancy

So much for the Beveridge Plan itself. It stands alone as a piece of practical and imaginative planning. Its fate will ultimately be decided by the answer to the question, Can we afford it? The reply can be made : Can we afford not to afford it? Can we afford to retain poverty in Britain? Such replies are true. A hundred years ago, there had to be poverty. Now there need be none. That is the lesson of the Beveridge Plan. But this must be proved in hard facts and figures. The Plan brings with it tremendous social assets. But there are liabilities on the other side. This is a re-allocation of the national income—albeit on a very modest scale. The question is: Is the expenditure envisaged in the Plan on the right scale in relation to our national resources, and does it accord with proper social priorities? If the scale is right, then all the rest follows automatically from it. There are secondary matters to be settled, such as the proportion of the cost which can appropriately be covered by insured persons' contributions and the proportion to be borne by general taxation. These matters are discussed at some length in the following chapter, which assembles the financial and statistical material which is needed for a fair appraisal of the Plan. Here we are concerned only with the problem of scale. It is the essence of statesmanship to get the big things right; the details then fall into line.

The right approach to the problem is to compare the social security expenditure with the national income. This is the real test. The following table sets out certain relevant figures:

Social Security and National Income *
(£ millions)

	1938-39.	1945.		1965.
	Actual.	Present Services.	Beveridge Plan.	Beveridge Plan.
Net National Income .	4,595	6,500		8,500
Social Security Expenditure	326	415	697†	858
(as % of National Income)	*7·1*	*6·4*	*10·7*	*10·1*

* Net national income figures and total cost of social security—including cash benefits, health services, administration—from table on p. 378 below.

† This figure could if necessary be reduced without interference with the Plan ; economies could be made in the cost of unemployment benefit, disability benefit and children's allowances. See p. 374.

Just before the war of 1939, expenditure on social security benefits and publicly financed health services absorbed 7·1% of the national income. On certain assumptions about the future size of the national income, the Beveridge Plan would increase this proportion to 10·7% in 1945; the proportion would then fall to 10·1% in 1965. But this does not compare like with like. Much of the new expenditure is simply a re-channelling of existing expenditure, and does not represent a change in allocation of resources. If we take both private and public social security provision together, thus including industrial assurance premiums and payments to private doctors, we find that the increase is from 11% in 1938 to 13% in 1945.[1] In a world which will surely be very social-security-minded, an additional allocation of 2% of the national income for these purposes is surely possible; indeed, it is conservative. There are other charges on the nation's resources. But this level of expenditure can be fitted in without serious difficulty, provided that the national income is fairly maintained and the Treasury continues its war-time practice of using Budgetary policy to attain real social objectives. It would be necessary to retain some of the war-time taxation; possibly between one-third and one-half of it, according to the level of expenditure on national defence and other social services.[2] But on balance it should be possible without undue difficulty to make the jump from 1938 to 1945, and after that time the expansion in the cost of the Plan would be more than balanced by the steady increase in the national income.

But will the national income be £6½ milliards in 1945 and £8½ milliards in 1965? These figures are based upon the Report's assumption that prices will be 25% higher than in 1938; this is really immaterial, for changes in prices would, of course, affect both the size of the national income and the social security benefits. The dynamic factors are the number of workers in employment and the level of productivity—the output per worker. At the moment, following the Beveridge Report, the main attention is concentrated upon employment. But productivity is equally important, as the experience of the pre-war period shows. In the fifteen years from 1924 to 1938, unemployment averaged 14%. Had it been as low as 5%, the total national income during that whole period would have been

[1] See below, p. 378. [2] *ibid.*, p. 387.

10% higher. That loss of income was, so to speak, the cost to the nation of unemployment. But in the same period the national income per worker at work rose by about 20%; [1] if throughout those fifteen years, therefore, productivity had been as great as it was at the end of the period, the total national income in the fifteen years would have been 10% larger—just the same increase as would have taken place if there had been full employment throughout. Productivity must be fostered just as carefully as employment. We must aim at increasing both. Maximum productivity may be the more difficult to attain. But it is clear that once the problem of mass unemployment has been conquered, and unemployment varies at worst between, say, 5% and 10%, the possibilities of advance by reducing unemployment further are very limited, and the whole hope of increasing human welfare is governed by the prospects of increasing productivity.

In the immediate post-war period, after the main demobilisation—which is what we really mean by the notional year 1945—the level of employment will certainly be high. By then, imported raw materials will be flowing into the country in reasonable plenty. Reconstruction building will be getting under way. There will be hectic activity in the shipbuilding industry. The munition plants will be turning over to peace-time work. The Treasury would be releasing the deferred pay claims, and thus providing the necessary stimulus to purchasing power if activity showed signs of flagging. There will be a strong "reconstruction" demand for exports. After the war of 1914-18 this period of intense activity did not last very long; it was over by 1921. This time it may be expected to continue longer. The Administration will be more adept in exercising the necessary control; the greater extent, both of destruction and of mobilisation of industry, means that the corresponding period of recovery will be longer. The difficult time may come later. But it seems reasonably certain that the immediate post-war years will be a period of substantial economic activity, with a high level of employment. The actual size of the working population will be somewhat larger than it was before the war, unless there are very substantial war casualties. There are certain minor elements of uncertainty, according to the extent to which women wish to

[1] *Studies in the National Income*, 1924-38, edited by Professor Bowley, p. 193.

continue to work and the aged postpone retirement, but on balance the working population should be higher, and the rate of unemployment will be appreciably below the 1938 level of 12½%—it may be little more than 5%.

The national income estimate of £6½ milliards is conservative in that it assumes that output per worker will be no higher than it was before the war. During the war, output per worker has risen substantially. Longer hours have been worked; less time has been lost in industrial disputes; under the stress of war there has probably been some increase in real efficiency. Much of this expansion will be lost as working hours come down to normal. There will be a switch from certain industries with very high productivity of labour—for example, the aircraft industry—to industries with relatively low productivity, such as textiles. The war-time pressure to efficiency will be eased. Nevertheless, it is extremely unlikely that output per worker will fall below pre-war level. There has been rapid technical progress during the war, an energetic introduction of labour-saving machinery, a considerable expansion of electric power consumption, an improvement of industrial welfare, and a good deal of education of management. These are gains which will not be lost. There are important factors on the other side. Income from foreign investments has been lost, and this reduces the real income per occupied worker; the terms of trade may move against us, for food and raw materials may be scarcer than manufactured goods. But on balance there is no reason to doubt that real income per worker will be up to the 1938 level. In Britain after the war of 1914-18, real output per man-hour in 1924 was 6% above the 1913 level; in France, the pre-war level was regained as early as 1921.[1] We shall do at least as well this time as we did then.

The assumptions underlying the estimate of £6½ milliards in 1945 are therefore well justified. We can thus assert with confidence that the Beveridge Plan is entirely feasible, and that the re-allocation of the national resources which it represents can be done without undue difficulty. In the longer view, the attainment of the Plan depends upon the product of full employment and increasing productivity. If employment remains at a high level, and productivity continues to increase at the rather moderate pre-war rate, then from year to year the provision of

[1] Clark, *Conditions of Economic Progress*, pp. 23, 99.

social security benefits and of health services will be a decreasing burden upon the national resources. If unemployment developed, and if for some reason productivity failed to increase, the burden might from time to time become considerable. This would not mean that we could not "afford" the Plan; it would simply mean that as a result of our failure to organise the national resources sensibly, we were having to go without a lot more things in order to abolish poverty. We must be quite clear what we mean here. The Report goes a little too far in stressing the assumption of full employment. The State would not "go bankrupt." Indeed, paying out unemployment benefit would help the national income to recover, for it would maintain purchasing power. What would happen would be that the general standard of living would fail to rise at the rate at which it should if the national resources were reasonably fully used. We should still prevent poverty. We should still maintain good health. But workers would be getting unemployment benefit instead of wages; there would be less goods and services available for public consumption. So people would be unnecessarily worse off. That is the whole of the matter. That is why there must be both full employment and a steady growth of productivity. The Plan can go on without them. But they are the conditions upon which social progress is founded.

Britain's Economic Environment

How can full employment and growth of productivity be achieved? Much is being written about them. There is a tendency, however, to assume that the post-war problems will be of the same kind as those of the pre-war world. This is certainly wrong. The post-war world is different. There is a danger that just as we went into the war mentally, and even physically, equipped for the 1914 war, so we shall go into the peace well prepared for the 1919 peace. We may then find that we have spent a lot of time discovering the answers to the wrong questions. Too little consideration has yet been given to Britain's post-war economic environment, and to the way in which the economic structure will fit into it. Yet this is the decisive point. It will determine whether we shall be able easily to maintain full employment. The experience of the past shows that this relation of a nation's economic structure to its economic environment—in other words, the impact upon the national economy of the fundamental economic forces of the time—plays the decisive part in the nation's economic progress. If the environment is favourable and the structure well adapted, full employment and an expanding standard of living are easily achieved. If, on the other hand, conditions are inherently unfavourable, tremendous efforts have to be made, and even then they may be unsuccessful. Britain's experience in the last century is a typical example; the world was being rapidly developed, and, by a combination of historical circumstances, Britain was first in the field, both in financing this development and in supplying manufactured goods. Later, however, and especially in the period between the world wars, Britain's previous advantages were lost, her industrial structure became old-fashioned, and there were fifteen years of considerable difficulty, with unemployment on an unprecedented scale.

During this century Japan has been able to achieve an amazingly rapid economic development—more spectacular than that of any other country; there was a huge world market for her products, and she had an abnormally low cost structure. The Soviet Union has worked in a favourable environment for securing full employment in industry, having an undeveloped country with tremendous natural resources and a vast surplus agricultural population; the Soviet economic and political institutions have been well suited for pressing through massive industrial expansion at great speed. Sweden's success in overcoming the trade cycle is attributable partly to the sensible policies of her Government, but the task was greatly eased by the strong demand which developed from Britain and the Continent for Sweden's basic exports—high-grade iron ore and timber products. France, on the other hand, had an altogether unfavourable economic environment in the pre-war world; the fiscal system was obsolete, industry backward, the quantity of scientific and technical research wholly inadequate; France's special products were in poor international demand. The French economic system needed revolution; it was completely out of harmony with the economic environment of the 'thirties. The position of the United States in the 'thirties was likewise out of balance; the excesses of the boom had left such a mess that even the most vigorous efforts of the New Deal could do hardly more than maintain a tolerable level of employment. Some countries were able to expand their economic life without difficulty; others encountered terrible trouble in even remaining where they were.

Where will Britain stand in the post-war period? The environment should be more favourable than in the period between wars, at any rate for the attainment of full employment. Two powerful forces should, over a period of years, contribute to the maintenance of a high level of economic activity. The first is the internal demand for building; not only is there a vast back-log of house-building to be made up, accentuated by air-raid destruction, there will also be a steady demand for new hospitals, health centres, schools and public buildings of all kinds. Enough building work is in prospect to keep an enlarged building industry fully occupied for probably fifteen years. The second force may be slower to come into operation, but it is more spectacular. The war in the Far East has released social and economic forces on a massive scale. This will certainly lead to tremendous industrial expansion throughout Asia. China will industrialise. So will post-war India. The Soviet Union will develop Siberia. The timing of this industrialisation is uncertain. But there is no doubt that it will come; its effects upon the world economy will be comparable to those of the opening of the North American continent in the last century. Here is a vast potential market waiting for British exporters. New methods of financing the development of backward countries, appropriate to twentieth-century political conceptions, would be needed; maybe the development will have to be financed on lend-lease lines. The essential point is that the motive power for an expanding world economy exists in Asia; if it can be set in motion, there will be no lack of markets for British industry in the next generation. Once Asia is determined to increase its standard of living, there will be a world scarcity of all high-class industrial products for as far ahead as we can see. These two big constructive economic forces should work in Britain's economic favour — the building back-log and the industrialisation of Asia. One might add a third, which is that the expansion of the standard of living in the world generally would be of definite benefit to Britain, for our main export trade is with countries with high incomes; the better off a country is, the more it needs British high-quality goods.

The economic environment should offer tremendous opportunities. Can the economic structure adapt itself to take advantage of them? In the period between the world wars large sections of British industry failed to adapt themselves to the change which was taking place. Other new industries developed with great power and originality—retail distribution, newspapers, electricity supply, radio, building and building materials, chemicals, rayon and certain engineering and allied industries. On the whole, the changes of structure which have taken place recently are favourable for the future. The coal industry has now contracted to a size which is in reasonable relationship with the long-term demand; the cotton industry has been contracted; this removes two of the sores on the pre-war economy. The steel, heavy engineering and shipbuilding industries have at any rate become accustomed to produce large outputs for a long period. There has been a big expansion of the chemical and light engineering industries. Large numbers of firms have learnt to do precision work; modern machine-tools have been installed; managements have been compelled to work in co-operation with one another, with consequently favourable effects upon the average level of efficiency; economy and efficiency in the use of fuel, power and raw material have been forced upon industry; new factories have been built on modern lines; there have been substantial developments in factory welfare. The net effect of the war has been to modernise British industry. There is still much to be done. But the technical and productive side of British industry will probably be sufficiently adaptable provided that the enterprising undertakings are not shackled by restrictive associations. There is much more doubt about the ability to seize export opportunities and to develop the necessary techniques for financing and developing Asiatic trade in conditions of far-reaching social change in that continent. It is certain that such trade will be financed and developed through Governmental agencies; it is far beyond the scope of private enterprise. But adequate means have not yet been devised to develop this with the necessary vigour; this is one of the large post-war problems awaiting solution. Similarly, in order to take advantage of the building opportunity, the building and building materials industries must be organised into a powerful instrument in much the same way as the engineering industries have been organised for armament production, and a proper framework of land use must be laid out, on the lines of the Uthwatt Report, so that this instrument should work effectively and uninterruptedly. If these things are done, the framework will be laid for an expanding economy.

Full Employment

The first step towards a full employment policy is to develop these two opportunities to the maximum. This implies action over the whole field of Government, political and diplomatic as well as economic. We must further with all means at our disposal the rebuilding of Britain, on the one hand, and the industrialisation of Asia and other backward countries on the other. As a necessary corollary to both we must develop education and training; steadily advancing technique is indispensable. If these two major opportunities are seized, full employment will be maintainable. We shall be swimming with the tide. By concrete action along these lines, rather than by vague trade treaties and pious resolutions for the reduction of tariff barriers, we can bring about the expanding world economy which is the only favourable economic environment for Britain.

Having got these big things right, we can plan full employment. We need not bother about intermittent unemployment—the temporary unemployment of people moving from job to job, seasonal workers and casual workers. This can be reduced, partly by stopping casual labour—one of Mr. Bevin's contributions—and partly by dovetailing seasonal industries into one another. It could be almost entirely eliminated by Essential Work Orders, but this is both unnecessary and undesirable; it is a good thing for workers to move from job to job. There is thus a rind of unemployment which represents about 3% and which is inevitable in a free and progressive economic system. Besides this rind, there is a hard core of possibly 2% which represents structural unemployment—caused by technical changes, long-term contraction of industries which have permanently lost their markets, and so on. The extreme case is the depressed area unemployment of the 'thirties, but unemployment of this kind arises continually in an active and developing society. This is very difficult to tackle. We cannot prevent it, for it is inherent in technical progress. Indeed, we want the structure of industry to change with the times; we want to stimulate the mobility of labour and encourage the expansion of some industries and the contraction of others. Otherwise, economic life becomes static and decays. Tremendous efforts must therefore be made to cope with these situations promptly and effectively. The displaced man must be found new work. This may be impossible without transfer, though the need to transfer can be reduced by the effective control of location of new industry. If a move is necessary, every possible assistance must be given. In almost all cases some re-training will be needed; this requires, as we have seen, a big expansion in Government training facilities and in general State supervision of training. It also requires a long-term economic pattern to show the direction in which these workers should be re-trained.

The bulk of pre-war unemployment, however, arose from general depression in trade. This is the mass unemployment which must be rooted out of our society. Its origin is the uneven flow of activity in the capital-goods and export industries. Employment in these industries falls; this reduces their workers' purchasing power; this reacts upon the demand for consumer-goods and thus upon employment in the consumer-goods industries, and so unemployment spreads like influenza. In the pre-war years, the capital-goods and export industries were chronically unstable. So there was mass unemployment. The remedy is to secure a steady employment level in these industries. This means control of the flow of orders to them. This can be done readily for the capital-goods industries—building and public works contracting; general, electrical and constructional engineering; shipbuilding and railway equipment industries. The building and public works programmes must in any case be State-planned. The railways and public utilities even before the war financed their capital expansions by loans under Government auspices, and they will in any case either become public corporations or remain under indirect State control. The ship replacement programme will be Government-financed. The capital sums involved in large industrial projects, such as new steel plants, are so large that private enterprise can hardly finance them ;[1] the State will in any case exercise control for other purposes, such as location. Thus the bulk of the output of the capital-goods industries comes under direct State supervision; there is no difficulty whatever in dovetailing these projects together into one stable long-term programme.

A substantial part of the export industries' activity can likewise be programmed—electric generating plants for India, railway equipment for China, an underground railway for Leningrad, steel plant for Australia, and so on. A large volume of smaller orders passing through the Government-cum-industry export agencies which will be handling trade with backward countries, can also be programmed. In the vulnerable capital-goods and export industries there will thus be a firm core of programmed activity. The unprogrammed residue—small in the capital-goods industries, but of course fairly large in the export industries—would fluctuate according to general trade conditions here and overseas. These fluctuations should be compensated by State action. If activity seemed to be falling off, marginal public works programmes could be speeded up, and more purchasing power could be released by tax reduction, food subsidies, or temporary increases of social security benefits. If, on the other hand, an unhealthy over-expansion seemed imminent, purchasing power could be siphoned off by Budgetary action. By these means the required stability of employment could be obtained. The techniques of programming present no problem; this would flow automatically from the war-time system of controls, maintained perforce in the initial post-war years to ration imported raw materials and other scarce factors of production. The techniques of compensatory financial action by the State are less clearly established, but there is a great deal of war-time experience to draw upon. A substantial body of opinion, hostile to direct State participation in industry, holds that full employment can be maintained by financial measures

[1] It is significant that *A National Policy for Industry*, the statement by 120 leading industrialists, which is intrinsically a plea for industrial self-government, in effect concedes this point. "The equipment of industry with up-to-date plant and machinery," it states, "is as much in the national interest as public works, and industry will be entitled to obtain financial assistance for industrial schemes if our view is accepted that service to the community must be its first aim."

alone; the financial levers are certainly enough to look after minor fluctuations around a planned core of activity.

Full employment can be achieved by this combination of policies. The State must take charge of the building programme in just the same way as it takes charge of the war production programme. It must link together all the capital development work of the Government agencies, public corporations and undertakings under its direct or indirect control. It must, in association with the industries concerned, take charge of the exports for the development of economically backward areas. All this work within the State's sphere of influence must be drawn into a cohesive and stable long-term programme. The relatively small trade fluctuations outside this sphere must be compensated by Budgetary policy which would adjust purchasing power accordingly. Structural unemployment must be handled by re-training and the encouragement of new industries. The whole of this plan stems directly from the war economy; the problems will have to be handled along these lines in any event in the initial post-war period if complete chaos is to be avoided. In other words, the peace-time full employment programme is an organic growth from the needs of war and immediate post-war. That is the normal pattern of new development of society.

Here we reach the crucial point. This is the course of events. But there is a choice between swimming with the tide and drifting with the tide. It is the difference between having a plan and driving it through or going through the motions of having a plan. This is the basic issue of post-war politics. To most rational beings, the choice is clear. The nation must know where it is going. We must have a long-term plan on a broad working basis. It need not be calculated in intimate detail. Nor does it involve State operation of everything. There must be a planned framework within which the economic system—public and private—can work. Otherwise everyone is in the dark. The sensible kind of plan is to fix a target national income of, say, £8 milliards for 1955; this would be divided appropriately between consumption and construction, and between various kinds of consumption and various kinds of construction. From this would flow the appropriate industrial structure and distribution between industries of the working population and the appropriate distribution of incomes to be achieved. The whole economic apparatus of the State—the building programme, the Budget, the re-training schemes, the price regulations, the State-controlled industries, the public-private export agencies, the banking policy and the rest—would then be geared to secure that result. Clear and definite social goals would emerge—the immediate abolition of poverty, a ten-year housing goal of four million houses, a national nutrition goal, an electrification goal of fifty milliard units a year, and so on. We shall have a planned economy whether we like it or not. The choice is between a good plan, energetically carried out, and a weak and indecisive plan.

Social Incentives and Social Change

The attainment of full employment and social security will lead to profound social change. The beginnings of this are already apparent in the war economy. The most important change is a gradual weakening of monetary incentives. The traditional exercise of industrial discipline through fear of the sack, poverty and destitution becomes much less effective. The fear of bankruptcy likewise ceases to be a menace to the business man;[1] in conditions of full employment, most companies can reasonably hope to secure a steady rate of return on invested capital. The trend of society in the last ten years has been very markedly in this direction. The growth of monopoly and trade associations has largely been an attempt by businesses to avoid or pool business risks; in rearmament and war there has been unanimous demand from industry that the State should perform the function of risk-bearing, by supplying all the capital for factory expansions, by guaranteeing loans, by pooling war risks, and in fact by taking all the responsibility which in a system governed by monetary incentives should be taken by the private capitalist. The risks of modern society, indeed, have become so vast that individuals can no longer take them. When they are taken collectively the nature of society changes. Opposition to the Beveridge Plan and to the implications of full employment is nothing more than an attempt to put the clock back, not to 1939—when these trends were already very well under way—but to 1929, or even to 1913.

[1] Wholesale business failures have fallen from 441 in 1938 to 36 in 1942; retail from 4,601 to 363. (*Economist*, 23rd January 1943.)

This blunting of the spur of monetary incentive raises the question of industrial discipline, enterprise and efficiency in acute form. This is emerging strongly in war industry. Factory managements are given to seek new methods of handling their staffs; they provide industrial welfare facilities; they strive through Joint Production Committees to associate the workers with the job of management; they try to build up a team spirit among the workers. The trade unions, for their part, find the scope of their work widening from negotiations of wages and hours and fighting for better conditions on the floor of the factory to the discussion and problems of factory efficiency and production planning. This has not yet proceeded very far; only the more far-sighted managements and the more advanced sections of the workers are yet seeing the problem at all clearly. But these are plainly preliminary attempts to build in the factories a new kind of worker-management relationship to replace the old sanctions. This will again react, as these things do, upon the industrial structure itself and then back again to the problem of incentives. The large and modern undertakings, with new factories and with ample funds to afford welfare provisions and to employ the best labour managers, are at a great advantage over smaller and more old-fashioned firms; they can keep their labour. The advanced firms drive out the backward firms, and the whole dynamic process gathers momentum.

In the past, efficiency has been associated with the idea of competition. The more efficient firm was the firm which could drive its competitors out of business. For this conception another is being substituted, much more closely related to the facts of modern economic life. In the war, attempts were made to improve the efficiency of a whole industry. Managers of firms making a weapon share their experience, visit each others' factories, learn how to do the job better. Efficiency tends to become separated from an individual firm's profit-and-loss account, and comes to represent a standard of management, on a professional rather than on a commercial level. Here again, only the beginnings of this have yet been seen in the war economy. But what has actually happened shows how industry can improve its efficiency under conditions of diminishing commercial risk. In such circumstances, furthermore, more and more able people concentrate their attention upon the problems of management and thus of efficient industrial operations on an all-industry basis—instead of upon problems of financial manipulation. Big jobs of organisation were already before the war beginning to have a greater appeal than big money. This is a natural consequence from the development of an industrial world in which the great majority of business men insist that the State should bear all big risks and in which the rate of taxation is correspondingly high.

Finally, the place of the State. We have already seen the broad economic function of the State in the achievement of full employment and social security. We have seen that this develops naturally from the war-time activities of the State. Its methods will be much less dictatorial. Its tempo will be less urgent. It will not need to call for the last ounce of human effort or to demand sacrifices of fundamental liberties. But it must drive through the two big jobs to be done—the rebuilding of Britain and the industrialisation of the backward areas of the world. We must therefore have a positive and enterprising State, well equipped with powers to control, with an organisation appropriate to its work, and with a high quality of men to lead and to act. When the State was the umpire between conflicting interests, appeasing one with a tariff or another with an increase in unemployment pay, it acquired negative and judicial habits. But now the State must be the creator of enterprise—no one else is willing to take the responsibility, and no one else can be given the comprehensive power. The creator must create, and not postpone or prevaricate; nor can a creative power be "impartial" in affairs of human welfare and national progress.

But even efficiency and enterprise are not enough by themselves. When risks are collectively borne, and when a new type of social incentive arises to replace the monetary incentives, there must be an altogether new bond of confidence between the State and the citizen. The successful working of the economic system depends upon this. Every man must feel that he is part of the show, that the State is run for his and everyone else's benefit, and that it is really a partnership of 47 million people. It is then simply his duty as a matter of enlightened self-interest to work as well as he can, to keep himself healthy, to pay his taxes, and in general to carry out his social responsibilities. On its part the State will provide him with every opportunity for advancement according to his abilities; it will look after him and his family when he loses his income; it will carry him through the recurrent crises of family life; it will see that he is in a position to get the goods and services which he needs to the extent of the contribution which he makes to society. This is the nature of the new social contract, which emerges from this growth of the war economy into a peace economy for full employment and social security. The State and the citizens must make this contract together, and both of them must understand its implications. Such a new basis for society, stated in formal terms, may seem a long way ahead. But it is on the way. Its economic foundations are being built, and they are sound foundations for the expanding economic environment and expanding economic needs of the post-war world.

Chapter XIII

SOCIAL SECURITY HOUSEKEEPING

By R. W. B. CLARKE

IF the British people are determined to rid themselves of poverty, they can do it. It is simply a matter of national housekeeping. The national resources can be laid out so that a minimum standard of living is available for everybody, enough to cover basic human needs. The only problem is to find ways and means of doing it. That the problem can be stated in this way is a sign of the times. During the last fifteen years there has been a tremendous growth in our knowledge of the way in which people live, of the social structure, and of the forces which work within it. We are therefore now able to think about social problems rationally and objectively; we are beginning to tackle social evils in very much the same realistic and unprejudiced spirit as that with which doctors fight disease. Sir John Orr and his fellow-nutritionists were among the pioneers of this spirit; in the Beveridge Report, the new way of thinking emerges with overwhelming force. The main cause of poverty is diagnosed as failure of earning power for certain specific reasons. It may be loss of income through unemployment, sickness or old age; it may be that income is not enough to provide properly for a family. The fundamental cure is to end unemployment and ill-health; old age is in any case unavoidable. But after organising the strongest possible offensive against unemployment and ill-health, we must still provide sufficient incomes for those who suffer loss of earning power, and we must help to cover parents' commitments by giving children's allowances.

The practical job falls into four stages. The first is to determine what income is needed to cover the basic human needs of families of various sizes. This can now be done much better than was possible a generation ago; not enough was then known about nutrition to formulate clearly human food requirements for the maintenance of good health; nor was enough known about the facts of poverty to enable basic needs to be laid down—apart from the pioneer work of Booth and Rowntree, these were not established until repeated social surveys had been conducted all over the country in the decade before the war. The second stage is to estimate the number of people who will lose their earning power in each year from each of the various causes; this is the field of the actuary and the social statistician, and here the experience of thirty years of social insurance and a flood of new statistical knowledge are of great value. The third stage is to compute the annual cost of providing replacement incomes; this shows the size of the slice of the national income which must be earmarked for these benefits. The fourth stage is to relate this to the national resources and to devise means of releasing the necessary amount of purchasing power from other purposes, either by direct levies as contributions or direct taxation or by indirect levies through excise duties and general taxes upon industry; at this last stage, the spate of recent studies of the size and distribution of the national income and the new ideas of public finance which have developed lately provide a rational foundation for policy. We can now deal with facts established by scientific methods instead of with unbacked assertions and prejudices.

Unless they are translated into practical quantitative terms, social security proposals remain vague aspirations, such as the Trades Union Congress proposal for 40/- a week unemployment benefit for a single man, and the National Federation of Old Age Pensions Associations demand for pensions of 30/- a week at 60. The level of benefits, the number of people who will have them, the burden upon the national resources and the best means of spreading this burden—these are the flesh and blood of a social security plan. When we planned in the middle of the war, many of the major facts were still unknown. We could not foretell the post-war price level; we could not say when the war would end or what further destruction would take place before its end; we did not know the scale of other pressing post-war claims upon the nation's resources. The detail of the calculations must therefore be regarded as provisional, as was emphasised by the Fabian Society, the only body to submit detailed financial estimates to the Beveridge Committee.[1] The Beveridge Report makes certain general assumptions—in particular the assumption that there will be no mass unemployment; it states very clearly and defin-

[1] Appendix, p. 446.

itely that the proposed rates of contribution and benefit are not firm figures, and that they are not an integral part of the scheme;[1] when the time comes to work the Plan, entirely different scales of contribution and benefit may be appropriate. But the shape of the calculation is of permanent application, and in fact we can make reasonably good guesses about the future.

THE MINIMUM STANDARD

The first stage is to determine the rates of standard benefit—the minimum income which will provide basic human needs. This means enough of the right kinds of food to keep good health, a home to live in, and a sufficient margin for clothing, heating and lighting, and incidental expenses. This minimum will, of course, steadily increase as the standard of living develops; the modern "minimum" diet is very much better than the bulk of the population had a generation ago, and the standards of clothing and incidental expenses are likewise related to the general standards of the time rather than to absolute subsistence levels. The minimum adopted in the Report was determined with the assistance of the best expert opinion—Professor Bowley, Mr. Seebohm Rowntree, Mr. R. F. George and Dr. H. E. Magee. One of the most useful by-products of this Report is this authoritative statement of minimum living needs in the conditions which prevailed just before the war.

The food needs are based upon the British Medical Association and League of Nations minimum dietaries; there is now almost complete agreement between the nutrition experts on what such diets should contain. The clothing needs are based upon social

[1] Report, para. 27. For the purpose of his calculations, Sir William Beveridge assumes that the post-war price level will be some 25% above that of 1938. Since May 1941, the Ministry of Labour cost-of-living index has been stabilised around a level of 200, or 28% above the average for 1938. At the end of 1942, retail food prices were about 15% above 1938, clothing prices were up by 85% to 90%, prices of fuel and light were up by 33%, and rent and rates were up by 2%. In fact, however, the prices of the whole range of goods bought by working-class families have risen more than the index suggests. Prices of foods which are not in the index, such as green vegetables, have risen by over 50%. The Treasury has concentrated its efforts upon keeping the index stable, and has subsidised certain products accordingly; the unsubsidised items have surely risen more. Retail prices of necessaries as a whole, therefore, are more like 35% above the 1938 level rather than the official increase of 28%. The current price level may be between 5% and 10% higher than the Report's hypothetical post-war price level; for a true comparison with present benefits, the Beveridge figures should be increased accordingly.

surveys, and are roughly equal to the present clothing ration.[1] Fuel and light and sundry household expenses are included at the normal rate of consumption of poorer families. A margin is added to cover incidental expenses and inefficient buying. The minimum weekly cost to cover basic needs except rent, at 1938 prices, is thus established at 12/6 for a single man or 11/6 for a single woman, 22/- for a married couple and 21/2 for an aged couple.[2] The cost of maintaining a child varies from 5/- weekly for an under-five to 9/- weekly for a boy of 14, or an average of 7/- a week.

This is well-trodden ground, and its main significance lies in the authoritative nature of the calculation. But then comes the first difficulty—the problem presented by the striking differences between people's rent obligations. Sir William Beveridge, after a very detailed review,[3] decides provisionally for a flat allowance of 10/- weekly for man and wife, and 6/6 for a single individual. But he regards this as unsatisfactory, and proposes that a further examination be made. The truth is that the nation's rent structure is in a shocking mess; whatever treatment one proposes in social security benefits, some anomalies will follow. It may be possible in the long run to get some sense into the rent structure. There will, however, always be tremendous differences between people's rent obligations; town rents will never be as low as country rents; the family man will never have the same rent as a single man living with his parents or boarding as a lodger. The Report suggests that this is a problem which can be settled rapidly. But this is clearly unrealistic. The rent

[1] The cost at 1938 prices of a typical lay-out of the clothing coupons, including boot repairs, would have been just under 1/6 weekly in working-class districts.

[2] The minimum weekly requirements at 1938 prices, excluding rent, are as follows :

	Food.	Clothing.	Fuel, light and sundries.	Margin.	Total.
Man	7/–	1/6	2/6	1/6	12/6
Woman . . .	6/–	1/6	2/6	1/6	11/6
Man and wife . .	13/–	3/–	4/–	2/–	22/–
Retired man . .	6/–	1/4	3/–	1/6	11/10
Aged couple . .	11/6	2/8	5/–	2/–	21/2
Youth, 15 to 17 . .	7/6	1/6	1/6	1/6	12/–
Child	5/11	–/10	–/3	—	7/–

It is noteworthy that a woman needs 1/– less than a man, because of lower physiological needs ; the most surprising point is that, contrary to previous calculations, an aged person needs very little less than a working adult. (Report, paras. 193 to 229.)

[3] Report, paras. 197 to 216. The facts quoted here are taken from this section of the Report, except where otherwise stated.

differences can be reduced. But they will always exist, and we must plan to reduce the resulting anomalies to a minimum.

The extraordinary variation of rent between regions is the first source of trouble. The regional average paid by industrial workers' households varies between 16/- a week in London and 7/6 in Scotland; the average agricultural householder pays only 4/7. This means that if rent is allowed for in the benefits at a flat rate of 10/-, the average London unemployed man will receive only seven-eighths of his minimum total requirements, while the farm worker will receive benefit at least 5/- in excess of his real needs. This seriously damages the careful calculations of food and clothing needs; these requirements are assessed to the nearest sixpence, but the difference between the actual rent need and the rent allowance is measured in half-crowns. The Report shows that in no part of the country would a 10/- flat allowance be within 2/6 of the actual rent for as many as half the households.

The regional variation, however, is by no means the whole of the difficulty. Within any region, the dispersion between rent needs is hardly less than that between the regions themselves.[1] Large families have to pay large rents; 6-room premises are about 3/- a week dearer than 3-room premises.[2] Nearly one worker in five either owns his own house or is buying it;[3] if such a man loses his income, he may be faced with the need to maintain heavy building society payments or he may have nothing to pay except local rates. Again, something like 250,000 households are provided with dwellings rent-free by employers: they have no rent liability when the wage-earner is sick.[3] These are simple illustrations of the type of variation which exists between the rent needs of different households. When upon these variations are superimposed the thousands of diverse household patterns which determine the actual rent obligation of the individual earner, the hopelessness of trying to tackle the problem by giving a flat rent allowance becomes even more apparent. Some single men and women live with their parents and make only a small con-

[1] Mr. Seebohm Rowntree states that in York in 1936, 18% of the families paid less than 7/– rent, 53% between 7/– and 10/11, 29% 11/– and over. (*Fortnightly Review*, February 1943.)

[2] From data given in the 1938 Report of the Unemployment Assistance Board, p. 198.

[3] *Ministry of Labour Gazette*, December 1940.

tribution to the rent; others live on their own. Some aged people live by themselves; others live with their children and have only a nominal rent obligation. In some families the wife is the main earner; in others there may be two, three or even more earners. At no point in the structure of rent obligations is there uniformity which would warrant uniform treatment; the attempt to impose it weakens the scientific basis of the Beveridge benefits. The flat allowance of 10/- a week creates anomalies which extend throughout the proposed system of benefits.[1] It means in effect that some people will be forced to seek supplementation of their benefits by assistance, while others will receive more than can be justified on basic human needs.

The one fact which is common to all these household patterns is that the rent is the first charge upon the household's resources. There is no doubt whatever that if the rent allowance included in the benefit is appreciably less than the actual rent paid, the incomeless household will go short of food or clothing. No adjustment can be made in the charge without a complete uprooting of the family; in most cases, indeed, there are no cheaper places to which the family can go. The 1938 Report of the Unemployment Assistance Board, discussing the problem created by high London rents, expressed the point clearly:

> "In many of these high rent cases the Board's officers feel reluctance to putting the applicant in funds to meet charges that seem so disproportionate to his normal means, and this reluctance is increased when regard is had to the frequently unsatisfactory nature of the accommodation. *The facts are, however, that in many neighbourhoods the rents are so uniformly high that the applicant has no option in the matter.*" [2]

[1] Four examples illustrate this:

(*a*) Guardian benefit, at 24/– weekly, includes only the single woman's rent element of 6/6; yet a widow with dependen children is surely more likely to have a rent comparable with a married couple.

(*b*) Benefits for a man with five children contain the same rent element as those for a man with none; nor does the children's allowance include a rent element.

(*c*) The gainfully occupied married woman's disability benefit is 16/–; it is assumed in fixing this that the married woman pays no rent; where this is untrue, there is a clear anomaly.

(*d*) The 20/– benefit for the single man of 18 to 20 is not enough if he is living by himself, but is probably generous if he lives at home.

[2] p. 78. Our italics.

When a man loses his income, indeed, he will certainly maintain his home for as long as he can, no matter what sacrifices have to be made.

The only way to tackle this problem and to satisfy the essential social need—which is simply to give the sick or unemployed man the firm assurance that the rent money will be there each week—is to provide a special rent allowance which would cover the actual rent for which the claimant is responsible, subject to a maximum fixed regionally; this would of course include rates and the interest element of building society payments.[1] This proposal was put to the Beveridge Committee by the Association of Municipal Corporations and the Fabian Society; it has been subsequently endorsed by Mr. Seebohm Rowntree.[2] The Report states the case for the proposal with great force, and rather surprisingly concludes by uneasily rejecting it. The proposal is a novel one in social insurance; the main argument against it is that it runs counter to the principle of equal benefits for equal contributions—a principle, the Report states, which "has a strong popular appeal and is much easier to defend than any departure from it."

It is generally accepted, of course, that this principle can be abandoned in the payment of dependants' allowances; a married man pays the same contribution as a single man. At any rate in the short run, the rent obligation is at least as fixed and unavoidable as the need to maintain dependants; that is proved by the fact that the household will cut its food in order to pay the rent. There is, however, some substance in a refinement of this argument, which is that although the rent obligation varies widely from household to household, the people with the bigger earnings do in general have bigger rents. The consequence of the proposal, it is argued, is that skilled workers as a whole would receive larger benefits than unskilled workers as a whole, although they make the same contribution. To those who regard the contribution as an insurance premium, designed on a precise actuarial basis to cover the benefits which the individual contributor will receive in his lifetime, this is a conclusive argument. Those on the other hand who regard the contribution rather as

[1] It is desirable to arrange for postponement of payment of capital element during unemployment or disability.

[2] *Fortnightly Review*, February 1943.

a weekly payment by which the contributor maintains membership of an all-in social security scheme, designed to cover him against all contingencies and financed primarily from general taxation—which is much nearer the reality of the Beveridge Plan —will be less impressed. It is, of course, anomalous to pay a larger benefit to the man with the larger earnings—although I suppose that even then it might be argued that the latter is likely to contribute more in general taxation. But the evidence set out in the Report suggests that the tremendous variations in rent are due much more to regional and other causes unassociated with the level of the household's earnings; the evidence of War Service Grants shows that households with 100/- to 120/- a week pre-war income pay on the average only 2/3 a week more in rent than households with less than 40/- a week, and this is confirmed by Mr. Rowntree's investigations in York.[1] On the whole, it seems incontrovertible that the anomalies which would be created by the payment of the actual rent would be altogether much smaller than those which follow from the payment of the flat allowance. From the point of view of "popular appeal," the underwriting of the home is surely immensely attractive, and would wholly outweigh whatever feeling there might be that contributions should be rigidly fixed to benefits.

The Report suggests that it might be practicable to fix a higher contribution and higher benefit in London and other high-rent areas, and lower contribution and lower benefit in agricultural areas. This differentiation would apply only to unemployment and disability; it is suggested that in principle the aged should adjust their rents as they approach pensionable age. This suggestion might create fewer anomalies than the flat rent allowance, but it is nevertheless unacceptable. The exclusion of the aged is not really justified, for the differences between the rents of aged Londoners and aged Norfolk men are hardly less than those between the rents of active workers in these places; the

[1] The evidence is based upon a sample of rents and pre-war incomes of applicants for War Service Grants. The rents varied from 10·2/– a week in the groups with less than 40/– a week and with 40/– to 60/– a week to 12·4/– in the group with 100/– to 120/– a week. Above this level, the rent increased more sharply with income, but this would of course be looked after by the application of the maximum. (Report, para. 209.) Mr. Rowntree states that in York in 1936, of the householders with less than 65/– a week, 52·6% paid less than 10/– a week rent, and 47·4% paid more; of those with more than 65/– a week, 42·6% paid less than 10/– rent, and 57·4% paid more. (*Fortnightly Review*, February 1943.)

pensioner can adjust his rent so that it is not abnormally high in relation to the level of rents generally in his region, but he cannot be expected to do more than that. The proposal to vary both contributions and benefits on a regional or occupational basis gives a mathematical sanctity to the contribution-benefit relation which it does not actually possess; it complicates the scheme unnecessarily; it provides only for regional differences in rent, and ignores the extremely important differences which arise from variations in household pattern—number of children, number of earners in household, and so on. Even after this complication of the contributions and benefits, the man with five children would still have the same rent allowance in his benefit as a man with none, and the second earner in the family would still receive benefit which contained full allowance for rent which he would not have to pay. This is a compromise proposal which has very little to commend it; it would be justified to alter the simplicity of the flat contribution only if this alteration solved the problem, and not if it added complexity without striking to the root of the matter.

It is indeed difficult to see any rational alternative to the payment of the actual rent subject to a maximum. The Report concedes that the administrative difficulties can be overcome; the Fabian Society at the request of the Beveridge Committee submitted draft regulations which set out the procedure in detail.[1] The main practical difficulty is to determine the rent for which a claimant is responsible when there is more than one earner in the household, or where there is a lodger or sub-tenant; the draft regulations show how this can be done. The regional maximum rent could be fixed; this would vary according to the size of the family, and it would be definitely lower for aged persons than for people of working age, because of the adjustment which aged people can be expected to make. In order to avoid the administrative task of assessing every claimant's rent, it would be possible to fix a standard benefit including a standard rent and then allow people to make claims as of right if their actual rent exceeded the standard level. If the standard were fixed nationally, as the Report suggests would be possible, the permissible excess could be, say, 100% above standard; if the standard were fixed regionally, as envisaged by the Fabian Society, the permissible

[1] See Appendix, p. 447.

excess could be, say, 50% for people of working age and 25% for aged people. This simplification would, of course, involve extra cost for the Exchequer; it is a one-way option, and those with abnormally low rent would thus receive an unnecessarily generous benefit. But this might be worth while if the extra cost of administrative time involved in assessing the actual rent in each case were substantial. This is a matter of administrative practice rather than of principle; my own opinion is that it would be simplest and most effective to provide the actual rent obligation.

There the matter stands for the present. The final step in the determination of appropriate benefit scales is to take the needs for food, clothing, etc., at 1938 prices, to add a rent allowance of 10/- for married couples and 6/6 for single individuals, 8/6 for aged couples and 6/- for single aged persons, and then to inflate the total to correspond with the assumed 25% increase in prices from 1938 to the hypothetical post-war level. The result is to establish a series of benefits based upon standard rates of 40/- a week for a married couple and 24/- a week for a single person. The minimum level for a woman is slightly less than for a man; a reasonable minimum rate for the aged would be appreciably lower—say, 37/- for a couple and 22/6 for an individual. The Report takes the view, however, that it is hardly worth while to differentiate between the benefit for a man and for a woman, and that the aged should have a slightly more generous "minimum" than those who are working, for their pensions must provide for long-term needs whereas the unemployed and the sick are able to postpone certain expenditure until they are at work again. The benefits of the Beveridge Plan are therefore uniform; they treat men and women equally; they provide the same for pensioners as for those whose earnings are interrupted. The cost of maintaining a child at post-war prices is estimated at an average of 9/- a week, of which it is assumed that 1/- is covered by allowances in kind, such as free and cheap milk and school meals, leaving a cash allowance of 8/- per child for those on benefit. The general children's allowance is at an average of 8/- for every child after the first. These allowances contain no rent element; the implication appears to be that a large family should have the same rent as a childless couple!

These benefits [1] may be compared with the present insurance and assistance provisions, which are of course designed for the present price level, some 5% to 10% above the Beveridge post-war level.

	Beveridge Benefit.		Present Provision.
Single man . .	24/–	Unemployment Insurance	20/–
		Unemployment Assistance	20/6
		Sickness Insurance * .	18/–
Man, wife, 3 children	64/–	Unemployment Insurance	41/–
		Unemployment Assistance	51/6
		Sickness Insurance * .	18/–
Widow, 2 children .	40/–	Widow's Pension * . .	18/–
Aged couple . .	40/–	Old Age Pension . .	20/–
	(ultimate)	Supplementary Pension .	37/–

* These would be supplemented in case of need by the Public Assistance Committees, whose rates in general are slightly below Assistance Board.

The present social insurance benefits are hopelessly inadequate; even the top assistance rates are appreciably below the minimum standard. Contrary to the general belief, however, old age pensioners are much more favourably treated than anybody else. Pensioners who are receiving supplementary benefit are in fact on a basic needs standard or near it; no other group of economically incapacitated are anywhere near this level. Families with children are particularly inadequately treated; the Assistance Board makes allowances varying from 4/9 for an under-5 to 7/9 for a boy of 14, and this is much better than the unemployment insurance benefit of 4/- for each of the first two children and 3/- for each of the rest; but the real need as measured by the Beveridge allowance is 8/-. It is a peculiar commentary on the social values of our society that it treats the aged best and the families with children worst.[2] One of the great merits of the Beveridge Plan is that it restores the

[1] The Fabian Society benefit standard was fixed exclusive of rent and at current prices. For the first three cases in the table, assuming rent at the Beveridge standard, the Fabian scheme benefits work out at 26/6, 70/– and 42/6 respectively; they are virtually the same as Beveridge when the different price level is taken into account. The Fabian allowance for the aged, at 33/6, is appreciably less, for the Fabian scheme contemplated paying benefit at a maintenance rate to nearly all the aged immediately, whereas the full Beveridge pension does not come into operation for twenty years. (Appendix, p. 446.)

[2] So highly is age regarded, indeed, that in the spring of 1940, when the survival of the British people literally depended upon vigorous and far-reaching mobilisation of the nation's resources, Parliament spent week after week in heated controversy on a new Pensions Bill.

balance of the social services, and throws the emphasis upon the needs of men and women under 45.

Only a small minority of workers who are earning receive less income than the Beveridge standard, when their earnings are credited with the general children's allowances. The man who is earning, however, has to pay contributions and will also have some travelling expenses; broadly, the rates of wages which would give him the same net income whether he was earning or not would be as follows:

Single man or woman . . .	30/– a week
Married man	46/– a week
Married man with children . .	54/– a week

If the contributions were reduced below the Beveridge level, this balancing point would be correspondingly lower; if general children's allowance was given for the first child, the difference between the man with children and the man with none would disappear. On the other hand, there are other expenses than those which are allowed for here which a man must incur if he is to enjoy a reasonably comfortable livelihood.

How do these rates compare with the present wage structure? The average earnings of men in the principal industries in July 1941 were 99/5 a week, equivalent on account of the extensive working of overtime to an average weekly wage of about 82/6.[1] Mining, agriculture, the railways, and certain other important services were omitted from this census; the effect of including them might be to reduce the average to about 80/- a week. This means that the average family man would receive a weekly wage about 50% higher than the Beveridge standard. At the lower end of the wage scale, however, there are wages near and below the standard. About one-tenth of the men earned less than 55/- a week;[2] perhaps one-twentieth earned less than 48/- a week. It appears, therefore, that rather less than 5% of the childless married men and less than 10% of married men with

[1] *Ministry of Labour Gazette*, December 1941, pp. 234-5. The level of wages in these industries is stated as being 18% above October 1938. The Ministry of Labour index of wage rates increased by 23% from 1938 to July 1941. The wage level thus corresponds fairly well with the Beveridge price level, 25% above 1938.

[2] Little is known about the dispersion of wages round the average : this estimate is based upon the London distribution in 1929, summarised by Bowley in *Wages and Income since 1860* (1937), p. 44. The implicit assumption is that wages in the country as a whole in 1941 were distributed round the average in much the same way as in London in 1929—a rather risky assumption.

children earn such poor wages that their income would be as great or even greater if they were unemployed on Beveridge benefit. The average woman's wage rate in the industries covered above was probably about 40/- a week; this average is no more than 40% above the standard, and probably appreciably more than 10% of working women receive wages which are no better than the Beveridge benefit. Women's wages are on the whole less adequate than men's wages, if the parent's position is safeguarded by children's allowances.

The Beveridge benefits accordingly are in reasonable balance with the wage structure. Over at least nine-tenths of the wage range, wages plus family allowances provide incomes in excess of the minimum standard. A small minority of workers are so ill-paid that they would have better incomes when unemployed than when working. This means that their wages must be raised. We cannot tolerate poverty as a normal feature of a man's working life. The concept of the national minimum must cover those who are working as well as those who are not. This problem of very low wages must be tackled; the obvious method of doing it is by the enactment of a national minimum wage, possibly with regional variations to look after rent differences. This would have to be supplemented, however, with an extension of Trade Boards and of trade union organisation; the national minimum wage is not itself enough to cope with the problem.

The Number of Incomeless People

The next stage is to determine how many people will be without incomes in any year. It is a pity that the Report handles this stage with such complexity; the complicated actuarial calculations tend to obscure the very simple concepts which are in fact involved. The process is in reality perfectly straightforward, but in the Report and in the Government Actuary's Appendix it appears as something of a mystery. Yet all that has to be done is to estimate over a period of years how many people will suffer from each of the various contingencies against which the scheme protects them.

The calculation begins with the classification [1] of the population of Great Britain in mid-1944, divided between the six Classes of the Report:

[1] Report, p. 194.

CLASSIFICATION OF POPULATION OF GREAT BRITAIN, MID-1944

Class.	Numbers in Thousands.		
	Men.	Women.	Total.
I. Wage- and Salary-earners	13,350 *	4,750	18,100
II. Others gainfully occupied	2,150	450	2,600
III. Housewives, including gainfully occupied	—	9,450 †	9,450
IV. Other persons of working age	1,000	1,300	2,300
V. Children under 15, or 15-16 at school	5,000	4,800	9,800
VI. Retired persons above working age	1,200	3,550	4,750
Total	22,700	24,300	47,000

* Includes estimated 500,000 peace-time strength of armed forces.
† Includes 1,400,000 gainfully occupied housewives, of whom perhaps one-half would register in Class I.

During the twenty years to 1965, the total population will first grow and then fall to rather below its present level. The number of children is expected to decline steadily; the number of aged will certainly expand fast—by some 40% between 1945 and 1965, according to the Registrar-General's estimates. The number of people of working age will decline slowly at first and then much faster; in 1965 it will be nearly 6% below the 1945 level.[1] This is the general demographic framework within which the scheme must be operated. How many of this population will need social security incomes each year?

Unemployment.—The Report assumes an average rate of 8½%, equivalent to an unemployment register of 1,500,000. From the point of view of this calculation this figure is unnecessarily high. The post-war rate of unemployment may be as high as this, or perhaps even higher; if national and international economic policy is handled sensibly, it should be less. But whatever the level may be, the Social Security Budget need take account only

[1] The Registrar-General's estimates for Great Britain (Report, para. 234) are:

	1945 ('000)	1955 ('000)	1965 ('000)
Children under 15	9,310	8,740	8,020
Men 15-64, women 15-59	31,480	31,130	29,760
Men 65 and over, women 60 and over	6,240	7,480	8,810
	47,030	47,350	46,590

of the inevitable unemployment. It must cover the short-term unemployed—the people moving from job to job, the seasonally unemployed, such remnants of casual labour as may remain after the war. It must cover the structural unemployment which is created when industries contract for technological and other causes. Unemployment of these kinds will always exist in a dynamic economic system; its extent is something over 5%—say, 1,000,000 men and women. All other unemployment is "depression" unemployment, and is a sheer waste of national resources. If it develops, the payment of unemployment benefits unbalanced by Government revenue has definitely constructive effects, for it enables mass purchasing power to be maintained and so increases employment; such benefits would pay for themselves in bigger tax yields from the increased national income. We should only plan our Budget to include inevitable unemployment; there is no need to find revenue to balance the cost of providing benefit for "depression" unemployed, for their benefit is properly financed by borrowing. The Beveridge figure of £110 millions a year is definitely higher than is necessary by this criterion; it could be reduced by perhaps one-third, or £35 millions, if inevitable unemployment is put at 5%.

Disability.—The Report assumes a rate of disability one-eighth higher than was recorded in National Health Insurance before the war; this appears to be equivalent to an all-age average of 3¾% to 4% for men and 4½% to 4¾% for women—some 800,000 people would thus be receiving disability benefit at any given time. This estimate is not too high; N.H.I. benefits have in the past been so inadequate—one-eighth of the men receiving them at any time have to supplement them by applying for Public Assistance [1]—that people have been literally unable to afford to be ill and away from work. A slightly higher figure would not be unreasonable, although on the other hand it must be remembered that a public medical control is likely to be more effective than the present system both in preventing and in curing illness. The Report estimates a cost of £57 millions in 1945, which will rise as the working population gets older and thus more frequently ill. This 1945 figure is somewhat smaller than the "normal" under the Beveridge Plan, for the new classes entering the scheme would not get benefit in respect of

[1] Report, p. 244.

chronic disability lasting more than one year until they had paid three years' contributions. Furthermore, the Plan itself excludes the short illnesses of the self-employed, which would probably cost an additional £2 millions a year. Finally, a difficult problem arises in the treatment of existing chronic cases; these must be linked with whatever old age plan is adopted, for, as the Report points out, it is clearly anomalous to put a married chronic invalid of 63 up from a present disablement rate of 10/6 a week to full disability benefit of 40/- a week and then when he is 65 to bring him down again to the level of retirement pension in that year of 26/6 a week.[1] Some £10 millions could be saved in the first year if existing permanent invalids were treated as being prematurely pensioned, and given instead of the full disability benefit the pension which they would be due to receive when they retired. This is of course only a transitional point; if retirement pensions on a full maintenance basis were introduced at once, it would not arise. For *industrial disability*, the cost is estimated at £15 millions a year in respect of some 100,000 people on benefit at any given time,[2] rather more than one-half of whom would be permanent industrial pensioners.

Old Age.—The number of aged people can be foreseen with some precision. All the men who will be eligible for pension in 1965 were well past 35 at the outbreak of war, and the possible changes in mortality rates are fairly well charted. The following table sets out the dimensions of the problem, with the figures rounded to the nearest 25,000:

NUMBER OF AGED PEOPLE
(Men, 65 and over; Women, 60 and over)
(Thousands)

	1945	1965
Men: 65 to 69	925	1,300
70 and over	1,150	1,650
Women: 60 to 69	2,500	3,450
70 and over	1,675	2,400
Total	6,250	8,800

[1] Report, para. 353. The extent to which the bulk of ill-health is concentrated upon chronic cases is not generally recognised; in Scotland in 1935-36, more than half the total volume of incapacity was represented by "chronic" cases—i.e. cases in which illness continued throughout the entire year. (*Report on Incapacitating Sickness in Scotland*, 1935-36, published by Department of Health for Scotland, June 1937.)

[2] Report, p. 244, gives 1942 number as 100,000; this would not be substantially changed.

Under the existing arrangements for State pensions and assistance, pensions of some kind would be provided in 1945 for some 4,000,000, or rather less than two-thirds of the aged.[1] Some 3,625,000 would receive contributory pensions of 10/- a week, payable to an insured man at 65 or an insured woman at 60, the insured man receiving 10/- for his wife if she is 60 or over. About 375,000 men and women over 70 would receive non-contributory pensions of 10/- a week on a means test basis. Of these four million pensioners, possibly 1,500,000 would receive supplementary pensions according to need. Broadly, therefore, the position is that one-quarter of the aged receive pensions which are supplemented to a maintenance level; another 40% receive contributory and "means" pensions at 10/- a week but do not receive further assistance; the remaining 35% have no State pension at all. A handful of the latter receive public assistance, either in institutions or in outdoor relief; a substantial number are wives of men below pension age; the remainder—well over 25% of the aged—depend entirely upon the provision which they have made for themselves. Many of them are no doubt in very difficult circumstances and are unwilling to apply for non-contributory pension or, if they are under 70, for public assistance. But they cannot even nearly all be regarded as being in urgent need. A great many people do provide for their own old age and are entirely independent of the State.

The Beveridge Plan for the aged is founded upon this fact. The Plan rejects the idea of an immediate maintenance pension for every aged person in favour of a steady widening of the scope of the contributory pension scheme until it covers the whole community, together with a gradual stepping up of the contributory pension until in twenty years it becomes a maintenance pension; in the meantime, those who need full maintenance get it on assistance terms. The population is in effect divided into three groups: those who are now eligible for contributory pension or will be eligible for it; those who will become eligible by the extension of the scheme to the whole population; those who are now or will become aged who are not eligible for contributory pension and either do or do not require assistance. In the long run these groups will merge together—in 1975 there will be very few aged without contributory pension at a full

[1] These facts are derived from those given in the Report, paras. 233-255 and p. 244.

maintenance rate. But in the transition period the three groups are treated in three different ways.

The first is the present contributory class, which is nearly the whole of the employed population. There are 19,000,000 people of working age and their wives in this class. Their pension is increased in 1945 from 10/- to 14/- (25/- for a married couple), conditional upon retirement. It is then stepped up by 1/- (1/6 joint) every two years, until the rate of 24/- (40/- joint) is reached in 1965. All aged in this group receive the same pension in the same year; a man who retires in 1955 gets 19/- and the man who retired in 1945 would get 19/- in 1955. The new pensioners and the old ascend the ladder together. The pension is subject to an increase of 1/- (2/- joint) for every year for which retirement is postponed. Existing pensioners continue at the 10/- rate until they retire. The immediate size of this group in 1945 would be the same as under the existing scheme—some 3,625,000 people would receive the pension, or 58% of the aged population. Their number would probably expand to over five millions in 1965, but not all of these would then be receiving pensions, for a significant proportion would still be working.

The second group is the new contributory class, which consists primarily of self-employed and unoccupied people, but also includes a number of employed persons who have hitherto been excepted, such as civil servants. There are 3½ million people of working age in this group. There would be no pensions for this class until 1955, when they would enter at the 14/- rate. This would be stepped up at 1/- every year until the full 24/- rate was reached at 1965, but this stepping up would not apply after a man had retired—the man who retires at 1955 would receive 14/- for the rest of his life, but the man who retires at 1961 would receive 20/-. The special increases for postponement apply equally to this group. It is difficult to estimate the numbers, but the number eligible for pension in 1965 might be more than one million.

The third group is the remainder—the present aged who do not have contributory pensions, the men of over 55 and the women of over 50 in 1945 who would not have time to qualify for new contributory pensions and so could contract out of paying contributions, the people who for one reason or another are disqualified from contributory pension—such as the people who are exempt from the whole scheme because they have no income to pay contributions. These would if they needed it receive assistance pension at a full maintenance rate. The finances of the scheme provide for 400,000 full assistance pensions in 1965.[1] The number of people in this group will be substantial at the outset—though only a small minority need the assistance pension—and will still be significant in 1965, but will gradually disappear in the course of time.[2] In 1975, there will be very few people still alive who were more than 55 years old in 1945; the only people in this class would then be the people who had failed to pay contributions, and as people pay contributions whether working or not and would find it very difficult to avoid paying them, the number would be very small indeed—certainly not more than 5% of the aged population.

The cost of the pensions on this basis works out as follows:[3]

ANNUAL EXPENDITURE ON THE AGED
(£ millions)

	EXISTING SCHEME.	BEVERIDGE PLAN.		
	1945	1945	1955	1965
Retirement pensions	94	126	190	300 †
Assistance pensions	57 *	39	33	25
	151	165	223	325

* £10 millions " means " pensions, £47 millions supplementary pensions.

† If there were no retirement condition and no special increase for postponement of retirement, the cost would be £330 millions ; if the pensions of new contributory classes were stepped up after retirement, the cost would be £315 millions ; if the pensions of the present contributory classes were pegged at the level at retirement, the cost would be £270 millions. These modifications would have some effect in 1955 but hardly any in 1945.

The Plan as it stands represents very little additional expenditure in 1945; the cost then rises as the pension is stepped up and as the new contributory classes come in. This scheme has certain

[1] Report, p. 199.

[2] In 1945, it would be about 35% of the aged population (58% in contributory group with 7% wives of men below pension age) ; in 1965, over 20% ; in 1975, not more than 5%. Many of these, of course, would still be working.

[3] Report, p. 197.

advantages in that it secures immediate financial economies; it also provides a breathing-space in which existing superannuation schemes can be adjusted; it provides free medical treatment for all aged people, and it provides an adequate pension on a uniform means test basis for those who require it. It can hardly be said that this is inadequate; the right way to adjust it, if adjustment is deemed necessary, is to speed up the transition period.

Much depends upon the extent to which the aged remain at work. In an ageing society it is obviously necessary that the working life should be as long as possible; we cannot contemplate a state of affairs in which a diminishing number of workers must maintain an expanding number of pensioners. In the relatively narrow terms of the finance of the pensions plan, if nobody continued work after retirement age, the cost of pensions in 1965 would be £330 millions instead of £300 millions, so that for the same outlay the pensions would have to be 10% lower. The real loss would be much more than this, for the national income would be lower and therefore the £300 millions figure would be a bigger drain upon the community's resources; the Government Actuary takes into account the fact that people continuing to work continue to pay contributions, but he does not take into account the fact that if people continue to work their incomes would be bigger than if they retired, that the national income would be bigger, and that the proportionate demand upon it for social security benefits would be much less. Failure to continue work to the extent foreseen by the Government Actuary would seriously increase the real cost of the Plan; on the other hand, a greater propensity to work by the aged would appreciably reduce the total cost.

How many of the aged will remain at work? If the people in the various age-groups showed the same propensity to work as in 1931, about 40% of the aged population would still be at work—this of course includes wives of 60 and over whose husbands are still working.[1] This proportion is perhaps unrealistically

[1] Census for 1931 gives 65·4% of men 65-69 gainfully occupied, 33·4% of men of 70 and over; 16·4% of women 60-64, and 8·2% of women 65 and over; 70% of men 65-69 are married, and 55% of men of 70 and over, and an allowance must be added for women 60 and over who are married to men below pension age.

high; people record themselves in the Census returns as "occupied" when in fact they are not. Also, the standard of living has increased very considerably since 1931, and as the standard of living rises, people tend to retire earlier. The Government Actuary estimates that just before the war only one-third of the male contributory pensioners were working;[1] whereas the over-all proportion for men recorded in the Census was nearly one-half. He considers that the introduction of retirement pensions will certainly reduce the propensity to work — this is incontrovertible — and on his assumptions it seems that the proportion of male contributory pensioners who will be working will fall from one-third to one-quarter. The gradual introduction of pensions for the self-employed will in general cause them to retire earlier; the Government Actuary estimates that self-employed men will retire at 70—so that about 45% of the aged in this group will still be working. On the whole, it is probably reasonable to forecast that one-quarter of the aged population will be working and three-quarters retired; unless special measures are taken, the proportion at work will fall as the years pass and the pensions are stepped up and new classes become eligible for them.

The Fabian Society suggested[2] that people could effectively be induced to remain at work by the payment of 10/- a week at 65 (or 60 for women) to all aged, followed by a retirement pension on a maintenance basis when they ceased work. A great many people give up work because their earning power is impaired by age—their speed is less, they may have more illness, and so on. A payment of this kind would tend to right this difficulty; it would certainly be a more effective inducement than the Beveridge increment of pension of 1/- a week for every year of postponement of retirement.

We can now give a rough indication of the cost of alternative proposals. The following table sets out some possibilities: the existing scheme, the Beveridge Plan and some variants upon it, the Fabian Plan, and more grandiose plans, culminating in the

[1] Report, p. 197. 55% of male contributors remained at work at 65, the proportion falling to 12½% remaining at work after 75. The Government Actuary expects that 50% will retire at 65, 25% between 65 and 70, and the rest between 70 and 75.

[2] Appendix, p. 434.

National Federation of Old Age Pensions Associations' demand for 30/- a week at 60.

ALTERNATIVE PENSIONS PLANS

	ANNUAL EXPENDITURE. (£ millions)	
	1945	1965
A. Existing Scheme	151	210
B. Beveridge Plan and variants:		
The Plan itself	165	325
The Plan without retirement condition	170	355
The Plan set forward ten years * .	200	360
C. Fabian Plan: lower retirement pension † for all retired aged, plus 10/– weekly for working aged:		
(i) One-third working	235	330
(ii) One-sixth working . . .	260	370
D. Universal Pensions at once:		
Beveridge pension for all retired aged .	280	390
Beveridge pension for all men at 65 and women at 60 . . .	335	470
30/– a week for all aged at 60 . .	580	820

* Rate for present contributory classes increased to 19/– single and 32/6 joint in 1945; other classes brought in immediately at 14/– and 25/– joint; full pension rates reached by 1955 instead of 1965.

† Retirement pension for all aged people of 15/– single and 25/– joint plus rent; 10/– weekly to working aged.

It is clear from this table that pensions for all aged people, contributory or not, are very expensive indeed. The Fabian pension is a bare minimum maintenance pension, and is linked with very attractive help for those who remain in work. But even if the aged showed their pre-war propensity to work, the Fabian scheme would cost £235 millions in 1945, compared with the Beveridge Plan at £165 millions or a speeded-up Beveridge cost of some £200 millions. The Beveridge Plan suffers from the defect that it fails to provide pensions on a maintenance level for the first years of operation, except for those who prove need, and indeed in the initial stages imposes a retirement condition for receipt of a pension which is only three-fifths of a maintenance pension. The Fabian Plan would provide maintenance pensions—albeit on a slim basis—for many who did not need them and had made perfectly adequate provision for themselves. This dilemma is inescapable. It would probably be best to link the schemes together, by speeding up the Beveridge transition and by giving a small payment to those who remain in work instead of giving them additional pension rights. But the extent to which this can be done depends upon the financial position; the provision of more generous pensions in 1945 should certainly rank behind the claims of other social security benefits and indeed of other social services such as education.

Housewives' Benefits.—The chief provision is against *widowhood.* About 75,000 women are widowed under the age of 60 every year; widow's benefit of 36/- a week for thirteen weeks would cost £2 millions. There are some 300,000 widows with dependent children; guardian benefit at the inadequate rate of 24/- a week would cost £19 millions a year. The continuation of the existing 10/- widow's pension to about 300,000 existing widows without dependent children would cost about £8 millions in 1945, and would gradually fall as these widows reached the age of 60 and passed to retirement pension. There would be some 200,000 widows under 60 without dependants who would be receiving no benefit at all; only a very small proportion would need State support.[1] The cost of these benefits is £29 millions, falling to £21 millions in 1965. The *marriage* grant, for 400,000 marriages a year at £10 maximum each, would cost £3 millions a year, but less at the outset, for it would take women some time to build up the necessary contributions—forty for each £1 granted, and only a proportion would ever get the maximum; the cost is so small and the advantage in encouraging marriage so useful that a rather more generous grant might be given. The *maternity* grant of £4 for each of 700,000 births a year would cost £2·8 millions; this grant is inadequate and we suggest £10, costing

[1] Of the 810,000 widows under 60 in 1942, 440,000 were receiving widows' pensions, and 370,000 receiving none. Of the former, 5·3% were receiving public assistance, of the latter, 2½%. There is certainly a great deal of poverty untouched by public assistance, but the proportion for the pensionless does suggest that the bulk of widows in the class ineligible for widow's pension are in fact fairly provided for. (Report, p. 244.)

£7 millions; the maternity benefit of 36/- a week for thirteen weeks for gainfully occupied mothers would, for some 180,000 a year, cost just over £4 millions, making £7 millions or £11 millions according to the size of the maternity grant.

Funeral Grant.—The allowance of £20 on the death of adults, with a lower rate for children, would cost £11 millions in a full year; there are roughly 600,000 deaths a year. At the outset of the scheme, more than half the deaths would be excluded—persons over 60 not being covered—and the cost would be £4 millions, rising to £12 millions a year in 1965.

National Assistance.—The Report puts the annual cost of the residual public assistance at £5 millions; this is necessary to cope with all sorts of contingencies which cannot be brought into a uniform pattern.

Administration.—The Report includes a total cost for administration of £24 millions a year—£18 millions for the insurances, £3 millions for assistance, and £3 millions for children's allowances. This represents about 4½% on the total benefits paid, falling to 3½% by 1965. This may be compared with existing cost to contribution ratios—much the same as cost to benefit ratios—of 9·3% for unemployment insurance, 16·9% for health insurance, 2·5% for contributory pensions and with industrial assurance cost ratios of 35%.[1] For unemployment assistance the ratio of costs to allowances paid is 12·8%.[2] There is a notable saving of administrative cost in an all-in scheme with no means test; in fact, the total cost of running a comprehensive plan is little more than that of the present system.

Children's Allowances.—The principles of children's allowances were dealt with in the previous chapter. Here we are concerned with the statistical basis of the choice between policies. There are three broad alternatives: (*A*) to pay an allowance for every child, (*B*) to pay stepped-up allowance for each child after the first, and (*C*), following the Report, to pay a flat rate allowance for each child after the first. The following table sets these out; it covers all children under 16, and it assumes that every child of an unemployed or sick parent gets 8/- a week:

[1] Report, pp. 277-86.
[2] 1938 Report of Unemployment Assistance Board, p. 53.

CHILDREN'S ALLOWANCES

	Total No. of children under 16. (m.)	ALTERNATIVE *A*.		ALTERNATIVE *B*.		ALTERNATIVE *C*.	
		Per child per week.	Annual cost. (£m.)	Per child per week.	Annual cost. (£m.)	Per child per week.	Annual cost. (£m.)
First Child	5·5	6/-	90	—	18	—	18
Second Child	2·8	6/-	46	7/-	52	8/-	58
Third Child	1·2	7/-	22	8/-	25	8/-	25
Fourth Child and over	1·0	8/-	21	9/-	24	8/-	21
Total under 16	10·5		179		119		122*

* The Beveridge figures cover children under 15 and those of 15 still at school; it is £110 m., or £208 m. if the first child is included. (Report, p. 202.)

There is very little difference in total cost between an ascending scale, such as Alternative *B*, and the flat rate proposed in the Report. The Beveridge figure of 8/- a week is an average of different rates for different ages, according to the needs of children of different ages and the allowances in kind available to them; this could hardly be linked with an ascending scale. On the whole, the ascending scale is preferable, because it actively stimulates population and is more simple for the parent to understand.

The most difficult financial point about children's allowances is their relation to income tax. The Report says very little about this, but at present rates of income tax it is of tremendous significance. Parents receive an allowance in their income tax assessments of £50 a child; to a person who is paying the standard rate of tax, this is equivalent to a children's allowance of 10/- a week per child. If children's allowances were introduced universally, it would clearly be less necessary to continue to give this income tax relief; it would be reasonable to allow parents the choice between receiving tax relief or receiving the children's allowance direct. There could thus be very considerable savings to the Exchequer to balance the cost of the children's allowances.

At the present admittedly abnormal levels of taxation, these savings to the Exchequer could be very large indeed. Tax relief to the effective amount of 6/- per child or more is being given in respect of 60% of the first children, 40% of the second children,

20% of the third children, and 5% of the fourth and subsequent children. This means that if each parent was given a choice between children's allowances as in Alternative *A* and his present tax relief, the parents of some 40% of the children would lose on one what they gained on the other, and would thus be no better off; allowances would have to be paid in respect of only 60% of the children; the net cost to the Exchequer of Alternative *A* (which covers every child) would be only £105 millions instead of £179 millions.[1] If Alternatives *B* or *C* were adopted, the corresponding saving would be much less—the net cost of either scheme would be about £95 millions instead of £120 millions. The singular fact is that the net cost of providing allowances for every child is at present tax rates very little more than that of providing for children after the first![2] And this arrangement of providing a choice between the allowance and tax relief does mean that the extra expenditure goes where it does most good—to the parents with large families and incomes of less than £500 a year and to parents with small families and incomes below £250. The position of the higher-income families remains unchanged.

It seems at first sight, therefore, that we could adopt Alternative *A* and link it with tax relief. This would be administratively practicable, as the Chancellor admitted in his White Paper, and it would yield the right sort of social result. At the same time, however, the spectacularly low net cost would be only transitory; as the abnormally heavy burden of taxation was lifted from the lower middle incomes, additional expenditure would be incurred in providing children's allowances for the people who were no longer receiving tax relief. At the pre-war tax rates, indeed, the net cost of Alternative *A* would be about £150 millions—only some £30 millions less than the gross cost. In view of this fact, it may be best to keep the children's allowance formally separate from the tax relief and to treat the latter on its merits; even with children's allowances, the bachelor or the childless couple would certainly have a greater ability to pay taxation than a

[1] These figures of net cost are consistent with those given by the Treasury in the White Paper on Family Allowances, 1942, Cmd. 6354.

[2] The reason for this is that Alternatives *B* and *C* provide bigger allowances for the second and subsequent children than Alternative *A*, and if *B* and *C* were adopted provision must still be made for the first children of incomeless parents—about one-sixth of all first children.

couple with children. On balance, Alternative *A* would probably still be preferable. But provision for the first child is not a matter of urgent social priority, and Alternatives *B* or *C*—preferably the former—would be adequate.

Public Health Service.—The cost of the comprehensive health and rehabilitation service is difficult to foresee. The most recent analysis of the cost of the nation's medical services is that of Medical Planning Research, which gives the following picture for 1938-39:[1]

COST OF MEDICAL SERVICES, 1938-39

(£ millions)

	Public.	Private.	Total.
Hospitals and other health services	52 (*a*)	23 (*b*)	75
Doctors' fees and salaries	10 (*c*)	38	48
Dentists and masseurs	3	9	12
Dispensed medicines	2	3	5
Total	67	73	140

(*a*) Hospitals, £11·7 m.; mental hospitals, £14·5 m.; tuberculosis, venereal disease, maternity and child welfare, school medical services, £14·3 m.; poor law medical service, £8 m.

(*b*) Hospitals, £17 m.; convalescent homes, £2·2 m.; district and other nurses, £2 m.

(*c*) N.H.I. payments, plus salaries of doctors employed in public service, apart from those paid by hospitals.

The pre-war cost of the medical services was thus about £140 millions, excluding the expenditure upon patent medicines, which was at least £20 millions a year. The total cost was roughly equally divided between public and private provision. In addition, the whole of the preventive services, such as notification of disease, and the whole of the contributory environmental services, such as sewage disposal, are publicly provided. During the war, the public sector has expanded; the Beveridge

[1] Interim General Report of *Medical Planning Research*, issued as a supplement to *The Lancet*, November 21, 1942. The most complete review, for a somewhat earlier period, is that of P. E. P., published in *The British Health Services*, pp. 387-93.

Report estimates the post-war public provision on the basis of existing services at £79 millions, compared with the pre-war figure of £67 millions.

This gives little indication of the cost of a comprehensive public medical service. Dr. Stark Murray works on the basis of the pre-war cost of £140 millions, excluding the new building of hospitals and health centres which would be required.[1] Medical Planning Research gives a comparable figure of £170 millions; the main difference is provision by Medical Planning Research for a considerable increase in nurses' pay and in the scope of nursing services generally. There is general agreement between these two authorities that there would be great administrative economies in a national medical service, and that the nation could get more and better medical service at the same real cost. Sir William Beveridge, after consultation with the Ministry of Health, has adopted a figure of £170 millions,[2] which represents an increase of about one-fifth on the pre-war total cost, and does not appear to be unreasonable in relation to other estimates. It would be necessary to provide a substantial building programme in addition; there will be resources for this when the immediate work of emergency house-building is completed.

The Report's estimate of £170 millions a year may be on the high side. There would be no cause for concern, however, if it proved too low. In every sense of the word, we can afford a great expansion of the health services. Not enough of the nation's resources are being devoted to this purpose. There are at any time some 800,000 people who cannot work because they are ill. Each of these people when working would make a contribution to the national income of at least £300 a year. If by so doing we could reduce the amount of illness by one-half, it would be worth while on a purely economic basis to spend an additional £120 millions a year on the provision of health services—that is, to increase the existing expenditure, public and private, by two-thirds. Public money spent on health services, like public money spent on education, literally pays for itself in increased national income. Intensified investment of national resources in health would yield a more than adequate return.

[1] Dr. Stark Murray, *Health for All*.
[2] Report, pp. 201, 204.

THE COST OF SOCIAL SECURITY

The third stage is to draw up the "liability" side of the Social Security Budget. This is a matter of collating the results arrived at with the corresponding prospective figures for 1945 on the existing cash benefit provisions, and with the Report's forecasts for 1965.

EXPENDITURE UNDER THE BEVERIDGE PLAN

	No. of Adult Beneficiaries at any Time in 1945 * (including Adult Dependants). (millions)		Annual Expenditure. (£ millions)		
	Full Maintenance Benefits.	Other Benefits and Grants.	Existing Services. 1945	Beveridge Plan. 1945	Beveridge Plan. 1965
Unemployment . .	2·1	—	84	110	107
Disability . . .	1·1	—	27	57	71
Industrial Disability .	0·2	—	13	15	15
Widows' Pensions (under 60) . .	0·3	0·3	12	29	21
Old Age Pensions .	—	3·6 †	151	165	325
Maternity Grant and Benefit . . .	0·05	0·7	3	7	6
Marriage Grant .	—	0·4	—	1	3
Funeral Grant . .	—	0·3	—	4	12
Children's Allowances	5·3		11	110	100
National Assistance .	—	—	15	5	5
Administration . .	—	—	20	24	23
Health Services . .	—	—	79	170	170
	3·75	3·9 benefits 1·4 grants	415	697	858

* This is the number receiving benefits at any given time in 1945 under the Beveridge Plan. The full maintenance beneficiaries receive benefits at the full Beveridge benefit rate ; the numbers in the second column refer to benefits, such as the Old Age contributory pensions, which are not enough for full maintenance, and grants, such as the marriage grant, paid during the entire year.

† Contributory pensions only ; some of these are actually supplemented to a full maintenance basis, and assistance pensions are given to people who are not eligible for contributory pension and are in need.

In its initial stages the Beveridge Plan will provide full maintenance at any moment for 3¾ million adults of working age; it will provide children's allowances at a maintenance rate for half the nation's children; it will give contributory pensions for nearly 4 million aged and widows, and will provide supplementation and assistance pensions for these and others of the

6¼ million aged who may need them; it will provide miscellaneous grants which will be received by about 1½ million people a year; it will give everybody a comprehensive and free medical service. The total expenditure in 1945 is estimated at £697 millions, compared with the prospective expenditure of £415 millions on the present services. The £697 millions figure may be on the high side. If only the inevitable unemployment were included, there would be a saving of some £35 millions; there is a possible saving of £10 millions in the benefits for permanent disability; a credit of some £10-15 millions could be allowed in the children's allowance figure in respect of savings in tax relief—it is perfectly easy, indeed, to pare the figure by £50 millions. Within the £697 millions framework, there is some scope for correcting certain inadequate benefits and for speeding up the old age transition. The increased cost in 1945 is mainly the result of the introduction of children's allowances and the comprehensive health scheme; these account for £190 millions of the increase of £282 millions—just over two-thirds. Of the rest, the increased expenditure upon disability is the most significant; there is very little increase in payments to the aged in 1945—the increase in contributory pensions is almost entirely offset by the reduced charges for non-contributory and supplementary pensions. In the following twenty years, however, the expansion in the total expenditure from £697 millions to £858 millions is entirely accounted for by the increased payments to the aged as the weekly benefits are stepped up and the new classes of contributor become eligible for benefit. The whole financial picture emphasises the underlying philosophy of the Beveridge Plan, which is to provide full maintenance and constructive allowances for the population of working age immediately after the end of the war, and to improve the conditions of the aged more gradually as the national income develops in the post-war years.

The Distribution of the Burden

This expenditure represents a burden upon the community. It is not a question of "cost" in the old-fashioned language of pre-war Budgets. It is rather the real cost in the sense of the effect upon the whole national economy of changing the flow of goods and services so that a substantially larger share goes to the aged, the unemployed, the sick and the other beneficiaries of the scheme. There are some folk who say that the nation "will not be able to afford" expansion of the social services because of the cost of the war; others will say that as the nation can spend fifteen million pounds a day on the war for month after month without any dire financial effects, the benefits which it can afford are practically unlimited. Both arguments are out of date; they are in artificial terms of money cost instead of in real economic terms. We should have learnt from the war that we must look behind the money façade. If the incomeless are to receive a bigger share of the nation's output, those who are in work and are receiving purchasing power in wages and profits must receive less. If there is unemployment in excess of the unavoidable minimum, of course, this is not precisely true, for social security payments to the unemployed would increase the national income by setting the unemployed resources to work. But we are assuming a high level of employment, and in that case there is clearly a limit to the extent to which people are ready to transfer their purchasing power to the economically incapacitated. The people will not accept more than a certain amount of taxation, and this applies equally to the wage-earner and to the well-to-do; if the worker's effective purchasing power is cut by taxation or by excessive contributions more than he thinks is justified, he will resist the scheme. The essence of political economy is to find the size of the transfer which will both right the social ill and secure common consent.

The most straightforward criterion of what the nation "can afford" is the proportion which the expenditure bears to the national income. The table on p. 378 compares the social security payments in the last thirty years with the national income. This proportion grew from 1¼% just before the last war to 3¾% in the middle of the 'twenties, to 6½% in the depression, and to 5¼% in 1938. To link this up with the Beveridge Plan we have to assume a post-war national income; the 1945 level is taken to be 40% above that of 1938, the result of a 25% increase in prices and also of a larger working population with less unemployment; the national income per head, it is assumed, will then increase at the annual rate of 1½%, which was actually achieved in the period between the wars.[1] The proportions then appear as follows:

[1] See above, p. 329 *et seq.*, for a full examination of these assumptions.

PROPORTION OF NATIONAL INCOME

	Cash Benefits. (%)	Total Social Security Cost including Health Services and Administration. (%)
1938 . . .	5·3	7·1
1945 . . .	7·8	10·7
1965 . . .	7·8	10·1

In the broadest terms, the 1945 expenditure contemplated in the Beveridge Plan is about 50% higher in relation to the national income than that of 1938. In the twenty-year period following the war, the national income may be expected to rise fast enough to absorb very comfortably the increased cost of the Beveridge pension scheme.

The forward step from 1938 to 1945 is not nearly so spectacular even as appears in these figures. Before the war, private expenditure upon medical treatment, medicines, voluntary hospitals and other provision against ill-health was of the order of 2% of the national income. The annual payments of industrial assurance premiums were about 1½% of the national income. There was substantial further voluntary provision against contingencies which are covered in the Beveridge Plan. Much of the additional proportion of the national income devoted to these public purposes is thus simply a change in the channel by which provision is made.[1] From the point of view of allocation of national resources, it is immaterial whether each citizen pays £1 a year for a private doctor or whether he pays £1 a year to the Government and the Government pays the doctor. There is no doubt, of course, that considerable voluntary provision will continue; not all the extra public expenditure envisaged in the Plan will be a simple replacement of existing private expenditure for the same purposes. But these percentages show perfectly clearly that the proportion of the national resources which is allocated to provision against these contingencies will not increase

[1] More services will be available for the same real cost; the most striking example is the tremendous gain to the public from the replacement of industrial assurance with a cost ratio of 37% by funeral benefit with a cost ratio of certainly less than 5%.

to nearly the same extent as the table suggests. The increase from 1938 to 1945 may be, say, from 11% (7% public plus 4% private) to 13% (10¾% public plus 2¼% private). But it will not be much more than that. The bulk of the expansion will be a re-channelling of existing private provision. In these real terms, the Beveridge Plan looks very conservative indeed; the nation could probably afford an even more far-reaching plan. There can clearly be no serious financial difficulty in operating a scheme of this scale. (See p. 378.)

The financial problem is simply one of diverting the required amount of current purchasing power from individuals into the common pool from which social security grants and benefits are paid. This is, of course, done partly by levying contributions and partly by the ordinary instruments of taxation and borrowing. The realities of this process are unnecessarily obscured by an unsound analogy with private insurance; the financial structure of social insurance is framed on the implicit assumption that the State for these purposes is a mammoth-size Prudential. Insured persons' contributions and contributions from their employers are paid into an autonomous fund, and are matched by contributions from the Treasury; the moneys in the fund are invested in Government securities to yield an "income" to the fund; there is a periodical actuarial review to determine whether there is a "surplus" or a "deficit," after which contributions and benefits are raised or lowered accordingly. There are good historical reasons why social insurance is financed in this way, but they should not be allowed to cloud the fact that the whole apparatus is nothing more than a fiction and has no real logical content. The pattern of social insurance is as different from private insurance as could be. Private insurance is a contract between two financially independent units—the client and the company. The client pays his premiums, which are based upon the actuarial risk and the rate of interest which the company can earn on its investments; the company's only financial resources are its premium and investment incomes. The State, on the other hand, has unlimited financial resources. Each year it pays from the social security pool what is required to meet the benefits, and it can in reality collect no more and no less from contributions, taxation and borrowing. If it collects more in order to build a fund against future expanded commitments,

SOCIAL SECURITY CASH BENEFITS AND NATIONAL INCOME: 1913 TO 1965
(£ millions)

	PAYMENTS UNDER SOCIAL INSURANCE AND ASSISTANCE SCHEMES.				BEVERIDGE PLAN.	
	1914-15	1926-27	1931-32	1938-39	1945	1965
Unemployment	0·4	50	111	90	110	107
Sickness	8·0	20	19	19	64	77
Workmen's Compensation	3·5	6	6	7	15	15
Old Age and Widowhood	10·0	38	76	94	194	346
Public Assistance (out-relief)	3·2	28	16	26	5	5
Marriage and Funeral Grant	—	—	—	—	5	15
Children's Allowances	—	—	—	—	110	100
Cash Benefits	25·1	142	228	236	503	665
Health Services				65	170	170
Administration				19	24	23
Total Cost *				320	697	858
Net National Income (calendar years) †	2,150	3,850	3,520	4,595	6,500	8,500
(Cost of Living, 1938=100)	(64)	(110)	(94)	(100)	(125)	(125)
Cash Benefits as % of Net National Income	1·2	3·7	6·5	5·3	7·8	7·8
Total Cost as % of Net National Income				7·1	10·7	10·1

* Beveridge Report, pp. 104 and 214. The Workmen's Compensation for 1914-39 is for seven industries only; the full 1938 figure was £13 m.; this is picked up in the percentages for 1938.

† Net national income at factor cost in these years; relative prices shown by Ministry of Labour cost of living index. 1938 national income is official estimate in Cmd. 6347; 1926 and 1931 from *Studies in National Income, 1924-38*, edited by Bowley, p. 81, adjusted to accord with Cmd. 6347 definitions; 1913 from Clark, *National Income and Outlay*, p. 232, adjusted for definition. 1945 national income assumed to be 40% above 1938, resulting from 25% price increase, 3% increase in working population, reduction in unemployment from 12½% to 5%. From 1945 to 1965 it is assumed that income per head rises at pre-war rate of 1½% per annum: Bowley, *op. cit.* p. 193.

all it can do with the fund is to invest it in Government securities —upon which incidentally it fixes the interest rate. The fund is thus nothing more than a collection of the Government's own promises to pay; when the time comes to meet these commitments, the amount of money which the State has to raise from taxation or borrowing is precisely the same as it would have been if there had been no fund at all. For example, suppose the pool must pay out £15 millions a week, and workers' and employers' contributions provide £5 millions a week. The State must then provide £10 millions a week, either by taxation or by selling Government securities. If there were a fund, the interest on which yielded £3 millions a week, the State would still have to provide £10 millions a week, for the £3 millions interest on the Government securities held by the fund is paid by the State. In other words, the State must operate on a pay-as-you-go basis. It has no alternative. It cannot set aside reserves for future contingencies, for the reserve can be only in the form of Government securities. So the process of the fund degenerates into mere book-keeping; indeed, its only purpose is to segregate the financial operations of the State from one another and to render much more difficult the task of getting a consolidated statement of the State's incomings and outgoings.

A strong case can nevertheless be made for operating the social security pool through a fund. It lends an aura of commercial respectability and actuarial rectitude to the Plan—a political consideration of some importance. The segregation from the rest of the national finances may reduce political pressures to increase the benefits in times of boom and decrease them in times of slump, and so may enable the Government to follow a more sensible economic policy than it could do if the scheme were financed as part of the Budget. These are advantages which cannot be ignored. But the big disadvantage is that the quasi-insurance structure encourages a certain obscurantism in public finance, and hinders the vitally important work of public education in these matters. Public controversy thus tends to rage round non-essentials and to miss the main points; at best this means that sensible policies have to be carried out in spite of public opinion rather than because of it; at worst it may lead to awful misconceptions based upon the analogy with private insurance such as those of the May Report in the summer of 1931,[1] and the subsequent legislation of the National Government—misconceptions which, as almost every economist would now agree, intensified the depression and caused altogether unnecessary suffering. On balance, it is probably best to call things by their right names and abandon the analogy with private insurance; now that economic knowledge is reaching the stage at which it can fruitfully be applied to public affairs, it is on the whole best to conduct the financial operations of the State with the utmost clarity and simplicity so that the maximum public understanding and the minimum technical mystery is achieved. It may be necessary for traditional reasons to have a Social Insurance Fund, but it must be made quite clear that the whole idea of the surpluses and deficits in the fund is artificial and is simply paper book-keeping.

Provided that the contributory principle is kept in the right setting, however, it is not only unobjectionable but also positively desirable. The evidence submitted to the Beveridge Committee revealed an overwhelming body of public support for specific contributions—although it must be remembered that the views expressed by such organisations as the Trades Union Congress General Council and the National Conference of Friendly Societies, to which the Report gives great weight on this question, can hardly be taken as evidence of the views of men and women of under 35, whose whole approach to social questions may be undergoing far-reaching change in the Services. The payment of contributions is certainly a convenient administrative machinery for determining who is entitled to which benefits, and it is a convenient and accepted means of diverting purchasing power to the State. Furthermore, it is something of a check upon irresponsible demands. We can therefore accept the contributory principle, subject to the condition that the contributions are low enough to enable them to be paid by every citizen without undue hardship and that benefits are paid for the whole period of loss of earning power, irrespective of the number of contributions made. In other words, the contributory principle is

[1] Sir George May, Chairman of the May Committee on National Expenditure, was associated with the Prudential; it was natural that the Government should call in a man of his experience, for it believed that unemployment insurance was fundamentally analogous to private insurance; it was inevitable that he should in those circumstances treat the problem in the same way as he would have treated a bankrupt insurance company.

a great advantage if it is conceived as a registration payment conveying the title to benefit; it is pernicious if the contribution is regarded as being mathematically linked to the benefit. In the latter case, indeed, the "ninepence for fourpence" fallacy appears; the essential truth that everybody contributes in two ways—as an insured person paying a flat rate contribution and as a member of the community paying direct and indirect taxation—is lost; people are deluded into thinking that their contributions pay for their benefits and thus they fail to understand why they are being taxed. As the scope of social insurance is spread to cover the whole population, the distinction between the "insured person" and the "community" vanishes; for the community as a whole the cost is not "one shilling for threepence" but "one shilling for a shilling," and people must be made to understand this. The relative proportion of the cost to be met from specific contributions or from taxation is purely a matter of fiscal technique; provided that the contribution is large enough to be an adequate registration payment—that is, large enough to represent some effort on the part of the contributor and to check artificial claims to benefit—no high principle is involved.

In the Beveridge Plan—and indeed in all social insurance schemes—the relation between the rate of contribution and the rate of benefit is entirely arbitrary. In order to earn the benefits which he would expect to receive during his whole lifetime, an entrant into the scheme at the age of 16 would have to pay a weekly contribution of 103·2d. for the whole of his working life from the age of 21, and somewhat smaller contributions between the ages of 16 and 21.[1] Even this is to some extent arbitrary; it assumes a rate of interest on the fund of 3%—i.e. that the State lends itself money at 3%; it excludes the cost of medical benefit and of children's allowances; it assumes that men pay for widow's benefit and women pay for marriage benefit, and it makes a number of other assumptions of this kind. It is then assumed that the State shall pay one-third of the cost of unemployment benefit and one-sixth of the cost of the other insurance benefits, except for marriage and funeral grant. When this is taken into account, the necessary contribution proves to be 79·7d. per week. It is then decided that nearly one-quarter of

[1] Report, pp. 188-9.

the cost of the health services should be charged to the contribution, which requires an extra 10d. a week, making 89·7d. a week in all. The contribution for an employed man is thus put at 90d. a week; it is assumed that the employer's contribution will look after one-half of all the insurance contributions except maternity and burial and marriage and will look after 15% of the contribution for the health service. The conclusion is thus reached that the employed man must pay 4/3 a week and that the employer's contribution is 3/3 a week.[1] The calculation bristles with assumptions and arbitrary determinations. Lastly, it is provided that the State stands the loss which is involved in admitting virtually the whole of the population over the age of 16 at the full rate of benefit although they have not paid contributions from the age of 16 to the present time. There is no actuarial virtue in these calculations; if one decided that the contribution should be 2/- or 10/- a week, one could go through precisely the same computation making the appropriate assumptions which would yield a result of precisely the same validity. If we assumed, for example, that the State should pay three-quarters of the unemployment benefit, one-half of the disability benefit, one-third of the pensions and all the maternity benefit, that the remaining cost, except in the case of funeral benefit, be divided equally between worker's and employer's contributions, and that the insured person should pay one-tenth of the cost of the medical service, the necessary contribution from the insured person would be 2/6 a week and from the employer 2/-. We could then provide, as the Government Actuary does, that the State should stand the loss on all the present population who will not have contributed on this scale since they were 16. This complicated apparatus, indeed, really means nothing at all; it means even less when we remember that the employer does not in fact pay the employer's contribution but passes it on to the community of insured persons in increased prices, and that the mass of insured persons also pay the State's contribution. In actual fact, the contributions are fixed, just the same as any other tax, according to what the insured person can afford and is willing to pay.

The Beveridge contributions thus have no intrinsic merit; they are no more linked to the actual benefits paid than would

[1] Report, pp. 152, 227.

be contributions of half the size or half as large again. They must be considered purely in relation to taxation policy and in relation to what people can afford. In principle, the insured person's contribution must be large enough to be an effective registration payment. Provided it is large enough for this, however, it should be kept as small as possible. This is so for two reasons. Firstly, it is in effect a poll tax and so is highly regressive in its incidence; it is a much larger burden upon the small incomes than upon the large. Secondly, it is to be universal and must cover virtually every member of the community whether earning or not; consequently it must not be so large that a substantial number of people cannot afford to pay it. On the other hand, the contribution does represent an established and acceptable form of taxation, and from the fiscal point of view it would be unwise to abandon revenue from a freely accepted but regressive tax in favour of one which is socially more just but less acceptable; working people understand the contribution better than they understand the income tax as applied to weekly wages. In the light of these considerations, what is the right level of contributions for the Beveridge Plan? The Beveridge proposal,[1] compared with the existing level of contributions, is as follows:

	Men (21 and over).			Women (21 and over).		
	Insured Person.	Employer.	Total.	Insured Person.	Employer.	Total.
Employed Persons (Class I)—						
Beveridge Plan	4/3	3/3	7/6	3/6	2/6	6/–
Existing	1/10	1/10	3/8	1/7	1/6	3/1
Self-Employed Persons (Class II)—						
Beveridge Plan	4/3	—	—	3/9	—	—
Persons not Gainfully Occupied (Class IV)—						
Beveridge Plan	3/9	—	—	3/–	—	—

There is not much doubt that the great bulk of employed men can quite comfortably afford the 4/3 a week which is required of them under the Beveridge Plan. The average industrial worker's household spent 4/8 a week per adult man in 1937-38 on compulsory insurance contributions, medical treatment,

[1] Report, pp. 152, 227.

industrial assurance premiums and similar expenditure; this is equivalent to 5/10 a week at the post-war wage-and-price level.[1] All but a small minority of employed male workers would certainly be able to afford the Beveridge contributions. But the lower tenth of wage-earners would have serious difficulties in paying this money every week; the fact that many of them do pay a similar proportion of their earnings in charges of this kind is not really evidence that every wage-earner can afford it. The Report recognises this,[2] and makes a tentative suggestion that the employer's contribution should be increased and the worker's reduced if the weekly wage is below a certain level. But this adds an administrative complication, and incidentally destroys the conception that there should be a flat rate of contribution which everybody should pay. The right policy is surely to fix the contribution at the rate which everyone can pay; if the bulk of workers can afford to pay more, they can pay more in taxation.

The employed woman's contribution of 3/6 a week is certainly too high. The average woman's wage is 40/- a week, or about one-half of a man's. A contribution of nearly 10% of the wage is assuredly more than women can fairly be expected to pay, given the present structure of women's wages. We have noted earlier that, in relation to human needs, women's wages are less adequate than men's when family allowances are paid, and contributions on this scale would make the disparity worse. The contributions required from people in Class II and Class IV likewise look high; the incomes of self-employed and unoccupied people vary tremendously and there is no doubt that many people in these classes could pay the contributions without any difficulty. But some of the poorest people in the community are in Class II, and many people in Class IV have no incomes at all; the Report recognises this by allowing people in these classes with incomes less than £75 a year to contract out of the scheme.[3] It is highly undesirable, however, that anyone should be able to contract out; the size of the contribution—3/- a week—will induce a great many Class IV women to contract out, and will present some difficulty to people with incomes slightly above the £75 limit. The level of Beveridge contributions is too high; one gets the impression that the Report started with the idea of a 4/3 contribution for the Class I man—which is reasonable for the bulk

[1] Report, para. 286. [2] Report, para. 408. [3] Report, para. 363.

of workers—and then fixed the other contributions *pari passu* without adequate consideration of their practicability.

The employer's contribution under the Beveridge Plan is two-thirds above the existing level. This too is excessive. The employer's contribution is not in general paid by the employer, but is passed on to the consumer like any other prime cost, and is indistinguishable in its effect from indirect taxation. It affects the costs of export industries and protected industries alike; it increases the prices both of luxuries and necessities; it is a tax for which no good case can be made. The Report suggests with some reason that as the contributions are collected through the employers, it is useful to retain an employer's contribution and so financially to associate employers with the scheme. Moreover, the employer's contribution is part of the structure now, and to remove it would sacrifice a tax which is already in existence and is accepted. Thus some employer's contribution may be retained. But it certainly should not be increased to anything like the level proposed in the Beveridge Plan. Apart from the fiscal argument, there is the further objection that social insurance lore requires self-employed and unoccupied persons to pay their own employer's contribution; if, therefore, the contributions for employed persons are laid out in such a way that a substantial part is covered by the employer's contribution, the corresponding contribution for self-employed persons may become very large. This actually happens in the Report; it is the basic reason why the Class II and Class IV contributions are so big; one of the reasons put forward in the Report for not allowing short-term disability benefit for Class II people is that it would increase their contribution beyond the level which they could afford to pay.[1] There is much to be said for having some employer's contribution. But all the arguments are in favour of keeping it very low.

To sum up, the Beveridge Plan contribution for employed men is too high for the worst-paid workers; the contribution for employed women is definitely too high; the contributions for people in Class II and Class IV are too high; the increase in the employer's contribution cannot be defended on rational

[1] Report, para. 119. The Class II and Class IV contributions are calculated with the same formula as Class I applied to the benefits which they receive (e.g. excluding unemployment benefit), but whereas the Class I contribution is split between worker and employer, the insured person has to pay the whole of the Class II and Class IV contribution.

grounds. The following scale of contributions might be more appropriate:

	Men (21 and over).			Women (21 and over).		
	Insured Person.	Employer.	Total.	Insured Person.	Employer.	Total.
Class I . .	2/6	2/-	4/6	2/3	1/6	3/9
Class II . .	2/6	—	—	2/3	—	—
Class IV .	2/-	—	—	1/9	—	—

Contributions on this scale would be ample to provide an effective registration payment; they would be within the capacity to pay of every person in every class; the contributions of the different classes would be in broad relationship to the benefits received—the ratio of each class's contribution to the others' is the same as in the Beveridge Plan. It would be possible, with contributions on this level, to reduce the income limit for exemption in Class II and Class IV from £75 to £50 or even less. This scale of contributions, indeed, would make the scheme really universal.[1] The employer's contribution remaining virtually at the present level, there would be no additional charge upon industry.

The lay-out of the total expenditure divided between the various sources of revenue is as follows:

Sources of Social Security Revenue

Source of Revenue.	1938-39	1945			1965	
		Existing Schemes.	Beveridge. Plan.	Alternative Contributions.	Beveridge Plan.	Alternative Contributions.
	(£m.)	(£m.)	(£m.)	(£m.)	(£m.)	(£m.)
National Exchequer and Local Rates * . .	221	280	366	497	534	662
Insured Persons . .	55	69	194	114	192	113
Employers . . .	66	83	137	86	132	83
	342	432	697	697	858	858

* From Report, para. 282. The table in the Report gives a separate item of "Interest" as a source of revenue, given as £9 millions in 1938-39 and £15 millions in 1945 and 1965; this is, however, interest on Government securities, which must be found from the National Exchequer, and so is in reality indistinguishable from other revenue from the Exchequer.

In the initial stages of the Beveridge Plan, 28% of the purchasing power required for the social security pool is siphoned from

[1] A possible alternative is to have three or four levels of contribution, according to earnings, and a flat rate of benefit; this in effect incorporates a taxation principle into the contribution. (Appendix, p. 451.)

insured persons' incomes as direct contributions, nearly 20% is derived from increased prices necessitated by the employer's contribution, and just over one-half is derived from general taxation. The proportion of the latter increases to some 63% in 1965. Under the alternative contributions which we have suggested, one-sixth of the total expenditure would initially be covered by the insured persons' contributions,[1] one-eighth by the employer's contribution, and just over 70% from general taxation, and the latter proportion would rise as it does in the Beveridge Plan. In the alternative plan, of course, the capacity of the bulk of the working-class to pay direct and indirect taxation would be much greater than in the Beveridge Plan itself; the burden on wage-earners as a whole would not necessarily be reduced, but it would be more fairly distributed between them.

It now remains only to relate the burden upon the National Exchequer to the post-war national income and outlay. Sufficient evidence has been put forward to show very clearly that the Beveridge Plan involves very little additional burden upon the national resources—indeed, the bulk of it represents a re-channelling of existing expenditure for these purposes. How does this fit in with the other demands which will develop after the war—the demands for expenditure of resources upon education, upon national defence, upon housing and upon public nutrition? The fear is already being expressed that the Beveridge Plan will take all the money that is available for the expansion of the social services. It is certain that there will be a permanently increased expenditure upon national defence compared with the period between wars; the service of the national debt will cost more; certain other expenditures may be heavily swollen. To forecast all this is a highly speculative business. But some sort of a guess can be made at the order of magnitude. The best way to get this is to analyse the future from the revenue end. In 1938, some 26% of the national income was siphoned through public authorities as direct and indirect taxation, local rates and social insurance contributions. In 1941, the proportion was 40%.[2] The post-war proportion of the national income devoted to taxation should lie somewhere between these two figures; the

[1] This is incidentally almost exactly the same proportion as is provided by insured persons' contributions under existing schemes.
[2] War Finance White Paper, 1942, Cmd. 6347, p. 6.

level of taxation will be permanently higher than in 1938, but it should be appreciably below the war-time level. We have conservatively assumed a post-war national income of £6,500 millions. The yield from taxation for the central government, local authorities and extra-Budgetary funds would therefore be between £1,700 millions and £2,600 millions. The total public revenue would be between £1,800 millions and £2,700 millions, credit being taken for the profits from local authorities' trading services, the net receipt from the Post Office, and other non-tax revenue.[1]

This is the cloth from which post-war public expenditure must be cut. We need not include, of course, the cost of physical rebuilding, for this is properly financed by loan—it is capital expenditure in the full sense of the word, and will yield income in the shape of rents; there is a "book asset" against the expenditure in the surplus in the War Damage Fund. But all recurring costs must clearly be balanced by prospective revenue —the revenue Budget, so to speak, must be in balance. The following table sets out the public expenditure—government, local authorities, and social security fund—in the calendar year 1938, together with a tentative lay-out of public expenditure in 1945:

EXPENDITURE OF PUBLIC AUTHORITIES, 1938 AND 1945

	1938 (£m.)	1945 (£m.)
National Defence (*a*)	350	500
National Debt Interest (*b*)	225	400
Social Security (*c*)	340	700
Education (*d*)	125	175
Housing (*e*)	50	75
War Pensions	40	75
Other Expenditure (*f*)	220	275
Total	1,350	2,200

(*a*) The proposal for 1945 is four times as much as in the years between wars, but is probably something like what would be required to maintain a powerful and up-to-date striking force.
(*b*) Estimate for 1942-43 is £325 millions.
(*c*) As given above.
(*d*) The 1945 proposal should be sufficient to provide a first-class free educational system.
(*e*) Mainly housing subsidies.
(*f*) Includes cost of administration, highways, local authorities' services, subsidies to industry, etc.

[1] £82 millions in 1941, Cmd. 6347, pp. 14, 15.

This suggests that if one-half of the war-time increase of taxation were maintained, the Beveridge Plan could be financed perfectly easily, with a comparable expansion of education, housing and other social services, with an expenditure upon national defence some four times greater than the rate in the period between wars and indeed appreciably above the level ruling in the period between Munich and the outbreak of this war, and with an expanded national debt. If a more conservative figure were included for national defence, and less spectacular expansions in the other services, it would be possible to work within a framework of £2,100 millions expenditure, which would require the retention of only one-third of the war-time taxation. These figures are not conclusive, but they show the orders of magnitude, and suggest very powerfully that there is no cause for alarm that the nation "will not be able to afford" both national security and social security and constructive social advance.

The analysis shows, indeed, that the whole question of what we can afford turns upon the size of the national income, and it is upon this that public attention must be concentrated during the post-war period. The Beveridge Report focuses attention upon full employment. That is essential. It is the stupidest form of waste to leave resources idle. But it is also necessary to keep up the greatest possible efficiency in the use of national resources, to increase output per worker, to weed out the inefficient concerns, to encourage all technical advance and to devise means of translating this technical advance into productive efficiency throughout industry. If we could attain a national income of £7,000 millions in 1945—which would involve an increase in output per head of only 10% above 1938—we could do this programme of public expenditure with very little more taxation than was needed before the war; if we could achieve £8,000 millions by 1950 we could take practically any expansion of the social services in our stride. This is the key to social security. To achieve it, the nation must go forward boldly with economic development, must adapt itself to its economic environment, and must regain the economic vigour and initiative which were allowed to decay in the period between the wars.

Chapter XIV

THE STAFF PROBLEM

By JOAN SIMEON CLARKE

THE Ministry of National Insurance will have to maintain close contact with numerous individual citizens, each of whom will judge the Ministry chiefly by his reception at the local office. It is of paramount importance to the Ministry that he should be welcomed and treated with consideration and interest. The reputation of the Ministry will depend largely on its local staff. These will have to be selected and appointed carefully, and it is essential to consider at the outset what sort of people they must be. But local staff, however suitable and expert, can only act within the framework of their Ministry's policy at any time. If the policy is ill-conceived, no local deftness will cover its deficiency. In 1934, for example, no soft speeches would have convinced the public that those receiving reduced rates under the new Unemployment Assistance Board were justly suffering loss of income. The Standstill saved the situation only after vocal sections of the public had decided that the Board had really tried to rob the poor. Even first-class staff (the newly formed Board was operating with a very mixed bag of out-station staff, many of them without relevant experience) would have been powerless to sell the public an unacceptable policy. On the other hand, in the long transmission belt carrying social policy from Whitehall to the private citizen, it is the interviewing officer who makes final delivery; if he is peremptory, hurried, irritable or stupid he will alienate citizens, and bungle the execution of policy however well thought out that policy may be. A National Insurance Ministry needs perpetual team-work between the planning and administrative Headquarters staff and the executives in all the local offices; each depends, for final success, upon the intelligent operations of the other. Each will benefit by close liaison—interchange between Headquarters and out-stations staff, Regional and local conferences, provincial officers of Headquarters type and calibre, an Intelligence staff which (among other duties) would explain policy to local staff, and, conversely, tell Headquarters planners how the public had reacted to new policy and what were current social trends.

The thesis of this chapter is that these various functions need persons specially equipped for their performance—that calculating widows' pension rates, relating size of benefits to population groups, estimating the effect of industrial planning on the volume of claims national and local, talking with deserted wives or pushing the malingerer back to work—that all these diverse jobs need special skills and special knowledge, and that both at its Headquarters and in its local offices the Ministry must appoint appropriate persons to exercise appropriate sorts of skill.

This cuts right across existing Whitehall theories and procedures; there seems to be a Civil Service tradition that if you set up tidy governmental machinery and recruit a body of intelligent administrators of high integrity, you can run anything —shipping, Cairo, coal-mines, pensions. The needs of economic planning in a technical age may prove this thesis wrong. Already the majority of higher appointments outside the Civil Service call both for technical specialisation and for background knowledge of economic, sociological, psychological or scientific processes. Certainly government requires a high degree of intelligence, and wide general knowledge (though not of ancient Greece); and certainly long years in the Civil Service do give an excellent apprenticeship in methods of administration; but technical information is usually picked up as a by-product, and there is no required knowledge of the fundamental forces in society.

This is not the place to argue the general case. Interchangeability of civil servants may be better than intensive specialisation; certainly the tradition of passivity is easier to maintain among the non-expert. After all, we have arrived fairly successfully where we are now. However, there is one field where the failure of non-specialisation is apparent, a field in which the Civil Service is increasingly responsible. The Social Services depend ultimately upon the contact of the administration, local or central, with individual citizens. The content of this contact may affect the whole life pattern of the citizen concerned; it may determine whether, for example, he is allowed to take work in a trade other than his own, whether (until it is repealed) the Act of Settlement shall be invoked for his removal to a distant home-town, whether he is entitled to an old age pension, whether he shall have a Council flat. Such decisions, being made all the time all over the country, may have profound effects on the health, wealth and happiness of the community. Even the few examples listed above impinge on problems of industrial and geographical mobility, employment policy, the aged in an ageing population, subsidised housing; also they impinge directly on the happiness and morale of the citizen affected. If he goes away feeling angry, thwarted and insulted, his discontent spreads through his household, his street, his neighbourhood. Such discontent, magnified and multiplied throughout the community, swells finally to condemnation of the Government itself. This process actually happened in the Black Coffin Riots of 1938; a stupid economic policy was emphasised by crude interpretation to the relevant sections of the public. Expert administrative staff can prevent these sorts of confusion by weighing up future policy according to known social data and modern social science principles. If we are to plan our national social and economic policies we must have persons qualified to plan at all the planning points. The "born organiser," or the clever solicitor turned administrator, may be brilliant people, but if they lack economic knowledge where economic knowledge is essential, they are wrongly placed.

Headquarters Staff

The success of the Ministry will depend on the extent to which the citizen's needs are satisfied having regard to his ultimate welfare, and on the extent to which major social policy is furthered at the same time. It is the Headquarters staff who will have to frame policy and to integrate that of the Ministry of National Insurance with national policies for health and population, education and employment, and with budgetary and industrial planning. They will have to estimate the social, economic, and psychological effect of any measures they may take. Conversely they will have to devise ways of promoting national policy through the Ministry's activities. To take a current example: the Assistance Board recently empowered its staff to pay special clothing grants to old age pensioners. This happened at a time when war needs urged us to reduce production of consumers' goods, and when the Treasury was steadily creaming off purchasing power from the community as a whole. No doubt the pensioners needed the equipment, but if this extra purchasing power, and more, had been pumped into the community through special grants in the depression it might have had a marked effect in stimulating trade. However, action was postponed till it was economically unsuitable and showed lack of foresight and of integrated thinking. These sorts of decision certainly call for skills other than administrative capacity. They will occur increasingly in the future when the National Insurance Ministry becomes a part of a nationally planned economy. We may imagine that at some future date the economic planners will wish to stimulate industry by temporarily increasing purchasing power. The Ministry's officials should be able to co-operate by working out a scheme which would have the most satisfactory economic and social effect on the community. Scientific policies, based on known facts, take the place of *ad hoc* administrative rulings. Constructive long-term thinking, and the exercise of the newer mental disciplines, becomes a governmental function of first-class importance.

How are these sorts of experts to be got into the Ministry? In peace-time some of those who really understand the social sciences are congregated in the Universities; others are engaged on social surveys and research. Since the war many of them are temporary civil servants; they have been called in not only because administration has increased in scope, but because the urgency of war-time planning calls for the right people in the right places. If later we are to plan for national well-being the same criterion must carry over. We must have first-class persons where their skills are needed. We must be prepared to take economists, sociologists, psychologists and statisticians into the Ministry of National Insurance at the higher salary ranges as temporary staff. We must be prepared to use suitable experts wherever they are to be found in the community. It is preposterous, for example, that an expert in social administration should be sent as government emissary to the West Indies, but that there should be no normal opportunity for him to occupy himself with government administration in this country. Such persons bring with them into government departments a range and depth of social experience which the professional civil servant lacks. In this respect they are likely at any time to be superior to the sociologist or economist who might, in a more enlightened future, be recruited straight into the administrative class from the University. It is true that mobility and interchange, to be discussed later, will help the latter to extend his knowledge, but there should always be scope inside the Ministry for older persons trained and experienced in the social sciences. The least part of their value to the Ministry will be its further integration with the wider community life; permanent civil servants are too segregated; there will be great advantages in the recruitment of persons of standing who have moved freely about in the community and who should be able to keep their outside obligations as local councillors, lecturers, writers. The Ministry will be enriched by their experience. Recognition of the need for social science experts must be established straight away so that they may be incorporated into the new Ministry as soon as it is formed. "Good administrators" brought in from the higher ranks of other Ministries to start the new one will not suffice. It is essential that at least some of those who administer at the highest levels should understand the nature and the purpose of the social services.

Headquarters experts will be occupied variously with direction of administration, with planning and with research. They will need to know what is being done both in quantitative and qualitative terms, and what its effect is nationally, locally and on various categories of the community. On the basis of the knowledge so acquired they will be able to plan future policy and to estimate its implications. Intelligence and statistics will be particularly important. All kinds of significant social facts, now unknown, may be discovered; we may learn, for example, what correlation there is between family allowances and the birth-rate, between old age pensions and industrial mobility, between maternity benefit and maternal mortality, between free medical service and days lost through sickness, between industrial training and criminal convictions. Sir William Beveridge emphasised[1] that the Division of Statistics and Intelligence must "make use not only of its own material but of the experiences of other countries in the same field." The pooling of various national experiences is of great interest and of great value. However, it is impossible to agree with Sir William when he continues: "The Ministry should be able to make grants for

[1] Report, p. 148, para. 398.

the carrying out of research in all matters where further knowledge might reduce the burdens on the Fund." It is really extraordinary that a man who relates his whole plan to the promotion of human happiness—a word rarely mentioned in official documents—should relate research to the mere reduction of the charges on a Fund which, as the previous chapter of this book shows, is little more than a book entry. There would be slight constructive purpose in a Ministry which measured its success by cash economising. The criterion for social research is its contribution to the sum of human welfare; this the research sections of the Ministry should be well equipped to further. We must emphasise that these sections of the Ministry will do more than collect statistics; economists, sociologists, psychologists, statisticians should be given facilities to do first quality social research and to collaborate with outside research bodies. Their monographs (similar to those of the Medical and Industrial Health Research Councils) should be major contributions to the pool of knowledge about modern society.

The actual collection of the raw material—research in the field—must necessarily be performed by staff of the Research Division of the Ministry; in this respect its set-up would be similar to that of the War-time Social Survey. Trained research staff would operate in the regions and districts. Their job would be both to report on significant facts coming to their notice, and to engage in definite pieces of field research at the instigation of their Division. They would work under the direction of the Regional Intelligence Staff which would probably be responsible for the first stage of co-ordinating the field research results before transmitting them to the Research Division at Headquarters.

The Research Division and its local staff must maintain close relationship with the Public Relations Division. There will be need for constant collection of data—research—and for constant information to the community—publicity. The Public Relations Division must tell the public what the Ministry is doing and, as far as possible, why it is doing this. The community will be perpetually interested in a social service Ministry, and it will have strong opinions about its operations. If the Ministry can be inspired by a constructive desire to improve social conditions, to promote health and to increase happiness, it will be able to take its policy to the public confidently and without that defensiveness which characterised the Assistance Board in its early years. It may be necessary to evolve a new technique of public relations. Public education should be furthered, the Ministry kept alive to current opinion, and a spirit of co-operation between the Ministry and the community gradually developed. If democracy is to have any governmental meaning in the future it should mean that the people begin to understand what the administration is about, and that the administration regards the public as a partner in its operations. As a producer of services the administration must be genuinely anxious to know how the community, the consumers, are affected. It is hardly necessary to stress that this will necessitate a reorientation of Civil Service outlook and a new type of Civil Service personnel.

Every local office should maintain close relations with the local community. The Assistance Board's Advisory Committee system,[1] modified, should be carried over to the new Ministry.[2] Staff in the local offices should be encouraged to think of themselves as part of the local community. Relatively senior staff transferred to offices in districts unknown to them should be given opportunities to visit local organisations and to meet local leaders and officials. Only in this way will they be equipped to work efficiently among the local population. The work of the whole Ministry will be enriched by friendly relationships between local offices and local communities all over the country. Similarly there must be sympathy between Headquarters and the local and Regional offices. This will be furthered by a flow of staff out from Headquarters to local and Regional offices and from these offices into Headquarters. This mobility and fluidity should be part of staff policy, although there should be no set rules for regularly moving on officers (like Nonconformist ministers) as soon as they had settled in a local office. Status and pay of Headquarters and Regional and local staff should be assimilated so that interchangeability be feasible and often practised.

Local Offices

The day-to-day work of local offices will fall into three broad categories. First, social administration, for which prototypes of the Headquarters administrative staff will be required. The

[1] See p. 159. [2] See Appendix, p. 453.

second will be routine checking of benefit claims and the payment of cash to which the claimant is entitled as of right. The third will deal with problems as diverse as human nature itself; this type of work will include the assistance section (or supplementation or emergency benefit, whichever word may be used) involving close knowledge of the claimants' home affairs; it will also include advice or information work, and attempts to solve the special problems of individual citizens arising in the daily work of the Ministry.

Staff dealing with the second category will need a high degree of special skill. Staff on the relatively routine work of the local offices will be equally important, but three months' instruction should serve to tell them of the functions of the Ministry and of their own part in it. They will need to be courteous, intelligent, and quick; they will need secondary school education and, if the gods are good, a sense of humour. The majority of them will be occupied in scrutinising claims for benefit and approving them. All this will be routine, but it must be pleasant. The atmosphere of the local offices is important. Let us not repeat the dreary dwellings of some Employment Exchanges or of most Relief Stations. Bright paint is as cheap as dark paint, bright faces pleasanter than scowling ones. All this is part of the presentation of the Ministry to the general public, and we must use imagination about the local offices. We shall need new buildings in the long view, a few flowers in the short view. Furniture is important, too. There is no reason why the scrutineers should not sit at their work with the claimant sitting also, even though the checking of a claim will normally be swift. It is a good idea to have a long table partitioned into little stalls as the Board does now; by leaning forward to the table visitors can have a semi-private conversation with little extra use of space. Claimants will not *need* to talk, but some of them may want occasionally to raise a point of difficulty. The scrutineer will have to be alert to sort out those who have a special problem or enquiry; she must recognise new points of principle as they arise; she should distinguish misery from trickery. The job will be about 80% routine with about 20% intelligence and intuition added. The spirit of this work will depend largely on the supervisors, and here we come back to the functions of the highly qualified staff members.

The possible division of duties and responsibilities will be clearer if we imagine the way a National Insurance Office actually might work. The citizen paying an initial visit to the local Insurance Office with a new claim might be received in the Entrance Section. This would be the time for the citizen to be welcomed to the office and to be made to feel that the administration was put there to co-operate with him. If it seemed that other social services would be of use these should be called into play. Two guiding principles should operate : first, that citizens who wanted to make a routine claim in a routine way and to treat the whole thing as a piece of simple business should do so; secondly, that those who welcomed the chance to talk to "an official" about their special worries should find there the sort of official who could both understand and help with their solution. The Entrance Section would then be staffed with those officials about whose qualifications the following pages are concerned. Claimants paying a routine visit subsequently would not need to come into this Section but would go straight to the scrutineers. However, if one of them wished to change the nature of this claim (e.g. from widows' to training benefit), or to transfer to a new address, or to remarry, or to complain of hardship or to depart in any way from routine repetition of a claim, he should be referred back to the Entrance Section, which would function, in effect, as a Welfare Section (and could be called such if the public did not mind the title). Part of the scrutineers' responsibility would therefore be to spot problems and to refer them to more highly trained colleagues. They should have constantly available the advice of trained supervisors with the same qualifications as staff in the Entrance Section. Also, the Assistance Section, involving the discussion of domestic details, would need skilled staff. Lastly, the Advice or Information Section suggested by Sir William Beveridge would also need trained personnel. Only those who have worked in such a war-time Bureau know how frequently straight questions from the public reveal problems deeply tangled in the social structure; to these no instantaneous answer can be given, although some solution, to be worked out with the questioner, may affect the welfare of whole families.

It is on those officers who make daily contact with the public that the reputation of the Ministry will largely rest. These will be divisible into two broad categories, the semi-trained and the highly trained, with clearly separated functions. Whatever way the local offices may be administered there will be need for these two types of officer at the point of personal contact with the public. Although discussing now the qualifications of the highly trained, I do not assume that all claimants will want any service other than routine—if they did, the staffing problem would be practically insuperable—but I do assume that some citizens will want time and trouble wisely spent; for them it is imperative that trained staff shall assist.

Basic Staff Requirements

Social service staff working at the point of contact with the public have to find a synthesis between the satisfaction of individual requirements and the furtherance of national policy. The social service staff must understand Government policy and thence the policy of their own Ministry. This involves a grasp of the economic principles underlying social administration, and of current social and industrial data. Especially in a planned economy social service workers must know what is being planned and why, which trades are shrinking and which expanding, the objectives of schemes for re-training and for industrial (and perhaps geographical) mobility, for public works programmes, and for the stimulation or reduction of consumption. The National Insurance Ministry will reflect these policies, and its staff will have the job of implementing them in their dealings with the public. Future social service staff must have enough knowledge of and interest in national policy to understand what is happening. And they must see their own individual jobs as integral parts of a co-ordinated social and economic programme.

That is the indispensable minimum of theoretical knowledge. In addition, social service staff must have practical knowledge of the social resources of the community, know which ones are relevant for which situations and how to call them into place, and they must know this in terms of their own districts. They should be acquainted with local geography, including schools, and know the prevailing rents in different quarters, and the main trades and rates of pay. All this information will be necessary some time or another. Citizens consult social service personnel with startling frequency; they expect immediate comprehension and sound advice; they assume that staff are sensible and well-informed. Such conversations may be outside the official's terms of reference as a benefit-assessor; they can never be outside the scope of welfare. Some citizens will take their benefit and go; others will like to talk. The staff must be qualified to answer if they do.

However, no amount of theory nor of practical knowledge will be effective without inherent qualities of intuition, friendliness and sympathy. Staff must be able to effect immediate contact and not only seem but *be* welcoming and warm; they must be sufficiently self-controlled and equable to avoid getting irritable when there is pressure of work; they must be interested in human beings and imaginative enough to understand how other people's lives *feel*. These qualities are found in great profusion among voluntary social workers. But there they are undisciplined. Novices are easily overwhelmed by their own sympathy; they identify themselves with the distressed citizen to such an extent that they become incapable of objective planning; they accept his own valuation of his history instead of working out, and maybe helping him to achieve, a balanced view of tricky situations. Fortified by an "official's" endorsement of his hard-luck point of view, the citizen may easily be harmed rather than helped by the contact. Proficient social service personnel must avoid this situation; they should be able to build relationships based on mutual trust and respect without having their intellects confused by sympathy or sentiment. A Ministry of National Insurance cannot be staffed by persons who batten upon their own good works. Old-style philanthropy has no more place in a new Ministry animated by purposeful constructive policy than has the spirit of the old-style Relieving Officer.

Lastly, all these qualities must be reinforced with personal and mental maturity, a product not only of age, but also of emotional development. The Ministry's staff will not be there as censors, and sooner or later they will be told unsavoury facts about other people's lives. They must be able to accept such histories calmly and without passing moral judgment, for to do so would be to throw a burden of guilt and distress on the confiding citizen, and, probably, to destroy his contact with the Ministry. Unhappy people need common sense as well as money or advice. The quality of uncensorious acceptance is a product of maturity which is a valuable asset to social service personnel.[1]

Clearly all these required attributes are not inherent in the chromosomes. Intellectual grasp of social and economic trends, plus detailed knowledge of community resources, must be added to native common sense, intelligence and friendliness; self-discipline, balance and maturity are essential. This combination of equipment can only be produced by training coupled with personal aptitude. This is the point at issue with the Civil Service. The Assistance Board till recently provided no relevant training for its staff; the Ministry of Labour, with similar but not identical requirements, has not done so either. The disastrous early history of the Board was partly the result of using unskilled personnel. Many Employment Exchanges have been unpopular because the public considered that their counter staff were ill-informed and brusque. We must plan for the future on the experience of the past. If we are to have a National Insurance Ministry playing a dynamic and constructive part, and integrated in the life of the community, if citizens are to feel confidence in this Ministry's care for their security and welfare — then we must start immediately to train its staff.

Here an immediate problem faces us. We must start planning from where we are now. There are already numerous out-station staff[2] in those public social services which would be absorbed by the new Ministry. The competence, experience and suitability of such staff varies; some of them have long practical experience in the social services; few have the intellectual training which will enable them to relate their detailed daily work to the development of a planned society. We must have a sensible plan for the selection and instruction of transferred staff, and we must be able to relate this to our future programme. At the least we must arrange for transferred staff—however great their practical experience in social service—to understand the role of their new Ministry in the national life. Carefully planned lecture courses will be essential. But the

[1] There is great advantage in employing suitably qualified married women on many sections of this work. There should be facilities for them to be appointed to the staff on a temporary basis, but with appropriate salary and status, after they have reared their families.

[2] See Appendix, p. 454.

transition difficulties can be met more realistically once we have established long-term policy.

Training Programmes

Training of social service personnel is in itself no new idea. Already training facilities exist in this country and in America (and before the war existed in some European countries). But whereas the Americans admit trained staff in large numbers to public welfare agencies, we do so only for Probation Officers, and to a lesser extent for Factory Inspectors, house property managers and the few almoners and psychiatric social workers who are in public hospitals. The great bulk of our trained personnel work for voluntary bodies of various kinds; at present there are no facilities for their admission to the Government Departments. The future problems are the relation of training programmes to public service requirements, and the adjustment of Civil Service entrance and conditions to admit of the establishment of social service staff so trained.

Social service training is provided in this country by 18 Social Science Departments of the Universities. Students take Certificates or Diplomas, but not degrees. The courses usually last two years, but are reduced for graduates; those with degrees taking the academic part of the course in one year instead of two.

The syllabus is similar to the majority of courses on both sides of the Atlantic. Students are required to attend University-standard courses on some or all of the following, though rarely pursuing them beyond the first-year stage:

> Economics, sociology, social psychology, psychology, industrial law, industrial history and organisation, public administration, criminology, psychopathology, machinery of government, social statistics, social insurance.

Equally important in the student's final reckoning is field-work under supervision. This is adjusted to the student's plans; intending almoners do a large proportion of practical work in hospitals, probation officers in the Courts, etc., in addition to general welfare work. Students have to work hard and to take an increasing amount of responsibility; "Social workers must learn to carry responsibilities which involve the welfare of human beings, and they can at first be safely entrusted with these responsibilities only when they are working under careful supervision," says the University of Chicago.[1] The Americans have studied the technique of supervision more carefully than we have. The English student works as the junior member of an office staff and is taught by a senior member of it who discusses the details of her work fully and frequently. The American supervisor has a different idea of her functions; she is a counsellor as well as an instructor; she is concerned with the wide implications of the student's work and with the student's personal adjustment in a period of rapid, and perhaps difficult, development. Meanwhile the student gains both in experience and in self-reliance, learning a great deal about the way that people feel and live and work, about the social service structure, and how to mobilise the various resources. Supervisors supply the Universities with full reports on their students, none of whom can qualify without satisfactory reports on field-work. This aspect of having the work on approval is not the least advantage of the field-work system; misfits in the social service field today are almost always among the older untrained ones who got there by mistake and then could not escape.

Recruitment to the Public Service

Even if all trained social service staff work in the public service there would not be enough of them to do all the appropriate work in the new Insurance Ministry and ancillary services. We must increase the number of trained personnel more rapidly than in the past, as well as giving them the chance to enter Government service. However, it is no good effecting expansion of training programmes without first adjusting methods of recruitment of social service personnel to the Civil Service, and secondly providing financial help to trainees.

Recruitment is complicated by the age of newly trained persons. Maturity is needed; this may not come with age but is unlikely to come without it, so that students are not usually accepted for training under the age of 19.[2] It is worth noting that at Chicago students are not permitted to do field-work if they are under 21. Then, the course usually lasts two years (including University vacations, which are unduly long but many

[1] University of Chicago, School of Social Service Administration. Announcements for the sessions 1941, 1942, p. 18.

[2] Although this has been reduced to 18 by most Universities since the war.

of which are occupied by full-time field-work). Experience teaches that short courses of limited content are not satisfactory. Grace Abbott, who knew the problem both from the public service and the University angle, said:

> "Training for all social work must be broad professional training and not the narrow vocationalism characteristic of the apprenticeship system. In any profession specialisation comes with experience." [1]

Clearly, therefore, social service staff cannot be recruited to the Civil Service under 21 years of age. Their recruitment must be adjusted to their age and to their training. Professional staff are not now recruited through any of the regular Civil Service examinations. Doctors, scientists, lawyers and engineers [2] join the service after their professional training is completed. Except for factory inspectors and probation officers, no such facilities exist for professional social service staff. The Civil Service has up to date tacitly denied that professional status or training is relevant for such persons. If the thesis of this chapter is conceded, the Civil Service will have to admit trained staff who are at least 21, and who could suitably be within the age-groups 21 to 25. (When the scheme is first started it will be advisable to recruit trained staff up to 35 with suitable pension adjustments so that a core of trained and experienced personnel can be built up at once.) Admission should be by open competitive examination plus competitive interview. The examination should be closely related to the principles and purpose of social service administration, and therefore to the content of the training courses. It would be senseless to recruit professional people through an examination in mathematics or classics, just as it is now senseless to recruit Ministry of Labour Third Class Officers through the Income Tax Inspectors' examination. The interview should be given by persons who had themselves been trained and experienced in the social services, and it should determine the candidates' personal suitability for the work. The various channels by which candidates should come to the examination will be discussed later.

Once admitted, professional staff must have professional status. At present both in the Assistance Board and in the

[1] Abbott, Grace, *From Relief to Social Security*, University of Chicago Press, 1941, p. 351.

[2] Post Office Engineers have efficient post-entry training.

Ministry of Labour, seeing and talking with members of the public is a lowly job. In future it must be recognised as skilled work needing professional competence. This will mean that the new staff must have entirely different status and grading from the Investigating Clerks to the Board.[1] They will be specialists, not clerks interchangeable among any of the routine jobs in the office. They should be paid (since pay is still a mark of status) no less than similar staff are paid outside the Ministry. Investigating Clerks (women) are now paid on the average £2 11/-[2] weekly minimum. London County Council Children's Care Organisers, trained staff of course, begin at £3 15/-[2] weekly while they are temporary; as soon as they are put on the permanent staff, after four to eight months, they get £200[2] yearly with pension rights, rising by £12 annually to £250,[2] and thence by further £12 increments if they are promoted to senior status and so on. These rates should certainly be considered minimal; an approximation to Burnham scale rates would be more just.

Expanding Training Facilities

A second problem must be tackled before training programmes can be realistically expanded. They are expensive. In England they are not degree courses, and it is difficult for even a bright student to obtain maintenance and tuition grants to cover all expenses. (It is a little easier in America where promising students can often get free or reduced tuition in return for part-time work.) The nature of the training also makes it relatively costly; fares to field-work and to visits of observation may run into several shillings weekly, plus the cost of lunches eaten at any available restaurant instead of at the cost-price students' places. 10/- weekly is a reliable estimate for fares, lunches, etc., for social service students in London. Specimen fees for the two-year Social Science course, including examination dues and other fixed charges, are, when averaged for a single year: London School of Economics £29 8/-, Birmingham University £20 11/-, Liverpool University £18 15/-. The total annual cost is difficult to reckon, especially as many students, particularly in London, live at home. Birmingham students usually spend a year resident in a Settlement during training, and for these the total annual

[1] See p. 149. [2] All figures excluding War Bonus.

cost, including residence and fees, is reckoned to be about £100. The University of Chicago's School of Social Science Administration makes careful estimates of students' annual costs, including tuition, fees, etc., rent and care of room, board, laundry, textbooks, etc., and incidentals; at pre-war exchange rates these estimates are: Low £164, Average £205, Liberal £300.[1]

Clearly, if suitable people are to have the training, full maintenance and tuition grants must be obtainable. These could be provided in two ways. First, the Local Education Authorities could make grants to school leavers in their areas, either direct, to those leaving school at 18+, or in the form of deferred bursaries, so that children leaving school at, say, 16, could do other work until they were 19, when they could take up their bursaries if they wished, subject to confirmatory interviews with the training school. The intervening three years could profitably be spent as unestablished staff in the National Insurance Ministry, which would give valuable grounding in clerical and administrative methods, but this should not be a necessary condition of such bursaries. Secondly, the State could make block grants to training schools to be distributed in tuition and maintenance grants to persons between the ages of 19 and 23. These bursaries and grants would ensure that the supply of trained staff could be adjusted to demand, and that within this limit suitable persons were not excluded by lack of funds, even though they might be giving up paid work to take the training.

Once financial help is available, we should increase the number of training facilities. It would be better to multiply centres rather than to enlarge existing departments, which, as the following samples show, cater for smallish numbers of students who can be well known to the teaching staff:

Training School.	Number of Students Registering for Two-Year Social Science Course.			
	1939	1940	1941	1942
London School of Economics	98	60	50	73
University of Birmingham	40	27	22	56
University of Liverpool	40	26	41	49

[1] University of Chicago, School of Social Service Administration. Announcements for the sessions 1941, 1942.

Provincial Universities in any towns large enough to provide instructive and varied visits of observation and sufficient scope for field-work should be encouraged to institute social science courses. Even the larger polytechnics [1] could organise such courses satisfactorily provided that properly qualified tutors and lecturers could be obtained, and specially if arrangements could be made for students to attend such lectures as economics and psychology given by first-class teachers in near-by Universities or University Colleges. Multiplication of training courses must not result in lowering of standards.

In-Service Training

This is the long-term view of social service training. Certainly professional training must develop along the lines already indicated. But we cannot expand University standard training overnight. Professionally trained staff will not be immediately available, and we shall have to start by reviewing present staff of those Departments which should be liquidated if a new Ministry is built. None will have received the sort of training postulated in this chapter as essential, although many will have real insight into social service problems. Public Assistance Staff, and a few of the Board's staff, will have taken the examinations of the Poor Law Examinations Board; however, these deal predominantly with the technicalities of Poor Law Administration—Settlement, Lunacy, etc. We shall have to staff these sections of our Ministry needing fully trained personnel with the best already available both inside and outside the Civil Service, plus others whose personalities and experience recommend them for the work even if they are untrained. Having selected our interviewing staff, we must devise a training programme sufficiently flexible to meet their diverse needs in the transition period.

We must avoid the dilemma which the Americans faced when they began to implement their Social Security Act; they found that "Thousands of people throughout the country as a whole were being put on staffs of public assistance [2] agencies and were assisting

[1] London University's Social Studies Diploma can be taken by evening students in a 4-year course, lectures being given in polytechnics and evening institutes by University lecturers, but there are not, and for evening students cannot be, adequate facilities for field-work as an integral part of the course

[2] American phraseology.

in the administration of the program, when they themselves had little background for the work undertaken."[1] The Social Security Board tackled the problem realistically, though late, by setting up a Division of Technical Training, and by evolving the system of In-Service Training which now operates. In this way staff get their training while they are actually employed and even on the job already. We can learn much from this, though training will not alter personalities. Whatever training scheme we may introduce here, we must insist that trainees should be first selected for the suitability of their qualities. The Americans emphasise this: "We see the need for continued insistence upon support for good personnel standards in the State and for continued *denial that training is a substitute for good personnel*."[2]

Nor is In-Service Training a permanent substitute for professional school training programmes to which post-entry training should be complementary. However, in the transition period a balanced In-Service training programme is the best which we can aim at. This will involve four main elements—supervised practical work, lectures, reading, visits of observation. Of one of these, "Supervision," says the Social Security Board,[3] "is not a sterile checking on accuracy of form-filling and rule-following, nor does it seek to force the minds and actions of staff into a common mould through exerted authority. Rather, it seeks to stimulate and release the individual's capacity to use his own knowledge and judgement in the performance of his duties." If, therefore, we need to institute In-Service Training as an emergency device inside our new Ministry of Social Security we must carefully select those who will supervise. Their job will be to see that all staff understand the place of the Ministry in the country as a whole, and the place of their own office both in the Ministry and in the local community. There must be opportunity for regular interviews, free from interruption, between the supervisors and individual members of the staff, in which not only the general policy and trend of the work can be discussed, but also the staff member's individual experiences, problems and achievements in her work.

Theoretical lectures must be given by University-standard

[1] Report of Division of Technical Training, Bureau of Public Assistance, Social Security Board, 26th January 1939, p. 12.

[2] *ibid.*, p. 13. Our italics.

[3] Division of Technical Training (v. *supra*) : Supervision as an Administrative Process Contributing to Staff Development, November 1940.

outside lecturers. If the Ministry is to be entirely self-reliant, on the American principle, in its In-Service training programme, it will not be able to give the broader background of modern knowledge which is essential. There will, of course, be difficulties in gathering staff together for lectures, especially in thinly populated districts. This could probably best be achieved by stationing trainees systematically in offices in University towns for at least a year so that they could either attend relevant lectures in the University during their office hours, or else have lecturers from the University come to a central building to give *ad hoc* courses to the trainees in that town. However it be arranged, there is no substitute for this type of academic lecture, and no formalities or conventions should be allowed to obviate its execution.

Thirdly, if the students are really to benefit from their training they will have to read in their spare time, and to write essays to be corrected and discussed either by their academic lecturers, or, through the post, by a correspondence tutor specially appointed by the Ministry. They will need help on the intellectual side just as they need help with practical and emotional problems from their supervisors.

Lastly, visits of observation should be an integral part of the training programme. Trainees must acquire clear mental pictures of those other social resources of the community which may at some stage supplement or qualify their work. They should visit Police Courts, Approved Schools, Borstal Institutions and prisons; hospitals and clinics; schools and technical institutes; homes for children and old people; institutions for the chronic sick and mentally afflicted; municipal housing estates and community centres. In addition they should see something of industry; it is difficult to talk intelligently to a factory worker if you have never been inside a factory.

This type of In-Service training programme approximates as nearly as possible to the normal professional training given in the Universities. In this it differs from American methods. On the other hand, American social service staff are encouraged to take "educational leave" while still in the public service, and to become students in Schools of Social Service. No reliable statistics are available to show the numbers doing this, though it appears that between two and three hundred members of

State staffs took educational leave in 1938, and that over a quarter of these received financial help from public funds. American University methods make this easier than would English ones. Students can attend the University for a term or two and then return to work. Later on they may return again to that University or another, and courses taken successfully during their previous period of residence will count towards their final qualification.

Expediency and convenience will determine the type of training most suited to this country; if trainees have the American type of In-Service Training they will need educational leave to attend academic courses in a recognised training school. Alternatively the Ministry will have to institute an internal training programme on similar lines to those suggested here, which will include an educational and developmental programme as wide as that given in the Social Service Schools. The argument is, of course, that this type of training is really necessary; any lesser version of it will turn out less skilled staff and so will ultimately detract from the efficiency of the whole administration. However pressing may be the need for trained staff, and whatever the administrative complications of instituting a high-standard training programme, we shall defeat our own ends if we reduce criteria.

There is an added reason for maintaining high standards of In-Service Training. If those trained in the Universities are to have the chance to enter the public service through competitive examinations and interviews, they will need to have a clearly defined relationship to those trained in the Service already. In fact, those who have received In-Service Training will have to compete with University-trained persons if they are to be admitted to do the social service interviewing, etc., for which their training has designed them. Whether such staff are trained in the Ministry or in the Universities, they will all need the same high qualifications and ability if they are to be entrusted with the business of representing the Ministry and its policy to the public. It is absolutely clear that In-Service Training must be as good as professional University training; the only criterion for appointment to social service positions must be fitness for the job. If they are to be appointed, those trained in the Ministry will have to be as good as those trained outside. In-Service

Training must provide a coherent, intensive and extensive professional course.

Finally, we must remember that the new Ministry will be judged not only by the excellence of a paper plan, not only by administrative competence, not only by lavish benefits, but also by the spirit of the staff, its spokesmen. They will provide the elasticity and resilience which human beings need. Sir William Beveridge himself emphasised [1] the need for:

> "Selection and training of staff with special regard to their functions in serving the public and in understanding the human problems with which they will be concerned."

This, he said, is "of outstanding importance."

[1] Beveridge Report, para. 385.

EPILOGUE

By LORD BEVERIDGE

On 10th June 1941 Mr. Arthur Greenwood, as Minister without Portfolio, announced in the House of Commons that he had arranged with all the Departments concerned for a comprehensive survey of existing schemes of social insurance which would be considered in due course by the Committee on Reconstruction Problems, of which he was Chairman; and that Sir William Beveridge had accepted his invitation to become Chairman of an Inter-departmental Committee which would conduct the survey, taking into account representations received from responsible organisations and persons concerned.

On 20th November 1942 a Report on Social Insurance and Allied Services arising out of the work of this Committee was signed by myself and presented to Sir William Jowitt, who, as Paymaster-General, had succeeded Mr. Arthur Greenwood as Minister concerned with Reconstruction Problems.

In September 1944 two White Papers (Cmd. 6550 and Cmd. 6551) were presented to Parliament setting out the proposals of the Coalition Government of that day for social insurance. The first of these papers, "Part I," covered social insurance generally (except for Industrial Injury) and Family Allowances. The second dealt with Industrial Injury. In March 1944 a White Paper setting out the proposals of the Coalition Government for a National Health Service was presented to Parliament.

On 1st August 1946 a new National Insurance Act became law. It had been preceded, by a few days, by a National Insurance (Industrial Injuries) Act, and in the year before by the Family Allowances Act, 1945; the way for these measures had been prepared by the passing in November 1945 of an Act to establish a Ministry of National Insurance. They have been followed by the passing, on 6th November 1946, of the National Health Service Act, designed to establish a comprehensive health service for England and Wales. A companion measure for health service in Scotland is before Parliament.[1]

[1] National Health Service (Scotland) Act, 21st May 1947.

In this Epilogue I shall review briefly the course of these events, compare the proposals made at various stages with the legislation which has resulted, and suggest some of the problems that remain for settlement.

The Origin of the Beveridge Report

The Inter-departmental Committee announced by Mr. Greenwood was duly appointed, with the following terms of reference:

> "To undertake, with special reference to the inter-relation of the schemes, a survey of the existing national schemes of social insurance and allied services, including workmen's compensation, and to make recommendations."

The Committee held its first meeting on 8th July 1941.

As circumstances led to the members of the Committee other than the Chairman receiving less than the normal recognition of their work, their names and offices should be placed on record in any account of what followed. These representatives were: Mr. R. R. Bannatyne, C.B., Home Office; Mr. P. Y. Blundun, Ministry of Labour and National Service; Miss M. S. Cox, O.B.E., Ministry of Pensions; Sir George Epps, K.B.E., C.B., Government Actuary; Mr. R. Hamilton Farrell, Ministry of Health; Mr. E. Hale, C.B., Treasury; Mrs. M. A. Hamilton, Reconstruction Department; Mr. A. W. McKenzie, Board of Customs and Excise; Sir George Reid, K.B.E., C.B., Assistance Board; Miss M. Ritson, C.B.E., Department of Health for Scotland; Mr. B. K. White, Registry of Friendly Societies and Office of the Industrial Assurance Commissioner. The number of these representatives and of their departments, all directly concerned with different aspects of a single problem, was in itself an illustration of the need for the Committees to look at the problem as a whole. The Secretary to the Committee was Mr. D. N. Chester, then engaged in the War Cabinet Secretariat.

The circumstances which led to these departmental representatives receiving less prominence at the end of their work than at the beginning were, in effect, the last three words of the terms of reference given above: "to make recommendations." Mr. Greenwood's original announcement in the House of Commons contemplated only a "survey," such as officials could make without embarrassing their Ministers. "Recommendations," however, would necessarily be proposals for action and would raise issues of policy. The Committee's first activity, beginning in June 1940, was "survey," obtaining from each of the departments concerned historical and descriptive memoranda. This took some months.[1] As soon as in November the Committee of civil servants were invited by a Chairman's memorandum to look at the last words of their reference and to consider the main questions on which they might be asked to make recommendations, it became obvious that they could not proceed any distance on this line without serious embarrassment. An official of the Ministry of Health could hardly sign a report proposing the abolition of the Approved Society system, and an official of the Home Office could hardly sign a report proposing the supersession of workmen's compensation, without obtaining the previous agreement of the appropriate Minister; still less could a Treasury official propose publicly a large increase of expenditure from taxes without knowing how the Chancellor of the Exchequer would react to this. On its original lines the Committee could not have produced any Report at all—except as the considered views of the Government.

So at the beginning of 1942 the character of the Committee was changed by correspondence between Mr. Greenwood and myself.

> "My dear Beveridge,—I have discussed with the Chancellor of the Exchequer the position of the departmental representatives on the Inter-departmental Committee on Social Insurance and Allied Services. In view of the issues of high policy which will arise, we think that the departmental representatives should henceforward be regarded as your advisers and assessors on the various technical and administrative matters with which they are severally concerned. This means that the Report, when made, will be your own report; it will be signed by you alone, and the departmental representatives will not be associated in any way with the views and recommendations on questions of policy which it contains. It would

[1] During these months, from June to the end of October, I was almost wholly occupied on another enquiry—into the use made of Skilled Men in the Armed Forces. My Report on this, presented in October 1941, was published in the following January.

be well that the Report should contain words to make it clear that this is the position.—Yours sincerely,

"(Signed) ARTHUR GREENWOOD."

"MY DEAR GREENWOOD,—Many thanks for your letter as to the work of the Committee on Social Insurance and Allied Services and the position of departmental representatives thereon. I had already communicated the substance of what you write to the Committee at their last meeting and will now circulate your letter.

"Needless to say, I entirely accept the view taken by the Chancellor of the Exchequer and yourself. I believe that in this way the departmental representatives will be even more useful than if they had to sign the Report and I shall encourage them within the Committee itself to express their views with complete frankness to me so that whatever I may say I shall say after getting the best possible advice.—Yours sincerely,

"(Signed) W. H. BEVERIDGE."

The change meant that I alone signed the Report; it was published as a Report by Sir William Beveridge and the hands of the Government were absolutely free in regard to it. The change did not mean that I or any one man could ever have made the Report or that the Committee were unimportant. Their contribution was absolutely vital. In the Report itself I had to make acknowledgments to them in carefully measured terms in order to avoid any appearance of committing the Government. On a later occasion, in a speech at Caxton Hall, I felt able to express the debt of the country to the officials more frankly.

"There is another remark often made about the Beveridge Report . . . and that is that the Report is a one-man Report. Now, it is true that the Report is signed by one man only—myself—so that I am the only person that can be hanged for it. No one else can be brought to book for anything whatever that is said in it. No one else is committed to it. But it is not true that the Report was made, or could have been made, by one man sitting and thinking and studying by himself. I had sitting with me a Committee representing all the Departments concerned with the problems under consideration—all the best experts in the Government service—and very good experts they are. They acted as a Committee in examining witnesses, in discussion and in criticism. They acted as my technical advisers. Without their help in all these ways the Report would have been a very different and much inferior document. I alone am responsible for all that it proposes, just as a Minister alone is responsible for everything that is done in his Department. I was like a temporary Minister for devising this particular piece of post-war reconstruction; I could not have done the job otherwise.

"Real Ministers would not be able to do much without their Departments. It has often been noticed how different are the speeches which politicians make when they are Ministers, with all the knowledge and ability of the Departments behind them, and the speeches which they make in opposition when they have nothing to trust to but their own intelligence and knowledge. Those opposition speeches sometimes are very flimsy and dull by comparison with the wealth of knowledge, the grasp of the subject and even the humour that is displayed by Ministers sitting on top of their Departments. Though it is the same mouth out of which the speech comes on each occasion."

Today, I can safely go one stage further and say that there are important points in the Report which would have been different if the Chairman had taken his own way without regard to the officials; there are whole sections which were re-written with a view to getting the maximum of free assent by experts.

The process by which the Report on Social Insurance and Allied Services came into being in November 1942 was, I believe, up to that time unique. It illustrates the convenient flexibility of British political institutions.

Substantial Adoption of the Report

The five Acts already passed by Parliament[1] amount substantially to an adoption of the Report. There are differences of language: "Social security" has disappeared in favour of "national insurance"; the housewife is described as a "non-employed person" and in place of sharing joint benefit with her husband as member of a team is still an "adult dependant" in

[1] Ministry of National Insurance and Family Allowances Acts, 1945; National Insurance, National Insurance (Industrial Injuries), and National Health Service Acts, 1946.

respect of whom her husband gets an increase of his benefit. But these changes of wording, however regrettable, are in the main differences of form; the housewife as a non-employed person gets much the same treatment under the Act as was proposed for her in the Report as a vitally useful member of a working team. There are differences of permanent substance also; the most important of these lies in the treatment of industrial injuries and is discussed below. There is a difference in the speed and form of transition to the new pensions, very important to individuals but not affecting the permanent structure. There are many minor differences. But all the differences together are small as compared with the substantial identity of what was enacted by Parliament in 1946 and what was written in the Report of 1942.

The six fundamental principles of social insurance set out in paras. 303-308 of the Report were flat rate of subsistence benefit; flat rate of contribution; unification of administrative responsibility; adequacy of benefit; comprehensiveness; classification. These are the principles underlying the National Insurance Acts of 1946. There is less unification in the Acts than was proposed in the Report as regards industrial injury. But this is a detail as compared with the acceptance of all the rest of the principles, including that of adequacy. The Coalition Government rejected this principle, in respect of amount and duration of benefits and by refusing to relate money rates in any way to cost of living. The National Insurance Act returns to the Report on all these points, most notably on the last of them. Section 40 of this Act provides for quinquennial review of "the rates and amounts of benefit in relation to the circumstances at the time of insured persons in Great Britain, including in particular the expenditure which is necessary for preservation of health and working capacity and to any changes in those circumstances since the rates and amounts of benefit were laid down by this Act or any Act amending it and to the likelihood of future changes."

The twenty-three principal changes of the existing schemes proposed in the Report were set out in para. 30. One only of the twenty-three—conversion of the business of industrial assurance into a public service under an Industrial Assurance Board—has failed hitherto of acceptance; this particular change was shown in the Report in brackets, as desirable but not essential to the whole of the rest of the Plan for Social Security; its fate has been shared by suggestions forming part of other principal changes and also bracketed, namely the use of Friendly Societies and the giving of a marriage grant. Apart from these bracketed items, the corrections needed in para. 30 of the Report to make it an accurate description of what is now the law are few and far between.[1] Nearly everything proposed in para. 30 has been done.

The three Assumptions of Social Security named in para. 301 were dealt with more fully in paras. 410-443. Two of them—Children's Allowances and Comprehensive Health Service—are already on the Statute Book. The third of them—Maintenance of Employment—has been accepted as a policy common to all parties in a White Paper of June 1944.

There is no need to labour the point of the extent to which the proposals of the Report have been translated into practice. It is of more interest to consider the points of difference between what was proposed and what has been done.

Industrial Injuries

The only large difference of permanent structure between what was proposed in the Beveridge Report and what has now been enacted relates to industrial injuries, that is to say accidents occurring or diseases contracted in the course of employment. Provision for such injuries, introduced first as workmen's compensation for a few industries in 1897 and generalised in 1906, was the oldest of the various schemes which came under review by the Inter-departmental Committee and differed in principle from the methods adopted in dealing with all other forms of interruption of earnings. The Workmen's Compensation Acts placed upon each employer individually a legal liability to compensate any employee for loss of earning due to accident or industrial disease "arising out of and in the course of his employment." The amount of the compensation, in contrast to the flat rate applying to sickness, unemployment and old age under the social insurance schemes, was related to the wages formerly

[1] All that is needed is revision of the last lines of change 4 (workmen's compensation) and of change 12 (condition of benefit to long-term unemployed), and omission of the word 'prolonged' both in change 7 (disability benefit for the self-employed) and in change 9 (assimilation of benefit rates). Change 8 (provision of training benefit) has been carried out in a different form.

earned, but could not fall below a minimum which at the time of the Report was 30/- for a single man or woman if wholly incapacitated. The cost, instead of being shared by the employer, the workman and the State, was borne wholly by the employer, who as a rule met the cost by insuring against his liabilities, either with an insurance company or through a mutual association.

The Report, while recognising the benefits conferred by workmen's compensation in the past, named a number of disadvantages and proposed supersession of the existing scheme of workmen's compensation and inclusion of provision for industrial accident or disease within a unified Social Insurance scheme, with the benefits determined not by litigation but by administration, with most of the cost borne by three parties, employer, employee and the State.

This change, one of the major revolutions proposed in the Report and affecting many vested interests, has been adopted in the legislation now approved by Parliament. This degree of agreement between the Report and what has been enacted is worth emphasising, particularly having regard to the circumstances in which this change was made. The system of workmen's compensation had been under criticism for some time, and when the Inter-departmental Committee began was under review by a Royal Commission appointed a year before. But at that moment the Royal Commission had come to a standstill, because the employers declared themselves unable through pressure of war activities to proceed with the preparation of evidence to the Commission. The appointment of the Inter-departmental Committee was to some extent due to this difficulty. As compensation to the Trade Union Congress for the blocking of the Royal Commission, the Inter-departmental Committee was established, with terms of reference expressly including workmen's compensation. The obstacle which had held up the Royal Commission was by-passed. The Chairman of the Inter-departmental Committee, disregarding the difficulty about getting formal evidence from employers about workmen's compensation, made the revolutionary proposal of superseding the whole system, and this was adopted.

The Report, in proposing to include provision for industrial injuries in the unified scheme of Social Insurance, examined the difficult problem, with strong arguments on each side, as to whether this implied that industrial injury should be treated exactly like every other cause of interruption of earning, with benefits the same as for unemployment and sickness, and with an identical method of meeting the cost. The Report recognised that in a scheme based upon subsistence needs the presumption was in favour of treating all equal needs equally; a workman disabled by an accident would have the same needs, whether the accident occurred in a factory or just outside it. On the other hand, the Report concluded that there were good reasons for adopting a contrary view, at least in regard to those who suffered lasting incapacity or death through industrial accident. The strongest of these reasons for differentiation was that the risk for industrial injury varies greatly from one industry to another; since the dangerous industries, notably coalmining, building, shipping, are important industries to which adequate supplies of men must be attracted, it was fair to compensate for the additional risk by making specially favourable provision for industrial injury.

Moved on the one hand by the desire to treat all needs equally, and on the other hand by the argument for making special provision for industrial injury, the Report proposed a compromise which would have made the benefit for all temporary injuries the same as for sickness and unemployment, but for any lasting injury would have provided a pension on a more generous scale and related to the wages which had been lost. This would have meant that in 90% of all cases of accident there would have been no need to determine whether the accident was due to industrial injury or not, and no need to enquire as to the wages formerly earned. The 10% of cases in which such determinations would become necessary would be those of greatest importance to the workman.

The Report proposed at the same time another distinction between industrial injuries and other causes of disability, namely in the method of meeting the cost of benefits. About two-thirds was to be met by social insurance contributions from employers, employees and the State raised equally from all industries and individuals; about one-third was to be raised by a levy on employers in industries specified as hazardous. In each of these industries moreover there was to be a statutory association of employers and workpeople specially concerned with safety, and having the power of distributing by a system of merit rating among individual employers, the total levy for which the industry was responsible. The object was in every dangerous industry to enlist the financial interest of employers, individually and collectively, in pushing safety methods to the utmost. The associations would have been empowered also to propose supplementary schemes of insurance against industrial injury adapted to the conditions of each industry.

In the method of meeting costs as in the proposals for rates of benefit, the plan of the Report was a compromise between strongly argued opposing views. The Trades Union Congress General Council, like the Fabian Society in this volume, while supporting the proposal to make compensation for industrial injuries a social service in place of a subject of litigation, held that the whole cost should continue to be borne by employers separately in each industry, in order by merit rating to maintain the financial incentive to reduction of dangers. The Mineworkers' Federation urged that the cost of all accidents, wherever occurring, should be pooled and be borne by all employers equally. Most of the employers' organisations opposed any large change of the existing system. One—the Shipping Federation—which favoured bringing industrial injury into a unified social insurance scheme, argued that there should be contributions by employers, employees and the State.

The Coalition Government's White Paper accepted the proposal of the Report to include provision for industrial injuries in a unified social insurance scheme with tripartite contributions; it rejected the proposal to assimilate rates of benefit for all temporary disabilities however caused and also the levy on hazardous industries. It made an entirely new departure in proposing that the benefit paid in case of industrial injury, while materially higher than for any other form of disability, should not depend in any way upon the earnings that had been lost. For total disability there should be a flat rate benefit of 35/- a week for a single man or woman, rising to 40/- after 13 weeks; for anything less the benefit should be a proportion of this determined by the actual physical injury—so much for a leg, an arm, a finger, etc.—irrespective of the effect of this injury on earning capacity. This was an adaptation to industrial injuries of the methods adopted in assessing compensation for war injuries.

The Labour Government has followed substantially the White Paper, with in the end an even greater differentiation between disability attributable to industrial injury and all other forms of interruption of earnings. Industrial Injuries are dealt with in one Act of Parliament and Sickness, Maternity, Unemployment, Old Age, Widowhood in another. Both schemes are on a contributory basis, with employer, employee and the State sharing the cost, and it is contemplated that the employer's and employee's contributions should be paid for both schemes together by one stamp on one insurance document. But the amount of the joint contribution, that is to say the value of the stamp, is not shown in any single figure anywhere. It has to be reached by adding together figures from two separate Acts of Parliament. It is for a man between 18 and 70, 9/5 (as compared with 7/6 in my Report), and for a woman between 18 and 65, 7/5 (as compared with 6/-). Of the 9/5, 4/4 is paid by the employer and 5/1 by the employee, by deduction from his wages. Of the 7/5, 3/5 is paid by the employer and 4/- by the employee, by deduction from her wages.

The benefit paid to a single man or woman incapacitated from work by industrial injury is 45/- a week as compared with 26/- a week in sickness or unemployment. But the differences between the two schemes are not confined to these differences of rates. They extend to administration and to conditions of benefit. There are separate Insurance Funds for industrial injuries and for other branches of national insurance. There are separate Advisory Committees to report on Regulations. The allowance of 16/- a week for an adult dependant is not paid in sickness or non-industrial accident if the claimant's wife is herself working and earning as much as 20/- a week; it is paid for industrial injury for a wife living with her husband however much she is earning. Even the provisions as to waiting-time, that is to say the first three days of not-earning, are different in the two cases; the first three days of sickness and unemployment get paid for if there are as many as 12 days lost earning in three months; with industrial injury they get paid for if there are 12 days lost altogether in six months. If the disablement is permanent or prolonged, further differences develop. For industrial injury disability is assessed on physical grounds alone, and a disability may be treated as 100% calling for a 45/- disablement pension, even though it does not destroy completely capacity for work and earning; if it does do this, the pension is increased from 45/- to 65/- a week. If the incapacity is such as to involve constant attendance, a further 20/- or 40/- a week may be paid.

All these differences of treatment between industrial injury and other misfortunes may depend on a difficult diagnosis of origin in a disease, on the place in which an accident happens, on the control of the vehicle in which the employee travels to or from his work. Two men of the same occupation, each with a wife earning wages, suffering the same physical damage by similar accidents may in one case get 26/- a week and in the other 61/- a week, becoming perhaps 81/- or more.

There is another way in which the new scheme may give rise to anomalies. The break with tradition and from the practice of all other countries in making compensation for industrial injuries independent of actual earnings is the most original contribution in either of the Coalition White Papers; the assessment of disability is to be purely physical. One object of this is to avoid the sometimes difficult and unsatisfactory calculations of what were the earnings before the accident; the result in many cases depended on the period taken into account and the chances of unemployment. Another more important object is to avoid what used sometimes to be described as "compensation neurosis," the feeling of the injured man that the sooner he recovered and the more he showed himself able to earn the less compensation he would get; I have myself come across a case in which a mother was obviously more anxious to get blood-money for her daughter's injured arm than to get the daughter trained for earning in some new way. Such extreme cases are rare. But in general it is clear that to make the rate of compensation vary inversely with actual earnings is a kind of means test, with all the discouraging effects on the individual that are inherent in every means test. So the authors of the White Paper on Industrial Injuries boldly cut away from earnings altogether. They proposed that compensation should be based on loss of physical faculty, the same for every one irrespective of his previous occupation or subsequent earnings. The sooner he could get over his physical loss—whether of a finger or a hand or a limb—and earn, the better for him; he would keep his compensation undiminished and enjoy his earnings.

This is an excellent idea. But it has its difficulties. An accident —say the loss of two fingers—may leave one man, as soon as his wound has healed, as capable as ever of his former work; the same accident may destroy completely the capacity of another man to work at his former occupation. Yet under the White Paper proposals both would get the same compensation. This point naturally was raised when the Industrial Injuries Bill was before Parliament. It has been met to the extent of providing that if an industrial injury makes it impossible for a man to pursue his former regular occupation, his disablement pension should be increased by 11/3 a week. Even with this it is clear that an identical injury to two men may leave one of them much poorer than before, while the other has a permanent pension added to undiminished earning capacity.

There is no escape from this if earnings are to be disregarded, so long as all industries and occupations are treated alike. The risk of industrial injury is one which varies extremely from one industry to another; the economic effects of any particular injury may vary even more from one occupation to another. There are industries—notably mining, shipping, building—in which the danger of accident, and others in which the danger of contracting disease, must be accepted as part of the conditions of employment. There is by contrast an even larger field of employment in which the risk of accident is probably less in the place of work than it is at home or on the way from home to work. The scale of provision now made for industrial accidents is not more than is needed for the dangerous industries. But it will lead to anomalies and sense of injustice in many cases. It is difficult to avoid the feeling that industrial injuries insurance would have had a smoother passage in future if the fundamental fact of differences between different industries and occupations in relation to it had been more fully recognised and more space left for the development of supplementary schemes for particular industries. Best of all, I still believe, would have been a combination of the Report's plan of differentiating between industrial injury and other misfortunes only where the injury led to prolonged disability or death, with the new idea in the White Paper of cutting away from earnings altogether, in determining compensation.

Old Age Pensions and other Differences from Report

Next to the treatment of industrial injuries, the most important difference between the Report and the Acts relates to pensions in old age. Yet here too the similarity between the Report and the Act is more important than the difference. The four chief novelties of the Report, of making insurance for pensions universal in place of confining them to special categories of employees under contract of service, of making pensions adequate for subsistence without means test, of making pensions conditional on retirement from work, of encouraging men to go on working while they can by increasing the rate of pension if retirement is postponed, have all been accepted. What has not been accepted is the form of the transition from the old system to the new.

The Report, adapting the precedent of the New Zealand scheme, proposed that pension rates should rise gradually to full subsistence level over a transition period of twenty years; the classes hitherto excluded from contributory pensions—self-employed, non-employed, civil servants and others with occupational pensions—would have to contribute for ten years before drawing anything and would reach full subsistence level, like the rest, after twenty years. The Report was written under strong argument as to the importance of keeping down social service expenditure in the immediate aftermath of war, before production and national income had been restored; it was made plain that there was nothing sacred about the precise period chosen for transition. The National Insurance Act cuts out the transition period altogether for one section of the population—those previously insured for 10/- pensions; it brings the rest of the population in for full pensions after ten years. Whether this is just as between the two classes is today hardly worth discussion; by the time that the Labour Government came to prepare their Bill the political pressure of the existing pensioners for full rates at once was very strong; in ten years time all will be the same for everybody.

There are many other differences between the Report and the Acts—in the treatment of widows, in relation to some other particular benefits, such as those for maternity and death. But these are variations of detail between substantially similar models. There is a more important difference—in the scale of the children's allowances, 5/- a week in the Act as compared with 8/- proposed by the Report. This represents a departure from the principle of freedom from want; the inadequacy of the 5/- paid for each child except one under the Family Allowances Act has been formally recognised in the National Insurance Acts, where the increase of benefit for the first child in disability or unemployment is 7/6. But particular rates of benefit are things which can be changed; section 40 of the National Insurance Act provides for periodic review and the advocates of better children's allowances will have their chance every five years.

In place of examining further the differences between the Report and the Acts, it is better worth while to discuss two points of greater importance in which both of them differ from the line taken by the Fabian Society. These are the treatment of rent and the level of insurance contributions. Each of them raises interesting issues of principle.

The Problem of Rent

With the existing rent structure and the wide variations of rent paid for identical accommodation by different families, a uniform cash benefit everywhere cannot with any accuracy meet subsistence needs. To enable the Social Security Scheme to do this, the Fabian Society (and in this they were joined by no less important a body than the Association of Municipal Corporations) proposed that the cash benefits, including pensions, should in all cases consist of a flat rate to cover the assumed cost of food, fuel, clothing, etc., for the family and of an allowance equal to the actual rent being paid in each case. This proposal was examined sympathetically in the Report in a special section on the problem of rent. The facts supporting the Fabian proposal were fully set out and the impossibility of meeting minimum needs by any uniform cash benefit not adjusted to rent was fully recognised. In the end the proposal was rejected, but the rejection was accompanied by suggestions of further consideration. The reasons which led to this attitude—that is to say the difficulties on the other side of adopting the Fabian proposal—are not perhaps equally recognised by the Fabians or in Mr. Clarke's chapter on Social Security Housekeeping. They are set out fully in the Report. As is argued there, the objections to meeting on Social

Security account the actual rent paid in each individual case are most serious in relation to retirement pensions, which may be drawn for many years on end. If the pension is fixed once for all at the time of retirement, with regard to the rent then being paid, there will be extreme lasting inequalities in the provision for old age, according as one old couple may have managed to secure good and expensive accommodation at the moment of retirement while another has failed to do so. If, on the other hand, pensioners are to be free at any time to change their lodgings if they can, and pay higher rent at the expense of the Social Insurance Fund, there will be a competition, in which the old with State subsidies will outbid the young for decent accommodation.

The Report examined accordingly, among other alternatives, a suggestion of paying actual rent only in sickness and unemployment, with uniform retirement pensions in all cases. Its failure to recommend any of these alternatives was not due to ignoring the weakness in relation to actual needs of uniform cash benefits. Its rejection of the Fabian proposal was provisional. It accompanied that rejection with the proposal for further examination of the rent problem and the possibilities of regional differentiation. It summed up: "The extreme variation of rents between regions, and in the same region, for similar accommodation is evidence of failure to distribute industry and population and of failure to provide housing according to needs. No scale of social insurance benefits free from objection can be framed while the failure continues. In this as in other respects the framing of a completely satisfactory plan of social security depends on the solution of other social problems."

In a money and price economy we cannot have freedom from want by redistributing purchasing power unless for all the necessaries of life, including houses, there is a genuine free market, so that each man has the option of paying less or more for worse or better accommodation. Such a free market in living accommodation can be brought about only by an immense development both of building and of transport, and effective redistribution of industry and of population. Unless a free market in housing can be brought about some form of subsidy to rents may be necessary. But the subsidy should be given as part of housing policy to all citizens while earning and not earning, and not, as part of Social

Security policy, only to those whose earnings are interrupted. This is the fundamental economic reason which, I believe, still justifies rejection of the Fabian Society proposal. In the legislation now in force the proposal is ignored completely, except in so far as the quinquennial review of rates and amounts of benefit required by Section 40 of the National Insurance Act may provide an occasion for reviving it.

The Level of Social Insurance Contributions

The Beveridge Report set out a "Plan for Social Security," using as its main method "Social Insurance." The present volume is concerned with Social Security; the Fabians do not, if they can help it or except for criticism, use the word "insurance." The Coalition White Papers rejected the word "security" as they rejected the aim of freedom from want; they set out proposals for "social insurance" which were deliberately short of security. The Coalition House of Commons, somewhat light-heartedly and unexpectedly, in the title of the new Ministry got rid of "social" and replaced "social insurance" by "national insurance." The Labour Government has accepted this and we now have National Insurance Acts.

This difference reflects a different approach to financial and fiscal problems.

"Social Security," as conceived in the Beveridge Report, is security organised or assisted by the State against those risks to which the individual will remain exposed, even when the condition of society as a whole is as good as it can be made. Social Security, on this definition, excludes measures of general application for improving the condition of society—full employment, minimum wages, factory laws, public health, housing, education and so forth. It is concerned with the individual, and in a money economy is primarily (not wholly) financial: it is essentially a process of re-distributing purchasing power so that at all times, in sickness, unemployment, old age, as well as in health and activity, the individual shall have an income for his needs; the term "security" implies that the income shall come as of right, not of charity, and shall be adequate in time and amount. Re-distribution of purchasing power, if it is to be effective, must be compulsory; it involves taxation—the State taking money away from people when they have it in order to hand money back to them when they need it. The taking away can be done entirely as part of the ordinary taxation of the country, without any special insurance contributions. One can have Social Security on a non-contributory basis, as they have in New Zealand; this is Social Security without social insurance. In proposing Social Security mainly, though not solely, by the method of "social insurance," the Beveridge Report took a line different from that of New Zealand. It proposed that a substantial part of the money required for benefits should be raised, not by general taxation taking account of capacity to pay, but by social insurance contributions, at a flat rate not adjusted for individual capacity to pay, levied both from insured persons and from their employers if they had employers. The reasons for taking this line were set out in paras. 272-276 of the Report on "Taxation and Contributions." The choice of the term "social insurance" was explained in paras. 20-26; it was meant to mark the development of a new type of human institution differing from voluntary insurance and not bound either to accumulate individual reserves or to adjust premiums to risks.

The Fabian volume, while not excluding social insurance contributions altogether, gives them a more restricted role than in the Beveridge Report. They are regarded essentially as a convenient means of identifying and classifying the insured population; the figures suggested by Mr. Clarke as the joint contribution of insured person and employer are 4/6 for an adult man and 3/9 for a woman. These compare with 7/6 and 6/- in the Beveridge Report, and 9/5 and 7/5 in the National Insurance Acts.

It may well prove that these last figures are harmfully high; they will certainly bear hardly on many small employers and self-employers. I have given reasons for holding that, even on the assumptions made in the Government Actuary's Report, too much is being charged to contributions and too little to general taxation. On the other hand, I believe that social insurance contributions have an importance far beyond that of merely registering the population. To raise some definite proportion of the total cost in this way—relating contributions to benefit rates —is the best safeguard, perhaps the only safeguard, against pressure otherwise irresistible to push up benefits unduly. The experience of the Labour Government with the Industrial Injuries Act is clear evidence of danger when those who expect to draw the largest part of the benefits realise that the cost will almost wholly be borne by others.

The Next Steps

The principle of redistributing purchasing power so that all citizens at all times on condition of service shall be above want has been accepted. The way in which the popular acclamation accorded to the Beveridge Report drove the Coalition Government to its White Papers is one of many illustrations of the way in which public opinion in this country can become effective. That bread and health for all at all times shall come before cake and circuses for any one at any time is the free decision of our democracy. The practical machine for giving effect to this principle has been established. There remains an immense task of administration in setting the machine to work. There remain for solution many problems.

Some of the tasks still to be done are no more than a rounding off of Social Security. However perfect any Social Security Scheme, some misfortunes and some individuals will slip through its meshes. There will be need for assistance taking regard of individual needs. The next Act of Parliament, already promised, is one to deal with Assistance, to take the problem from Local Authorities into the hands of some National Assistance Authority.

Another minor measure for which there is need is some plan for dealing with the problem of alternative remedies, for adjusting claims at common law or under the Employers' Liability Act to the new scheme of Social Security.

More important than these roundings off of Social Security are the things that lie outside it.

First and greatest of these is full employment of all our productive resources as effectively as possible. This means maintaining the National Income in real terms, in terms of goods and services. The National Insurance Acts represent a financial operation; they are concerned with purchasing power over goods, with means, not with ends. At their best they can ensure only that whatever goods there are they should be distributed as between rich and poor, as between times of earning and not earning, so as to put necessities before comforts. Social Security does not itself affect the general standard of living directly. That depends upon output, and output depends upon full productive employment of our resources.

Equal to this in importance is the problem of redistribution of industry and population so as to avoid congestion in towns and squalor in town and country alike. This is the condition of raising the standard of living where now it is lowest—in relation to housing. It is also, as has been shown above, a condition of making any system of uniform cash benefits equal to the task of abolishing want.

There remains a third fundamental problem. The minimum needs of all men, as animals, are much the same. The needs of different men, as men, for happiness are not the same, any more than are their productive capacities. The third of the main principles laid down in the Report in regard to Social Security was that Social Security must be achieved by co-operation between the State and the individual. The State should offer security for service and contribution. "The State in organising security should not stifle incentive, opportunity, responsibility; in establishing a national minimum it should leave room and encouragement for voluntary action by each individual for himself and his family." This principle has an application extending beyond Social Security. There are many evils, material and moral, which we cannot extirpate from society without using the powers of the State, that is to say, of the organised community, in fields hitherto thought to have been outside the proper sphere of State action. On the other hand, we cannot have a good society if everything is done by the State. The central problem of the immediate future at home is how to preserve voluntary action in a planned society.

APPENDIX

Memorandum of Evidence submitted to the Beveridge Committee by the Social Security Sub-Committee of the Fabian Society. This was supplemented by oral evidence.

I

OUTLINE OF THE SCHEME

The Practical Implementation of Social Security

1. The anomalies and deficiencies of the social insurance and allied services are well known to the Committee, and this paper does not refer to them. They are so striking and so deeply rooted in the structure of these services that major reconstruction will be necessary if they are to be eliminated. Such a reconstruction cannot stop at a mere rearrangement of existing contributions, benefits, and paying agencies; it must be accompanied by a reassessment of the social functions which the cash services can and should perform in modern society. In this paper a detailed scheme is put forward, embodying what we believe to be the basic principles upon which these services must henceforth be founded.

2. First, the social insurance and allied services are only one facet of social policy in the broadest sense; they are one of many instruments by which society attains its social objectives. A constructive social policy aimed at providing the maximum public welfare must be linked with a positive economic policy to make full use of the nation's resources, a positive health policy, a positive education policy, a positive housing policy, a positive population policy. These fields are outside the Committee's terms of reference, but the cash services cannot be separated from them; unemployment benefit is inextricably linked with unemployment, health insurance with medical services, family allowances with population objectives.

3. Second, too much emphasis has in the past been placed upon the cash aspect of the insurance and allied services, and far too little upon the need for positive and constructive services to keep people productive and healthy or to restore them rapidly to work and health. Such constructive services must be the hub of the whole affair. There must be a free public medical service and there must be an improved placement, training and rehabilitation service. Without them, it is impossible to frame a satisfactory system of cash payments. The purpose of the cash payments for sickness and unemployment is to provide for people who lose their earning power for one reason or another; this cannot be done adequately or justly except as an integral part of positive action to restore that earning power.

4. Our proposals are based upon this premise. They aim at providing sufficient maintenance for those who temporarily or permanently lose their earning power—that is the simple service which the community owes its members. But they fully recognise the profound reciprocal obligation upon the citizen to co-operate fully in the restoration of his earning power. The obsolete "cash" criterion with its poor law connotations on the one hand and demands for unlimited payments "as of right" on the other, is replaced by a new "social" criterion, by which society provides full maintenance for its economically incapacitated members, but does so only to the extent to which its members are willing to accept their corresponding social obligations. The emphasis passes from "cash" to "work" and "health." Social Security is thus conceived in positive and creative terms rather than as merely fending off misery or destitution by money payments.

5. In this context, the insurance-cum-assistance type of scheme is clearly outmoded. In the process by which a man is entitled to insurance benefit "as of right" for a period of 26 weeks, and may then receive assistance only after a stringent investigation of his financial position, the real needs of the case—restoration of earning power—are completely eclipsed by the financial considerations—the number of contributions paid, the number of weeks' benefit received, the amount of savings at the man's disposal. If the rates of benefit and the conditions of assistance are "generous" there is grave danger of waste of public funds and of moral deterioration of those publicly maintained for long periods; if the benefits are small and the conditions of assistance "strict," hardship and injustice and social bitterness are created.

6. For the contingencies of unemployment, sickness, disablement and widowhood, we therefore propose a flat rate benefit, at a level adequate to cover reasonable needs, paid for an indefinite period with no needs test. The flat rate would be exclusive of rent, and the actual rent of the client would be paid, subject to a maximum. This would give the worker real security against the economic effect of these contingencies. He would know that his rent was covered, and that he would have enough to live on. He would also have the assurance that the resources of society would be directed to the restoration of his earning power. We propose also very strong sanctions against the malingerer or the slacker; refusal to co-operate with the placement, re-training and rehabilitation service or with the public medical service would be dealt with very severely. This "social" sanction is likely to be far more effective and just and constructive in dealing with the asocial individual than a "financial" sanction can possibly be.

7. Provision for old age requires special treatment. It is clear that society must provide adequate living standards for the aged; the removal of the fear of poverty in old age is an essential constituent of the health and welfare of people in their working years. But the

changing age-distribution automatically rules out the extremely generous schemes which are being canvassed in some quarters; it would be a fundamental error in social policy unduly to divert resources to the aged at the expense of the young. Our proposals are therefore framed on the assumption that adequate maintenance must be provided for the aged, but that every possible effort must be made to induce old people to remain at work for as long as it is possible for them to do without detriment to their health. We therefore suggest a double-deck scheme, by which gainfully occupied men of 65 and women of 60 receive a 10/- weekly pension while they continue at work, to compensate for the loss of earning power as they get old. They should be able to retire after that date on a pension which provides sufficient maintenance (paid as a flat rate plus rent) but is not so high as actually to encourage them to leave work. As an incentive to supplementation of pension by work we should regard as "retired" those earning less than 10/- per head weekly. We also propose an unsubsidised State superannuation scheme to which people could voluntarily contribute.

8. The social security scheme should be comprehensive, covering all gainfully occupied persons; there is no case for omitting the self-employed, who are equally liable with others to sickness, disablement, old age and widowhood. Nor is there any reason why one upper income limit rather than another should be chosen; it is desirable on social grounds that these services should be available to all, and the absence of an upper income limit simplifies administration and avoids difficult border-line cases. Benefits in respect of loss of earnings would, of course, be subject to direct taxation in the same way as any other income. Part-time workers, working between 15 and 30 hours weekly, should be included on a half-benefit basis, and this could also apply to such marginal cases as those shopkeepers' and farmers' wives who are in effect partially employed by their husbands.

9. It is clearly impossible to link contributions with benefits in a scheme of this kind. Such link is possible only in an insurance-cum-assistance scheme. If the benefits continue indefinitely, or indeed if the bulk of the cost is borne by the State, the contributions are in reality no more than a tax of a rather regressive type. The employer's contribution is in any case indefensible except as a convenient and accepted form of indirect taxation; it is actually a tax on employment which can be justified only if the employer is regarded as having some responsibility for the employment, health and maintenance in old age of his employees. No useful purpose is served, therefore, by the continuance of specific contributions, except in so far as they represent a more acceptable system of taxation than the direct taxation of workers' incomes. The policy to be followed depends largely upon the extent to which war-time income tax on wage-earners' incomes becomes an accepted part of the fiscal system. It must be clearly recognised that most of the cost would have to be borne by the workers

themselves. If in peace-time the great mass of working-class incomes can be included in the income tax we should prefer this as a method of financing social security than the tripartite system of contributions by employers, employees and the State which has hitherto prevailed.

10. In addition to these cash services which are aimed at compensating for temporary or permanent loss of earning power, we propose a number of allowances to be available to all people whether gainfully occupied or not, to meet contingencies which require additional expenses. These include family, maternity, marriage and burial allowances. The case for family allowances is now generally accepted; adequate maternity allowances are clearly necessary, not only to cover the working mother's compulsory absence from work, but also to cover the incidental expenses of all mothers; a small marriage allowance would remove an important obstacle to early marriage, and thus possibly to the raising of larger families; burial allowance, together with control or municipalisation of the undertakers' services, would strike at the root of the asocial exploitation of the fear of a "pauper's funeral" by the industrial assurance companies.

11. Provision must also be made for the payment of emergency benefit to people who come outside the scope of the scheme—e.g. wives of men in prison or aged people who had never been gainfully occupied and become needy—and to supplement the incomes of people who for justifiable reasons are unable to manage on the basic benefits provided. Means would, of course, be taken into account in the assessment of these payments. The emergency service would supply the necessary elasticity in the scheme as a whole, and would also provide an important field for positive welfare work.

12. We contend that it is possible within the limits imposed by the prospective size of the national income and the willingness of the public to accept taxation, to provide rates of benefit which would be adequate for reasonable maintenance of the economically incapacitated and their dependants, and also to provide the constructive allowances set out in para. 10. The proposed scales are set out in paras. 23-5 of the detailed recommendations. The total annual cost may be roughly estimated at the order of £600 millions, or about 9½% of the net national income at current prices; the corresponding pre-war proportion was about 5%, but some 1½% of the national income was then devoted by the workers to voluntary protection—through industrial assurance, friendly societies, etc.—against contingencies which would now be borne by the scheme. This projected lay-out of the national dividend seems to us both practicable and desirable; it does not seem too generous when we consider that at any given time one-quarter of the adult population is directly or indirectly affected by one of these contingencies. We must again add, however, that these scales are entirely dependent upon the adoption of a constructive and forward-looking national economic

policy, for unless the national income can be maintained at a high level such benefits clearly cannot be paid. And the stages by which the scheme is introduced should necessarily be planned to accord with the progress of economic reconstruction.

13. From the administrative point of view, the scheme as a whole has great simplicity. All these services should be administered by a Ministry of Social Security, with a Minister responsible to Parliament. This Ministry would absorb the functions of all social insurance and assistance agencies, including the Ministry of Pensions. The whole complex apparatus of National Health Insurance would be cleared away; the Ministry of Labour would be able to concentrate its attention upon the expansion of its placement, training and rehabilitation service; the Ministry of Health would be able to concentrate upon the building of a free public medical service; the Assistance Board would be completely absorbed; the Public Assistance Committees would lose all their cash-paying functions. There would certainly be a great saving in administrative effort, and a consequent increase in administrative coherence, simplicity and efficiency.

14. Workmen's compensation should not be included in the comprehensive social security scheme, for there are real advantages to be secured from retaining the employer's financial interest in the safety of his workmen. But it would be administered by the Ministry of Social Security. Employers should be required compulsorily to insure in a State-operated scheme; the premiums would be merit-rated according to safety conditions. Claims should be settled by administrative procedure instead of by the present time-wasting and money-wasting reference to the Courts. The entire machinery of insurance against employers' liability would be removed from the sphere of profit-making. There would be no adverse interest financially opposed to the payment of each claim.

15. War pensions and personal injury allowances are not included in the comprehensive scheme, for the community's obligation to provide a proper livelihood for the war-disabled and for war widows is on rather a different plane from its obligation to the economically incapacitated. The payments should provide something more than the bare minimum for healthy existence. The administration of these payments, which is now unduly complex, should come under a special division of the Ministry of Social Security, and special attention should be paid to the needs of the war-disabled when the rehabilitation services envisaged in para. 3 are being established.

16. Finally, throughout the whole field, great importance must be attached to the staffing of the Ministry of Social Security. It is essential that the men and women at the point of contact between the Ministry and the public should be trained for social service work; otherwise the spirit of constructive welfare can never appear. It is essential also that those responsible for policy should be fully aware of the role which the social services can and should perform in developing the public welfare. Great changes are taking place in the attitude of

the public to the State and to the social services; it is vitally necessary that the administration should adapt itself to these changes and develop new types of personnel to meet new requirements.

II

DETAILED RECOMMENDATIONS

I. Provision against Unemployment, Sickness, Disablement, Widowhood

17. The scheme protects all gainfully occupied persons and their dependants against economic insecurity arising from unemployment, sickness, disablement, widowhood. Benefits adequate for the maintenance of the citizen and his dependants must be available for the full duration of the contingency; the same rate of benefit should be paid in respect of all these contingencies. There must be no upper income limit and no test of need. All gainfully occupied persons must be included, with no "excepted" employment. Those working between 15 and 30 hours a week should be classed as part-time workers, and should receive half-benefits; shopkeepers' wives and daughters could be placed in this category. People who are working but who derive more than a certain proportion of their income from "unearned" sources (other than social security benefits) would not rank as "gainfully occupied."

18. *Unemployment benefit*, continuing for the whole period of genuine unemployment, should be linked with a placement, training and rehabilitation service, operated by the Ministry of Labour. This service should after a period review the industrial position and prospects of the citizen; if there was no prospect of re-employment in his original trade, the service would provide training and other rehabilitation facilities. The period before positive action of this kind was taken would depend upon the circumstances; the position of a youth of 18 or 19 in a blind-alley occupation would be reviewed in this sense almost at the outset of his unemployment, whereas that of a highly skilled worker in a cyclical industry would not be reviewed for a substantial period. Formerly self-employed persons claiming unemployment benefit would, of course, receive it if they were willing to co-operate with the placement service, and take other jobs if offered. Failure to co-operate with the placement and rehabilitation service would mean loss of benefit or other deterrent treatment, subject to a right of appeal (see paras. 41-2).

19. *Sickness benefit* should likewise continue for the whole period of unfitness for work, the distinction between sickness and disablement benefit disappearing. Here again the emphasis must be laid upon the restoration of the citizens to health. Only a free State medical service can provide sufficient services. Eligibility for benefit should

depend entirely upon the opinion of the State medical service whether the citizen is fit for work. The abolition of the "panel" system and the supersession of private practice by the State medical service would remove any financial interest which doctors may now have in giving decisions unduly "favourable" to their patients; the State medical service should be able to say fairly and frankly whether a man is fit for work or not. Society would be protected against the malingerer by measures analogous to those provided for unemployment above.

20. *Disabled men and women*, if gainfully occupied before disablement, should receive benefit indefinitely. Blindness should not be regarded as a separate disability. Congenitally disabled and those who were disabled before they could have been gainfully occupied would be regarded as gainfully occupied for this purpose. "Percentage pensions" should be paid to those whose earning capacity is partially impaired, the pension being related to the degree of economic incapacity from which they may be expected to suffer in the occupation they are able to follow, subject to a maximum. There should be a specialised placement service for disabled persons, together with specially organised diversified workshops as necessary. Supplementation should be paid in case of need to those whose living expenses are increased on account of their disability.

21. *Widows* of gainfully occupied men and gainfully occupied widows should receive full benefit for as long as they have dependent children. Widows without dependent children should receive benefit for the first three months of their widowhood. At the end of that period, if they were not working, they would receive unemployment, sickness or disablement benefit as was appropriate, subject, of course, to the conditions set out in paras. 18 and 19 above. *Orphans* would receive a total rate of 10/- weekly.

22. The standard rate of benefit would be exclusive of rent. The total payment made would include the full rent for which the citizen was responsible, or of course the rates and the interest element of building society payments and Schedule A tax liability if the citizen was buying or had bought his house; the rent allowance would be subject to a maximum, fixed regionally. A scale would be necessary to apportion the rent paid for a dwelling in which there was more than one earner. Provision would also be necessary to prevent the exploitation of this situation by landlords. The separate allowance for rent presents some administrative difficulties, but it has the real social advantage that the citizen can feel that his rent obligations will be met, whatever the contingency, and it is in any case necessary because rents are so very diverse that it is impossible to provide a flat rate benefit including rent which is neither unjust to the worker with a high rent nor unduly wasteful of the public funds.[1]

23. It is proposed that the standard weekly benefit, excluding

[1] For further elaboration, see Supplementary Evidence, p. 456.

rent, should be 20/- for a man, 18/- for a woman, 13/- for the wife or other adult dependant; family allowances (see para. 31) should be made up to 9/- for each child whose family is being maintained by Social Security benefits. These rates are based upon the cost of the B.M.A. diet and the Bristol Survey allowances for clothing and fuel and light, re-priced at the prices of the winter of 1941-42 (see Annex A). The woman's benefit is fixed below the man's on physiological grounds.

II. Provision for Old Age

24. A benefit of 10/- weekly should be paid to all gainfully occupied men at the age of 65 and to gainfully occupied women at the age of 60. This would be paid as compensation for loss of earning power with increasing years. Male pensioners still earning should have an additional 5/- weekly for non-gainfully occupied wives over 60.

25. On retirement from work at any time after the age of 65 for men or 60 for single and widowed women, a further pension of 5/- weekly plus rent would be paid, and married pensioners would then be entitled to 10/- weekly in respect of their wives. The effect of this double scheme would be that a married man of 65 or over could receive a retirement pension of 25/- weekly plus rent; a single man of 65 or over or a single or widowed woman of 60 or over could receive 15/- weekly plus rent. Gainfully occupied married women of 60 or over should receive an extra 5/- weekly when they and their husbands retire, making, for these couples, a total of 30/-. These benefits may be regarded as adequate to provide reasonable maintenance, although they are below the rates for the other contingencies (see Annex A). To encourage supplementation of these pensions by part-time work, earnings of less than 10/- weekly per head should be disregarded.

26. These benefits are confined to the gainfully occupied. In order to qualify for them, a man or woman would be required to have been eligible for social security benefits continuously for the five years preceding application for the pension. This would in effect cover everyone except those who had been living on private means or on the generosity of relatives—for example, a widow who had been widowed at the age of 50 and had no dependent children, and had then lived on private means, would not be eligible at 60 for a pension, but a similar widow who at the end of three months' widowhood (see para. 2) had been deemed incapable of work and had received full or partial disablement benefit ever since would be eligible at 60. Men receiving other benefits would pass to old age benefit at the age of 65, and single and widowed women at 60; those receiving unemployment or sickness benefit would be allowed to continue at those rates of benefit on the understanding that they were willing and able to resume work, with a reasonable prospect of obtaining employment.

27. It must be stressed that the financial possibility of providing adequate benefits depends to a very large extent upon the proportion

of old people who would want to retire on pension at the stated age. Measures must be devised to induce them to remain at work as long as possible without detriment to their health. As longevity increases, the age to which people are capable of useful work should also increase. The achievement of this requires both propaganda designed to show old people that the community needs their continued work and the investigation of the practical problems of employment of old people.

28. The conditions for benefit set out in para. 26 are sufficiently clearly defined to determine in the long run whether a given person is or is not eligible for benefit. But at the date of introduction of the scheme there would clearly be considerable difficulty. People should be entitled to these benefits if they could demonstrate that they would have been eligible if the scheme had been in force when they reached pensionable age. All insured persons and all those being maintained by public and charitable funds would automatically be eligible; a series of *ad hoc* decisions would have to be taken about other categories of people.

29. A voluntary unsubsidised scheme for the provision of superannuation benefit over and above the statutory rate should be made available through the Post Office. The amount of additional pension that could be provided would depend on the amount of contributions and interest standing to the credit of the individual on his attaining the age of 65. It is estimated that, assuming interest at the rate of $2\frac{1}{2}\%$, a contribution of 1/- a week paid continuously from the age of 20, or of 2/6 a week from the age of 40, would purchase an annuity of 10/- a week at the age of 65. In the event of the death of the contributor before that age, the amount of the contributions and interest would be payable to his estate. A special advantage of this scheme would be that employers who desired to supplement the State pension provision could be encouraged to make contributions on behalf of their employees instead of running an individual scheme of their own. This would remove a serious obstacle to industrial mobility imposed by self-contained superannuation schemes.

III. Provision of Constructive Allowances

30. Allowances must also be provided for the whole population in respect of the following contingencies which involve increased expenditure: parenthood, maternity, marriage, burial.

31. *Family allowances* are now accepted as the best single means of combating a lowered standard of living due to the obligations of parenthood, and their introduction is in any case a necessary part of positive population policy. We propose that allowances should be made for each dependent child under the school-leaving age and for older children receiving full-time education, and that the allowance should increase for the third and fourth children, both in order to encourage the raising of larger families, and also because large families

will contain a high proportion of older children, who are much more expensive to maintain. The family allowance should not cover the whole cost of maintaining a child, but it should make a substantial contribution. We propose allowances of 6/- weekly for each of the first two children, 7/- for the third, 8/- for the fourth and subsequent children. The 6/- allowance is roughly equivalent to that provided at the present time to all income tax payers with an income of £4 a week or more in respect of their first child. As stated in Annex A, para. 7 (*e*), if it were necessary to reduce the total cost of the scheme we should omit family allowances for the first child.

32. The allowances should be paid to the mother in cash at the Post Office. The existence of these allowances should not be allowed to check the energetic development of services to children in kind—milk in schools, school meals, etc. Income tax assessments should be adjusted so that parents in effect receive either the family allowance or the income tax rebate, whichever is the greater. This presents certain difficulties, as the White Paper on Family Allowances [1] points out, but it is the adjustment most likely to be generally acceptable.

33. *Maternity allowance* must be provided for all gainfully occupied women for a period of six weeks before and after childbirth; withdrawal from industry should be compulsory for this period; the allowance would be the same as sickness benefit (see Annex B). These payments could suitably be made dependent upon certificates proving ante- and post-natal medical supervision. In addition to the weekly payment for gainfully occupied women, a lump sum of £10 should be paid to all women at childbirth for the general expenses of the new baby. The system of Home Helps should be extended as a service in kind, not only for maternity, but also for temporary sickness and disability.

34. *Marriage allowance* of £15 should be paid. Marriage is a severe strain on the resources of those in lower-income groups, and if we desire to reverse present population trends, we should not only remove financial obstacles to child-bearing and child-rearing, but also smooth the path towards earlier marriage as a preliminary step. This allowance would be payable throughout the entire population.

35. *Burial allowance* of £15 should be paid. This would serve the very useful purpose of countering the abuses of industrial assurance. It is at the same time necessary that strong efforts should be made to reduce the excessive level of funeral costs (see Annex C) by control of undertakers' prices or by municipalisation. The undertaking services are bound to expand in the coming years, and it is highly desirable that the State should ensure that the community secures the fullest advantages of concentration of undertakers' concerns over large areas and the consequent quantity production of accessories

[1] Family Allowances, Memorandum by the Chancellor of the Exchequer, May 1942, Cmd. 6354.

without being subjected to monopoly price policy by the undertakers' associations. Local authorities should therefore be required to make schemes for the regulation of charges, and in default of satisfactory co-operation from private firms should be required to provide municipal burial or cremation at a standard acceptable to the local *mores* at a reasonable price.

IV. Provision for Emergency Benefit

36. Emergency benefit should be granted in cases of sudden emergency or in respect of circumstances outside the provisions of the scheme. This would cover the sort of emergencies represented by applications of P.R.D. relief in war-time; it would cover people outside the scheme, such as wives of men in prison, or widows who had lived on private means and generosity of relatives, and had lost their investments; it would cover cases in which people were unable for justifiable reasons to maintain themselves upon the basic benefits provided (e.g. disabled people with special expenses). Payment of these benefits would be made only after full investigation of financial resources and other circumstances, and it would be desirable to allow local officers a substantial degree of discretion in payment. This provides the necessary element of elasticity which must exist in any social welfare scheme.

V. Workmen's Compensation

37. Workmen's compensation should not come within the comprehensive scheme. It should remain a charge on industry, but employers should be required to insure in respect of all employees in a State-operated insurance scheme. This should apply to all employers, but industries which wish to form mutual associations for workmen's compensation insurance, on a non-profit-making basis, should have the option of contracting out. Premiums should be merit-rated according to the safety provisions in the place of work. Workers should have full facilities to complain of deficient safety arrangements and to suggest improvements; the importance of safety prevention must be stressed throughout. The only reason for separating workmen's compensation from other contingencies is the desirability of using the financial provisions to induce employers to improve their safety arrangements. The administration would, of course, work in close co-operation with the Factory Inspectorate and Mines Inspectorate.

38. All claims should be settled by a Workmen's Compensation Commission without going before the Courts. These Commissions should be regional, with an umpire in London. We believe lump sum settlements to be undesirable, for experience shows a tremendously high proportion of failures in the one-man businesses in which these lump sums are invested. Rehabilitation and the provision of appliances

would be dealt with by the services provided in accordance with para. 3. There should, of course, be no upper income limit for beneficiaries.

39. The Ministry of Social Security (see Section IX) would be responsible for administration; payments would be made through its offices, and in general would be equivalent to the standard social security payments.

VI. War Pensions

40. War pensions are likewise separate from the civil provisions of the scheme, for injury or loss of life in war is an altogether different type of contingency. All armed forces and civil defence pensions, including those administered by other agencies than the Ministry of Pensions, should be paid through the Ministry of Social Security, and the Ministry should take over all administration.

VII. Residual Service

41. There must be a residual service for those who voluntarily place themselves outside the scope of the scheme, by failure to co-operate with the placement, training and rehabilitation service or with the medical service. Claimants who, for example, refuse to accept suitable jobs which are offered them but nevertheless require financial assistance would pass to the residual service as a result of a determination by an Adjudicating Committee, which would be similar to the existing Courts of Referees with suitable modifications. The Committee would be furnished with the fullest particulars about the claimant, and would decide whether the claimant's objections to the job or to the rehabilitation procedure proposed were valid. Deterrent measures, where suitable, could include payment in kind, payment to another member of the household, or institutional treatment. Some elasticity would be allowed in the application of these deterrent measures.

42. Appeal machinery would be created to enable decisions of the Adjudicating Committee to be challenged at a high level where (*a*) the Committee is not unanimous, or (*b*) the Chairman gives leave to appeal, or (*c*) the Ministry of Social Security wishes to get a decision on an important point of principle.

VIII. Financial Provisions

43. The financial provisions of the scheme are analysed in Annex A. Broadly, the scheme is estimated to cost something less than £600 millions a year, which, it is believed, is within the capacity of the nation's financial resources to bear without undue strain.

44. No definite recommendations are made concerning contributions. The benefits are not linked with the payment of contributions according to an insurance principle, so that contributions in these terms become no more than a specifically allocated direct tax of a

somewhat regressive kind. The financial requirements of the scheme are such that a considerable part of the cost would have to be subscribed by the wage-earners themselves, either by contributions or by direct and indirect taxation. A number of possibilities are discussed in Annex A, but the suitability and acceptability of direct taxation of low incomes is not yet sufficiently established to enable us to state whether public opinion would prefer that method to the well-established method of weekly contributions deducted from wages. In any event, the evidence suggests that benefits are being increasingly dissociated from contributions in the public mind, especially among young men in the armed forces. No great shock would thus be felt by public opinion if the existing contributory basis was abolished overnight.

45. When the Social Security scheme was introduced, all existing social insurance funds would automatically pass to the Ministry of Social Security. They could be used either to provide for some of the immediate costs which would be incurred, or to contribute to the income of the Ministry. A firm resistance to increases in benefit in times of exceptional prosperity would be necessary both from the Minister and from the Chancellor of the Exchequer; it is hardly conceivable that either they or Parliament should be so ignorant of current techniques of public finance as to attempt to cut the benefits in periods of relative depression; payment of unemployment benefit at an adequate rate at such a time would, of course, be of positive benefit in maintaining the public purchasing power and in stimulating industrial recovery.

IX. Administration

46. The whole scheme should be administered by a Ministry of Social Security, under a Minister responsible to Parliament. The Ministry would be responsible for the payment of all public moneys under the scheme. It would absorb the functions of all existing public agencies in this field. The Ministry would work in close collaboration with the Ministry of Labour, which would continue to be responsible for placement, training and rehabilitation, though on a greatly expanded scale; with the Ministry of Health, which would be responsible for the free public medical service, and with the Treasury, which is responsible for public financial policy.

47. The Ministry would have regional and local offices, directly responsible to headquarters. The community should co-operate with the work of the Ministry through local and regional Advisory Committees. There should also be a Central Advisory Committee with functions analogous to those performed by the Consultative Committee of the Board of Education.

48. The Ministry should at every point in its administration consider the welfare of citizens as a definite objective. Special welfare departments should be set up in larger offices to handle citizens' personal problems, to give advice, etc.

49. The Ministry would inevitably inherit its local and regional premises from such existing institutions as the Assistance Board, Insurance Committees, etc. The provision of adequate buildings to provide proper atmosphere and facilities should be effected as soon as conditions permit.

50. Special attention should be paid by the Ministry to research, intelligence, and the collection and examination of statistics in the field of the social services, both at home and abroad. In addition to itself carrying out certain types of investigation, the Ministry should sponsor research by independent bodies and should be receptive to suggestions based on their findings. The Ministry must also have a comprehensive public relations policy covering its relations with official and voluntary bodies, with organised and unorganised groups, and with individual citizens. Public relations are important in the social services; failure to understand this has seriously embarrassed the Assistance Board from its inception.

51. Consequential changes resulting from the creation of the Ministry would be the dissolution of the Assistance Board, the Approved Societies, the Insurance Committees, the Pensions Committees, the Ministry of Pensions (which would become a Department in the new Ministry). The Ministry of Labour would be concerned with placement, training and rehabilitation only, and would cease to administer benefits to the unemployed. Similarly the Ministry of Health would have responsibility for the organisation of health and medical services, but would no longer supervise the payment of Sickness or Disability Benefit, nor Widows', Orphans' or Old Age Pensions. These duties would be absorbed by the new Ministry, which would also relieve the Department of Customs and Excise from responsibility for Old Age Pensions administration. The cash-paying functions of Public Assistance Committees would also be transferred. These bodies would, in the first instance, supply staff for the new Ministry; ample numbers are available (see Annex E).

52. In the longer view the staff engaged on the social service work of the Ministry must have knowledge of the method and outlook of the social services, and understanding of the role of the social services in the national life. They must also have the personal qualities which will enable them to make satisfactory contacts with citizens coming within the sphere of the Ministry. With this end in view we propose that recruitment for the Ministry's staff shall be (1) from those with professional social service training, (2) from those wishing to transfer from other Departments, for whom a scheme of in-service training should be developed, (3) from mature persons with relevant knowledge or experience who would be recruited for the higher posts (see Annex E, paras. 4 and 5). The success of the Social Security scheme depends upon the development of positive co-operation between the Ministry and the public, and this depends very largely upon the quality of the staff, both in the field and in policy-making at headquarters.

ANNEX A

FINANCIAL ESTIMATES AND POSSIBILITIES

1. This appendix seeks to establish, in very broad terms:

(a) The cost of providing adequately for primary needs;
(b) The probable cost of the social security cash benefits;
(c) The relation of this cost to the national economic resources.

Many of the estimates are inevitably highly speculative, but it is nevertheless considered necessary that some attempt should be made to provide some quantitative basis for policy.

Cost of Primary Needs

2. The B.M.A. diet for an adult male was priced at 7/4 weekly by the Bristol Survey [1] in May-June 1937; this result was broadly confirmed by the Crawford Food Enquiry.[2] The Ministry of Labour food price index increased by 22% to the end of 1941. This gives a current cost of 9/- weekly for the B.M.A. adult male diet.[3] But the price of foods not included in the index has risen much more, and a figure of 10/- weekly is probably needed to buy a diet equivalent to the B.M.A. diet. The B.M.A. diet is considered deficient in milk, but this deficiency should be made good by social distribution.

3. Clothing, fuel, light and cleaning materials, on the Bristol Survey basis, and adjusted to the price increases given by the Ministry of Labour index, cost 8/- weekly for an adult male. A further 2/- must be added to cover miscellaneous expenses—such as newspapers, tobacco, stamps.

4. An allowance of £1 a week, excluding rent, may therefore be regarded as a reasonable minimum for an adult male. The corresponding figure for an adult female is 18/-; for a married couple 33/-. The cost of maintaining a child varies according to age; it is not less than 7/- for a child under 5, and 11/- for a boy of 13. We propose to give family allowances (see p. 440, para. 31) of 6/- weekly for each of the first two children, 7/- for the third, 8/- for the fourth and subsequent. For children whose families are being maintained wholly by Social Security benefits we should make these sums up to a flat rate of 9/- per child.

5. For men of 65 and over and women of 60 and over, the minimum weekly maintenance cost, on the same basis as in paras. 2 and 3 above,

[1] *The Standard of Living in Bristol.* University of Bristol Social Survey, 1938.
[2] *The People's Food,* by Sir William Crawford, K.B.E., and H. Broadley (Heinemann, 1938).
[3] See Annex F, p. 455.

is 15/- excluding rent, or 25/- for an aged couple. The figure is lower because of the old person's lower food and clothing needs. However, we propose to pay 30/- on retirement to aged couples in which both partners qualify as gainfully occupied persons, and to allow aged persons to rank as "retired" if their earnings are under 10/- weekly per head.

6. A "minimum standard" cannot be given for rent, for the variations are too great. The scheme provides for a special rent allowance, covering the rent for which the citizen is responsible, subject to a maximum which would be fixed regionally. For statistical purposes we assume an average of 7/- weekly for each wage- and salary-earner (derived from the 1938 Ministry of Labour family budgets); 5/- rent is allowed for single aged persons, and 7/6 for aged couples.

Cost of the Social Security Scheme

7. The following table[1] sets out a very approximate estimate of the annual cost of the scheme:

	£m.
Unemployment (*a*)	85
Sickness and disablement (*b*)	95
Old Age (*c*)	225
Widows and Orphans (*d*)	40
Family Allowances (*e*)	100
Miscellaneous (*f*)	25
Administration (*g*)	25
Total	£595 millions

(*a*) Assumes 1,000,000 unemployed, or 5% of occupied population, with assumptions about men's dependants as in footnote.

[1] Population structure extrapolated from pre-war refers to the end of 1942, as follows:

	Males (m.)	Females (m.)	Total (m.)
Total all ages	22·6	24·4	47·0
Children under 16	5·3	5·2	10·5
Adults, 16-64	15·4	16·6	32·0
Aged, 65 and over	1·9	2·6	4·5
Occupied, 16-64	14·7	5·8	20·5

Each occupied man has 0·6 adult dependants (aged no longer being dependent) and 0·7 children. We assume there are 0·8 million widows under 60, each with 0·3 dependent children; 0·6 million single and widowed women of 60-64; 0·8 million married women of 65 and over; 1·2 million married men of 65 and over.

Costs of (*a*), (*b*) and (*d*) are for men of 16-64 and women of 16-59 only; costs of these allow for supplementation of family allowances to bring total children's allowances up to a flat rate of 9/- each per week.

(*b*) Assumes average incapacitation of 14 working days a year—4·3% for men and 5·0% for women—applied over whole of occupied population. Latest figures for Department of Health for Scotland give 10·92 days per male and 12·45 per female in 1935-36, but rate is rising. This costs £80 millions. Additional allowance of £15 millions to cover those who do not appear in the Census as "occupied," but who would be eligible for benefit (e.g. congenitally crippled, and those who though originally "occupied" have ceased to record themselves as such).

(*c*) Assumes 95% of men of 65 and over and 85-90% of single and widowed women of 60 and over eligible for benefit. Assumes 25% of eligible men of 65 and over, 20% of eligible women of 60-64 and 6% of eligible women of 65 and over are still at work, thus only receiving 10/- weekly and not full retirement pension; this is one-half the extent to which these classes recorded themselves as "occupied" in the 1931 census.

(*d*) Assumes 200,000 widows under 60 with 250,000 dependent children (including orphans); their benefits would cost £15 millions. Large part of remainder aged 45-59 and would be difficult to restore to work. Assumes full benefits have to to be paid to 60% of them, or percentage benefits (for disablement) to a larger proportion; this gives extra cost of £25 millions.

(*e*) Assumes that parents receive either the family allowance or the income tax rebate, whichever is the larger. The cost is the net addition, but makes no allowance for time-lag in income tax assessment. It includes all children under 16, on the assumption that the school-leaving age should be raised to 16; if, however, it is fixed at 15, the cost is £90 millions. If the total cost of the Social Security scheme had to be reduced we should omit family allowances for the first child.

(*f*) Maternity benefit for working mothers £1½ millions; maternity allowance for all mothers £7 millions; marriage allowance £4½ millions; burial allowance £9 millions; emergency benefit £3 millions.

(*g*) 5% of estimated cost allowed for administration.

8. The total cost is therefore something less than £600 millions per annum. The most important single item in the cost is old age, and substantial reductions could be achieved if a larger proportion of the aged could be induced to work for a longer period; a great deal would depend upon the extent to which childless widows of 45-59, single and widowed women of 60-70, men of 65-70 and disabled folk generally could be brought on to an effective earning basis. Of

the total cost, some 55% is in respect of people who have ceased to make any positive contribution to the nation's economic life. It is clearly necessary to reduce this proportion as far as possible.

9. These calculations do not take account of the cost of the public medical service. The excess over the present cost to the community of medical services would not be great in relation to the figures in this section. Its financing would be partly a technical problem of diverting to the State purchasing power now used for purchasing medical services; it would partly depend on the extent of adaptation of existing private and public medical and health services (hospital, maternity and child welfare, school medical and tuberculosis services, etc.).

10. The total number of adults who would be maintained by benefit at any given time is of the order of 9,000,000, or one-quarter of the adult population.

Relation to National Resources

11. The proportion of the cost of cash benefits to the national income increased from 1½% in 1913-14 to 5¼% in 1938, when it stood as follows:

	Net National Income. £m.	Cash Benefits. £m.	Proportion.
1938 War Finance White Paper 1942 (Cmd. 6347)	4,595	240	5¼

The net national income at current prices in 1941 was estimated in the White Paper (Cmd. 6347) at £6,338 millions. If the national income can be maintained at this level in the post-war period the Social Security scheme represents some 9½% of it. Admittedly the national income in 1941 was swollen as a result of long hours of work, a very low level of unemployment, and the employment of women who would not normally seek paid work. On the other hand, productivity was reduced by war conditions, such as the black-out, air-raids, the use of less efficient labour to replace men in the army, shipping difficulties and the dislocation of international trade. We are throughout assuming that a constructive policy in other spheres will avert the recurrence of large-scale unemployment and permit technical productivity to increase rapidly once the first period of reconstruction is over. Hence it seems on the whole reasonable to relate the cost of our proposals to the 1941 level of national income; if money values change greatly either upwards or downwards we should revise the scale of our benefits, and the relationship of their total cost to the National Income would not be affected.

The following considerations should be taken into account in deciding whether it is practicable to increase in this way the percentage of the national income used for social security:

(*a*) A higher level of taxation than that ruling before the war will probably be acceptable. If the State increasingly takes on the function of risk-bearing and enterprise, this removes the central long-term objection to high taxation.

(*b*) Substantial sums are spent in voluntary provision against contingencies against which the scheme will protect people; subscriptions of this kind were before the war equivalent to some $1\frac{1}{2}$% of the national income. Furthermore, considerable sums are spent in providing for relatives, who would now be looked after by the scheme.

(*c*) Public opinion is demanding a much greater measure of security, and this scheme is something like the minimum which can be said to represent "social security" on the cash provision side.

12. In Budgetary terms, the scheme would involve the retention of about 30% of the additional taxation imposed in the war. The following table sets this out:

	£m.
Net National Income (White Paper Cmd. 6347) 1938	4,595
1941	6,338
Total public revenue in 1941, including accrued taxation liabilities (*a*)	2,557
Total public revenue in 1941 at 1938 taxation level (*b*)	1,648
Estimated cost of Social Security scheme . . .	600
Cash payments in 1938, inflated according to the increase in the national income from 1938 to 1941 .	340
Additional cost . .	260

(*a*) War Finance White Paper 1942; section E. The public revenue includes local rates and social insurance contributions, for these are equally direct and indirect taxation with the Central Government's taxation.

(*b*) Public revenue in 1938 was £1,194 millions or 26% of net national income; 26% of £6,338 millions is £1,648 millions.

Broadly speaking, rather more than one-half of the cost of the scheme would be covered by devoting the same proportion of the estimated post-war national income to social security payments as was provided in 1938; the remainder would require additional public revenue equivalent to about 30% of the extra taxation imposed in 1941 compared with 1938. One cannot say at this stage how far other governmental expenditures will require to be developed, and will need a share of the public revenue. But this scale of social security provision does not appear to be *prima facie* unreasonable.

Contributions

13. The scheme itself does not require workers' and employers' contributions as an essential part of its administration. Eligibility for benefit would not depend upon the payment of certain numbers of contributions. In these circumstances, contributions simply represent a convenient and accepted form of taxation—the workers' contributions are direct taxation, the employers' contributions indirect taxation. We recommend the abolition of employers' contributions. Employers so relieved will be able either to increase wages or to reduce costs and thence prices. The retention of workers' contributions inherently depends upon the extent to which direct taxation of low incomes is likely to become sufficiently acceptable to remain incorporated in the fiscal system after the war. The income tax is by far the most equitable of all taxes, and if the wage-earners can be induced to accept it, it is by far the best way of raising the public revenue.

14. If contributions are deemed to be required, then a basic contribution of 3/6 weekly for men and 2/6 weekly for women, with half-rate for youths of 16 and 17 and for part-time workers and for occupied men over 65 and women over 60, would yield about £150 millions, or one-quarter of the total cost. This would likewise cover roughly one-third of the benefits which would be provided for the gainfully occupied alone—unemployment, sickness, disablement, widows' pensions and old age. This may be compared with the present workers' contribution of 1/10 for men and 1/7 for women. The average working-class family spends at least as much again on insurance premiums, payments to friendly societies, pension funds, etc. So this scale of contributions would be within the range of all but the poorest workers.

15. A system of graduated contributions might be substituted. Much the same result would be achieved by contributions of 4/6 weekly for people with incomes above £7 a week; 3/6 for people between £4 and £7; 2/6 a week for people below £4; with 6d. a week less for women. The choice between these means of providing finance should be left until more experience is available of the acceptability in the long term of income tax on low incomes.

16. It is noteworthy, however, that the 1941-42 rates of income tax, applied to the gross income of people with less than £250 a year, yield something over £100 millions. Workers' contributions to social insurance yield some £55 millions. Consequently, the existing levels of taxation on low incomes, together with the existing workers' contributions, would cover about the same as the larger contribution systems set out in paras. 13 and 14. But this would provide only one-quarter of the whole cost; much of the rest would inevitably fall upon the low-income groups, either in direct or in indirect taxation.

ANNEX B

MATERNITY BENEFIT

1. Maternity benefit under National Health Insurance introduces the "double benefit" whereby the insured married woman may get more than the insured unmarried mother, although the need of the latter may be presumed to be greater.

2. The maternity benefit is supplemented by many other payments or subsidies which local authorities are empowered to make, but these are very unequal in scope and incidence.

3. A bad feature of existing arrangements is that pregnancy as such is deemed not to be "sickness" within the meaning of the National Health Insurance Acts. Some doctors put expectant mothers "on the panel" a few weeks before confinement, but it is more or less a matter of chance unless complications exist.

4. The position is particularly bad for women normally engaged in insurable employment by firms (of which there are many) who for various reasons dismiss or suspend women known to be pregnant. Such women are frequently disallowed Unemployment Insurance Benefit because they cannot satisfy the Anomalies Regulations relating to married women on account of their condition, although not eligible for Sickness Benefit.

5. They are thus left suspended between the various social insurance schemes and unable to earn even though able to work. They are left without wages and deprived of any compensation at a time when they have to bear a heavy additional expenditure arising out of their own needs and those of the expected child.

ANNEX C

FUNERAL COSTS

1. The sum of £15 recommended for Burial Allowance will suffice at the prices prevailing in London in April 1942 for earth burial in a common grave, hearse, coffin, one car and undertaker's services. At 1942 prices the average working-class expenditure on funerals is about £18.

2. Undertakers' charges are as high as this because (*a*) they include an element of compensation for the risk taken in paying interment fees in advance on behalf of the client; (*b*) the prevailing prices are kept high by the needs of the small undertakers whose overhead costs are high in relation to their turnover and who are protected by the policy of the British Undertakers' Association; (*c*) coffins, handles,

etc., are produced in small quantities instead of being made by more efficient methods on a large scale.

3. Earth burial in a common grave averages about £1 10/- in London, and the cost may include: Cost of grave, fee for grave-digging, fees to clergy, fees to verger, tolling bell. There is clearly scope for full investigation here; burial fees (including those paid to the clergy) vary not only according to the size of the grave to be dug, but also according to its location.

4. Cremation costs in London vary from £3 3/- to £7 7/- and could be reduced if crematoria were used more. Apart from the initial capital cost, they can be run more cheaply than burial grounds, and can operate for increased numbers at reduced costs, whereas a cemetery actually diminishes its capital at each burial (most municipal cemeteries operate at a loss). Two medical certificates are required by law before cremation. "The alternative doctor's" certificate often costs a fee of £2 2/-. (Stoke-on-Trent charges £4 4/- for all cremation services including Medical Referee.)

5. The working class insures heavily (at the expense of current consumption of food, etc.) against charges which are thus greatly in excess of actual costs of the relevant services. (See also Wilson and Levy, *Burial Costs and Funeral Reform.*)

ANNEX D

ADVISORY COMMITTEES

1. The purpose of local Advisory Committees would be to enable senior officers of the local office of the Ministry of Social Security to keep in close touch with leaders of local public opinion, and to provide opportunity for discussion of local matters which fundamentally affect the work of the Ministry. The Committees should provide facilities for the ventilation of complaints and for transmission to the officers of comments and suggestions.

2. The Committees should have no executive powers; above all, they should never function as Case Committees. The officers of the Ministry must be responsible to the Ministry, and to no one else.

3. The Regional Advisory Committees should consist of the chairmen of the local Advisory Committees within the region, together with the senior officers from the regional office of the Ministry; their functions should be similar to those of the local Committees.

4. Members of all Advisory Committees should be paid for loss of remunerative time, and should have travelling (and, where necessary, subsistence) allowances.

5. Some members of the local and regional Advisory Committees should be nominated by the local authorities, and if Regional Councils are established, by them also.

ANNEX E

TRANSFER AND TRAINING OF STAFF

1. It is impossible to forecast the numbers of headquarters staff which would be needed for the Ministry, but the transfer of functions from other Departments would liberate about 6,000 officials from the headquarters of these various Departments. The 6,000 officials are at present employed as follows: [1]

Ministry of Health Insurance Dept. (excluding inspectorate)	2,000
National Health Insurance Audit Dept.	400
Ministry of Labour Unemployment Insurance Dept.	60
Ministry of Labour Finance Dept.	300
Ministry of Labour Umpire's Offices	10
Assistance Board	570
Ministry of Pensions	2,700
	6,040

Some staff would also be available from Customs and Excise, if they were released from responsibility for administering non-contributory Old Age Pensions.

2. The following number of officials would be available for local administration:

Assistance Board [1]	12,800
Ministry of Pensions [1]	1,000
Public Assistance	3,000
Ministry of Health Inspectorate [1]	800
	17,600

There are also some 13,300 officials in the local offices of the Ministry of Labour, a substantial proportion of whom would be available for transfer, but it is difficult to estimate the number.

3. It is probable that the fusion of the cash services will lead to a substantial reduction of administrative effort and cost, especially if the Ministry adopts the most up-to-date methods of mechanised record-keeping and administration.

4. Although, as stated above, officials can be drawn from existing Departments, it must not be assumed that a staff of adequate quality can be provided by this means. A major difficulty in establishing the organisation is likely to be the lack of suitably *trained* personnel. In the long run, the success or failure of the scheme will depend largely upon its staff, and upon the relations which they are able to establish with the public. It is therefore necessary that energetic

[1] Civil Estimates, 1942-43.

steps should be taken both to introduce trained staff and to provide facilities for training the existing staff in social service work.

5. The staff responsible for social service work should be recruited as follows:

(*a*) From those with professional social service training, selected by open competitive examination plus competitive interview. Age of entry 21 to 25. This group would include:

(i) Those whose studies were privately financed.

(ii) Those awarded by their local education authority a "deferred bursary" adequate for full maintenance when they left school, and who had done clerical work as unestablished staff in the Ministry until they were old enough to take the course. (Social service training cannot usefully be given before the age of 19.)

(*b*) From established staff in this or other Departments who, wishing transfer and having suitable personal qualities for social service work, should be given post-entry training within the Ministry of Social Security.

(*c*) From more mature persons possessing relevant knowledge or experience, recruited for the higher posts by competitive interview. Appropriate salary scales would be offered to attract them into the public service.

ANNEX F

B.M.A. SUGGESTED ADULT MALE RATION FOR ONE WEEK[1]

Item.	Quantity.	Item.	Quantity.
Beef	1 lb.	Sugar	1 lb.
Minced meat	½ lb.	Jam	¾ lb.
Bacon	½ lb.	Potatoes	5 lb.
Corned beef	½ lb.	Peas (dried)	¼ lb.
Liver (ox)	¼ lb.	Tea	¼ lb.
Eggs	2 oz.	Oatmeal	½ lb.
Cheese	½ lb.	Yeast	—
Milk	1¾ pts.	Rice	¼ lb.
Fish (cod)	¼ lb.	Syrup (treacle)	½ lb.
Butter	¼ lb.	Cabbage	1 lb.
Suet	1 oz.	Beans (butter)	¼ lb.
Lard	¼ lb.	Barley	½ lb.
Flour or	4½ lb.	Fresh fruit and green vegetables	1 serving daily
Bread	7¼ lb.		

[1] British Medical Association. Report of Committee on Nutrition, 1933.

SUPPLEMENTARY EVIDENCE

Submitted at the Request of the Beveridge Committee

RENT ALLOWANCES

The Inter-Departmental Committee invited the witnesses appearing on behalf of the Fabian Society Sub-Committee to amplify their Memorandum on the subject of rent allowances, with special reference to the scales to be allowed and the administrative methods which might be employed. The following additional Memorandum was therefore submitted.

A. Administrative Provisions

1. The object of a rent allowance is to safeguard the stability of the home in time of distress or lowered earning power. The attainment of this aim must form an indispensable element in a genuine programme of social security. It can be achieved only by a specific allowance unless the standard rate of benefit is raised to an impracticable level.

2. In order to simplify the practical operation of the scheme it is suggested that all claimants should be entitled to an allowance, based on an assumed rent liability, without proof of actual liability. This assumed rent would be fixed separately for each locality and would vary with the number of the claimant's dependants. Claimants would be able to claim a higher rent allowance on proof of actual liability up to the maxima described in the next paragraph.

3. In granting these higher allowances a distinction can be drawn between long-term and short-term liability for rent. It is unreasonable to expect a household to reduce its expenditure on rent during a contingency such as unemployment or sickness, which may be expected to last for only a few weeks or months, whereas in the case of old age the contingency is one of long duration, and the persons concerned may reasonably be expected to reduce their liability for rent, if it is unduly high, by moving to other premises. We propose, therefore, to pay those who are claiming benefit on account of unemployment, sickness, disablement, etc., an amount up to, say, 50% above the appropriate figure of assumed rent liability, on proof of actual liability. Persons receiving old age pensions at the retired rate would be entitled to receive up to, say, 25% above the appropriate figure of assumed rent liability, on proof of actual liability.

4. Proof of the actual liability for rent would normally be made by means of producing the rent book or lease. Persons who have bought a house through a building society or by means of a loan under the Small Dwellings Acquisition Act, or by similar methods,

would be treated on the basis that the interest, insurance, redemption charges and Schedule A Income Tax are equivalent to rent.

5. The rules for attributing liability for rent would follow those which now exist for establishing dependancy under Unemployment Insurance, except that a married man living with his wife would in all cases be deemed to be responsible for the rent, except where the wife could prove that she was in fact discharging the liability. Thus, a man would be deemed to be paying the rent in respect of his wife, and also for children and other dependants for whom he could claim unemployment benefit. Under our scheme, these rules would apply equally for sickness, disablement, etc.

6. In the case of a tenant with lodgers or sub-tenants, simple rules would be laid down, such as that where food and service is provided for an inclusive sum, one-third of such sum would be treated as a payment in respect of the rent and deducted from the liability for rent of the tenant. Where a furnished room is let without food or service, three-quarters of the weekly payment would be deemed to be paid in respect of rent. Married children or other relatives occupying part of the premises let as a whole to the father or mother would be required to apportion liability for the rent by agreement between themselves and submit a joint declaration to the local office of the Ministry of Social Security. This would have to show the number of rooms occupied by each household and the total rent. To some extent a miscalculation, whether intentional or otherwise, would not in the long run affect the total liability of the State to any considerable extent, since if one party thereby became entitled to claim too large a share of the total, the other party would be able to claim only a proportionately smaller share when his turn came, unless he could show that a change in circumstances had occurred. A safeguard against abuse would have to be provided, and the Ministry might have to employ Rent Officers who would have a right to bring cases before the Court of Referees if they considered the apportionment or any other aspect of a rent claim to be inadmissible.

7. The same rules as those suggested in para. 6 for arriving at the actual rent liability of a tenant would be used to determine the rent liability of sub-tenants, lodgers, etc.

8. A specimen rent form follows (Section C), showing the questions which a claimant would be required to answer.

B. Scale of Allowances

Detailed information for drawing up a standard scale of rent is already in the files of the Assistance Board, but the following figures have been used to work out a specimen scale for the purposes of illustration:

1. Mr. Seebohm Rowntree in *The Human Needs of Labour* gives the rent charged by certain local authorities for three bedroom

non-parlour houses in November 1936. The maximum charges vary from 9/4 in the case of Ipswich to 23/4 for London. The more usual charges outside London are from 12/- to 15/-.

2. The Ministry of Labour inquiry into the Expenditure of Working Class Households in 1937-38 gives:

Industrial Workers: Average rent, 10/8; Average number of rooms, 3·9.

Agricultural Workers: Average rent, 4/9; Average number of rooms, 4·0.

These figures cover wide differences in rents, and a considerable number would be at least half as much again for the whole country, and even more for the large towns.

3. The Assistance Board gives an additional allowance for rent where it exceeds one-quarter of the scale rent of assistance. The practice appears to be to take the actual rent into account up to a maximum of 12/6 for a single person and 22/6 for a married couple in the London area. Where a person lives with another household the share of rent is assumed to be 5/-.

Appendix IX to the Report of the Board for 1938 shows the amount of rent paid compared with the number of rooms occupied. From this table the larger proportion of cases appear to fall within the following limits:

No. of Rooms.	Amount of Rent.		
	England and Wales.	Scotland.	London.
1	5/– to 7/5	2/6 to 4/11	10/– to 13/5
2	,,	5/– to 7/5	,,
3	,,	7/6 to 9/11	,,
4	7/6 to 9/11	,,	12/6 to 14/11
5	,,	,,	20/– and over
6	10/– to 12/5	5/– to 7/5	,,

4. The above information enables us to produce the following outline table of assumed rent, but figures for different regions could easily be interpolated from the statistics available to the Assistance Board:

	Single Person.	Married Couple.	Married Couple with 1 Child.	Married Couple with 2 Children.	Married Couple with 3 Children.	Married Couple with 4 Children.	Married Couple with 5 Children.
London .	10·0	12·0	13·6	15·0	16·0	17·0	18·0
Large town .	8·0	10·0	11·0	12·0	13·0	14·0	15·0
Country .	4·0	6·0	7·0	8·0	9·0	10·0	11·0

This "assumed rent" scale allowance could be increased up to the actual rent paid on proof of the claimant's rent liability, with an upper limit, in the case of pensioners, of 25% above the scale, and in the case of sick, unemployed, and other short-term claims, of 50% above the scale.

C. Rent Claim Form

Claim for a rent allowance in respect of the following premises (address) ....

1. (*a*) Name of Tenant ....

   (*b*) Name of Landlord ....

   (Persons who own their houses do not answer this question but complete item 6 below.)

2. (*a*) Weekly rent .... (*b*) Rates (if not included in rent) ....

3. State the names of all persons living in the premises for rent of which claimant is liable. Those for whom you claim Dependants' Benefit should be entered in the left-hand column; any others in the right-hand column.

Dependants.	Other Persons.

4. Are any rooms let to lodgers? If so, give particulars of number, weekly payment made, and whether they are let furnished or unfurnished, and whether service and meals are provided.

5. If the premises are shared with persons other than your dependants or lodgers, what contribution towards the rent do such persons make?

Declaration as to Apportionment of Rent

We declare that liability for the rent of the above premises may be deemed to be shared between us in the following manner:

Name.	No. of Rooms Occupied.	Share of Rent.	Signature.

6. Particulars to be given by persons owning their own houses:

(*a*) Have you a mortgage or loan outstanding on the house? If so, state the amount, and name of person, local authority, Building Society, etc., who advanced the money..........
....

(*b*) State amount of weekly payment due in respect of above mortgage or loan..

(*c*) State amount of Ground Rent (if any).....................

(*d*) State amount of insurance premium on house................

(*e*) State amount of Schedule A Income Tax...................

SELECT BIBLIOGRAPHY

LITERATURE on the Social Services covers the ground unevenly. On Poor Law history, for example, much has been written, but on Old Age Pensions very little. Even with these limitations this bibliography is not exhaustive. The following classified lists indicate a minimum only in each subject; and, as discursive reading is also advantageous, Section I contains books dealing generally with the Social Services, their function and their history.

1. GENERAL

Social Insurance and Allied Services, Report by Sir William Beveridge, 1942, Cmd. 6404. H.M.S.O.
White Paper on Social Insurance, 1944: Part I, Cmd. 6550, H.M.S.O.; Part II, Cmd. 6551, H.M.S.O.
Abbot, Edith, *Public Assistance*, Vol. I (Vol. II in preparation). University of Chicago Press, 1940.
Abbott, Grace, *From Relief to Social Security*. University of Chicago Press, 1941.
International Labour Office, *Approaches to Social Security*. 1942.
M'Gonigle and Kirby, *Poverty and Public Health*. Gollancz, 1936.
Political and Economic Planning, Report on the British Social Services, 1937.
Rowntree, B. Seebohm:
The Human Needs of Labour. Longmans, Green & Co., 1937.
Poverty and Progress. Longmans, Green & Co., 1941.
Simey, T. S., *Social Administration*. Oxford University Press, 1937.
Spring Rice, Margery, *Working Class Wives*. Pelican, 1939.
Wickwar, W. Hardy, *The Social Services*. Cobden-Sanderson, 1936. O.P.
Williams, Gertrude, *The State and the Standard of Living*. P. S. King & Son Ltd., 1936.
Wilson and Levy, *Burial Reform and Funeral Costs*. Oxford University Press, 1938.
Social Work Year Book (U.S.A.). Russell Sage Foundation, New York.
Social Security Board (U.S.A.), Annual Reports.
Third International Conference on Social Work, 1936, Report. Le Play House Press.
New Survey of London Life and Labour, 1932. P. S. King & Son Ltd.
White Paper on Employment Policy, 1944, Cmd. 6527. H.M.S.O.
Social Denmark. Allen & Unwin, 1946.
The Superannuation Act, 1946. H.M.S.O.
The National Insurance Act, 1946. H.M.S.O.
Potter, Douglas, *The National Insurance Act*, 1946. Butterworth, 1946.
Report by the Government Actuary on the Financial Provisions of the National Insurance Bill, 1946. H.M.S.O., Cmd. 6730.

International Labour Office:
International Survey of Social Services, 1936.
International Labour Organisation and Social Insurance, 1936.
Approach to Social Security, 1942.
Blackshaw, W., *The Community and Social Service.* Pitman, 1939.
Bourdillon, A. F. C. (ed.), *Voluntary Social Services.* Methuen, 1945.
Family Welfare Association. How to help cases of distress : a year-book of information respecting the statutory and voluntary means of relief. King & Staples. (In progress.)

2. Public Assistance

Hadden's *Relieving Officer's Handbook,* Dumsday and Moss. Hadden Best & Co. Ltd.
Jennings, W. I., *The Poor Law Code and Law of Unemployment Assistance.* Chas. Knight & Co. Ltd.
Webb, Sidney and Beatrice:
English Poor Law History: Part II, The Last Hundred Years. Longmans, Green & Co., 1929.
English Poor Law Policy, 1910.
Minority Report of the Royal Commission on the Poor Law, 1905-9.
Morgan, W. E., *The Future Institutional Service.* National Association of Administrators of Local Government Establishments, 1944.
National Assistance Bill, 1947. House of Commons Bills, 1947-48. No. 7. H.M.S.O.
National Assistance Bill, 1947. Summary of the Provisions, Cmd. 7248. H.M.S.O.

3. Workmen's Compensation

Butterworth's *Digest of Workmen's Compensation Cases* (2nd ed.).
Levy, Hermann, *Back to Work: The Case for the Partially Disabled Worker.* Fabian Research Pamphlet 56, 1941.
Rackham, C. D., *Factory Law.* Nelson "Discussion" Series, 1939.
Robson, W. A., "Industrial Relations and the State: The Reform of Workmen's Compensation," *Political Quarterly,* Sept.-Dec. 1930.
Willis, *The Law of Workmen's Compensation* (latest ed.). Butterworth & Co.
Wilson and Levy, *Workmen's Compensation,* 2 vols. Oxford University Press, 1939-41.
Holman Gregory Report, Departmental Committee on Workmen's Compensation, 1920. H.M.S.O.
Home Office Memorandum on the Workmen's Compensation Acts, 1925-38. H.M.S.O.
Stewart Report, Committee on Certain Questions arising under the Workmen's Compensation Acts, 1938. H.M.S.O.
Thompson, W. H., *Workmen's Compensation Up to Date.* Labour Research Department, 1944.

Shannon, N. P., and Potter, D., on *The National Insurance (Industrial Injuries) Act*, 1946. Butterworth's Emergency Legislation Service, 1946.
Workmen's Compensation. Interim Report of the Departmental Committee on Alternative Remedies. H.M.S.O., Cmd. 6580, 1945.
Second Report. H.M.S.O., Cmd. 6642, 1945.
Final Report. H.M.S.O., Cmd. 6860, 1946.
Disabled Persons Employment Act, 1944. H.M.S.O.
Inter-departmental Committee on the Rehabilitation and Resettlement of Disabled Persons, Report, 1943. H.M.S.O., Cmd. 6415.
International Labour Office, *The Training and Employment of Disabled Persons.* I.L.O., 1945.
Ministry of Labour and National Service, Rehabilitation and Resettlement of Disabled Persons, Report, 1946. H.M.S.O.
National Insurance (Industrial Injuries) Bill, 1945, Explanatory Memoranda, Cmd. 6651. H.M.S.O.
Workmen's Compensation Acts, 1925-1945, Memo. on. H.M.S.O., 1946.
National Insurance (Industrial Injuries) Act, 1946. H.M.S.O.

4. National Health Insurance

Political and Economic Planning, Report on the British Health Services, 1937.
Robson, W. A., *Justice and Administrative Law* (Chapter III). Stevens, 1947.
Ministry of Health, Annual Reports.
Annual Reports of the Chief Medical Officer, Ministry of Health.
Royal Commission on National Health Insurance, Report 1925, Cmd. 2596. H.M.S.O.
Report of the Government Actuary on the Fourth Valuation of Approved Societies, Cmd. 5496. H.M.S.O.
National Health Insurance Act, 1936. (26 Geo. V and 1 Edw. VIII, ch. 32.)
Medical Benefit Regulations, Statutory Rules and Orders, 1936, No. 1163.
Harris, R. W., *National Health Insurance in Great Britain*, 1911-1946. Allen & Unwin, 1946.
A National Health Service, Cmd. 6502, 1944. H.M.S.O.
Sinai, Anderson and Dollar, *Health Insurance in the United States.* Commonwealth Fund, New York, 1946.
Levy, H., *National Health Insurance: a Critical Study.* Cambridge University Press, 1944.
Macnalty, A., *The Reform of the Public Health Services.* Oxford University Press, 1943.
Ministry of Health, Hospital Survey Reports, H.M.S.O. (In progress.)
Inter-departmental Committee on Dentistry, Interim Report, 1944, Cmd. 6568. Final Report, 1946, Cmd. 6727. H.M.S.O.

National Health Service Bill, 1945. Summary of the Proposed New Service, Cmd. 6761. H.M.S.O.
National Health Service Act, 1946. H.M.S.O.
Orr, D. W. and J. W., *Health Insurance with Medical Care: the British Experience.* Macmillan, 1938.

5. Unemployment Insurance and Assistance

Beveridge, W. H.:
Unemployment, a Problem of Industry. Longmans, Green & Co., 1931, or latest ed.
The Past and Present of Unemployment Insurance, Barnet House Papers, No. 13. Oxford University Press, 1930.
Unemployment Insurance Statutory Committee, Political Pamphlet No. 1. London School of Economics Publication, 1938.
Burns, Eveline M., *British Unemployment Programs, 1920-1938.* Social Science Research Council, Washington, D.C., 1941.
Chegwidden and Evans, *The British Employment Exchange System.* Macmillan & Co., 1934.
Emerson and Lascelles, *A Guide to the Unemployment Insurance Acts* (latest ed.). Longmans, Green & Co.
Gibson, M. B., *Unemployment Insurance in Great Britain.* Allen & Unwin, 1931.
Hill, Polly, *The Unemployment Services.* Routledge, 1940.
Millett, John D., *The Unemployment Assistance Board.* Allen & Unwin, 1940.
Pilgrim Trust, *Men Without Work.* Cambridge University Press, 1938.
Royal Commission on Unemployment Insurance, Final Report, 1932, Cmd. 4185. H.M.S.O.
Ministry of Labour, Annual Reports.
Unemployment Assistance Board, Annual Reports.
Unemployment Act, 1934. (24 & 25 Geo. V, ch. 29.)
Ministry of Labour and National Service, Tables Relating to Employment and Unemployment in Great Britain, 1939, 1945 and 1946. H.M.S.O., 1947.

6. Old Age Pensions

Wilson and Mackay, *Old Age Pensions.* Oxford University Press, 1941.
Commissioners of Customs and Excise, Annual Reports.
Ministry of Health, Annual Reports.
Assistance Board, Annual Reports.
Increase in Old Age, Widows' and Blind Persons' Pensions, Cmd. 6878, 1946. H.M.S.O.
Old People's Welfare. National Old People's Welfare Committee. Revised edition, 1947.
Nuffield Foundation, *Old People: A Report.* Oxford University Press, 1947.
Pensions Increase Act, 1947. H.M.S.O.

7. Blind Welfare

The Education of the Blind (Report of the Joint Committee of the College of Teachers of the Blind and the National Institute for the Blind). Allen & Unwin, 1936.

Handbook on the Welfare of the Blind in England and Wales, Ministry of Health, February 1939. H.M.S.O.

A History of Blind Welfare in England and Wales, National Institute for the Blind, Bulletin No. 7, 1934.

Blind Persons' Act, 1920. (10 & 11 Geo. V, ch. 49.)

Richmond, Lawrence, *Local Authorities and the Welfare of the Blind.* Law and Local Government Publishers, 1938.

Blind Persons' Act, 1939. (1 & 2 Geo. VI, ch. 11.)

Twelfth Report of the Advisory Committee on the Welfare of the Blind to the Ministry of Health, 1934-37, April 1937. H.M.S.O.

Wilson, J. F., *Voluntary Organisations for the Welfare of the Blind* in A. F. C. Bourdillon's *Voluntary Social Services.* Methuen, 1945.

8. Finance of the Social Services

Hicks, U. K., *The Finance of British Government, 1920-1936:* Chapters III (Social Expenditure), XII (Unemployment Expenditure). Oxford University Press, 1938.

Widows', Orphans' and Old Age Contributory Pensions Bill, Report by the Government Actuary on the Financial Provisions of the Bill, 1925, Cmd. 2406. H.M.S.O.

Report of the Committee on Pensions for Unmarried Women, 1939, Cmd. 5591. H.M.S.O.

Public Social Services, 1940, Cmd. 5906, H.M.S.O. (Latest published return of expenditure on the Social Services.)

Report by the Government Actuary on the Financial Provisions of the Bill relating to Contributory Pensions and Health Insurance, 1940, Cmd. 6169. H.M.S.O.

Ministry of Health, Annual Reports.

Unemployment Assistance Board, Annual Reports.

Unemployment Insurance Statutory Committee, Annual Reports.

National Income and Expenditure of the United Kingdom, 1938-1946. H.M.S.O., Cmd. 7099, 1947.

(See also other sections. There are no books dealing solely with the finance of the social services.)

9. Industrial Life Assurance

Actuaries, Journal of the Institute of, vols. 65 and 66.

Ansell, Charles, *Friendly Societies*, 1850. O.P.

Dinnage and Hills, *Industrial Assurance Organisation and Routine.* Pitman, 1934.

Walker and Woodgate, *Principles and Practice of Industrial Assurance.* Pitman, 1933.

Webb, Sidney, *New Statesman* Special Supplement on Industrial Assurance, March 1915.
Wilson and Levy, *Industrial Assurance.* Oxford University Press, 1937.
Annual Reports of the Industrial Assurance Commissioner, with Statistical Summaries: 1930-31, H.C. Papers 133; 1933-34, H.C. Papers 116.
Industrial Assurance and Assurance on the Lives of Children under ten years of Age, Report and Minutes of Evidence, 1931-33. (Cohen Report.)
Departmental Committee on the Business of Industrial Assurance Companies and Collective Societies, Report and Minutes of Evidence. Report 1920. (Parmoor Report.)
Assurance Companies Act, 1946. H.M.S.O.

10. Economics of Social Security

Bowley (ed.):
Wages and Income since 1860. Cambridge University Press, 1937.
Studies in National Income. Cambridge University Press, 1942.
Clark, Colin:
National Income and Outlay. Macmillan & Co., 1937.
The Conditions of Economic Progress. Macmillan & Co., 1940.
Findlay Shirras, and Rostas, *The Burden of British Taxation.* Cambridge University Press, 1942.
Hogben, Lancelot, and Others, *Political Arithmetic.* Allen & Unwin, 1938.
Orr, Sir John Boyd:
Food, Health and Income. Macmillan & Co., 1936.
Fighting for What? Macmillan & Co., 1942.
Reddaway, W. B., *Economics of a Declining Population.* Allen & Unwin, 1939.
Rowntree, B. Seebohm, *Poverty and Progress.* Longmans, Green & Co., 1941.
New Survey of London Life and Labour. P. S. King & Son, Ltd., 1932.
The Standard of Living in Bristol. University of Bristol Survey, 1938.
Social Survey of Merseyside, edited by D. Caradog Jones. University Press of Liverpool, 1934.
Political and Economic Planning, Report on the British Health Services, 1937.
6th Report on Incapacitating Sickness in the Insured Population in Scotland, 1935-36. H.M.S.O.
White Paper on Family Allowances, Cmd. 6354. H.M.S.O.
White Paper on War Finance, Cmd. 6347 (Analysis of the Sources of War Finance and an estimate of the National Income and Expenditure in 1938, 1940 and 1941). H.M.S.O.
Financial Statement 1942-43, H.C. Paper 78, April 14, 1942. H.M.S.O.
Report of the Government Actuary on the 1940 Pensions Bill, Cmd. 6169. H.M.S.O.

Sickness, Absence and Labour Wastage, Medical Research Council, 1936. H.M.S.O.
Report of New Zealand Social Security Department for 1941-42.
Williams, Gertrude, *The Price of Social Security*. Kegan Paul, 1944.
de Schweinitz, Karl, *England's Road to Social Security*. University of Pennsylvania Press, 1943, and Oxford University Press, 1944.

11. Family Allowances

Ginsburg, Louis, *Parenthood and Poverty*. Fabian Research Pamphlet 43, 1939.
Rathbone, Eleanor:
The Disinherited Family. Allen & Unwin, 1936.
The Case for Family Allowances. Penguin, 1940.
Titmus, R. M., *Poverty and Population*. Macmillan & Co., 1938.
International Labour Office, *Methods of Family Living Studies*. 1940.
White Paper on Family Allowances, Cmd. 6354. H.M.S.O.
Family Allowances Act, 1945. H.M.S.O.
Family Allowances Act, 1945, Memorandum on the Effect of the F.A.A. on the Workmen's Compensations Acts, 1925-1945. H.M.S.O., 1946.
Myrdal, A., *Nation and Family*. Kegan Paul, 1945.

12. Administrative Personnel

Cohen, Emmeline, *The Growth of the British Civil Service*. Allen & Unwin, 1941.
Finer, H., *The British Civil Service*. Allen & Unwin, 1937.
Hill, Leonard, *The Local Government Officer*. Allen & Unwin, 1938.
Macadam, Elizabeth, *The Social Servant in the Making*. Allen & Unwin, 1945.
Martindale, Hilda, *Women Servants of the State*. Allen & Unwin, 1938.
Robson, W. A. (ed.), *The British Civil Servant*. Allen & Unwin, 1937.
Report of the Departmental Committee on the Qualification, Recruitment, Training and Promotion of Local Government Officers, 1934. (Hadow Report.)
Report of the Royal Commission on the Civil Service (Tomlin Commission), 1929-31.
Publications of the Division of Technical Training, Bureau of Public Assistance, U.S.A., Social Security Board.
Younghusband, Eileen, *Report on the Employment and Training of Social Workers*. Carnegie United Kingdom Trust, 1947.
Training for Social Work. Nuffield College. Oxford University Press, 1946.
Report of Conference on the Selection and Training of Social Security Staff. Social Security League, 1944.
The Reform of the Higher Civil Service. Fabian Society, 1947.
Greaves, H. R. G., *The Civil Service in the Changing State*. Harrap, 1947.

NOTES ON THE AUTHORS

LORD BEVERIDGE, K.C.B., C.B.; Director of London School of Economics and Political Science, 1919-37; Master of University College, Oxford, 1937-44; Chairman of Inter-departmental Committee on Social Insurance and Allied Services, 1941.

BARBARA CASTLE, M.P., B.A. (Oxon.); Member of Parliament for Blackburn since 1945. Former member of St. Pancras Borough Council and the Metropolitan Water Board.

ROSALIND C. CHAMBERS, B.Sc.Econ. (London); Lecturer in Sociology, London School of Economics.

JOAN SIMEON CLARKE, B.A. (Cantab.); Social Science Certificate, London School of Economics; Post-graduate student of the School of Social Service Administration, University of Chicago, 1938-39. Formerly Research Secretary, Fabian Society, and Secretary, Social Security League.

R. W. B. CLARKE, B.A. (Cantab.); Frances Wood Prizeman of the Royal Statistical Society, 1932; Formerly Assistant Editor of the *Financial News*. Author of *The Economic Effort of War*, *Britain's Blockade*, etc.

EMMELINE W. COHEN, B.A. (London); Author of *The Growth of the British Civil Service*.

W. McG. EAGAR, C.B.E., M.A. (Oxon.); Secretary-General of The National Institute for the Blind; Secretary of the British "Wireless for the Blind" Fund and of The Moon Society; Clerk to the Governors of Worcester College for the Blind, and of Chorleywood College for Girls with Little or No Sight. Joint author of *The Land and the Nation*, *The Towns and the Land*, etc.

LOUIS GINSBURG, M.A., F.F.A.; Author of *Population Movements*, *Parenthood and Poverty* (Fabian Research pamphlets).

HERBERT W. MARSHALL; Relieving Officers' Certificate of the Poor Law Examinations Board; an Assistant Public Assistance Officer.

CLARA D. RACKHAM, M.A., J.P.; Alderman of Cambridgeshire County Council; Member of the Royal Commission on Unemployment Insurance, and co-signatory of its Minority Report; author of *Factory Law*.

WILLIAM A. ROBSON, Ph.D., LL.M., B.Sc.Econ. (London); Barrister at Law; Professor of Public Administration at the University of London. Member of National Insurance Advisory Committee. Author of *The Government and Misgovernment of London*, *The Development of Local Government*, *Justice and Administrative Law*, *Civilisation and the Growth of Law*, etc. Editor of and contributor to *Public Enterprise*, *The British Civil Servant*, *Population and the People*, etc.

GERTRUDE WILLIAMS, B.A.; Special Lecturer in Economics, Bedford College, University of London. Has written several books on social and economic subjects of which the most recent are *The Price of Social Security: a study of Labour Mobility* and *Women and Work.*

INDEX

For Product Safety Concerns and Information please contact our EU representative GPSR@taylorandfrancis.com
Taylor & Francis Verlag GmbH, Kaufingerstraße 24, 80331 München, Germany

www.ingramcontent.com/pod-product-compliance
Lightning Source LLC
LaVergne TN
LVHW011103300926
849160LV00008B/266

9781032205199